Lectures in the
History of Political Thought

Michael Oakeshott, *Selected Writings*

Volume I (2004):
What is History? and other essays
edited by Luke O'Sullivan, 0-907845-83-5

Volume II (2006):
Lectures in the History of Political Thought
edited by Terry Nardin & Luke O'Sullivan, 1-84540-005-4

Volume III (2007):
The Concept of A Philosophical Jurisprudence:
Essays and Reviews 1926–52
edited by Luke O'Sullivan, 1-84540-030-5

Volume IV (2008):
The Vocabulary of a Modern European State:
Essays and Reviews 1953–88
edited by Luke O'Sullivan, 1-84540-031-3

Michael Oakeshott

Lectures in the History of Political Thought

Edited by
Terry Nardin and Luke O'Sullivan

ia

imprint-academic.com

Published in the UK by Imprint Academic
PO Box 200, Exeter EX5 5YX, UK

Published in the USA by Imprint Academic
Philosophy Documentation Center
PO Box 7147, Charlottesville, VA 22906-7147, USA

ISBN 1 84540 005 4 (cloth)
ISBN 9 781845 400934 (pbk.)

A CIP catalogue record for this book is available from the
British Library and US Library of Congress

imprint-academic.com/idealists

Contents

Preface

This second volume of Michael Oakeshott's *Selected Writings* comprises the previously unpublished lectures Oakeshott gave at the London School of Economics and Political Science during the late 1960s, shortly before he retired as Professor of Political Science. Oakeshott had begun to prepare the lectures for publication, then abandoned the project. Among his papers, now in the Oakeshott archive at the LSE, was a photocopy of a typescript that he had corrected by hand and parts of which he had evidently had retyped. Copies of a slightly earlier typescript were circulating privately. We have used the LSE copy of Oakeshott's revised typescript, but we have checked it against copies of the earlier typescript and relied on the latter when the revised typescript was incomplete or unclear. We have not been able to find the originals of these typescripts.

The volume is a joint effort. Terry Nardin prepared a working transcript from the typescript in circulation. Luke O'Sullivan revised that transcript in the light of the revised typescript and other material in the archive. Both editors worked on the Introduction, with Nardin revising O'Sullivan's draft. The indexes were prepared by O'Sullivan. Keith Sutherland at Imprint Academic did much to improve the physical appearance and layout of the text.

The editors are grateful to the LSE for consenting to the publication of material from the archive. We are also grateful to those who have supported the project, including Kenneth Minogue and Timothy Fuller, whose gift of Oakeshott's papers established the archive, and the many well-wishers at the Michael Oakeshott Association, who helped publicize the *Selected Writings*. We want to thank the staff of the LSE archive, particularly Sue Donnelly and Anna Towlson, for their help. Thanks, too, go to David Boucher, James Cotton,

Robert Grant, and John R. Parr for sharing their copies of the lectures and other information. Finally, we are grateful to Imprint Academic, whose support for Oakeshott scholarship has been central to the growing interest in Oakeshott's thought during the last few years.

Editors' Introduction

Michael Oakeshott was appointed Professor of Political Science at the London School of Economics and Political Science in 1951. Soon thereafter he established an annual course on political thought. We do not know what topics he took up at first. Teachers of political thought often focus on canonical works, and Oakeshott may have begun this way. His course was aimed at undergraduates new to the subject, and for such students the most suitable materials are the 'classics' – texts that have, for one reason or another, outlived their original contexts. Such texts, Oakeshott at one time thought, are especially suitable for teaching how politics can be understood historically or philosophically.[1]

Oakeshott's lectures, we are told, 'laid bare the subtleties of Hobbes and Hegel, Mill and Green' and 'were packed with students from all disciplines' across the LSE.[2] 'Running from Plato to John Stuart Mill', the course soon 'became more or less the centre of gravity in that vast school'.[3] But later the focus seems to have shifted from texts to contexts. The last version of the lectures, which we present here, is a study of ideas in relation to their contexts, not a study of texts. Nor is this study of contexts a continuous story; it is an exploration of four particular contexts, the political experience of the ancient Greeks, the Romans, the medieval Europeans, and modern Europeans – 'different peoples, at different times, in different intellectual and physical circumstances, engaging

---

[1] Michael Oakeshott, 'The Study of "Politics" in a University', in *Rationalism in Politics and Other Essays*, ed. T. Fuller (Indianapolis: Liberty Press, 1991).

[2] Robert Grant, *Oakeshott* (London: Claridge Press, 1990), p. 19.

[3] Noël O'Sullivan, 'In the Perspective of Western Thought', *The Achievement of Michael Oakeshott*, ed. Jesse Norman (London: Duckworth, 1993), p. 105. John R. Parr, who attended the course around 1960, records that Oakeshott gave separate lectures on Plato, Aristotle, St. Paul, St. Augustine, St. Thomas Aquinas, Machiavelli, Montesquieu, Locke, Burke, Bentham, and Mill.

in politics in different ways and finding different things to think about it'.[4] The result is a study of the political thought of these peoples, not a tour of the classics.

Those who attended the lectures remember their intellectual substance and vivid presentation. Oakeshott had something to say and could say it well. 'The course showed with what sureness of touch he married a commanding vision of the various styles of doing politics in the Western world, their vocabulary and idiom, with the requirements of an undergraduate audience, generally new to this kind of subject'.[5] A former student describes Oakeshott as a 'polished, stylish lecturer' whose 'lectures (delivered from very full notes) were invariably well constructed, and interesting'.[6] Others confirm that he preferred lecturing from a detailed script, which he would then abridge or embellish as the occasion required.[7] 'He raised his voice sufficiently to be heard by everyone' but 'he did not project it forcefully or vary his tone very much; perhaps he disdained any oratorical devices'.[8] Maybe so, but he knew that lectures are performances. 'A particular feature was the opening of the lecture. Other lecturers traditionally walked down the centre aisle of the theatre, but Oakeshott had found a mysterious back entrance that enabled him to appear through the curtain behind the lectern, greeted each time by a storm of applause'.[9] Reading the lectures, one can imagine Oakeshott at his podium and enjoy, vicariously, the experience of being among his audience.

For Oakeshott, that audience was emphatically one of listeners, not readers. During his lifetime, Oakeshott would not agree to publish the lectures. But the typescript shows evidence of revision with an eye to publication. Several of the medieval chapters, for example, break from the pattern of short paragraphs crafted to be spoken, and seem to have been done after Oakeshott retired in 1968. That he allowed the lectures to survive amongst his literary remains is further

---

[4] 'Introduction', p. 33.

[5] Elie Kedourie, 'A Colleague's View', in Norman, pp. 99–100.

[6] Russell Price, 'A Choice and Master Spirit', in Norman, p. 29.

[7] Grant, *Oakeshott*, p. 19; Kenneth Minogue, Introduction to *Morality and Politics in Modern Europe: The Harvard Lectures* (New Haven: Yale University Press, 1993), p. xii.

[8] Price, 'A Choice and Master Spirit', p. 29.

[9] Noël O'Sullivan, 'Perspective of Western Thought', p. 105.

evidence that he was not decisively opposed to their surfac-
ing posthumously.[10] Fortunately, they are a pleasure to read
– crisp, cogent, clear, and engaging. Although they do not
contribute directly to current scholarship, the lectures fully
merit inclusion in a series of his selected writings.
Oakeshott's readings of the historical scholarship and classic
texts offer views on Greek, Roman, medieval, and modern
political thought that students and teachers will find illuminating and stimulating. Moreover, and perhaps more impor-
tantly in the present context, they shed new light on
Oakeshott's own thinking. They do so not least because they
enrich our picture of his self-conception as a teacher as well
as a scholar of political thought. The aim of this introduction
is, therefore, not only to give some idea of the content of the
lectures, but also to indicate how they relate to the rest of his
work. The first lecture is particularly worthy of close attention, after which we shall look in turn at each of the four periods he discusses.

Oakeshott's Introduction (Lecture 1)

Oakeshott declared in his opening address that the course
was intended as 'an historical study'. Coming from a man
with an abiding interest in the nature of historical inquiry,
those words were more loaded than usual, and it will pay us
to attend to them. Since the 1920s, Oakeshott had been revising his view of history as a distinct mode of theoretical
understanding, and we are entitled to see this view as pre-
supposed in his description of history as 'a mode of thought
in which events, human actions, beliefs, [and] manners of
thinking are considered in relation to the conditions, or the
circumstantial context, in which they appeared'.[11]

This was a subtle way of alerting his audience to what we
might call his 'one-damn-thing-after-another' view of the
historical process. His philosophy led Oakeshott to conceive
of historical events as related to one another only by other
events. Any attempt to reveal the overarching unity in historical events, anything like Hegel's argument that the whole

---

[10] Oakeshott 'put no restrictions on what was to be done with his papers when
he bequeathed them to Shirley Letwin'. Timothy Fuller, 'Editor's Introduction'
in Michael Oakeshott, *The Politics of Faith and the Politics of Scepticism* (New
Haven: Yale University Press, 1996), p. ix.

[11] 'Introduction', p. 31.

human past was the story of the development of freedom, lay beyond the remit of historical knowledge. Hence his remark to his students that 'I cannot detect anything that could properly correspond to the expression "*the* history of political thought"', an expression that he mercilessly dissected at length elsewhere.[12]

It is also worth underlining that Oakeshott was challenging any version of the belief that a clear direction of 'progress' was visible in the history of political thought, aiming thereby to cut across traditional distinctions between 'left' and 'right' in the interpretation of the history of political ideas. Hegelian, conservative, liberal, Christian, socialist, and Marxist thinkers have all entertained a belief that history was necessarily moving in a certain direction, but this was not the kind of view that Oakeshott thought a historical analysis of politics could support.

Such beliefs were usually inspired, in Oakeshott's view, by the assistance such grand narratives offered in furnishing justifications of particular courses of political action. They were part of the subject matter facing anyone concerned with political thought, but the aim of historical inquiry was to study them, not engage with them on their own terms. And in these lectures, Oakeshott's approach was anything but partisan. Anyone coming to them expecting a blast of polemic on the issues of the day will be disappointed; it took over two-thirds of the course to get to the modern world, and the first half was devoted entirely to Greece and Rome.

Oakeshott was equally keen to impress upon his students that he was not offering a 'scientific' history of imagined 'causes' and 'effects'. 'The geographical conditions of ancient Greece, or the institution of slavery, or their religious beliefs, did not cause the Greeks to think about politics in the way they did'. Such considerations he described as contextual, not causal. That is to say, he thought of historical relations as carrying mutual implications rather than strict entailments; hence the analogy of the dry stone wall that he used to characterise them elsewhere.[13] This is entirely consistent with his

---

[12] Michael Oakeshott, 'Political Thought as a Subject of Historical Enquiry', *What is History? And other essays: Selected Writings*, vol. I (Exeter: Imprint Academic, 2004), pp. 403–21.

[13] See Michael Oakeshott, *On History and other essays* (Oxford: Basil Blackwell, 1983), p. 94.

long-held view that history could make no claim to be 'scientific' in the manner of the natural sciences.

Another important qualification concerned the meaning of the adjective 'political' in the expression 'political thought'. This should not be taken to mean, Oakeshott emphasised, that there was a special kind of thought with an exclusive subject matter, 'politics'. Politics, like other human activities (Oakeshott instanced bringing up children, building houses, and banking as examples), could itself become a subject for discussion. When and if this happens, the questions people ask could either be directed to devising 'appropriate courses of action' and 'reasons for recommending them', or aiming 'to understand, to make more intelligible, to interpret, or to explain'.

So far as Oakeshott was concerned, there was a clear distinction between practical and theoretical approaches to politics. He was presupposing a certain conception of political activity in which politics are not natural to human beings but pretty much a necessary feature of any complex society not ruled in an entirely arbitrary fashion. For politics to appear, however, certain conditions must obtain. The existence of societies of language-using humans that provide the rudiments of existence but yet have no politics worth speaking of was perfectly intelligible. Put simply, politics was not a 'primordial' activity like eating or sleeping, but something that emerged gradually and imperceptibly over a long period.

Not only did 'politics' need a community of human beings, then; it also needed a community in which there were differences over 'common customs or rules of conduct'. Societies must have some way of dealing with disagreements over their arrangements before 'politics' could appear. This had the further consequence that politics required that the rules of a community 'must be understood by the members…to be capable of being determined by human deliberation and action'.

This was vital, Oakeshott thought. If it were really believed that 'the ruling authority itself, the law and the instruments of government, are all utterly unalterable – not merely difficult to change, but by their nature incapable of being changed' – there would be nothing to talk about. It is the essence of politics to be 'concerned with deciding between alternative courses of action and with instituting change… and persuading or inducing those who have the authority to act to make certain choices and not others'. If these things are held to be impossible, there can be no politics.

Behind these beliefs lay something like the view (and here Oakeshott may have learnt from Hegel) that humanity was unique in being able to acquire a 'second nature' through history and education. Only this could explain how political communities were brought into being. He shared, in other words, Hegel's sense of the historicity of human experience, and it indelibly coloured his view of how politics should be studied.[14] Even the philosopher would be unwise to ignore history, on the view Oakeshott was putting forward.

The relevant period was roughly the last three thousand years. Only during that time, Oakeshott claimed, had 'associations which provide in a significant degree the conditions for political activity' been in existence. Furthermore, he was explicit that 'politics' was 'in the main, a European invention'. No doubt accusations of Eurocentrism cannot be entirely forestalled on this point, even allowing for the qualificatory 'in the main', but Oakeshott was not tub-thumping: he immediately went on to describe politics as 'Europe's somewhat embarrassing gift to the world'. Moreover, he did not see anything like three thousand years of continuous European political history, as he explained elsewhere. Politics had emerged but 'often been submerged, or half-submerged, again' in European history.

Oakeshott's division of his subject into four 'relatively self-contained' eras of political thought was partly intended to reinforce this point. He wanted to emphasise the discontinuity between these 'memorable passages', as he called them; to his mind, for example, Greece and Rome had been very different, and labelling them both as examples of something called 'ancient' politics without further qualification was simply misleading. This attitude mirrors the historiography of the 1960s at large, which was increasingly sceptical in tone; in the history of science, for example, a similar insistence that the transitions from ancient to modern science were not part of a single story of progress, that Aristotle was not to be understood simply as an erring Galileo, was becoming widely accepted.

---

[14] For Oakeshott's account of Hegel's political theory see *On Human Conduct* (Oxford: Clarendon Press, 1975), pp. 256–63.

Oakeshott's attention to language also reflected wider historical and philosophical trends, such as the 'linguistic turn' in philosophy and the humanities that took place in the 1950s and 1960s. There was no set of words that was inherently 'political', no political language simply as such. Moreover, one always had to ask whether the words one was interested in were uttered 'in the service of political decision and action' or whether those who used them had in mind an 'explanatory' enterprise not directly connected to some practical course of action. In either case, one is usually dealing with words belonging to a complex vocabulary. One reason Oakeshott singled out the periods he did was that he believed that each had produced its own distinctive complex of political words, and he devoted considerable time to identifying the terms he felt were most characteristic of the period in question. When he turned his attention from these constituents of practical speech to 'political theory', he made clear that he was not discussing theories of how to act more effectively in politics, but suggesting historical and philosophical explanations.

In his philosophical writings Oakeshott always argued for a categorial difference between practical and theoretical (scientific, historical, philosophical) activity, and it was this insistence that lay behind his admonition that 'we should do well to avoid confusing practical political beliefs and arguments' with 'attempts 'to explain political activity, either historically or philosophically'. To help his students grasp the difference, he offered the distinction between religion and theology, between 'beliefs, sentiments, and longings' and 'a system of abstract ideas'. The analogy is not perfect, because theology, in the end, remains the servant of religion, while Oakeshott did not see history and philosophy as shackled to practice. The main point was to warn students that they should distinguish between 'a writer like Machiavelli or Locke and a writer like Hobbes or Hegel'.

In subsequent lectures, however, Oakeshott gives surprisingly little attention to individual writers. Indeed, those lectures compose a history of political thought remarkably free of political thinkers; only Plato, Aristotle, Augustine, and Aquinas are deemed worthy of lectures of their own (Plato and Aristotle each get two). No modern thinkers, not even Hobbes or Hegel, probably the modern political thinkers Oakeshott most admired, got their own. Perhaps this was because he felt that the contributions of modern political thinkers largely reformulated ancient and medieval ideas in the face of new problems, amounting to little more than old wine in new bottles. However that may be, even those thinkers he did discuss at length individually were always presented as philosophers whose political thought was part of a more general world-view embracing religion, ethics, science, and much else. As we shall now see, for Oakeshott the key to the history of political thought lay in the contextual approach.

Greek Political Thought (Lectures 2–10)

In referring to the 'political experience' of the ancient Greeks, Oakeshott distinguished between 'what actually happened' and 'what the Greeks themselves came to believe had happened'. These things might coincide, but they by no means always did so, even though Oakeshott believed the Greeks were right to recognize themselves, as he believed we must still recognize them, as 'the inventors of "politics"'. It did not matter for his purposes whether or not the Greeks' 'awareness of their own politics' coincided with the truth; the important thing was that this awareness had provided a 'myth or legend' that sustained their 'confidence in themselves'. As he saw it, the emergence of the *polis* around 1000 BCE was followed by the emergence of a narrative in which the Greeks told themselves a story of a union of tribes, the result of which was not itself a tribe but a self-consciously novel form of association.

All the features of the tribe – customs, gods, a chief or ruler – were transformed in becoming part of the *polis*. Just as 'Hellas' was the community of Greek-speakers, and not merely an area of the Mediterranean, so the *polis* was more than just a place. A *polis* offered protection, worship, and lawfulness, the 'justice' that Plato was to examine. Most of all, it offered the 'life of talk' that the Greeks believed made them 'superior to all other peoples'. This life was centred in the *agora*, the scene of 'the endless palavers which constitute half of Homer's *Iliad*', where the *demos*, the people, or more accurately, those of the *demos* who were *politai*, citizens, came to settle their own affairs – a privilege they believed was denied, for example, to the Persians.

Aristotle described the relationship between citizens as a kind of 'friendship', a relationship between equals, in contrast to the hierarchy of tribal and family relationships. Oakeshott emphasized that the equality under consideration here was an artificial one; notoriously, Aristotle was anything but a believer in natural equality. The significance of the artificial equality of the *polis* was that it was produced and maintained by persuasion, not force. Greek 'politics' consisted in precisely this process of mutual accommodation through discussion. This was true, Oakeshott argued, even in the early days of the *polis*, when a king or *basileus* ruled. Even though 'the right to speak on public occasions was confined to the king and his immediate counsellors', an assembly of citizens was still called 'to listen to deliberations about policy and about legal judgments, and they were participants in so far as they were there to be persuaded'.

In later times, the Greek cities famously came to know a variety of forms of government. So precarious was Greek politics that the belief arose that 'political forms and arrangements were essentially unstable', in a fashion that was, at best, cyclical, and certainly not progressive. There were, however, characteristic political forms, beginning with aristocratic oligarchies in which noble blood was claimed as a title to rule, but later often involving the dominance of the wealthy. There also emerged democracies in cities like Athens, where the original assembly had been 'transformed into the ruling authority' (always restricted to male citizens, a minority of the inhabitants). And from time to time there were tyrannies, which Oakeshott was careful to distinguish from despotisms. Where a despot was regarded as having no right to rule, the rule of the tyrant was autocratic but regular. The tyrant 'was a man, often a successful magistrate or military commander, who was pushed forward and endowed with authority; either by a shaky oligarchy, as a defender of its threatened privileges, or by a democratic faction intent on dislodging an oligarchy'. He differed from the despot, according to Oakeshott, in that he did not rule for his personal gratification and 'rarely subverted the ordinary laws of the *polis*'.[15]

The insistence on this distinction reflects Oakeshott's belief that constitutional issues had an important part to play

---

[15] 'The Political Experience of the Ancient Greeks', p. 58.

in understanding politics; the phrase 'power politics' he would doubtless have found very under-determined. Not only were power in the sense of force and power in the sense of right distinct from one another, he told his students, the sources of the right to rule had changed many times in the periods he was considering. Sensitivity to such distinctions was crucial to historical and philosophical understanding.

Oakeshott has been criticized for ignoring the violence of ancient history, particularly in the case of the Romans; his admiration of Roman law, for example, is said to have blinded him to the destruction wrought by Roman armies in Gaul and elsewhere as they extended imperial rule.[16] And superficially, it is true that his synthetic style can make things appear so neat and coherent that he is in grave danger of oversimplification. But if one reads carefully, one sees that Oakeshott in fact placed war absolutely at the centre of political history, especially in the modern world. He told his students quite clearly and unambiguously that 'preparing for war, fighting a war, or recovering from a war' had been the norm in modern Europe, and that 'modern governments owe their extraordinary power more to war than to any other single circumstance.'[17] We should not underestimate the radicalism of a view that declared, in a fashion similar to Marcuse at the time, that the technology of power in the modern world could transform the modern state into a police state.

Greek politics was faced with a stark choice that Oakeshott himself was inclined to regard as inescapable, the choice he once described as between 'jaw jaw' and 'war war'. The Hobbesian in him regarded either talk or violence as the only means available of resolving human disputes, and the very existence of politics was at least a victory for talk. He admired the Greeks for having brought into precarious existence a concept of government by persuasion.

Oakeshott may have regarded the assumptions he found reflected in the Greek distinction between political life in the *agora* and the life of the worker in the household or *oikia* as sound, but he did not hide from his students the fact that those fortunate enough to be accepted into the political

[16] See Perry Anderson, review of *Rationalism in Politics*, 2nd edn., *London Review of Books*, 24 September 1992, pp. 7–11.
[17] 'The Generation of a Modern State', p. 373.

sphere as self-determining agents were always a minority. His lectures were conventional in their view that neither Plato nor Aristotle had wanted to defend anything like what we know as modern democratic citizenship.

The lectures were eccentric, however, in dealing with Aristotle before Plato. One reason for this lies in Oakeshott's view that Aristotle had established a 'hierarchical map of human activity' which 'with a few amendments scribbled on it by later thinkers' had provided the 'context of all European political thought for two thousand years'.[18] At the base of this Aristotelian scheme was 'a place for getting a living and carrying on the human species'; next came a 'place for *politike* (the activity of making and sustaining a *polis*)'; and at the summit lay 'the activity of understanding and explaining'. Another reason for treating Aristotle first was that his thinking lay closer to the mainstream of Greek political experience, which it sought to categorize and rationalize, than Plato's effort to reshape that experience in the light of radically different ideas.

Whatever attachment to the Aristotelian framework Oakeshott may have had, it did not prevent him from recognizing that classification, because it 'entails the choice of a principle', is always 'an ambiguous and somewhat arbitrary activity'. For example, Aristotle had arrived at his influential categorization of constitutions into monarchies, aristocracies, and polities by combining the principles of there being one, or few, or many rulers, and of ruling as being either for the benefit of the rulers or the ruled. Aristotle's *Politics*, Oakeshott cautioned, was not to be read as if composed entirely of this sort of logical analysis. Using a phrase he also applied to Hegel's *Philosophy of Right*, he described it as a 'supremely miscellaneous' work, sometimes philosophical in its use of ideal types, sometimes empirical or quasi-historical in its use of examples, sometimes practical in its effort to diagnose the causes of political failure. Although Oakeshott is slightly inconsistent about the details, it is clear he saw Aristotle as engaged in several different kinds of inquiry.[19] All this is entirely consistent with Oakeshott's own theory of modality, which recognized different forms of knowledge.

---

[18] 'Aristotle (2)', p. 129.

[19] Compare 'Aristotle (1)', p. 113, and 'Aristotle (2)', p. 116, where first three and then four Aristotelean approaches to politics are distinguished.

If it is possible to discern traces of Oakeshott's own thought in his remarks on Plato and Aristotle, it is harder to do so in the treatment of stoicism and epicureanism with which he concluded his lectures on the ancient Greeks. This might seem odd; after all, epicureanism was notoriously associated in the early modern world with scepticism of the sort espoused by his beloved Hobbes, and Oakeshott himself attributed an 'ironic' character to philosophical thinking in *On Human Conduct*. Furthermore, in his personal life, Oakeshott was a rather epicurean character, preferring in his retirement a quiet retreat in the countryside and the company of friends to the bustle of London. Yet there was nothing unusual in his argument that both stoicism and epicureanism were responses to the increasing dependence of the Greek cities on external powers. We might, however, note his suggestion that circumstances to which stoicism was an intelligible response had arisen more than once in European history. Whether this was true of epicureanism, he did not say; perhaps he considered it, like stoicism, a permanent possibility.

Roman Political Thought (Lectures 11–15)

Oakeshott gave only half as many lectures on the Romans as he had on the Greeks, probably because he regarded their achievements in political thought as more practical than speculative; by common agreement, there were no Roman political thinkers of the stature of Plato or Aristotle. He was, however, keen to stress that the phrase 'the ancient world' involved 'one of the most misleading generalizations ever made' insofar as it implied that the Greek and Roman political experiences were indistinguishable.[20] Where the Greeks never really discovered how to secure political stability, the Romans excelled at the art of maintaining their state. It is not hard to discern admiration in the description of them as 'a conservative people supremely capable of learning from experience',[21] or in his claim that if the Greeks were the inventors of politics so far as Europe was concerned, it was the Romans we must thank for our conception of 'law'.

Singling out the transition from republic to empire, Oakeshott argued that the Romans were supremely good at

---

[20] 'The Political Experience of the Ancient Romans (1)', p. 176.
[21] 'The Political Experience of the Ancient Romans (2)', p. 206.

exploiting the ambiguity inherent in all political speech. It was because of their skill in this that the empire took root, though one may convict him of exaggeration in saying that it did so 'without opposition or serious misgiving'. This belief in the importance of language in politics ensured that an interpretation of Roman history in which socio-economic class was the governing principle found no favour with Oakeshott. Revealingly, given his admiration for Roman politics, he drew the comparison with eighteenth-century England, which, he believed, had also been ruled by 'family connections' and which he elsewhere implied had been the high-water mark of English political achievement.[22] To see Roman politics as simply the struggle between plebeians and patricians was to ignore the extent to which 'organizations of opinion about policy' cut across such divisions, just as they had in England. The great Roman families had also been 'organizations of interests', but they had never, in Oakeshott's opinion, been only that.

This emphasis on family separated the Romans from the Greeks, for 'all that is most representative of Greek thought expressly rejected the understanding of the *polis* on the analogy of a family or a household'.[23] But the principle uniting this extended Roman family was not 'engagement in a common enterprise' (for example, the mission of world domination with which Rome is often associated); it was 'respect for the *mos majorem*, ancient customs, and respect for the law'. Much of the strength of this principle was derived from its religious character; for Oakeshott, 'the *populus Romanus* was a *curia* (a religious society) composed of *curiae* (religious guilds)', and Roman politics 'never ceased to have an element of religious ritual.'[24]

In his account of Roman government, Oakeshott emphasized the distinction between *res publica*, the 'public concern' in which all Romans shared, and the *civitas*, or the Roman state. The belief in a Roman *res publica*, 'the destiny or *fortuna* of the Roman people', had made Rome not only, like Athens, a political community, but also a civil or legal community, 'a community which recognized itself as private individuals or families joined together in the enjoyment of rights and duties

---

[22] See *Morality and Politics in Modern Europe*, p. 109.

[23] 'Roman Political Thought (1)', p. 211.

[24] 'Roman Political Thought (1)', p. 213.

in respect of one another'. This notion of civil community, he claimed, had not emerged so clearly in Athens as in Rome, but it was essential to 'the sort of community we should be at home in', for the distinction between private and public communities was also crucial in modern political thought.[25]

The key term as far as Oakeshott was concerned was *lex*. This 'positive and historical' conception of law emerged from older ideas of *fas*, law as imposed by religious duties, and *jus*, law as a kind of moral rule. The significance of *lex* was that it 'stood for a law known to have been made at a certain time and a written down law', the equivalent of a modern statute. In this sense the Romans could be said to have arrived at a conception of sovereign authority that never fully emerged in Greece. 'A "sovereign" authority is not merely one that has no contemporary superior, but one which is emancipated from the past.'[26]

Roman thought also differed from the Greeks in understanding government as a combination *auctoritas* ('authority') and *potestas* ('legal power', which blended 'leading' with 'administration', in other words, the executive power). Etymologically, *auctoritas* and *auctor* were derived from the verb *augere*, meaning to increase, augment, 'add lustre to'. The *auctoritas* of the *auctor*, then, was that of a founder: Romulus was the *auctor* of Rome, and his *auctoritas* was believed to have been passed down through all subsequent generations. It was, however, the authority of a teacher or adviser, not a commander, and it was, so far as the institutions of Roman government were concerned, located chiefly in the senate, which was thought of as 'composed of *patres*, the "fathers" of the *populus Romanus*'.[27]

Commanding or ruling required *potestas*, power not as sheer force (*potentia*) but legal powers distributed amongst the various offices of state, each of which bore 'the right and the duty to do certain things'. Not only could 'all the rights and duties which pertained to all the different current officers of state' be subsumed in the concept of the total *potestas* available to government, the *potestas* of an office could be distinguished from the office to which it belonged. 'Thus, Augustus was successively endowed with the *potestas* of a

---

[25] 'Roman Political Thought (2)', p. 224.
[26] 'Roman Political Thought (3)', p. 245.
[27] 'Roman Political Thought (2)', p. 227.

consul, of a proconsul, of a tribune and of a censor', even though he was legally barred from holding those offices.

The significance of the principate, according to Oakeshott, was not just that an unprecedented amount of *potestas* was concentrated in the hands of a single individual, but that *potestas* and *auctoritas* were for the first time combined. The consequence of this development was that the distinction between the two was blurred; 'the later jurists tended to ignore [it], regarding the will of the *imperator* as supreme, and not worrying to consider very much how he became endowed with this supremacy'. Even then, however, a Roman emperor did not automatically become a despot exercising what the Romans called *dominium*, rule based solely on ownership; Caligula's declaration that 'I can treat anyone exactly as I like' was 'a desperate departure from the traditions of Roman government' that was not typical of a Roman emperor.[28]

Whatever one makes of this reading of the Roman political vocabulary, it is significant for understanding Oakeshott's own thought; in particular, the words we have been discussing were crucial to his mature political philosophy. The reader of the essay 'On Civil Association' in *On Human Conduct* will immediately notice that it uses many of the same Latin words to denote key ideas, and there is certainly a monograph waiting to be written by someone suitably qualified on their importance in Oakeshott's thought.

Roman politics was decisively altered not only by the end of the republic but also by the emergence of Christianity. This 'introduced a tension between religion and politics which had never before existed' in Roman experience, and was, Oakeshott thought, an ultimately victorious challenge to the foundational 'myth' sustaining that experience. In his introduction to an edition of *Leviathan* some years before, Oakeshott had argued that the Christian myth of the fall had fuelled the imagination of thinkers from Augustine to Hobbes, and he makes that argument again in his lectures on medieval political thought. The notion that a society requires such a myth if it is to have the cohesion necessary for civil association, however, is one that he never really worked out in detail; it is the source of some unresolved tensions in his thought.

---

[28] 'Roman Political Thought (2)', p. 236.

In the modern world, as Oakeshott's theory of modality implicitly recognizes, an irreducible plurality of viewpoints is the norm, but this plurality precludes the shared background he believed the Roman and Christian social myths had provided in ancient and medieval times. Hence, the possibility of maintaining the practical analogue of civil association, that is, government through the rule of law, is also adversely affected insofar as this depends on the existence of such a shared background. Yet in his theory of civil association, Oakeshott remarked only that it required the existence of some shared values, without ever really giving his attention either to the means of their generation or the form they ought to take.

Oakeshott could have replied that these were contingent, historic matters beyond the strict remit of political philosophy. But if one seeks outside his strictly philosophical writings for anything like a new 'myth' appropriate to modernity, one finds only the negative view that contemporary societies are united mostly by their acquisitiveness, as in his retelling of the Tower of Babel story.[29] Modern nationalist doctrines were similarly incapable of providing the right kind of 'glue' for civil association, as these lectures make clear.[30] Again, however, although he appears to have believed (unlike Carl Schmitt) in a form of patriotic sentiment that did not rely for its viability on excluding others, he never worked out this belief in detail.

To return to the lectures themselves, Oakeshott argued that the end of the Roman world could not be precisely dated, but that the universal extension of Roman citizenship throughout the empire marked a significant stage in its decline. The smaller the personal connection with the myth of the original foundation, the harder it became for individuals to experience it as a motivation for action. The Roman world ended, he seems to have thought, because its inhabitants lost the will to defend it – a conclusion reminiscent of Collingwood's remark that civilizations 'die in the night'.

Medieval Political Thought (Lectures 16–22)

Oakeshott extensively revised the medieval lectures around the time he retired, perhaps with an eye to publication, add-

---

[29] See 'The Tower of Babel', *On History*, pp. 165–94.

[30] 'The Authority of Governments and the Obligations of Subjects (2)', pp. 444–6.

ing a lecture on 'The Medieval Theory of Empire' and considerably expanding his treatment of Augustine and Aquinas. That his respect for medieval political thought matched his admiration of the Romans will not surprise those familiar with his published writings. This respect registered the unpromising beginnings of the medieval world, which emerged from the ruined fragments of the western Roman empire. The connection between the Roman and medieval civilizations was never entirely sundered, however, and in the lectures Oakeshott can be found emphasizing the linguistic and intellectual survivals. The Latin language and the Christian religion were, to his mind, two important bases on which medieval Europe was raised.

Oakeshott saw Christianity as supplying a sustaining 'myth' on which virtually all Europeans could draw for their self-understanding, and from the Latin language those who were literate gained 'a past-relationship with a Roman civilization in terms of which they came to understand themselves'. Oakeshott had made clear at the start of his lectures on Greece that the subjectivity of historical actors was not decisive in deciding what had really been going on at a particular time in history. Nevertheless, what people believed they were doing was still a component of whatever may have been going on, and we must attend to these beliefs when evaluating the place of institutions in the history of political thought. For Oakeshott, institutions were 'patterns of conduct, manners of behaving'.[31]

Early medieval politics characteristically lacked such settled patterns. Oakeshott believed that unlike Greek and Roman politics, medieval European politics began not from tribal associations but from an anarchic host of competing claims to rule advanced by rival 'noble' families. Medieval history was in a sense the history of the formation of institutions, like parliaments, which had no exact earlier equivalents. Despite the chaotic situation that followed the collapse of Roman authority, Oakeshott had no sympathy for the idea that the medieval centuries were the 'dark ages': 'the view that this was a period of European history of even compara-

---

[31] 'Medieval Political Experience', p. 265.

tive stagnation has nothing whatever to be said in its favour', he flatly declared.[32]

A foundational medieval belief was that the right to rule was God-given, in the sense that 'for men to be in subjection to other men, was so remarkable a situation that it could be justified only by supposing that this right to rule came from God.' Christian belief acted, in other words, as a limiting force in medieval arguments about the authority of governments. For Oakeshott, the ideas of absolute monarchy and divine hereditary right are characteristically early modern, not medieval: 'the belief in a hereditary right to rule is one of the signs that medieval politics has come to an end.'[33]

He also argued that medieval authority was no more directly linked to ownership than Greek or Roman beliefs about authority had been. Though medieval monarchs were usually amongst the greatest landholders in their kingdoms, it was not because of this that they were considered legitimate rulers. It was a 'great achievement of medieval political thought' to have grasped the distinction between *dominium*, authority in virtue of the lordship that came from ownership, and *potestas*, authority derived from a ceremony of investiture and exercised over vassals acknowledged to have privileges of their own.[34]

Discussing the Romans, Oakeshott had emphasized that 'the most fundamental of all distinctions in political thought is the distinction between "force" or "violence", and "authority"'; between *potentia*, which is physical, and *potestas* or *auctoritas*, which is mental; between "might" and "right"'.[35] He claimed that, even in its earliest days, the medieval world was never without some kind of law, but that it underwent a process analogous to that which occurred in ancient Rome and which Athens had never quite completed: the creation of a positive law in which the societies concerned emancipated themselves from the binding force of custom.

This process was assisted by 'the penetration of medieval Europe by Roman legal ideas', which Oakeshott described as

---

[32] *Ibid.*

[33] Oakeshott deleted this remark in the lecture on 'Medieval Government', but see p. 268.

[34] 'The Authority of Governments and the Obligations of Subjects (3)', p. 462.

[35] 'Medieval Law', p. 294.

having an 'ambiguous' quality. While those ideas 'seemed to proclaim an autocrat', they also suggested that the ruler 'owed his position to popular approval and authority'. Moreover, while attributing to government the power of 'remoulding the law of a community', they invoked 'the more familiar notion of rulers owing their authority as lawmakers to their subjects.'

That is not to say that medieval government was democratic in the modern sense, any more than Greek or Roman government had been. Oakeshott saw the primary activity of medieval government – the means by which a medieval polity was maintained – as providing justice through a hierarchy of courts, not pursuing policy under centralized direction (one of the distinctive features of modern government). Parliaments, which acted as both 'assistants and critics of royal government', provided 'the medieval answer to the problem of how to reconcile the belief in the fixity of law with the need for legal innovation'.

Parliaments not only gave advice, Oakeshott claimed; they also embodied the principle of consent. This is obviously a controversial point, but a very important one given the tendency of political theorists to regard consent as an early modern, usually Lockean, concept. In arguing that 'the feudal principle that a man's rights may not be altered without his consent' was 'already there in the organization of a feudal society', Oakeshott was detaching consent from its exclusive association with modern liberal democratic thought. Indeed, he claimed that it was often derived by medieval thinkers themselves from their reading of Justinian's Institutes, for example in the statement that *quod omnes tangit, ad omnibus approbetur*, or 'what touches all must be approved by all'. Similarly, 'representation' becomes not a modern notion, but a medieval one; thanks to the feudal hierarchy of reciprocal obligations, 'the possibility of one man "representing" others and both speaking and consenting on their behalf presented no puzzles or difficulties. Men "represented" others long before anyone began to think about "representation", or to talk about a principle of representation'.[36]

Before we leave the medieval lectures, we should note how Oakeshott handled the two thinkers in this period to whom he devoted entire lectures, Augustine and Aquinas.

---

[36] 'Medieval Parliaments', p. 315.

As Christian thinkers, both believed in a 'natural law' that was in fact divine in origin and 'absolute in its authority, above kings and emperors'. Refined by successive generations, it became 'much more speculatively satisfactory than the older notion that made law must not conflict with the ancient customs or that what was Roman was good.'[37]

Christian natural law, being theologically inspired, also departed from ancient, particularly Aristotelian, thought, in regarding political community as by no means 'natural' to human beings. In early Christian thought, government was no more than a regrettable expedient, necessary only until the imminent onset of the last days. Augustine, writing when this particular apocalyptic expectation had begun to subside, provided a 'sanctification of the imperial Roman government', of the '*pax Romana* seen *sub specie aeternitatis*', which saw some positive virtue in civil order, even if it was only a shadow of heavenly justice. The Hobbesian inspiration for Oakeshott's reading of Augustine is visible in his description of the *pax* of the earthly city as 'an unmistakable mitigation of the war of all against all which would otherwise spring from the unhindered self-preference of each man.'[38]

Augustine, as a man with urgent practical problems to solve, was engaged in a different kind of thinking than Aquinas, whose main aim was to reconcile Christian and Aristotelian thought in the light of Aristotle's rediscovered writings, which provided 'an explanation of human character, human activity, human virtue which seemed to conflict radically with the accepted Christian one'. To bring Christian and Aristotelian thought together, Aquinas had to modify the relationship between grace and humanity's earthly existence so that the two were no longer sharply opposed in the manner that Augustine had described. Political life could once again be seen as in some sense 'natural' to human beings. Though not the 'total' activity it had been for Aristotle, it ought nonetheless to be free from 'ecclesiastical control or supervision'.

The education necessary for salvation was a matter for the church, but the care of subjects, 'the protection of their rights and the custody of their laws', was in civil hands. Oakeshott's interpretation of Aquinas's writings on the *lex civilis*

---

[37] 'Medieval Law', p. 294.
[38] 'Medieval Political Philosophy (1): Augustine', p. 335.

reveals once more his ability to find his own political philosophy reflected in the ideas of earlier thinkers. He not only read Aquinas as arguing that 'the relation of civil to natural law...is the negative relationship of a rule which lays down what seems to be convenient in the circumstances to a principle which gives no specific guidance but must not be rejected' – an argument analogous to his own account of the relationship between law and a broader moral code – but saw the positive conclusions of Aquinas' *prudentia politica* as very much in line with his own.

We may conclude this section by quoting Oakeshott's summary of Aquinas' political creed. That 'not all sin can conveniently be made punishable as crime; that what cannot be abolished except at too great a cost must be tolerated; that the expectations of subjects (even if they are not manifestly just expectations) must not be peremptorily overridden; that the *lex civilis* is not an instrument of "salvation" but only of *civilitas* and *bene vivere*; and that to correct an evil in a manner which may destroy the *fides* (mutual trust) and the *amicitia utilis* (bonds of affection) which hold society together, is political suicide' were all Thomistic conclusions compatible with his own views on civil association and the rule of law.[39]

Modern Political Thought (Lectures 23–33)

Enough has been said to support the view that modern Europe, to Oakeshott's mind, was best understood as following the often divergent paths laid down in the medieval period. Although he acknowledged that the modern state enjoyed a 'sovereign' combination of exclusive secular and religious authority in a way no medieval monarchy had ever done, Oakeshott nevertheless saw it as built 'of materials got from the ruins of a medieval castle and a medieval abbey'.[40] Rather than emphasize the discontinuities between medieval and modern politics, he preferred to stress the continuities; rulers of modern states were just 'thinly disguised prince-bishops' or 'godly princes'. The Reformation in particular had allowed earthly monarchs to acquire the authority previously wielded by the church.

In the forging of this new combination, there slipped in a confusion between *jurisdictio* and *gubernaculum*, the activities

---

[39] 'Medieval Political Philosophy (2): Aquinas', p. 358.
[40] 'The Generation of a Modern State', p. 375.

of ruling and of pursuing policy, first in legislation and then in 'specifically judicial processes', that made the modern state an ambiguous entity and explains why the modern 'policy' state continually threatened to become a 'police' state. The confusion was fueled by the exigencies of war, warfare being the arena of policy in which the end is most easily taken to justify the means.

These conflicting tendencies at work in modern European politics were already obvious in the attitude of early modern rulers to the diversity that Oakeshott believed had been typical of medieval societies. Both 'the disposition to generate solidarity by destroying diversity' and 'the disposition to generate solidarity by containing diversity' could be seen at work, but the former was more usual; guild, ghetto, and gypsy alike felt its impact.

Persecution was, in other words, nothing new; the goal of a racially homogenous state, like the mono-confessional state, was at least as old as the sixteenth century. There was, Oakeshott implies, continuity between Spanish efforts to purge the kingdom of Muslims and Jews (1492, which marked both the fall of Granada and the expulsion of the Jews, is a symbolic date) and Hitler's Aryan project. There was class persecution too: 'The aristocrat exiled because he conflicted with the desired solidarity of a state is a familiar figure in modern European history, from the fifteenth to the twentieth century.'[41]

Why, then, did the sovereign state, which had the potential to produce a singularly repressive form of government, draw so much support? Oakeshott's answer was that only a 'sovereign' state offered emancipation from the hindrances of medieval society. Given the obvious dangers of such a state, compounded by the ever-increasing material power it could wield in addition to its legal sovereignty, an urgent question quickly became 'How can a government be constituted so that it may safely be trusted with "sovereign" authority?'

It could not be answered, Oakeshott argued, without some view of the kind of institution a state was. Manifestly, it was not a 'natural' one. 'A modern European state was so empirical a construction, was so manifestly a contingent collection

---

[41] 'The Generation of a Modern State', p. 380.

of human beings, that to seek a "natural" unity in it would seem to deny its most notable feature'.[42]

But if the state were admitted to be in some sense artificial, a variety of responses were still possible. For some, it was like a joint-stock company; indeed, the popularity of the very term 'association' as a description of a human community gathered under the aegis of a state indicated that the medieval world was ending. The influence of economic analogies was far reaching, to the point that Oakeshott thought it had 'come to supersede all others in importance'. The dominant view was that a state was an association united in 'the exploitation of the natural resources of the world' – an 'economy' or a 'factory'. Arising first in a religious context in the writings of authors such as Bacon, only the materialism had survived.

It is easy to see how this understanding of modern European political thought was transposed into the scathing metaphor of the Tower of Babel mentioned above, but in the lectures Oakeshott avoided breaking into a tirade, only noting that a third understanding had become increasingly widespread: one that took the state to be neither natural, nor artificial (in the sense of being entirely the product of design), but the historic product of innumerable choices. Thinkers such as Ferguson, Hume, Burke, Vico, and Hegel viewed the state as, like the European landscape itself, 'a blend of "nature" and "art", a blend of the "necessary" and the "chosen"...in which the "given" and the "made" are indistinguishable.'[43]

Oakeshott clearly felt himself closest to this strand of thought, describing as it did a state that is 'neither a god to be worshipped nor a formless chaos to be merely endured' but 'something for which we are conditionally responsible'.[44] It is therefore worth examining his remarks on how such a state had been thought to generate authority. He argued that questions like 'Why ought I to submit?', 'What would absolve me from my duty to submit?', and 'By what authority does a ruler rule?' employed 'the logic of right' rather than 'the logic of fact'.

---

[42] 'Interpretations of the Modern European State (1)', p. 414.
[43] 'Interpretations of the Modern European State (2)', p. 426.
[44] 'Interpretations of the Modern European State (2)', p. 427.

The searches for an original contract or divine endowment that were so prominent in the seventeenth and eighteenth centuries at least recognized that questions like these must be answered with reasons that point to an ultimate source of the right claimed.[45] The answers may make reference to a shared framework of legal rules, but they must not be reducible simply to the existence of sufficient force to ensure compliance. Oakeshott summed this up succinctly by saying 'Power does not have "reasons"; "right" does not have a cause'.[46] That is, the questions have to do with why I *ought* to obey, and to force me to obey without also having the right to use force would violate their terms. Although, as Hume had long ago remarked, lawful government supervened on force, it was not the product of force; although authority tended to generate power, the reverse was not the case. A qualitative shift was required for the move from might to right.

A cogent argument in terms of right can always be rejected, even if it cannot be refuted, but at this point, as Hobbes also believed, civility has broken down and we are in imminent danger of violent confrontation. Authority was so important because it was the only possible 'cohesive' belief about government. Oakeshott's argument admits that everything governments *do* is controversial, but insists that for there to *be* government at all, it must be possible to disagree with a policy but still acknowledge the government's right to carry it out.

The confusion between power and authority, Oakeshott felt, lay at the heart of the direction modern politics had taken. Until 'quite recent times', most claims to authority were in religious terms, but Europeans had ceased to share a Christian worldview that made them tenable. More modern claims to rule – for example, by virtue of membership of the proletariat or of an 'enlightened' elite – nevertheless used the same narrative structure in the speculative philosophies of history they created for themselves. For both Marxist and *philosophe*, the past was oppression and the future deliverance.

The belief in 'progress' could be said to share this structure, and it has sometimes been regarded as a characteristic liberal belief. But that a regime is 'progressive', cannot, on

---

[45] 'The Authority of Governments and the Obligations of Subjects (3)', p. 466.
[46] 'The Authority of Governments and the Obligations of Subjects (3)', p. 456.

Oakeshott's view, confer authority (though it may win approval), for authority cannot stem from anything government does. This is why he told his students that 'what is called "Liberalism", in its general or European sense' had 'systematically obscured' the problem of authority.[47] The remark is all the more striking because Oakeshott himself can, as he acknowledged, be read as locating his own political philosophy in the liberal family. The lectures, then, reinforce the view that the complex theory of civil association in *On Human Conduct* is best understood as an effort to dispel this obscurity for the benefit of liberalism. It is certainly true that he persistently singled out the writings of English Whig and liberal authors like Locke, Bentham, and J.S. Mill as suffering from it.

For Oakeshott, a more promising liberal answer to the problem of authority, one that observed the 'logic of right', was that authority derived from popular consent. That left undetermined what was to count as consent or how to assess it, but it was at least an answer couched in the correct terms. The logical incoherence of merging the discourses of authority and policy had not, however, prevented episodes of despotism. In the French and Russian revolutions, for example, governments had used their authority to pursue some goal – overthrowing feudalism or destroying the bourgeoisie – in which all were obliged to participate.

Insofar as governments had imposed such goals, however, they suppressed the identity of a modern European state as an association in terms of the rule of law, one in which individuals were to be left to their own devices unless these caused a disturbance of the peace. The final lectures were devoted to this subject, focusing on the confusion between a government confined to 'providing the conditions in which its subjects may pursue their own chosen and various ends', and one dedicated to 'organizing its subjects in the pursuit of a single, premeditated end or purpose'. This is the distinction presented in *On Human Conduct* as an omnipresent and definitive tension between 'civil' and 'enterprise' association. In the lectures Oakeshott spoke of 'telocratic' and 'nomocratic' forms of government, but the distinction is the same.

---

[47] 'The Authority of Governments and the Obligations of Subjects (1)', p. 433.

In a telocratic, goal-oriented state, activities are 'permitted only in relation to the chosen end and only in so far as they contribute to this end'. Even art becomes 'an adjunct of policy'. This view finds, at bottom, no difference between communism and fascism, and one must acknowledge that asserting the fundamental identity of these supposedly starkly contrasting ideologies of 'left' and 'right' remains controversial. Oakeshott's reply was always that 'left' and 'right' were categories of practical politics wholly inappropriate for detached theorizing; one of the virtues of his approach is its ability to cut across them.

Oakeshott focused in particular on what happened to law in a government undergoing a telocratic drift. Legality 'is recognized to have no independent virtue, but to be valuable only in relation to the pursuit of the chosen end.' It is subordinated, that is, to the pursuit of whatever is held to be the 'common good' or 'social purpose', which is always 'a substantive condition of things'. Ceaseless technological and industrial advance had only encouraged the faulty inference that because a government had the power to pursue an overarching policy, it therefore should. Oakeshott saw this view of government as an ultimate explanation of European colonialism and imperialism, even going so far as to say that 'in Europe, it may be recognized as governing a European "state" as if it were a colony.'[48] He also thought that in the twentieth century, the telocratic perspective had continuously infiltrated the notion of the 'welfare state', a confusion made possible because the nomocratic view he favoured also acknowledged an obligation to provide for those unable to provide for themselves.

Standing in the way of a complete victory for telocracy was the continuing pluralism of modern European states. Communities holding 'a variety of religious and moral beliefs, and 'engaged in multifarious and rapidly changing activities, occupations, and enterprises' were not promising material on which to impose a single 'condition of things'. Since attempts to interfere with 'the freedom to make choices for themselves' were likely to antagonize European citizens, none of the unmistakably telocratic regimes that the twentieth century produced had survived.

---

[48] See 'The Office of Government (1)', p. 477.

We should note that Oakeshott's 'nomocratic' government is not to be simply identified with the 'minimal' or the 'non-interventionist' state; the distinction he was driving at did not concern the size of government or the frequency of its actions, but their character. A government could employ many people and be vigorously active without forsaking its adjudicatory and peacekeeping role. Historically, governments had often been driven in a nomocratic direction by the clash of two or more telocratic perspectives; the only way to escape the 'civil war of telocracies' which he thought had characterized the seventeenth century was to move towards a 'substantively neutral legal order' that shied away from explicitly promoting one or the other conception of godliness.

This view may perhaps be taken as a reworking of what is sometimes called the history of toleration, underlining the essentially liberal nature of Oakeshott's account. The readings he presented in his closing lecture of Kant, Bentham, and Adam Smith in the light of this history of nomocratic ideas on government only reinforce this impression. Nevertheless, he remained insistent to the end on the ambiguous character of the modern European state, and never resorted to arguing that the nomocratic perspective, which he transparently preferred, would, could, or even should win the day.

It may, to borrow a phrase, be easy to conceive of a better series of lectures on the history of political thought, but it is probably not so easy to write one.[49] Oakeshott's effort shows him to have been as aware as any Marxist or Foucauldian of the importance of material factors like land ownership or technology, but to have persistently rejected the belief that these were necessarily decisive in favour of an historical perspective to which agency and contingency were ineliminably important. Overall, the lectures are the most successful sustained piece of historical thinking of all his works, in the sense that they stick to the explication of the key terms and institutions of the period in their contexts. While he often drew parallels with later eras in his accounts of the Greek, Roman, and medieval periods, it cannot be said that his treat-

---

[49] See John Passmore, review of Roger Scruton, *From Descartes to Wittgenstein* (London: Routledge, 1981), *Times Literary Supplement*, 19 February 1982, p. 182.

ments of them were mainly concerned with their significance for us; their relevance as the source of much of our own political thought and vocabulary is taken for granted, and the focus is on understanding them in their own right.

A Note on the Texts

During his own lifetime Oakeshott made these lectures available to colleagues and friends. It appears that he initially consented to their publication, and then changed his mind, for the photocopies in the Oakeshott archive of the lectures dated 1968–9 on which this volume has largely been based (LSE 1/1/21, folders 2–5) had clearly been prepared with this aim in mind. Each page had been numbered, and a title page and table of contents supplied. However, it was clear that the version at LSE 1/1/21 could not be published just as it stood.

This first effort at publication left some pages absent or misplaced, and there were numerous autograph sheets and marginalia not integrated into the main body of the text. While this volume of the *Selected Writings* was in preparation, a more legible but incomplete set of photocopies of the lectures (covering Greece and Rome only) was deposited at the Oakeshott archive (LSE 19/1). In addition, the editors had access to some slightly earlier versions of the lectures dated 1966–7 which remain in private circulation. In the cases where there were gaps, deficiencies, insertions, etc. in the version at LSE 1/1/21, then, we sought guidance from the alternate versions. The main source of each text is given in a note at the end of each lecture.

It is unknown whether the original MS of the 1968–9 lectures from which both LSE sets were taken survives, but this final series appears not in fact to have differed greatly overall from the versions given in the three previous years, though there are often significant differences of detail. Oakeshott altered the whole of the first lecture extensively, for example. He also entirely rewrote other important parts of the series, including the first three sections of the first Aristotle lecture, the account of Plato's myth of the cave, and the first section of the lecture on 'Medieval Government' (previously given the more specific title of 'Medieval Kingship'). The 1968–9 version also included three lectures on medieval political thought which were either not present in the circulated versions ('The Medieval Theory of Empire') or appeared in a much more condensed form (those on Augustine and Aquinas) as 'Medieval Political Philosophy'.

In most cases, Oakeshott worked on the 1968–9 version simply by making additions and deletions to the typescripts he had used for the 1966–7 lectures in his own hand, though in case of the 'Introduction' he had an entirely fresh typescript made. In some cases, however, the 1968–9 version contains copies of autograph sheets that were obviously intended to replace sections of the typescript, even though these had not been crossed out. Unfortunately, it is not entirely clear in all cases exactly where the revisions were to begin, and the only solution has been an educated guess based on the context, as in the section on Plato's early life.

Moreover, in all the versions of the lectures, some passages were placed in brackets, the significance of which is not entirely clear. They cannot always be assumed simply to be deletions, as there are also plenty of crossings-out which unmistakably do signify deletions. It seems most likely that the brackets sometimes indicated passages to be omitted if the lecturer was running short of time. Such bracketed passages have therefore been retained here unmarked, on the grounds that the text as it now stands is to be read, and not heard. The deletions themselves have generally been treated as authoritative, as there is no reason to think they were not made by Oakeshott himself, but in a few cases, where the final version of the lectures omitted some passages from the earlier versions that gave a more extended discussion of the same point, these have been retained as they seemed to expand rather than alter the thought involved.

As in volume 1, the aim was to make a good text publicly available rather than attempt a fully annotated critical edition. Transcription was generally unproblematic; some portions of the lectures were in manuscript, others in typescript, but Oakeshott's handwriting remained good throughout his life, and the intentions of his amendments were usually unmistakable. In a few cases, some of the marginalia proved illegible, usually either because the original photocopy had been taken with insufficient care, or because of the poor quality of the copy.

Once more, the general layout of Oakeshott's original text has been retained as far as was consistent with presenting it in an editorially coherent manner. Throughout, where

Oakeshott used section numberings, or inserted section breaks, these have also been retained, but with a consistent and simplified format to produce a more readable text.

Oakeshott's own footnotes and the small number of editorial notes have been kept separate, with the latter appearing as endnotes. These are restricted to giving the location of the version used. In the few cases in which it proved impossible to see exactly where Oakeshott meant to place corrections, additions, or notes, this has been noticed while inserting such emendations amongst his footnotes. In the main body of the text, obvious mistakes in punctuation, spelling and grammar have been silently corrected.

The use of capitals for offices (King or king) in the text was inconsistent, and lower case has generally been preferred here, except for titles held by specific individuals; the popes, but Pope Innocent III. Abbreviations have also been expanded, so that, for example, 'xvii century' becomes 'seventeenth century'. Ampersands have been replaced by 'and', and superscripting has been ignored. The underlinings in the text were so extensive that they have usually not been replaced by italics, except in the case of double underlinings or other instances where emphasis was clearly intended. Double quotation marks have been replaced with single quotation marks except for quotations within quotations. Words and phrases in languages other than English (chiefly transliterated Greek and Latin) have been placed in italics to make them stand out in the text.

One

Introduction

1

What I have to offer you in these lectures is best described as a study of political thought, or aids to the study of political thought.

In the main, it will be an historical study.

First, we shall be concerned to find out what has actually been believed and thought and said about politics, or in the idiom of politics, from time to time and from place to place, among some of the peoples of Europe during the last three thousand years.

Secondly, we shall be trying to understand and account for these beliefs and ways of thinking by relating them to the circumstances of their appearance. And this is what I mean by an historical study.

History I take to be a mode of thought in which events, human actions, beliefs, manners of thinking, are considered in relation to the conditions, or the circumstantial context, in which they appeared.

This circumstantial context, however, is composed of other events, actions, and beliefs, just as the context of a word in a sentence is composed of other words from which we gather its meaning on that particular occasion.

That is to say, history is not a mode of thought in which we understand events, actions, and beliefs as examples of the operation of general laws, but one in which we understand events, actions, and beliefs in relation to things of the same kind – namely, other events, actions, and beliefs. The question the historian is out to answer is: What is the significance of this event, or action, or belief in the context of events and beliefs in which it appears.

Now, I have described what we shall be doing in this way because I do not want you to think that I am suggesting anything so specific as a relationship of cause and effect between the conditions or the circumstances in which a belief appeared and the belief itself.

For example, the geographical conditions of ancient Greece, or the institution of slavery, or their religious beliefs, did not cause the Greeks to think about politics in the way they did. These are merely part of the context which helps to make ancient Greek political beliefs more intelligible to us.

An historical study of political beliefs cannot, then, supply anything like a final explanation, or even anything that could properly be called a 'justification' of these beliefs.

We must be content if, in the process, these political beliefs and thoughts become a little more intelligible to us, and a little less mysterious, than they often are.

The point of view here is that nothing which men have thought or done is intelligible except in its own context of circumstances.

And the enterprise here is to make one event or belief more intelligible by seeing it in a context of other events or beliefs.

2

But, although this is to be an historical study, I want to avoid the appearance of putting before you anything like a continuous history of European political thought.

Adventurous books have been written in this style, but I do not think that any of them is really satisfactory.

Some people have believed that there is something to be called 'the history of political thought' which reveals a kind of cumulative achievement of European peoples gradually acquiring a 'truer' (or at least, a less erroneous) understanding of politics, or even a progressively more intelligent manner of considering and answering political questions.

It has even been believed that the history of political thought may be understood as the story of the 'mistakes' the human race has made in thinking about and practicing politics. And that in studying this history we may learn ourselves to avoid these mistakes.

I do not, myself, think this is so. I cannot detect a history of political thought which reveals a gradual accumulation of political wisdom and understanding. Indeed, I cannot detect anything which could properly correspond to the expression '*the* history of political thought'.

What I think I can see is different peoples, at different times, in different intellectual and physical circumstances, engaging in politics in different ways and finding different things to think about it.

And sometimes I think I can see some sort of an explanation for these different peoples having had the thoughts which they did have. And that is about all.

Consequently, I am inclined to direct your attention away from anything like a continuous story of European political thought, and towards the study of the political thought directly connected with some of the different and more memorable passages of political experience which the histories of European peoples have to show.

I will tell you later which these passages are.

Each of them I regard as a relatively self-contained political culture, and therefore as the proper context for political beliefs. *(distinct!)*

3

Now, a certain amount of unnecessary mystery has gathered round this expression: 'political thought'.

Some people speak and write of it as if it were a special kind of thinking; and in this way they make it more difficult to understand than it really is.

Others are disposed to include in it everything that has ever been thought or said or written about the human condition; and in this way they make it appear less specific than it really is.

But as I understand it, 'political thought' is *not* a special and mysterious kind of thinking with standards and manners peculiar to itself; and it is thinking about something quite specific, which should not be confused with anything else, namely *political* activity.

Most human activities are capable of being thought about and reflected upon; and in certain circumstances they are apt to be thought about.

We think about bringing up children, building houses, breeding horses, about fishing, and about banking.

Each of these activities provokes questions peculiar to itself, but in every case the common objects of thought are being pursued.

We think in order to devise appropriate courses of action and in order to find reasons for recommending them. We reflect in order to understand, to make more intelligible, to interpret, or to explain.

Political thinking is people pursuing these common objects of thought but in connection with a specific activity, different from any other; an activity called politics.

4

We begin, then, with an experience, the experience of a political life and political activity. Without this there can be no political thought.

Consequently, in order to be able to recognize political thought, we should have at least some provisional ideas about the political activity which is its necessary condition.

There are, of course, a great number of different kinds of human activity.

Some of them are primordial, like eating and drinking. Others are more sophisticated, like writing poetry, travelling in foreign countries, buying and selling, and curing diseases.

Political activity is, in the first place, to be understood as *one* among the numerous activities which have become characteristic of human beings.

Moreover, it belongs to the more sophisticated rather than the primordial activities. It is an acquired, rather than a 'natural', activity.

 Everybody, in order to live, must somehow get a living; but there have been many peoples who have had no 'politics', and who are consequently innocent of political thought.

Now, every kind of activity requires certain conditions for its appearance and practice. And normally these conditions do not appear suddenly and complete. They emerge gradually, and at a certain point the activity appears unmistakably with the emergence of the conditions which make it possible.

In order to be an accountant, you need a manner of doing business which uses accounts, which uses ledgers and account books, and you need to be familiar with certain invented mathematical techniques.

At what point in the emergence of all this does the man we now call an 'accountant' appear?

In order to be an astronomer you need not only the stars but also questions of a certain sort to ask about them, and instruments and techniques to help you find the answers.

At some point, not exactly to be discerned, the activity of mere star-gazing turns into astronomy. It is a question of the emergence of the necessary conditions in a sufficient and significant degree.

Our question is: What are the necessary conditions for the emergence of the activity we call 'politics'? What are the conditions required for the appearance of 'politicians'?

I think we may distinguish three important conditions for the appearance of a political experience.

Forgive me if I verge upon the obvious.

(1) Political activity is possible only where there is a plurality of human beings.

The solitary inhabitant of an island might write poetry, he might be a farmer or a geologist; the conditions for each of these activities are present. But he could not be a politician.

But political activity requires more than a mere plurality of human beings; it even requires more than a number of human beings living in close proximity to one another.

It requires an association of human beings.

Now, what constitutes an association is the recognition of common customs or rules of conduct. It is these rules of conduct which give the singleness or unity to an association which makes political activity possible.

But, on the other hand, an association of human beings in which there is no diversity of feeling, sentiment, belief, attitude, and activity could not generate a political experience.

This is why we are apt to think that a genuinely tribal society, which certainly has rules and customs, is not one in which politics is likely to appear. Such a society may have the necessary unity, but it rarely has the necessary diversity.

And this is why societies which admit a large variety of beliefs and activities among their members are apt to have a large place for political activity. And that is why associations capable of politics are apt to be, like the states of modern Europe, artificial associations which bring together in a single society people of diverse origins and cultures.

Politics, from one important point of view, may be said to be the activity in which a society deals with its diversities.

And, consequently, a society without diversities is apt to be a society without politics.

(2) The second condition for the emergence of political activity is the presence, within an association of the sort I have described, of some authority recognized to be the official custodian of the law of the association and the official director of the common affairs of the association. In short, a government of some sort; a ruling authority.

From one important point of view, political activity is itself concerned with the government and the instruments of government of a society. For these instruments constitute the recognized means by which a society deals with its diversities. And politics is deliberating on how, and upon what, to set these instruments to work.

As we shall see, it is quite possible to have government without politics, but it is impossible for there to be politics without government.

Another way of stating this condition for the emergence of political activity is to say that it is possible only in an association which has recognized a distinction between 'public' and 'private' and has acquired a specific authority whose office is concerned with 'public' affairs.

(3) But before political activity can appear a *third* condition must be satisfied.

Either the ruling authority itself, or the common law of the association, or the public policy being pursued, *or* all these, must be understood by the members of the association to be capable of being determined by human deliberation and action.

In other words, political activity is concerned with government, the instruments of governing, and with public policy. And it can appear only when what it is concerned with is understood to be amenable to human choice and decision.

This is, perhaps, the most important of the conditions of political activity.

It means that there is no place for 'politics' in an association whose members firmly believe that the ruling authority itself, the law and the instruments of government, are all utterly unalterable – not merely difficulty to change, but by their nature incapable of being changed.

And it means there is no place for politics in a world believed to be wholly determined by natural necessity.

If choice about human conduct is, for one reason or another, believed to be impossible, if there were no imaginable alternative to what is happening, and if that alternative could not be chosen by human beings, then politics would be impossible.

Politics, then, is an activity between human beings. We do not do politics with gods (unless we imagine the gods to be just like human beings), and we do not do politics with animals.

And the chief assumption about human beings which 'politics' entails, is that they are capable of determining their actions by taking thought.

Now, although politics without government is impossible, there is a distinction to be made. Ruling itself is not doing politics.

A ruling authority may engage in political activity either in relation to other ruling authorities, or in relation to its own subjects; but when it does so it is doing something other than ruling.

The reason why politics presupposes the possibility of alternative courses of action, and the possibility of change, is because it is an activity precisely concerned with deciding between alternative courses of action and with instituting change.

Politics is not ruling; it is thinking about what should be done and persuading or inducing those who have the authority to act to make certain choices and not others.

Thus, although a society may have certain rules and conventions about who should be listened to in deciding about its public affairs, or may suppress the utterance of opinions about its public affairs, in principle, 'politics' is not an activity confined to rulers, and it is an activity different from that of ruling itself.

These conditions, which must be satisfied if there is political activity at all, tell us, then, that there are certain intellectual and historical situations in which politics cannot appear.

But they tell us something more.

They tell us not to expect political activity to be merely present or absent, but to expect it to appear in varying degrees of significance.

They tell us to expect it to be a gradually emerging activity whose appearance anywhere cannot be exactly dated or assigned to any universal cause.

They tell us that political activity is like other activities in that it emerges imperceptibly with the emergence of the conditions which make it possible.

And lastly, they tell us to expect political activity not only to appear in varying degrees of significance, but also (according to circumstance) in varying degrees of intensity; and to expect it to be either a continuous activity or a merely intermittent activity.

5

Now, associations of human beings of this sort, associations which provide in a significant degree the conditions for political activity, have existed for about three thousand years.

This sort of association of human beings has been more common in some parts of the world than in others.

In many parts of the world, during these three thousand years, human beings have lived in communities of one sort or another in which there was no recognizable form of political activity – not because it was arbitrarily forbidden, but because the current beliefs about law, government, and the world in general allowed no place for it.

But the part of the world where associations of human beings capable of political activity have been commonest is what, generally speaking, we now call Europe.

'Politics' may be said to be, in the main, a European invention; it is Europe's somewhat embarrassing gift to the world.

But even in Europe, during the last three thousand years, there has been no continuous history of political activity.

It has emerged here and there, and it has often been submerged, or half-submerged, again. The best that can be said is that, in this part of the world, politics have never been allowed to lie submerged for any great length of time. Political activity has been as constantly rediscovered and reinvented as it has been lost or allowed to lapse.

For the most part, in the history of Europe, political societies (that is, associations of human beings which provide the conditions necessary for political activity) have emerged out of tribal societies. But there has been no uniform pattern in this emergence.

Some tribal societies have transformed themselves and have acquired the character of political societies by having to deal with changes forced upon them from the outside. But the commonest occasion for the emergence of a political society has been when a number of tribes have united to compose a new association.

And this has been not only the commonest occasion but also the most characteristic and the most decisive occasion. For a union of tribes is manifestly not itself a tribe, its law cannot be a tribal law, and its rulers are not tribal rulers: it is an association which provokes, almost inevitably, a new attitude to law, to government, and to the activity of governing and being governed, an attitude favourable to the emergence of political activity.

Such unions of tribes have, on some occasions, been the result of the choice of the tribes themselves (this was often the case in ancient Greece); on other occasions (in ancient Rome, for example, and in Scotland) it has been imposed by a conqueror. But wherever it has taken place it has been not only a momentous event, but also an exceedingly difficult achievement often taking many generations to accomplish.

Nor do we need to go to far distant times to observe the difficulty and the uncertainty with which a political society emerges from a union of tribes: the counterpart to what happened in ancient Greece and ancient Rome has been happening with an increasing momentum for the last sixty years in Africa and is taking place before our eyes.

6

Now, the relevance for us of these remarks about the conditions in which political activity and a political experience can appear is that they are also the conditions for the appearance of political thought.

There are, as we shall discover, many different levels of political thinking, but political thought may be said to appear, first, as deliberation directly connected with political activity: thought, that is to say, in the service of political decision and action.

And just as nobody acts unless he believes that the world is such that it may be acted upon and changed, so nobody deliberates about what should be done unless he believes that there are alternative courses of action open and that he is capable of making a choice.

In short, the assumption of political deliberation is that what goes on in the world is not determined solely by natural necessity, but is amenable to human choice. Now, when political thought appears as deliberation in the service of political action, the appropriate expression of this thought will be in words of a certain kind.

They may be words which simply express an opinion or a belief about what choice should be made; or they may be words which compose themselves into an exhortation, an advice, a warning, or an argument designed to recommend or to persuade or to justify.

In short, it would not be unreasonable, in looking for 'political thought', to look for it first in political speeches and debates and in the utterances of rulers, statesmen, and their advisers.

Many of these political utterances are directly concerned with decisions about what to do in specific political situations; and their vocabulary is often the vocabulary of ordinary practical activity.

The words used are the ordinary words we use whenever we recommend a certain course of action or predict its consequences – whenever we advise, warn, admonish, or restrain.

They are words which are not by any means peculiar to political thought, discourse, or argument.

But wherever 'politics' has established itself as one of the current activities of a society, wherever a significant political experience has emerged, a specifically political vocabulary has also emerged.

Sometimes the words in such a political vocabulary are new – invented in the course of political thinking – and have an exclusively political reference: words like 'state' or 'citizen' or 'empire'.

Sometimes they are the ordinary words of practical discourse which have been given a specifically political meaning: words like 'freedom', 'power', 'right', 'revolution', 'tyranny' – none of which were, in the first place, political words.

Now, this practical political vocabulary is of the utmost importance.

It is these words which express political beliefs. It is these words, and the way in which they are used in political argument or in the expression of political opinions, which tell us how a people thinks when it thinks about politics.

Every significant political experience has its own political vocabulary.

To be able to use that political vocabulary is the first of the political arts.

And, in the end, the only means we have of coming to understand any political experience, our own or that of another time and people, is by listening to the political utterance and by getting to know its political words and how they are used.

But all these political vocabularies, besides containing comparatively simple words, words which they are apt to share with the general vocabulary of practical discourse, contain some words which stand for larger and more generalized political thoughts.

Words, for example, like 'democracy', 'liberalism', 'nationalism'.

- Sometimes, they are collective words, which stand for complicated beliefs which may be taken to pieces and their components examined.
- Sometimes, they are used as if they were specially compelling reasons for pursuing a recommended policy, or specially compelling justifications for having done what has been done.

But, what is important, is that they all belong to this practical political vocabulary, used whenever political matters are discussed, debated, or argued about.

What we have to try to discern is their place and their significance in the arguments and utterances in which they appear.

The study of political thought may, then, in the first place, be understood as the study of political deliberation, discourse, and argument.

And what is to be studied is not only deliberation, discourse, and argument about matters of greatly varying dimensions – ranging from what shall be done tomorrow, through (for example) master-plans for the British economy, to questions such as: what is the ground of a ruler's authority to rule.

What is to be studied is also the different kinds of argument which are apt to appear in political discourse.

And the object of the study is to understand the thought embedded in this practical political deliberation and discourse, and to discern the assumptions it reflects, by putting it into its context of beliefs about the world and human beings.

In studying political thought, what we are seeking is something which may perhaps be called the intellectual organization, the organization of ideas, arguments and methods of argument, of a political experience.

What we are seeking is to understand political utterances in their place in what may be called the political culture of a people.

A history of thought is a history of men thinking, *not* a 'history' of abstract, disembodied 'ideas'.

7

Now, if it is reasonable to look, first, for political thought in the utterances which exhibit deliberation about practical political matters, and in the utterances in which practical political beliefs and policies are argued about, this is not the whole of the matter.

Not all thought is the servant of action.

And, besides the practical political thought – whose design is to diagnose political situations, to recommend responses to be made to them, to choose and to decide what shall be done or to defend or justify in argument what has been done – besides all this, there is another kind of thinking whose design is to understand and to explain.

In order to distinguish this kind of thinking about politics from the practical kind, it has often been called theoretical thinking: and so we have the expression 'political theory'.

But unfortunately this word 'theory' has become deeply corrupted, especially in connection with politics; and I prefer not to use it.

I shall call it, instead, *explanatory* thinking.

No significant political experience has appeared in the world without having provoked thought of this explanatory kind about politics.

And in connection with politics this impulse to understand and to explain has appeared in two different modes: historical and philosophical.

I do not propose, now, to explore further the nature of this explanatory thought about political activity.

My main point is to warn you that in this study of political thought we shall come across writers and pieces of writing which are not concerned to recommend or to defend practical political beliefs or policies, but which are concerned to explain political activity, either historically or philosophically.

And I want to suggest that we should do well to avoid confusing practical political beliefs and arguments with these other explanatory political theories and arguments. They belong, I think, to two different histories.

8

Now, this distinction between practical political sentiments, beliefs, ideas, aspirations; and theoretical, or explanatory, thinking about politics is important.

To have it in mind enables us to recognize the difference between different sorts of ideas, arguments, utterances.

It enables us, for example, not to mistake an argument designed to defend or justify a policy or a recommendation for an argument designed to explain or make it intelligible.

It enables us to distinguish between, for example, a writer like Machiavelli or Locke and a writer like Hobbes or Hegel.

It is a distinction more or less parallel to the distinction between religious beliefs, sentiments, and longings, and a theology in which these beliefs are transformed into a system of abstract ideas.

And what we are concerned with in this study of political thought is both the explanatory 'theories' which have emerged (and which correspond to a 'theology'), and the sentiments, beliefs, and aspirations which belong to practical political thought, and which correspond to the sentiments and beliefs of a popular religion.

9

Now, I have said that this study of political thought is to be, mainly, an historical study.

That is, we shall be trying to understand political beliefs and utterances as components of a political culture, and trying to understand political cultures as components of more general cultures – beliefs about the world in general, moral, religious, and social beliefs.

And I have said, also, that this study is not to be a continuous history of European political thought.

The view I am taking is that political thought (both practical and explanatory) takes place always in relation to a particular political experience – that is, belongs to some specific political culture.

And I design to concentrate this study upon four different political experiences or cultures, each highly developed, each with a vocabulary of political ideas of its own, each exhibiting its own characteristic political sentiments and beliefs, and each profoundly reflected upon.

- The city-states of ancient Greece.
- The ancient Roman republic and empire.
- The feudal realms of medieval Europe.
- The states of modern Europe which began to emerge in the sixteenth century and which constitute our own political experience.

Each of these constitutes a specific political culture different from the others. And if you are more interested in our own political culture than any other, I think you will find some interest and profit also in exploring and trying to understand these earlier political experiences.

Editorial Note

LSE 1/1/21, file 2, fos. 1–15. Photocopy of a typescript with autograph corrections.

Two

The Political Experience of the Ancient Greeks

1

I have said that our study of political thought is to be a study of the sentiments, beliefs, habits of thought, and ideas which compose the intellectual organization of each of four great European political experiences.

It is to be a study of the way in which the peoples concerned in each of these four political experiences thought when they thought about government, the instruments of government, and public affairs.

2

I want this morning to begin by saying something about the political experience of the ancient Greeks. This, so to speak, is the subject and the immediate context of Greek political thought.

By this I mean two things, which coincide with one another on some points, but which do not necessarily or always coincide.

- What actually happened to the ancient Greeks: the story of their politics. This, of course, has been pieced together by later scholars. It is what present-day historians of ancient Greece write about.
- What the Greeks themselves came to believe had happened to them; their own view of their political experience.

This may properly be called the myth or legend of Greek politics – not because it is necessarily untrue, but because the important thing about it is not whether or not it is historically true, but that it represents the Greeks' own awareness of their own politics. It was one of the means by which they understood themselves and expressed their confidence in themselves.

Every people awakened to political self-consciousness constructs a myth, an imaginative interpretation of how this came about.

The myth of modern English politics, for example, began to be constructed in the seventeenth century, and it is something to which our current political arguments and attitudes are always returning, and which is always in a process of enlargement and revision.

Like ourselves, the Greeks constructed a legend of their own political fortunes, and to understand it is an important part of understanding what they thought about politics.

Indeed, the construction of this legend was one of the most notable achievements of their political thought. And in considering it we shall be considering one level of their political consciousness.

It must, however, be recognized that these ancient Greeks, when they came to live in specifically political societies, gave remarkably little thought to their past.

The legend of Greek politics is, in fact, remarkably thin and unelaborate. They kept few records, they had no official historians, and they were unimpressed by precedent. They rarely looked to the past for the authority for current conduct. They never thought of themselves, as we sometimes think of ourselves, as borne along on a stream of events which flowed towards a better condition of things.

What we have to consider, then, is a mixture of history and legend, of fact and myth.

3: The Land

We are concerned with a people of mixed descent who lived in the Mediterranean peninsula we know as Greece, in the islands of the Aegean archipelago, and in some parts of Asia Minor.

Later the Greek world (the world of Greek-speaking peoples and of Greek political institutions) included settlements on the Mediterranean coast as far west as Marseilles.

The mainland peninsula is a little smaller than Scotland.

It is a land of rocks and mountains; it has few plains and no considerable rivers. It has a hard, poor soil, from which the Greeks spoke of themselves as 'tearing their living'.

Herodotus: 'Poverty has always been the foster-sister of Greece.'

For the Greeks, the sea was as important as the land: it was a coastal, island civilization, exposed and full of movement.

4: The People

The earliest identifiably 'Greek' inhabitants of this land are called *Achaeans.* They were reputed to have come from the East; Asia Minor.

They were clans or tribes (*genos*) of semi-nomadic shepherds who gradually settled down and took to agriculture.

Each of these tribes was (or believed itself to be) the descendant of a single progenitor: the tie of the tribe was the tie of common blood. A tribe was an extended family.

When they settled, a tribe became a tribal/household'. One has to think of a civilization not unlike that revealed in the Scandinavian Sagas – households, possibly living in hutments, but living a genuinely 'communal' life. And to the tie of kinship were added:

- the sharing of a common roof, a common hearth, and a common table;
- a common 'law' (which may be supposed to have emerged from more primitive taboos);
- a common religion; a 'family' religion, the worship of ancestors.

There were also tribal chiefs. And attached to each tribe there were probably domestic slaves, men of other races, and often prisoners of war.

These tribes were often at war with one another; but it was not beyond their skill to make temporary alliances with one another. And in the course of time there emerged some more permanent local unions of tribes.

Reputedly, the purpose of these unions was defence. And where such unions appeared there was often a fortified stronghold of some sort, a military organization, and some subordination of chiefs to a chief of chiefs.

But, about the year 1100 B.C. this land, occupied in this manner, suffered an invasion from the north.

The invaders were a relatively barbaric people, known as Dorians.

The immediate result of this invasion was the destruction of the emerging organizations of Achaean tribes, and a relapse into separate and often hostile tribal units.

The later result was a mixture of the Achaean and Dorian peoples.

The ancient Greeks, as we know of them, were largely a mixture of these two peoples.

They became a highly individual people, very unlike their neighbors. They were unusually tolerant, they escaped the exaggerations of authority and servility common among their oriental neighbors. They were a curious, restless, sociable people – above all fond of talk.

Many centuries later there emerged a legend in which the different characteristics of the Greeks were attributed to the different strains – Achaean and Dorian – of which they were composed.

The Achaean element was believed to supply the restlessness, the instability, and the curiosity of the Greek character; its easy fascination with what was new and its delight in change, its sense of humour. The Dorian element was believed to supply the dour, more severe and disciplined, and conservative element.

Athens was reputed to be a predominantly Achaean settlement; Sparta a mainly Dorian settlement. The one supremely loquacious; the other, of the opposite disposition, who added the word 'laconic' to the vocabulary of Europe – Sparta, Lacadaemon – dour and brief of speech – like the Scots.

5: The Early *Polis*

These ancient Greeks believed that their political experience began with a momentous change in their manner of living.

Upon these patriarchally governed tribes or village-households, whose unity was one of kinship, whose law was tribal custom, whose religion was a family religion, there supervened a new idiom of life: permanent unions of tribes.

These permanent unions of tribes were recognized as something new.

Each of these unions was composed of a diversity of tribes, and consequently it could not be understood on the analogy of a tribe. Its laws were something different from tribal custom; its religion could not be a family, tribal religion, and government could not be tribal, patriarchal government. The unity of each was not the blood and 'milk' unity of a tribe.

The name the Greeks gave to these new social and religious communities was *polis*. It is a word somewhat misleadingly translated 'city' or 'city-state'; but by calling it *polis* they recognized it as the beginning of a political life.

The process in which these *poleis* emerged is, of course, obscure and was slow. But in the course of six or seven centuries they became the common feature of the Greek-speaking world.

Spread from Asia Minor to the western Mediterranean, there emerged about 1,500 of them, each with a character of its own, each with a passion for independence which was never broken down, but each recognizing itself as 'Greek' and later as a particle of what came to be thought of as 'Hellas' – perhaps in somewhat the same manner as we think of ourselves as sharing in something more than merely geographical, called 'Europe'. But 'Hellas' was, above all, the world of those who spoke Greek.

Of some of these 'city-states' we know only their names and their locations. Others, like Thebes and Corinth, had long and famous histories. But the two we know most about are Athens and Sparta.

You may read in Book I of the *Politics* of Aristotle an account of how he thought these 'city-states' had emerged, and the reasons he found for their emergence.

Or, here is Plato's poetic, mythical description of the beginnings of Greek politics, a description which perhaps may be taken to reflect a dim memory of the first Achaean attempt to form unions of tribes, an attempt destroyed by the Dorian invasion.

He says that in ancient times the tribes which inhabited Greece strove to congregate and for mutual protection to live together in *poleis*. But when they first began that sort of life they 'lacked the art of living together in a *polis*', and consequently disputes arose between the component tribes and they dispersed again.

But *Zeus* (that is, the chief god of the Greek pantheon), fearing that the human race would perish, sent Hermes to teach them 'the art of living together in a *polis*'.

This art Plato describes as 'the art of resolving differences', the 'art of being just to one another'. The art of taking account of one another. For Plato, the *polis* and 'justice' were counter-

parts of one another. And we shall see later what this association of the *polis* with 'justice' meant to the Greeks.

A *polis*, then, began as an association of tribes, and its tribal
composition was only very gradually modified. It was a very
long time before people began to forget their tribal loyalties.

But, from the beginning, the Greeks recognized a *polis* as a
new creation, and a creation peculiar to themselves. In the
end, what distinguished the Greeks from all other peoples
was *polis*-life.

Polis-life was 'political' life, and they thought of themselves as the inventors of 'politics'. The first words of the
Greek political vocabulary were the words they used to
describe the unique features of this new kind of life. Let us
consider them.

6

The tribe had originally been a self-sufficient household-community, what the Greeks called an *oikia*. It has a law
and gods of its own, a chief who was at once father and ruler,
and lands of its own. It was a community in which there was
no distinction between 'private' and 'public'.

Now, when these household-communities associated with
one another to compose a *polis*, they did not disappear; they
changed their character.

The *oikia*, the household-community, was transformed
into a 'private' family community, engaged in getting its living by cultivating its lands. And this transformation took
place because the 'public' life of a *polis* had been superimposed upon the old, self-sufficient *oikia*.

In short, in the *polis* the distinction between 'public' and
'private' appeared for the first time: henceforward every
man had two lives – his 'private' life as a member of his family household community, and his 'public' life as a citizen of
his *polis*.

The word *polis* itself has several connotations.

It was a fortified place. In Homer, the adjectives applied to
it are 'high', 'well-walled', or 'well-built'. Often it had a cita-
del, like the Acropolis of Athens.

It was a holy place. Religion moved out of the *oikia* into the
polis: it was a 'public' activity. A *polis* was guarded by divine
powers, worshipped not on the family hearth, but in the
'public' temple. And the gods of the hearth and home, often

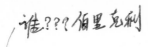
without changing their names, changed their character and became gods of the *polis*.

But a *polis* was not only something geographical; it was recognized as a number of households (and later as a number of 'private' individuals) associated together under a common *law*. 'It is its citizens, and not its walls, that make a *polis*', said Pericles. Law, like religion, had moved out of the *oikia* into the *polis*, and, in doing so, had changed its character. The customs of the tribe were superseded by the law of the *polis*.

Situated in every *polis* was an open space, called an *agora*. 集会 This was a market-place, a place of worship, of social intercourse and of public meeting. It was at once the emblem and the situation of the 'public' life of a *polis*. Indeed, *agora*-life, 'public' life, *polis*-life, and political life were, for the Greek, all expressions signifying the same thing.

It was in respect of having an *agora*-life that the Greeks believed themselves to be superior to all other peoples: the Persians, for example, governed by despots, were recognized to have no *agora*-life – that is, no *politics*.

For the moment, we may understand this *agora*-life as essentially a life of talk. The *agora* was the place where public affairs, *polis*-affairs (as distinct from 'family-affairs') were deliberated and discussed.

And an *agora* was so essential to the Greek way of life that even the camp of a Greek army in the field was laid out to have an *agora* where, for example, the endless palavers which constitute half of Homer's *Iliad* took place.

In later times, in Athens, the *agora* became so intimately connected with 'public' life that its use as a mere market-place was resented. Buying and selling corn and wine were similar activities to 'politics', but vastly inferior.

The next important word in this early political vocabulary of the Greeks is the word *demos*.

A *polis*, with its *agora*, was the centre of a tract of land. And this countryside (the cultivated land of the family-households) was known as the *demos*. The adjectives applied to it were 'plump', 'well-covered' (referring to the covering of the soil over the rock) and 'fertile'.

From being this 'countryside', the word *demos* came to stand for those who inhabited it and worked on it – the peasants – as distinct from the urban population of shop-keepers and citizens.

And later still, *demos* came to mean the ordinary, non-noble, people, wherever they lived. It is with this meaning that it appears in the word 'democracy' – the rule of the ordinary people; what medieval England called 'the commons'.

There is one more word to be noticed at this point – the most important of them all. The word *politai*: 'citizen'.

With the emergence of a *polis* there had emerged a new sort of human life – the 'public' life of the *agora* contrasted with the 'private' life of the *oikia*. But with the *polis* there came also a new sort of man: with the 'city' came the 'citizen'.

A 'citizen' is a man who knows himself, not as a member of a family-household or of a tribe, but as a member of a *polis*. The 'citizen' is a man in respect of his participation in *agora* life, the public life of a *polis*.

Every *polis*, even until near the end of this civilization of Greek cities, had rules which defined the qualifications of being a 'citizen'. And 'citizens' were distinguished from those too young to have any life outside that of the family-household, those who were resident foreigners in the *polis*, slaves, and generally speaking women – none of whom were, in any strict sense, 'citizens'.

But 'citizenship' was recognized as something much more important than a mere *status*. A 'citizen' was a new sort of person who had come into being with the *polis*; but what had also come into being was a new sort of human relationship – the relationship of 'citizen' to 'citizen'.

Clearly this relationship is different from the relationship of tribesmen to one another; it was not a 'family' relationship. What is it?

Centuries later, Aristotle, reflecting upon what the emergence of *polis*-life had brought with it, came to the conclusion that there were two essential characteristics of the 'citizen' to 'citizen' relationship: it was a relation of 'friendship' and it was a relation of 'equals'. And in saying this Aristotle believed himself to be pointing out important differences between *polis* and tribal or family relationships. Let us consider what he meant.

(1) 'Citizens are friends of one another.' Now, in saying this Aristotle did not mean that citizens do, or should, love one another deeply; what he meant was that, unlike the relation-

ships with a family, the relationship of 'citizen' to 'citizen' was one of choice.

Family relationships – those characteristic of the tribal household – the relationships of husband, wife, son, daughter, brother, sister, cousin etc., are relationships based upon kinship. Except in the case of husband and wife, choice does not enter in.

And the other relationship of the family-household (that of master and slave), though it is not a relationship of kin or blood, is certainly not a relationship of mutual choice.

'Citizens', then, are *not* blood-brothers to one another; they are free associates of one another. And just as the tribes which associated with one another to compose a *polis* did so by choice, so the relationship of citizen to citizen was to be recognized as a social and not a biological relationship; choice, not necessity.

This relationship of 'friendship' characteristic of the citizens of a *polis* was said by Aristotle to be 'watery' when compared with the blood and milk ties of a tribe or a family – at least 'watery' in the early history of a *polis*. But, weak or strong, it was a relationship which distinguished a *polis* from a tribe. It was, as Aristotle understood it, a supremely human relationship.

(2) 'Citizens are equal'. What did Aristotle mean when he recognized the relationship of 'citizen' to 'citizen' to be unique because it was a relationship of 'equals'?

Here, again, what he was trying to do was to distinguish the specifically *polis* relationship from family or tribal relationships.

The structure of a family or a tribe is hierarchical. There is not only the hierarchy which gives precedence to the head of the family, there is also the hierarchy of the 'generations'. Sons, perhaps, have precedence over daughters, elder brothers over younger; and so on.

But, outside the family-household, in the *polis*, in the *agora*, all this disappears. Fathers and grown-up sons meet, not as fathers and sons, but as something else – as citizens. In the *agora* all are contemporaries of one another.

Deference may be paid to age or to reputed wisdom; the holders of certain officers may have specific authority; but all this is quite different from the hierarchical structure of a family.

Of course, Aristotle did not believe, and no Greek was disposed to believe, that men were literally and naturally the equals of one another. What he discerned was that, with *polis*-life, and in the *agora*, there had emerged an artificial, or conventional equality, in which those who might be subordinates elsewhere (in the family, for example) ceased to be subordinates.

7

This, then, was the incipient vocabulary of political ideas in the emergent *polis*: *agora, demos, polis*.

And to them we may add now some traditional beliefs about how a *polis* emerged from tribal societies — beliefs which reflect an appreciation of the need for some creative act to produce so unprecedented a way of living as *polis*-life.

It was believed that each *polis* had a founder, often thought of as a semi-divine person. But what was more significant than the mere fact of a 'founding father' was the work attributed to this founder.

The essence of a *polis* was to be a real union of tribes and not merely a temporary alliance. And Aristotle voiced the common belief when he said that the activity of the founder of a *polis* was that of 'introducing' the tribes to one another and 'making them acquainted with one another'; making them 'at home' with one another. The work of a founder was like the work of a good host.

In the imagination of the Greeks the *polis* emerged, not in an activity of violence or conquest, but in an activity of persuasion. *Polis*-life was a sort of life in which persuasion had superseded the violence of tribal life, indeed, the violence of 'nature'.

And, of what had the host to persuade his guests? He had to persuade them to live together as a single community; he had to persuade them to surrender their tribal autonomies; he had to persuade them to compose or to resolve their differences; to accommodate themselves to one another.

A common law of the *polis* had to be elicited from the customs of the component tribes; a religion of the *polis* had to be elicited from the ancestral religions of the tribes. And it was only by 'persuasion', by 'agreement', that a durable *polis* could be established.

In short, as Aristotle understood it, the task of the founder of a *polis* was to teach the tribes who were to compose it, not

how to impose themselves on one another, not the arts of violence, but the art of accommodating themselves to one
another, the art, as he says, of 'being just to one another' – in
short, the art, as the Greeks understood it, of *politics, politike.*

A *polis*, you will notice, had the essential ingredients of
political activity: unity and diversity. The diversity was at
first tribal diversity; and the unity was only slowly acquired.

8

The political experience of the ancient Greeks was, then, in
the first place, the experience in which a political community
was constructed out of communities of a different sort; an
experience in which the potentialities of this *polis*-life were
explored; and an experience in which this *polis*-life spread
itself over the whole Greek-speaking world.

This experience of creation entered deeply into the Greek
political imagination, and it was profoundly reflected upon
by historians and philosophers.

But, secondly, this political experience of the ancient
Greeks was an experience of governing and being governed,
and experience of variation and change in the constitutional
structure and arrangements of a *polis.*

This part of their experience also received what may be
called an imaginative interpretation and entered into the legend of Greek politics.

And this also generated a vocabulary of political words
and ideas relating to the structure and organization of
government.

(1) The earliest kind of *polis* we know anything in detail
about is the city-state of which Homer writes, round about
1,000 B.C.

It is a *polis* which shows very clearly its tribal origins and
constituents. It was an organization of families; an organization in which there was the 'private', domestic world of the
household; and the 'public', political world of the *agora.*

It was ruled by a king – a *basileus.* The office of king was
usually hereditary; and his business was to be the pivot
round which the whole 'public' life of the *polis* revolved.

He was leader in time of war; he was the interpreter of the
unwritten customary law of the *polis*; he was the judge who
heard and decided legal disputes; he was the chief actor in

the religious activities of the *polis*, making the communal sac-
rifices to the gods of the *polis*.

In all this he was supported and advised by a council of
nobles (*boûle*); they were, probably, the heads of the constituent tribes, the patriarchal chiefs of household-communities.

They were the first 'men of the *agora*'. They met the king in
public council in the *agora*, where all the public life of the *polis*
took place. Homer's *Iliad* is full of descriptions of this
agora-life, with its councils of war and councils of judgment.

In addition to this council of nobles, there was an assembly
of citizens (*ecclesia*). This was usually called together by the
king when he had some important public announcement to
make, or on the occasion of religious ceremony. It, also, met
in the *agora*.

In earliest times, it would appear, the right to speak on
public occasions was confined to the king and his immediate
counselors. The ordinary citizens were an audience. But they
were an audience there to listen to deliberations about policy
and to legal judgments, and they were participants in so far
as they were there to be persuaded.

Here, then, in this earliest kind of *polis* were already the
three features which, throughout their history, the Greeks
considered to distinguish themselves from others: an executive head, a council, and an assembly of citizens.

(2) This monarchical structure did not last very long,
although naturally it lasted longer in some cities than in
others.

What supervened upon this primitive *polis*, ruled by a
king, was (usually) an aristocratically governed *polis*, in
which the heads of the noble families shared between them
the duties of the king.

It was a gradual change, although in some places there
may have been revolutionary moments. Kings retained their
religious functions longer than any others; and before the
office of *basileus* disappeared altogether it often became an
elective and an annual office.

(3) But in some of the cities of Greece there was no extensive
landed aristocracy to succeed to the kingly office. And in others, such as Sparta, which was preeminent for its ethnic divisions, the group who superseded the king was determined
by race.

Aristocracy, strictly speaking, was the rule of a *polis* by those who were of noble blood. But even where a genuine aristocracy established itself, it soon had to defend itself against those who claimed a share in ruling on account, merely, of their wealth or by reason of some other qualification which singled them out.

Aristocracy, in short, opened the door to a great variety of oligarchical governments, the most common of which was what the Greeks called a *timocracy* – that is, the rule of the wealthy.

In all oligarchies, the council of oligarchs was the supreme magistracy. It might be relatively numerous, or it might be a very select number of citizens: Athens was ruled at different times by a council of 1,000 and by a council of 400.

Under an oligarchical constitution the assembly of citizens often survived, but it usually became less important than it had been under kings and aristocracies.

(4) The only other regular constitutional form known to the Greek cities was called a *democracy*.

In a democracy, that original assembly of citizens (which in the monarchical *polis* had been little more than an audience) was transformed into the ruling authority. In this assembly all the important questions of policy were argued; and it ruled through committees and magistrates appointed or elected from among its members.

No citizen above a certain age was excluded from the assembly, but in every *polis* the citizen body was never more than a small part of the total population.

For example, Athens as a democracy had a population of about 170,000. But of these, only about 40,000 were citizens, only about half of them played an active part in politics.

Nevertheless, the records that have come down to us of the meetings and the details of the Athenian assembly are the first great records of European political talk.

(5) These, then, were the regular forms of government known to the Greeks. And there were few of the Greek cities which did not, at one time or another in their history, have governments in each of these forms.

But there was one other kind of government which, from time to time, made its appearance in a *polis*. It was recognized to be irregular, and it never lasted very long. It was called a *tyranny*.

A Greek tyrant was an autocrat, but he was not a despot. He was a man, often a successful magistrate or military commander, who was pushed forward and endowed with authority; *either* by a shaky oligarchy as a defender of its threatened privileges, *or* by a democratic faction intent on dislodging an oligarchy.

During his period of rule he usually depended upon a body of personal retainers; he was apt to live in some magnificence, but he rarely subverted the ordinary laws of the *polis*.

In short, a tyranny was the sort of government which was apt to intervene between periods of oligarchic and democratic government.

9

The Greek political experience, so far as the forms and instruments of government were concerned, was an experience of frequent, often revolutionary, change. Of the cities of Greece, Sparta alone enjoyed constitutional stability for more than an insignificant number of years.

This experience of perpetual change became reflected in the legend of Greek politics in the belief that political forms and arrangements were essentially unstable.

There is a belief which belongs to our own legend of politics that political change may be regarded as in some sense progressive – that the movement of political change has a direction and that it is pointed towards something that *we* call 'democratic' government.

The ancient Greeks had no such belief. What they believed was, rather, that every *polis* might be expected to go through an endless cycle of constitutional change. And that, for example, the achievement of democratic government was only a prelude to the reappearance of an oligarchy of some sort.

10

In the fifth century B.C., Hellas, the world of the Greeks, was, after a history of about 700 years, composed of numerous city-states.

Some were more powerful than others; some more adventurous and expansionist; some even acquired what were thought of as 'empires'. Among them, from time to time, there were alliances, leagues, confederacies, and hegemonies. They were often at war with one another. They were surrounded by enemies against whom they combined with great reluctance. They managed, however, to defeat their most powerful enemy, Persia.

What would have happened if these city-states had been left to themselves for another century or so is impossible to say. Perhaps just one more century of ringing the changes on the various forms of government. But, in fact, they had no such opportunity.

In the middle of the fourth century there was emerging in the north of the Greek peninsula a military power which in the course of fifty years was to conquer the whole Greek world, and to transform this civilization of independent city-states into a civilization of dependent and insignificant municipalities.

This military power was the armies of Philip and Alexander of Macedonia. And whatever independence survived the conquest of Greece by the Macedonian armies was later destroyed by the armies of Rome.

Thus came to an end the political experience of the ancient Greeks and its most notable achievement, the politics of the Greek *polis*.

These Greeks, who were later to be recognized (as they recognized themselves) as the inventors of 'politics', so far as Europe is concerned, were in some ways less successful than any other people we know of at accommodating themselves to one another.

It seems almost as if they were so enchanted with what they had invented – 'politics', *agora*-life, *politike* – that they did not think of it (as others have thought of it) as a means to an end, but as itself an end.

They cared much more for 'politics' than for government; and much more for political discourse and debate than for devising durable arrangements and institutions.

They were rather like the French of modern times; a loquacious people who would rather be defeated than stop talking politics.

Editorial Note

LSE 1/1/21, file 2, fos. 16–31. Photocopy of a typescript with autograph corrections.

Three

The Greek Image of the World

1

We have considered, very briefly, the political experience of the ancient Greeks; both what happened to them, and that aspect of their interpretation of what happened which they expressed in what I called the legend of Greek politics.

Now, what a people thinks of any of the experiences which come its way, and the intellectual organization which it gives to those experiences, is usually profoundly conditioned by its feelings, beliefs, and ideas about the world in general.

And I want this morning to say something about the way in which the Greeks thought of the world in which they lived, and their relation to that world, in so far as it is relevant to understanding their thoughts about politics and government.

Part, at least, of the unique character of their political thought derives from the peculiar way in which they thought about the world in which they lived.

I will begin by saying something about the way in which they understood what we ordinarily call the 'natural' world.

2

The word they used to indicate this world, in the most general sense, was the word *cosmos.* And they used this word in very much the same way as we use the expression 'the material world'. It stood for the aggregate, the sum of 'natural' things.

Now, one of the most remarkable things about the Greeks is that, from very early times, they came to understand this *cosmos* as a self-contained, self-moved order of things.

For them, it was not an order which had been created by a god, and whose components, and the movements of these components, represented the will of a creator.

The *cosmos*, to them, was a world of things which had come into being by itself, and which moves and changes according to its own internal and necessary laws, and for which nobody could be thought to be responsible.

Thus, the *cosmos* had nothing which could be called a 'ruler' or a 'government'. And thus, also, it offered to the Greeks no analogy by which they could understand the political world, or the activity of governing a *polis*. In the later history of European thought, peoples were often accustomed to think of the universe as 'governed' by a God who had created it. Christian thinkers acquired this belief partly from the Old Testament. And consequently they could think of human rulers on the analogy of God, and of God on the analogy of a human ruler. The Greeks had no such beliefs. But, if they did not connect the *cosmos* with government, they did make a connection between the *cosmos* and the social order.

A great scholar once wrote: 'The relationship between Greek thought about the *cosmos* and their thought about politics was always a reciprocal one: the *cosmos* was understood in terms of justice, law and fate, and the political order was thought of in the same terms.'[1] As we shall see, the words justice, law, and fate had, first, a cosmological meaning and only secondly a social and political meaning.

Nevertheless, although they thought of the *cosmos* as a self-contained, self-moved order of things, the Greeks never though of it as a mechanical order – like a clock, or a system of weights and pulleys, or an engine.

They never used the analogy of a machine in trying to understand the *cosmos*. Nor did they use it in trying to understand anything else, like a political constitution, or a system of government. The expression 'the machinery of government' would have been entirely foreign to them.

This, I suppose, was because they had no experience of machines of any degree of complication. The analogy, so to speak, was not available to them.

For them, the *cosmos* was alive; it was an organism, like an animal or a plant. An organism in the strict sense; that is, a whole which has no 'government' because its vitality is distributed in all its parts. Its most obvious feature was the

---

[1] W. Jaeger, *The Theology of the Early Greek Philosophers*, p. 140, cp. Burnet, *Early Greek Philosophy*, p. 151.

change and movement it displayed, and where the Greeks saw movement they understood there to be life.

The *cosmos*, then, was understood to be itself a living organism, composed of living organisms. It consisted of things which were generated, lived, decayed, died, and disappeared from the scene, or were transmuted into other things, in an endless, purposeless, circular movement according to its own inherent and necessary laws.

But, in the course of time, they came to make an important distinction, which Aristotle and other philosophers explored and greatly elaborated.

The *cosmos* was understood to consist of two parts, specially separated.

There was, first, *houranos*, the 'sky'. This was a world of permanent, changeless bodies, which neither came into being nor passed away, and which moved according to absolutely fixed and changeless laws. We may call it, perhaps, the world of the astronomer. A world in which nothing new ever appeared, and in which nothing irregular ever happened.

Secondly, there was the earth itself, the world (as they thought of it) 'beneath the moon'. This sublunary world was a world of contingency and of uncertain happenings, in which entirely new things could appear. It was not ruled by fixed and absolute laws. Indeed, almost anything could happen in it. This world was the world of human life. And many of the happenings in it could be recognized as the results of human choices and actions.

Others have believed there to be a close connection between these two worlds, what went on in the 'sky' determining what went on in the human world: the Greeks were disinclined to recognize much of a connection here.

Now, this belief about the world inhabited by human beings gave the Greeks the feeling that they lived in a world which, so to speak, allowed them initiative and freedom of movement.

And (in the end) they came to think of 'politics' as the supreme example of 'free' human movement, movement which sprang from human deliberation and choice.

Thus, we may say that they imagined the world in which they lived as a world in which 'politics' was possible, because it was a realm, not of necessary law, but of contingency. It was a world, *not* of examples of the operation of changeless laws, but of 'events', 'happenings'.

3

Now, besides this word *cosmos*, the Greeks had another word which they were apt to use somewhat differently: the word *phusis*.

We translate it 'nature'; and our words 'physics' and 'physique' are derived from it. It was a word which came to be incorporated in the Greek political vocabulary itself (as, of course, the word 'nature' belongs to our own political vocabulary in such expressions as 'natural law' and 'natural rights'). Consequently, there will be a lot more to be said later about its political meaning.

But, before it became a political word, it was a word with a more general meaning.

The *cosmos* consisted of things (*ousia*), all of them alive, and each having a specific character of its own; and the specific character of a particular thing they called its *phusis*, its 'nature'. Thus, a 'man', a 'horse', a 'tree', and a 'stone', each had a 'nature' of its own, which distinguished it from all other things. We often use the expression 'human nature' in just this way – attributing a specific character to human beings as such.

Each thing, therefore, had its own individual 'nature'. And if you wished to understand any of the things which composed the world around you, the question you asked yourself was: What is its *phusis*? What is its nature?

The Greeks understood that this question could be answered in various different ways, some of which yielded more important information than others. It could be understood as, for example, the question: 'What is it made of?'

But they (or their philosophers) reached the conclusion that, since each of these individual 'things' was alive and moved and changed, the most important form of the question: 'What is its nature?' was 'How does it behave and move?' What is the principle of its behaviour? What constitutes a thing is the way in which it behaves.

When Aristotle asked himself the question: 'What is the nature of the *polis*?' or 'what is the nature of justice?' what he was seeking was the specific character of a *polis*, or the specific character of 'justice'.

The *cosmos*, then, was a mixture of law and contingency, necessity and freedom; and in that part inhabited by human beings, the contingency was more significant than the law.

This allowed human beings considerable freedom of choice and action, and permitted *politike*, political activity.

4

There was, however, according to Greek belief, a set of beings who did not belong to the *cosmos* at all, a set of beings wholly free from the laws of natural necessity. These were the gods.

We are not concerned with the earliest religious beliefs of the Greeks. Like most other primitive peoples, they worshipped their ancestors, and their gods were tribal gods.

But in the course of time, the Greek-speaking peoples acquired some common beliefs about what they called 'the divine powers'. And although these beliefs changed with changing circumstances – the rural gods of the trees and rivers became the urban gods of the *polis* – their main outlines remained relatively unaltered, and in the course of time they were organized into what may be called a 'popular theology'.

The gods of the 'public' or common religion were many, and they composed a kind of family or 'household'. They lived on Mount Olympus. The head of the 'household' was Zeus – '*the* god'. And his subordinates bore some, perhaps vague, relation to him: they were his sons or daughters, his wives, brothers, brothers-in-law, etc.

In short, these gods were understood to be in many respects not unlike human beings. Human passions and emotions, virtues and vices, were attributed to them. But they lived in a different sort of world.

They lived, remote, on Mount Olympus. They had not made the *cosmos*, they were not responsible for what went on in it, and they could not in any proper sense be said to rule or control it. But they were concerned with human beings and their conduct; and the destinies of individual human beings were, in some respects, in their hands.

They constantly interfered in the lives of men, sending them good or ill fortune, helping or hindering human enterprises. But their most important power was to dictate what the Greeks called 'the fate' of each man.

A man's 'fate' was though of as a thread or cord (spun, cut off, and tied by appropriate gods) which 'bound' him. The imagery of 'fate', for the Greeks, was the imagery of spinning and weaving. Once *Zeus* had 'bound' a man, he could never be unloosed from his 'fate'.

But this belief was, in fact, less 'fatalistic' than it seems. Not all things in a man's life belonged to his 'fate.' Nothing contrary to his 'fate' could happen to him, but there was much in his life which was 'loose', 'beyond what is fated', *huper mellon*.

A man's fate chiefly concerned the time and manner of his death. To be 'fated' was rather like being condemned to die at a certain time and in certain circumstances. What happened in the interval between birth and death was by no means 'fated' – although a great deal of it might spring from the temporary good-will or ill-will of the gods.

Human beings, the inhabitants of the sub-lunar world, were then, subject to natural necessity and to the 'law' of their fates, but they remained, to a significant degree, 'free', masters of their own conduct.

With respect to human beings, then, the main office of the gods was to provide them with their 'fates'.

Beyond this, the gods were thought of as powerful, they were believed to understand the *cosmos* better than human beings understood it, to be wiser, and to have some knowledge (but by no means complete) of the future.

Consequently, tribes, cities, and individuals sought the protection of the gods, worshipped them, invoked their good-will, and sought the enlightenment of their wisdom. Each *polis* had a special tutelary divine power, worshipped in its temple.

The gods would sometimes visit the human world, disguised as men; and sometimes they would speak to men in their dreams or as a voice from a cloud. But their home was remote from the abodes of men; they did not, like the gods of the Romans, inhabit the temples where they were worshipped.

The relationship of human beings and the gods was rather oddly understood. The gods were not awful beings, to be feared. But, they were certainly not to be trusted. Human beings were often thought of as the playthings of the gods, who could be malicious, and who would sometimes go out of their way to make human life difficult.

This reflected itself in a characteristic feeling of despondency and pessimism; but there was very little resignation in the Greek temperament.

Their 'fates' they knew would catch them up in the end. But they had a great urge to try their luck, and to live dangerously. Their heroes were men who did not submit tamely; they were men of 'revolt', whose enterprise was to outwit the gods. The supreme human hero was, of course, Prometheus, who defied the Gods and tried to steal their wisdom.

The gods of Greece, then, were not part of the *cosmos*. They were immortal. They were not subject to the endless process of change, nor was their conduct governed by inflexible laws. They were 'free'; free from death and free from natural necessity.

Nevertheless, they were not exactly capable of *politike*, 'political' activity. It is true that they made speeches to one another, it is true that they deliberated and made choices and performed actions. But they knew too much about the future for them to be comparable to human beings.

The essence of *politike*, as the Greeks understood it, was deliberating, choosing, and acting in circumstances where no more than a rough guess could be made about the consequences. And this the gods could not do because they knew too much about the future.

5

There was, then, for the Greeks, a *cosmos* composed of things each with its own 'nature' or 'way of behaving'. The law of this *cosmos* was the law of natural necessity: an endless cycle of unavoidable, purposeless change.

And there was the world of the immortal gods.

Between these worlds lay the world of human beings. What were human beings understood to be like?

Aristotle said that human beings were neither gods nor beasts; and from one point of view, this saying contained all that the Greeks believed about human beings.

That they were not gods was obvious. And, as we shall see, it was believed to be very important that human beings should not mistake themselves for gods.

In one respect they were undeniably like beasts. They belonged to a world ruled by natural necessity. As a race, they were part of this endless cycle of procreation, birth, life, growth, and death.

But, in another respect, they were more like gods. As individuals they were capable of choice and action, and thus (to that extent) emancipated from the law of natural necessity.

In short their situation was strangely ambiguous. In the world ruled by natural necessity, and therefore not like the gods. But above the world of natural necessity (in virtue of being able to choose and to act), and therefore not exactly like beasts.

Now, the emblem of human freedom from natural necessity, freedom from having to obey the inexorable laws of the *cosmos*, such as it is, was recognized to be the power of 'artifice'.

The distinction between the 'natural' and the 'artificial', 'nature' and 'art', was one which Greek philosophers often reflected upon; but the distinction itself was recognized in popular thought.

The Greeks never quite rationalized this human power of 'artifice' in a doctrine of the freedom of the human will. They merely understood human beings to be capable of a kind of activity which was determined neither by the laws of natural necessity, nor by the 'fates' imposed upon them by the gods.

This activity was seen to be the power of interrupting the natural order of the *cosmos*, and of imposing themselves on that order. The power of using the *cosmos* and the things which composed it in order to achieve chosen human purposes.

The power of artifice appeared in two main forms:

It was the power of making artifacts, of fabricating things out of the materials provided by the *cosmos*: they could make things such as ships, ploughs, temples, and weapons, which did not exist in the 'natural' world.

These artifacts represented human designs, chosen purposes, or the means to achieve chosen purposes.

This human power of fabrication immensely impressed the Greeks. They saw in this world of artifacts a world created by human beings, evidence of at least a partial emancipation from 'natural necessity', a release from having merely to accept the world as they found it.

But this freedom from natural necessity appeared, also, in a much more significant activity than that of *making* things – things which, after all, were made out of materials of the 'natural' world and which were, therefore, half 'natural', so to speak.

Fabrication represented only a partial release from natural necessity: the artist or the workman had to accept the material and conform himself to what could be made out of it.

A much more complete release was understood to be displayed in the activities of speaking words, making choices, taking decisions and performing *actions*. Here there was no limiting material, and no interruption – one action was the spring of another in a continuous process of living as a human being.

In speaking and acting human beings were seen unmistakably to step outside the world of natural necessity and into a world of freedom which comes from choosing and acting.

And this is why the Greeks believed that *politike*, 'political activity', was the supremely and uniquely 'human' activity. 'Politics' is choosing and acting, not choosing and making. Politics is *doing actions*, not *making things*.

As they understood it:

(1)   Political activity emerged when human beings, by choice, superimposed *polis*-life upon life in the family-household.

The relationships of life in the family life were 'natural', 'biological', relationships of blood, and not of choice. But in *polis*-life men thought, chose, decided and acted for themselves. Moreover, they contracted a new relationship with one another, that of the 'free' relationship of citizen to citizen.

(2)   Political life took place in the *agora*, outside the world of the 'household'. The 'household' is 'nature'; the *polis* is artifice.

(3)   Political life consists of speaking – expressing opinions, engaging in argument designed to persuade, taking decisions and performing actions. It consists, not of responses dictated by natural necessity, but of actions which were chosen because there was always an alternative to them.

Fabricating, speaking, choosing and performing deeds, then, were understood as the uniquely human activities.

In respect of these, men could be recognized as higher than the beasts. And if they lacked the 'wisdom' and the 'prescience' of the gods, this very lack was part of the specification of *politike*.

'Politics' is choosing and acting when there is an alternative, and when the outcome of action is always in some degree uncertain.

In 'action', two things have to be chosen: the *purpose* or *end* aimed at, and the *means* to achieve it.

Politics, in respect of its being the exercise of choice, is something of which animals are incapable. In respect of its uncertainty it is something of which the gods are incapable. In respect of both it is uniquely human.

6

Human beings, then, endowed with certain unique powers, find themselves in a world governed in part by natural necessity, but for the rest, full of contingencies and opportunities for choice and action.

Taking this view of things, the obvious questions to ask are: How can we control these contingencies? Are they mere contingencies, or is there some regularity in them? What do we know, or what can we learn, about the world in which we live which will reduce the uncertainty of it?

The Greeks did think they knew something about the world of contingencies, and therefore something about how human beings should behave if they were to choose and to act in a way that was likely to be successful.

What did they think they knew about the world and themselves which would be some sort of guide to making choices and performing actions? For our information on this we will go to the Delphic Oracle.

At Delphi, on the gulf of Corinth, there was a famous and ancient temple of Apollo. And men in difficulties, with practical puzzles to solve, men who did not know quite what to do for the best, went to consult the priestess of Apollo. They went from all over the Greek world.

In the course of time some of the pronouncements of the priestess became famous: they were regarded as true (though often obscure) precepts about human conduct, based upon a profound knowledge of the human condition.

These sayings were, of course, reputed to come from Apollo himself; but they may be regarded as the wisdom the Greeks had acquired for themselves, in the course of their experience, about what to do and what not to do in this puzzling world of contingencies.

The most famous of these Delphic pronouncements was *gnothe seauton*: 'know thyself.'

This precept was understood as a moral precept addressed to the race of human beings. It meant: 'Each of you, understand that you are a man and nothing more than a man; and behave accordingly'. Know your 'nature'.

It was a precept chiefly designed to point out the difference between men and gods: 'Know that you are a man and not a god'.

Men, the Greeks knew as well as anyone else, are sometimes apt to believe that they possess divine powers: we are acquainted with aberrations of this sort, and we call it *megalomania* or *paranoia* (both Greek words). It happens in ordinary life; and it happens in politics. And it is the greatest mistake that a man can make.

This precept, then, pointed out, not only the illusion of believing you are a god, but also that whoever has this illusion will only spread disaster and unhappiness all round. It expressed a profound suspicion of anyone who set himself up to be more than a man, and the belief that the conduct of anyone who did this was out of touch with the realities of human life.

The second, and hardly less famous, saying of the Delphic oracle carried this piece of practical wisdom a step further. It was a cryptic saying: *meden agan*; 'nothing too much', or 'Do not attempt what it is beyond human powers to achieve'.

From one point of view, it was a precept enjoining 'modesty' and 'humility': 'Do not run to extremes'; 'keep the middle way appropriate to human beings who are neither gods nor beasts'. And this virtue of 'modesty' (*sophrosune*), 'unpretentiousness', was one of the most highly regarded of all human virtues.

At first, no doubt, this feeling that extremes were to be avoided in human conduct sprang from a superstitious fear of the jealousy and the contempt of the gods for a man who tried to be either more or less than a man. But later it became a rational suspicion of all excess in human life.

Excessive pride in human beings the Greeks called *hubris*: it was the pride that portends a fall. And the belief that it spells disaster in practical affairs was the heart of the moral attitude of the Greeks.

Let me illustrate its bearing upon ordinary and in political life.

In the story of Croesus as it appears in Herodotus, Croesus was the richest man in the world. He came to a bad end. And the moral of the story is that excess in any direction is something to be avoided because it portends disaster. The Greeks didn't believe that the downfall of Croesus was *caused* by his excessive wealth, they believed that his excessive wealth was a reliable *sign* that he would fall.

Xerxes, a prince who for a time enjoyed overwhelming power and success, was overtaken by *Nemesis* – disaster. He was too powerful for a man. Don't make an alliance with him; he will fall. Compare this with Machiavelli: don't ally with one more powerful than yourself; he will swallow you up.

The essence of Greek tragedy is a 'revolution' in which a man in a seemingly impregnable position of wealth, honour or happiness is overthrown. Oedipus, from the height of happiness, is hurled, through no fault of his own, into indescribable suffering. He was just *too happy*.

Thucydides ascribed the political disasters which overtook Athens to the *hubris* of the Athenians – to their trying to do too much, to their having 'imperial' pretensions.

Great power, great pride, great happiness, great riches or great good fortune – all these are foreign to the human condition and intimate a cataclysm to follow.

This, of course, does not mean that the Greeks always lived up to their own standards of moral wisdom. No people has ever done this. It means that this is what they thought about the human condition in their calmer moments. The legend of Prometheus is the legend of a man who sought divine wisdom and had in consequence to suffer a fate worse than death – punishment.

As the Greeks understood it, then, human beings inhabit a world of contingencies, of events and happenings which are not governed by necessary laws, but in which some rough regulations can be discerned.

Human beings lack the wisdom and the foreknowledge of gods. But, unlike beasts, they have powers of reasoning, speech, choice, and action; the power of designing and making things and doing things for themselves.

They will be successful (or are more likely to be successful) if they understand the sort of world they live in and the sort of beings they are themselves, and conform their conduct to their condition.

'Politics' is their unique capability because 'politics' is making choices and performing actions in a world whose structure and operation allows this sort of activity. But it is wise to know yourself and the world in which you have to act.

7

The Greek image of the world and of the human condition was one that contained a strong element of pessimism, or at least despondency.

Their gods were not notably friendly; and the world was not notably reliable. But the gods were many, and you were very much down on your luck if they were all, all at once, unfriendly or malicious; and the world did display some rough regularities; it fulfilled some expectations.

The proper business of human beings in the world was to use whatever skill, cunning, or cleverness they had to outwit the malice of the gods and to make themselves at home in the world.

'Politics' was the supreme example of human beings doing just this, using whatever freedom from natural necessity they enjoyed in order to make a recalcitrant world conform to their notion of a 'good life'.

And, in this respect, the greatest achievement which the Greeks credited themselves with, was the invention of *polis*-life. They recognized it as the sort of life which men were uniquely qualified to live; the sort of life which employed *all* that distinguished men from both gods and beasts; the pursuit of the human good by making choices and performing actions.

Editorial Note

LSE 1/1/21, file 2, fos. 32–44. Photocopy of a typescript with autograph corrections.

Four

The Political Thought of the Ancient Greeks (1)

1

So far, we have been concerned with two main topics:

- The political experience of the ancient Greeks.
- Some of the beliefs current among the Greeks about the world in general, about their gods, and about the human condition.

These beliefs supplied the context and a large part of the intellectual apparatus of their political thought. This is where they found the general ideas and the analogies to be used in giving an intellectual organization to their political activity.

These beliefs were often vague and ambiguous; they slurred over difficult questions – and there is incoherence at the edges.

But these are common characteristic of all political beliefs and sentiments. It does not make them less useful. Indeed, a belief which has ceased to be vague and ambiguous has lost most of its practical usefulness. In politics, beliefs need to be persuasive, not necessarily coherent.

As we shall see, it was these beliefs which were later sifted, criticized, and given a greater degree of coherence by such philosophical thinkers as Plato and Aristotle.

We are concerned with a people who, in a remarkably short period of time, passed from a mythological manner of thinking to a highly sophisticated and rationalistic way of thinking about these things.

But even the sophistication of fifth-century Athens reflected the earlier mythology. It is as impossible to understand how Pericles and Cleon thought about politics without understanding the earlier mythology, as it is impossible to understand seventeenth-century English political thought without knowing something about the Old Testament from which it drew so many of its ideas.

'The *cosmos* was understood in terms of law, justice, and fate, and the political order was thought of in the same terms' (Jaeger). So I propose to begin with the ideas of law and justice.

2

Law is a certain manner of regulating human conduct. And in most societies its forerunner is taboo.

'Taboo' is the belief that wrong or anti-social conduct will be followed automatically by an inescapable penalty. To perform the act is to incur the penalty; the passage from one to the other is a natural process. The act itself, if it is bad enough, kills, as if it were poison to the doer.

But where the regulation of conduct in a society is by 'law', a breach of the law is followed not by an automatic and inescapable natural penalty, but by the declaration, in a court of some sort, that the law has been breached, a declaration that the penalty will be such and such, and the execution of the decision of the court. Here, if the penalty is death, it is the sentence of a court or a judge – human decision has been interposed between the act and suffering the penalty.

We are concerned with the ancient Greeks when they had arrived at the notion of the legal regulation of conduct: the beginning, so to speak, of the history of Greek law.

The word used by the Greeks to express their first notion of law is *themis*.

Now, in the religious mythology of Homer, *Themis* is a goddess. She is the daughter of *Uranus* and *Ge* (Heaven and Earth).

This girl (of the most ancient and respectable lineage) became one of the wives of *Zeus*, the chief god of the Greek pantheon. By *Zeus* she became the mother of *Dike* justice.

Zeus, like other Greek gods, was a multiple personality; he had many powers, many different appearances, as well as many wives. But as the consort of *Themis*, he is the god of the social order, and their offspring is Justice.

But even as early as Homer, the word *themis* had acquired another and much more material meaning. Indeed, nearly all the abstract words in Greek – words like 'law' and 'justice' –

began life as concrete things, and they never quite lost their concreteness.

According to Homer, there was in the *agora* of the primitive *polis* something which he calls 'a *themis*'. It was an object of some sort; a pillar of stone, it has been conjectured, inscribed with some precepts about human conduct. And from meaning this inscribed pillar of stone, the word *themis* came to mean the fundamental laws and customs of a *polis*.

Such inscribed stones were a common feature of a Greek *polis* until quite late times. It was from them that the Athenians of the fifth and fourth centuries learned the law which they administered in the *Heliaea*.

Often enough, in early times, the word *themis* was used, not as a noun, but as an adjective. Homer, for example, says: 'It is *themis* to be hospitable to strangers.' *Themis*, then, stood for what is right and proper in human conduct.

Now, the questions we must ask ourselves are: Where did these early Greeks think that *themis* came from? How did a society acquire its laws and customs? And, what was the authority of a *themis*?

Every *polis* had a divine patron; and *themis* was understood, in the first place, to be 'a voice or utterance of the gods', as Homer says. A society does not make its own laws; they are a divine gift and an expression of divine wisdom.

But, in what manner did the gods speak? How did human beings come to know and to understand these divine utterances?

Now, part of the paraphernalia of the Homeric king was a *sceptron*, a scepter. It was, of course, a staff of office, distinguishing the king and representing his authority. Like the mace in the House of Commons, or the seal of the Lord Chancellor.

But it was also recognized as a source of inspiration, a magic wand. And it was by possession of this scepter, perhaps even by holding it in his hand, that the king was able, as Homer says, to 'extract *themistes* from Zeus.'

The process of law-acquiring, then, was thought of somewhat after this fashion:

- The god, or *Zeus*, utters a 'voice'; makes a general pronouncement about human conduct. Sometimes he is asked to do so, sometimes he does so gratuitously.

- A man, a king, qualified by birth and office, and the magic power of the *sceptron*, hears this utterance.
- The king publishes or pronounces it to the people.

In this process what had been a wise observation extracted from the gods becomes a rule of human conduct.

Themis, then, is an indication of right or proper conduct for human beings which represents divine wisdom. It is a divine law in so far as it emanates from *Zeus*; it is a human law in so far as it reaches a community through a human agent and in a process of 'hearing', 'understanding', and 'declaring'.

And it is on account of this human agency that error may creep in. The interpreter of divine wisdom may make a mistake; he may mishear the 'voice' of *Zeus*. If he does so, what he declares will be, not a 'true' *themis*, but what Homer calls a 'crooked' *themis*. Thus, even the earliest Greeks had an explanation for what is in the experience of all men – a bad or an unworkable law.

Now, it is important to understand that, as the Greeks thought of it, *themis* was the expression, not of an arbitrary divine will, but of divine wisdom. The gods were not powerful beings; they were wise or intelligent beings who were credited with knowing a bit more about the world than human beings. Their word was not itself law; it was wisdom.

And, in this respect, what these early Greeks thought about law contrasts with what another people – the ancient Hebrews – thought about it. Law, for the Hebrews, was a divine command, the command of the creator of the world: 'thus saith the Lord', disobey at your peril. Here no mistake is possible; you did not hear in order to understand, but only in order to obey. (Though even here there was a human agent and there might be a counterfeit agent – a 'false prophet'.)

Law, for these Greeks, was much more like a divine insight into the way in which the world works than a divine command. The gods, of course, had not made the world; but they often understood it better than human beings. Human conduct, then, is 'right' when it conforms to this divine insight.

And how marginal the difference between this early Greek notion of law and 'taboo' is, may be seen in this:

Themis may be accepted or rejected by those to whom it is given. If it is a 'true' *themis* and is accepted and followed, the conduct of human beings will accord to the 'nature' of the world, and they will automatically prosper and be happy. If they reject it, they will be living in a make-believe world, their conduct will conflict with the 'nature' of the world, and they will automatically be frustrated and suffer misfortune. *Nemesis* will overtake them, not as the *ad hoc* punishment of a god who has been disobeyed, but as the inevitable consequence of being out of touch with the world they inhabit.

3

These early Greeks, then, knew that they had a law, and they had some not inadequate beliefs about its 'nature' and where it came from.

Themis was *not* something that had been made; it was something which had been discovered, understood, and declared.

This earliest word for law in a *polis* harked back to the more ancient law and custom of the tribe. *Themis* was, so to speak, a tribal word, carried over into the *polis*, but never quite at home there.

Consequently it was not long before another word for law, another understanding of law, emerged which was more appropriate to the conditions of *polis*-life.

This word was *thesmos*. It was a word which, from being a colloquial expression meaning a 'custom', or 'use', gradually acquired the specific meaning of a formal 'law'.

Now, the change from *themis* to *thesmos* entailed no fundamentally new conception of law. *Thesmos* was still understood as a rule of conduct which, if followed, would make for prosperity, peace, and happiness, because it represented accord with the way the world worked.

And *thesmos* still retained the connection between law and divine wisdom.

What was *new* about it, what made it more appropriate to the facts of *polis*-life, was that it pointed to a new notion of how law was acquired and declared.

Each tribe which, in association with others, went to compose a *polis*, brought with it its own *themistes*, its own tribal law.

No doubt there were similarities; but there were differences also. And the law of a *polis*, if a *polis* were ever to acquire a law of its own, had to be a common law which had somehow to emerge out of this diversity of tribal *themistes*.

And *thesmos* was this, so to speak, first law of the *polis* as such, a law which never itself had been a tribal custom, but had emerged out of diverse and conflicting tribal laws.

And our question is: How did these early Greeks of the *polis* understand the process in which a *polis*-law, *thesmos*, emerged from a diversity of tribal *themistes*?

As the Greeks understood it, this process was one of 'doing justice' to the various tribes and their tribal *themistes* who entered the union of a *polis*.

No doubt, the most venerable, the most generally accept-able, the most useful of these tribal *themistes* became the *thesmos* of the *polis*: a selection, because it could be nothing more. This, if you remember, is the manner in which the common law of England emerged from the local customs of Anglo-Norman communities.

But the profound idea which emerged from this under-standing of the process was the idea of a law emerging from a judicial activity, from the activity of 'doing justice' to the dif-ferent tribes and their different tribal laws.

We shall have to consider later what the Greeks thought about 'justice' and the process of 'doing justice'. But it is clear at once how this idea of *thesmos* gives meaning to Aristotle's conception of the role of the 'founder' of a *polis*.

The 'founder' of a *polis* was an *oikistes*, a host, who 'intro-duces' the tribes to one another, who makes them 'at home' with one another, who 'does justice' to each of his guests, and teaches them the art of 'doing justice' to one another, the 'give and take' of social intercourse.

A *polis*, then, was understood to emerge, *not* in acts of vio-lence, not as the stronger tribe imposing itself upon the weaker, but under the guidance of a man, practiced in the art of persuasion, whose office is not exactly that of a 'lawgiver' but rather of a 'judge' who 'does justice' to the claims of rival tribal laws for recognition in a *polis*.

This is the significance of *thesmos*. It is tribal *themis* made appropriate to a *polis* by being subjected to a judicial process.

The 'founder' of a *polis* 'does justice', not so much to per-sons, as to tribes. And to 'do justice' to a tribe is finding a way of assimilating its customs to those of other tribes. The result is *thesmos*.

And, perhaps, very imperfectly, there is hidden in this idea of law as *thesmos*, the idea that law is something which human beings establish for themselves. This law is elicited, not so much by 'prophets' from the 'gods', as by judicious human beings from the customs of men.

But if there is something dramatic in the movement of thought from tribal *themis* to the *thesmos* of a *polis*, it must be understood not merely as an achievement, but as the beginning of a long process.

For law, even in the most conservative societies, never stands still for very long. Any society which is to understand itself must have an understanding of legal change. And this has often proved the most difficult aspect of human association to understand.

There will, of course, be small adjustments to take account of new circumstances. And these may be thought of as 'doing justice' to the emergent circumstances, recognizing and providing for them.

There is, usually, great reluctance to believe that genuinely 'new' law is being made: the laws are too important to the stability of a society to be thought of as being merely at the disposal of each succeeding generation.

Nevertheless, there come times in the history of most societies when their law gets into a muddle; when it becomes obscure or inapplicable. This, for example, was very much the case towards the end of the fifteenth century in England; and in responding to it some new ways of recording law were invented.

And in the history of most Greek cities, and notably in the history of Athens, there came times when their law had got into a similar sort of muddle.

In operation, over the years, the meaning of the simple precepts inscribed in stone in the *agora* had become obscure. They had been subject to 'interpretations', and it was only 'lawyers' who knew what the law was.

In these circumstances there is often a general demand that the law shall be taken out of the hands of near-priestly interpreters and custodians and published. And such a demand was made in Athens and other Greek cities – as it was made, as we shall see later, in Rome.

In response to this demand, the task of putting the law in order and writing it down was assigned to a commission of trustworthy men, or even to a single man.

Such a man was called a *thesmothete* – a settler of *thesmos*.

Originally *thesmothete* signified a 'judge', one who settled cases under the law; but here it signified a man who was to 'judge' the law itself – to adjudicate between the divergent interests which the law either represented or neglected and thus to restore peace and unity to the *polis*.

The most famous of these *thesmothetai* was Solon in Athens; but he had his counterpart in many other cities.

The qualities which a *thesmothete* was recognized to need were (1) 'wisdom.' Divine inspiration was required for success; and (2) disinterestedness.

He might be radical, like Draco; but, if he is to be successful, he must 'do justice' to all the interests involved.

The appointment of a *thesmothete*, then, assumed the conception of law which was contained in the word *thesmos*: law comes into being by 'doing justice' to divergent current rules. The office was clearly a 'judicial' office.

But it brought the Greeks nearer to the belief that 'laws' could be made, and a belief in *human* responsibility for law.

4

Themis and *thesmos*, then, represented two important stages in the history of Greek thought about the law of a *polis*.

But, about a couple of centuries after Homer, a new word for law appears in the Greek political vocabulary: the word *nomos*.

Now, when *nomos* became the current word for 'law', it carried with it two relatively new ideas.

(1) Law as *nomos* was essentially man-made. It was the product of a 'legislative' process rather than a 'judicial' process.

    Nomos is a decision about what shall be required and expected from citizens, and a direction to the magistrate to enforce certain conduct by imposing a penalty for the breach of it. The decision is made by men making or agreeing upon a rule.

(2) The human response embodied in *nomos* was understood to be a response of reason. *Nomos* is a rational solution of a social problem in terms of a rule of conduct.

Nous and *logos* (intelligence and reasoning) were always clearly connected with *nomos*. To make *nomos* it was not enough to *will* that people shall behave in a certain way and to have *power* to make them do so. The maker of *nomos* had to have *knowledge*.

Thus, when *nomos* replaced *themis* and *thesmos* as the ordinary word for 'law,' an essentially human, rational, almost secular idea of 'law' had replaced an essentially religious idea.

Now, the declarer of *themis* was recognized to require 'knowledge' to perform his office: he required to be divinely inspired.

The declarer of *thesmos* must have knowledge; something not far removed from divine inspiration.

What sort of 'knowledge' does the maker of *nomos* require?

The Greeks were in no doubt about the answer to this question: the legislator required a knowledge of *phusis* – 'nature', 'the natures of things', 'the principles according to which the things of the world moved and behaved'.

Polybius, for example, has this sentence: 'Lycurgus established his laws [in Sparta] because he was able to foresee by the light of reason the course which events normally take and the principle of their movement.' The 'normality' of nature is turned into a 'normality' for human conduct.

But what the 'legislator' needed to know was not merely something in general about the things which compose the *cosmos*, he had to know, understand, and take account of the 'natures' of those items in the *cosmos* which were immediately related to his *polis*.

Solon's laws for Athens, for example, were based upon the observation that Attica was good land for olives and vines but bad land for corn. Here was a piece of essential information about the 'nature' or 'physique' of Attica.

But further, the 'legislator' must not only know the geographical and economic circumstances in which his laws are to operate, he must know something about 'human nature'. And not merely about 'human nature' in general, but about the particular 'nature' of the people of his own *polis*.

Herodotus, for example, says that each 'people' has a *phusis* of its own. And it is not to be expected that laws which will be appropriate for Egyptians will be appropriate for Greeks. Nor, indeed, are all Greeks alike. Aristotle said Greek laws are no good for Scythians.

When Solon was asked by a flatterer whether he had given the Athenians the most perfect laws, he replied, 'No, but those most suited to their *phusis*.'

Thus, when 'law' was recognized as *nomos* it appeared as something closely related to local circumstances, and as something that men make for themselves and for which they are responsible.

'Every *nomos*,' said Demosthenes in the fourth century, 'is an invention; it is a resolution of well-informed and sensible men.'

5

Now, the emergence of 'law' understood as *nomos*, though it was a considerable intellectual achievement, brought with it some disadvantages and difficulties.

- Unavoidably it had a tendency to diminish respect for law. If law is recognized as a man-fabricated convention designed to meet certain local circumstances, it inevitably becomes something less imposing than a reflection of divine wisdom.
- The connection it recognized between *nomos* and *phusis*, 'law' and 'nature', had hidden in it ambiguities which puzzled Greek political thought for generations to come.

The justification of 'law' in terms of its conformity to 'nature' was a theme which proved itself to be the source of endless confusions, and first raised the question of the connection or lack of connection between 'ought' sentences and 'is' sentences; between value and fact.

Nevertheless, the Greeks were never eager and intrepid lawmakers. They would often make subordinate decrees about the conduct of citizens; but 'laws' – even when they were thought of as *nomoi* – were never easily or hastily made or changed. They were a people who could with confidence inscribe their laws in stone.

6

Now, any understanding of 'law' has as its counterpart some beliefs about 'justice'.

The Greek word for 'justice' is *dike*. But *dike* was not in the first place an abstract noun: it stood for something that people *did*, for a kind of conduct.

What we want to know is, not so much, the meaning of the word 'justice', but what Greeks meant when they recognized a man to have 'acted justly'.

In the mythology of ancient Greece *Dike*, like *Themis*, was a goddess. Indeed she was the daughter of *Themis* and *Zeus*. And her character appears in the company she kept. She had two sisters: *Eunomia*, the goddess of orderliness or harmony, and *Eirene*, the goddess of peacefulness.

We know what being 'orderly' is, and what being 'peaceful' is; what sort of conduct is being 'just'?

Originally, it meant something very informal; namely, behaving appropriately, doing the sort of thing which belongs to one's 'nature'.

The *phusis* or 'nature' of a man is the 'principle' of his conduct; it is what makes him behave in a 'human' manner.

The *dike* or 'justice' of a man is the conduct itself, the particular actions which are appropriate to his 'nature'.

For example, if it is the *phusis* of a lion to be fierce, then it is the *dike* of a lion to exhibit fierceness in its behavior: to roar, to snarl, and to paw the air.

If it is the *phusis* of a man to be rational, then it is the *dike* of a man to act deliberately and thoughtfully, because deliberateness and reflectiveness are exhibitions of rationality.

'Justice', then, was a word which stood for the particular ways in which a thing's 'nature' properly expressed itself.

Thus, it was a word available to describe a particular aspect of all *actions* – namely, their relation to the 'nature' of the actor. Actions which conform to the 'nature' of the actor are 'just' actions.

But it was a word available also for describing a particular activity, the activity of considering particular cases – the activity of 'judging' actions.

For 'judging' is concerned with eliciting the propriety of a particular action; and what appears in 'judging' is a pronouncement about the 'fitness' or 'justice' of a particular action. And its 'fitness' is its appropriateness to the 'nature' of the actor.

Now, a 'judge', in the narrow sense, is a man who sits in a court of law, who considers particular cases, and deals out 'justice'.

His task is to consider particular actions in relation to a *law*, and to decide upon their propriety in relation to that law.

Here, a specific *nomos*, a 'law', has taken the place of the less specific *phusis* as the criterion to be used in judging. But if the *nomos*, the specific rule of law, is itself understood to be a reflection of *phusis*, to judge an action in relation to a 'law' is to judge it in relation to 'nature'.

Dealing out 'justice' in a court of law is, then, to be recognized as only a special instance of the more general activity of considering particular actions or situations and pronouncing upon their propriety.

The activity of a judge is concerned with a particular case; and it is a threefold activity.

- He knows and states what the law is. This is the criterion by which he is to judge.
- He indicates, or points out, the divergence from the law which has happened in the particular case before him. He identifies the 'act' as an act of 'injustice'.
- He does something designed to restore the situation to normal, to what it ought to be. He does something to undo the injury perpetrated. This he does by imposing what is believed to be the appropriate penalty.

Thus, 'punishment' is not thought of in any of the difficult and complicated modern formulas of 'deterrence' or 'reform', but simply in terms of putting right what has gone wrong.

Dike, 'justice', consists of finding out the appropriate restitution in a particular case. It is giving the disordered situation its 'due'.

And to sue for 'justice' in a court is to ask for some wrong or injury you have suffered to be redressed.

Now, if 'justice' is understood in this manner, it is not difficult to see why the Greeks thought of the union of tribes who composed a *polis* as having been achieved in an activity of 'doing justice' – the 'founder' of the *polis* being recognized as a 'judge'.

Every *polis* began in disorder – the disorder of multiple and conflicting tribal laws, customs, religious cults, and interests. The process of making a single community out of this disorder and diversity could be recognized as a process of 'doing justice' to each item of this diversity. It was a process of reconciliation.

This is the significance of Aristotle's statement that: 'it is *dike* which draws men together and makes a *polis*.'

And 'justice' might almost be called the father of that family of beliefs which made the experience of *polis*-life intelligible to the Greeks.

In short, it is not going too far to say that, as the Greek thought of it, *polis*-life, 'political' life, *agora*-life, was a continuous activity of 'doing justice'.

And in order to participate in *polis*-life, the art which had to be learned was the art of citizens being just to one another. It was *dike* that transformed tribal *themistes* into the *thesmos* of a *polis*; it was *dike* which above all else distinguished a *polis* from a tribe. It is a *polis*-word; a word appropriate to circumstances in which men who recognize themselves as citizens arrange their relations with one another.

Consequently, it cannot surprise us that, when Plato came to set down his reflections on *polis*-life, he should have done so in a work called *Concerning Justice* – for this is the proper title of the work we call the *Republic*.

The political experience of the ancient Greeks was, first, an experience of creating a political community, what they called a *polis*.

Secondly, it was an experience of governing and being governed – an experience of variation and change in the constitutional structure of a *polis*.

The government of the earliest city states was monarchical: a king, a council of nobles, and an assembly of the *demos*.

These early monarchies were succeeded by what the Greeks called aristocracies: the rule of a nobility.

There were two other regular constitutions known to the Greeks:

- Oligarchies – the rule of a select number of self-appointed citizens, mostly determined by wealth.
- Democracies – the rule of a *polis* by its assembly of citizens from which only those too young to participate in politics were excluded. Although it has to be understood the 'citizens' in a *polis* were, in later times, only a minority of its total population.

Besides these regular constitutions, there was one other kind of government known to the Greeks. They called it a *tyranny*.

A Greek tyrant was an autocrat, and usually the representative of an oligarchic or a democratic faction. He never lasted very long. It was the sort of government which was apt to intervene between periods of oligarchic and democratic rule.

From this point of view, then, the Greek political experience was one of perpetual change, and this reflected itself in the belief that all political forms and constitutions were essentially unstable and non-durable.

By the end of the fifth century B.C., Hellas, the Greek-speaking world, was composed of large numbers of these independent city-states.

By soon after the middle of the fourth century B.C., this whole civilization of city-states had been destroyed, first by the invading armies of Philip and Alexander of Macedon, and later by those of Rome.

The independent cities of Greece were reduced to municipalities in a vast military Empire. Greek 'politics' came to an end.

The ancient Greeks, then, present themselves to us as the inventors of politics, so far as Europe is concerned.

And it sometimes seems that they were so enchanted with what they had invented – *politike*, *agora*-life – that they regarded it as itself an end.

Certainly they cared very much more for politics than for government, and much more for political debate and discourse than for devising durable arrangements and institutions.

Editorial Note

LSE 1/1/21, file 2, fos. 45–62. Fos. 45–59 are photocopies of a typescript with autograph corrections; fos. 60–2 are photocopies of autograph sheets.

Five

The Political Thought of the Ancient Greeks (2)

1

I have said something about the sentiments, beliefs, and ideas which the ancient Greeks connected with what they understood as *politike*, 'political activity': the nature of *polis*-life and the central place occupied by notions of 'law' and 'justice' in their understanding of a *polis*.

I want, this morning, to begin by considering what they thought about 'government'. They were much more interested in keeping up the momentum of change than in enjoying stability.

I said that they were a people who gave a good deal more attention to 'politics' than to 'government'; nevertheless, they did have some interesting and characteristic thoughts about 'government'.

2

We must begin by excluding two words which, although they are Greek and were used to describe something like 'government', were never used in connection with the government of a *polis*.

The first of these words is *despotes*. This, for the Greek, meant not a 'ruler' in the proper political sense, but a 'master'. It was used in two allied connections.

It stood for the relation between an 'owner' and his property or his slaves. A man was never a 'despot' in relation to another man unless that other man was actually or metaphorically his 'slave'.

Thus, *despotes* referred to the internal arrangements of an *oikia*, a 'household'. And even there it was restricted. The

head of a household was *despotes* only in relation to his property and his slaves, not in relation to his wife and children.

Now, many peoples have tried to make sense of the activity of ruling a state by seeking an analogy for it in the activity
of managing a family or a household. And some peoples
have incorporated the word 'father', 'head of a household',
into their political vocabulary and have used it to indicate
the character of a political ruler and his relation to his
subjects.

Pater patriae, 'father of his people', was one of the titles of
Roman emperors. 'Patriarchy' is a bastard word we use for
'fatherly rule' outside a family. And *papa*, long before it
became changed into 'pope', was a word for 'fatherly rule'.

But it is safe to say that the Greeks found the analogy of
domestic rule unenlightening when they came to consider
the character of a political ruler. And they indicated their
rejection of this analogy by refusing to use the domestic
word *despotes* when referring to the ruler of a *polis*. Even a
Greek *tyrant* was not *despotes*.

But, secondly, the Greeks observed around them peoples
among whom the ruler-subject relationship seemed to be
very like that of an 'owner' or 'master' to his estate and
slaves. This appeared to them to be so in Egypt and in Persia.

Consequently, they used the word *despotes* to indicate this
sort of ruler.

What they meant was that he was not a ruler in a political
sense at all. By calling the king of Persia *despotes* they meant
that he was quite unlike a *basileus* (the king of a *polis*), and
that he was really a man who owned an estate and slaves,
and that he controlled them, *not* in an activity of 'ruling', but
by 'violence'.

In short, the king of Persia was recognized to have 'power'
over his subjects, but he did not 'rule' them. He was a 'potentate', not a 'ruler'.

And it may, perhaps, be said that, in denying 'rulership',
in the proper sense, to a 'despot,' the Greeks were beginning
to make the supremely important distinction between
'power' and 'authority'. 'Ruling' in the proper sense is not
merely exercising 'power', it is exercising 'authority'; but
being 'despotic' was a matter of 'power' alone. Or, to put it
another way, the subjects over whom a 'despot' exercises
'power' are *not* free men, they are not even 'men' in the strict
sense at all, they are pieces of 'property'.

The second word we have to exclude is the word *hegemon*, and its companion *hegemonia*.

Properly translated, this means 'leader' and 'leadership'. It was used by the Greeks to describe a relation of one *polis* to others in a league or confederation of cities, or to describe a relation of one tribe to others in an alliance of tribes.

But the ruler or rulers of a *polis* were *never* said to exercise 'hegemony' over those they ruled.

In a democratic constitution there was often a man who was recognized as a 'leader' – like Pericles in Athens. But he was never *hegemon*.

And, here again, *hegemonia* was rejected as a word for 'ruling' a *polis* because it was understood to mean control by superior power. 'Hegemony' was 'supremacy' based upon superior power, and was therefore distinguished from 'government'.

A *hegemon* was 'mighty'; and to be 'mighty' was *not* characteristic of the 'ruler' of a *polis*.

3

Now, these exclusions begin to tell us something about what the Greeks believed the 'government' of a *polis* to be, and about the office of 'ruler' of a *polis*.

And we may learn more by considering the words they did use for this activity and office. The words *arche* and *archon*.

Like most of the other words whose meanings we are considering, the word *arche* did not begin as a political word.

It emerges as a verb, and it means 'to make a beginning', or 'to take the initiative'. To be the first to speak, for example; or to do something which sets in motion a course of events. The carrying off of Helen to Troy by Paris was said to be the *arche* of the Trojan war.

Indeed, perhaps the nearest equivalent in English to this word *arche*, which is often translated 'government', is the word 'cause' in a non-technical sense.

Now, it is at once obvious how appropriate this word *arche*, with all these colloquial connections, must have seemed to the Greeks as a description of the activities of the *basileus*, the 'king' of the primitive *polis*.

This man, distinguished by royal blood and the almost magical scepter of office, called together his noble councillors, discussed matters of policy with them, reached decisions, summoned the *demos*, and made the necessary public pronouncements.

He was the mediator between gods and men in the discovery and interpretation of law; he was a judge, a leader in war, and a priest. He was the man to make the first sacrifice in public religious ceremonies.

The most notable thing about him was not his powers as an executive, but that he spoke first. He took the initiative and made the beginning. It was he who drew attention to situations which needed a public response. He set things in motion.

'Ruling', then, was understood to be an activity of this sort; this is the significance of *arche*.

But the Greeks had another word for a man who 'set things going'; the word *orchamos*. But there was a world of difference between an *orchamos* and *archon*. An *orchamos* set things going by an act of violence, by giving them a push. An *archon*, a ruler, on the other hand, did it in speech; *not* the speech of command but of deliberation.

This, then, is *arche* – 'ruling' in a *polis*. The *basileus* was the first kind of *archon* known to the *polis*. But he was something more than merely the first; he was the model for the Greek notion of 'ruling.'

The later rulers – the aristocrats, the oligarchs, the democratic assemblies, the councils and the committees, the holders of specialized *archonships*, and the tyrants – all, in their various degrees and manners, exemplified this notion of 'government'.

It was a peculiar notion of 'government', in which 'ruling' was only marginally distinguished from *politike*, 'doing politics'.

Both *politike* and *arche* were activities which belonged to the *agora*; both were a matter of speech, of words: both were distinguished from violence, the mere exertion of force.

That 'governing' itself, and not merely 'politics', should have been understood as a matter of persuasion, is both odd and characteristic of the Greeks.

We often think of 'government' as mainly concerned with laying down the law and enforcing the law. And we are apt to think of the authority of the law as in some way deriving from the authority of the government.

But the 'government' of a Greek *polis* had very little to do with the making of law. There was always an aura of sacredness about the laws of a *polis*, which were rarely changed and then only with great reluctance.

And even the enforcement of law was apt to be thought of in terms of 'persuasion'. The obedience of the citizen (as distinct from that of the slave) was thought of as *peitharaxia*, based upon persuasion. He obeyed, not because he was commanded to do so, but because he had been talked to, and because he had perhaps himself contributed to the talk.

Arche was an activity predominantly *not* concerned with making law, but with the conduct of the affairs of a *polis*; and this often concerned the relations of one *polis* with its neighbours.

Arche was deliberating and deciding upon policy. ~not command!~

There is one other word connected with 'government' to be noticed, which seems to introduce a note of command rather than deliberation: the word *kurios*.

Much later, in the New Testament, this is the word used in addressing Jesus which we commonly translate 'lord'. And in the Athenian political vocabulary it was used in a manner which has suggested to some translators the word 'sovereign'.

Aristotle says that in a democracy the assembly of the *demos* is '*kurios* even over the laws'. But I think it is a mistake to use the modern word 'sovereign' here. *Kurios* means something more like having 'supreme and indisputable custody of the laws'.

Now, there is something very individual in this conception of government. It clearly reflects the belief that the exercise of *arche*, 'ruling', is the exercise of authority.

But if you were to ask: who did the Greeks think had authority to 'rule', and where did he get this authority from? you would be asking a very difficult question.

We know that they did not think the authority to rule in a *polis* was analogous to authority in a family or a household. It was *not*, like a father's authority, natural.

We know that they did not regard their gods as in any proper sense 'rulers', or that the source of an *archon*'s authority was in any sense 'divine'.

We know that they distinguished between the authority of a ruler and the authority of the law; and that something like a sacred authority attached to the law itself.

We know that, like many other peoples, they were sometimes inclined to think that men of notable wisdom should be regarded as having some authority in a *polis*. And this was a notion greatly elaborated by Plato.

But I think it is very difficult to find in their notion of a 'democracy', for example, any clear idea that the whole citizen-body had any natural or inherent right to *arche*.

If they had a theory of 'democracy' it was much more the belief that every citizen should be allowed to talk and that every citizen should be eligible to hold office.

In short, the Greeks (unlike many other peoples) were hazy about where the authority to rule came from and about how it could be properly acquired. And they could, perhaps, afford to be hazy about these matters because they had so firm a belief in the inherent authority of a relatively unchanging law of the *polis*.

As we shall see later, European thought applied itself to the question of the authority of rulers, and this question often became the centre of their thought, only when ruling became associated with making 'law'.

4

I want now to say something about the beliefs which centred round another very important word in the Greek political vocabulary: the word *eleutheria*, which we translate, 'freedom'.

What specifically did *eleutheros*, a 'free man', and *eleutheria*, 'freedom', mean for the Greeks?

In the Greek mythological manner of thinking, in which notable human activities and attributes were personified in the character of a god, Dionysus was given the title of *eleutheros*, 'free'. He was the god of wine; and no doubt 'free' here signified 'uninhibited'.

This primitive notion of 'freedom' may not be terribly important when considering 'freedom' as a political idea; but it does give us a significant hint. It suggests that the condition of being free is achieved in a process of 'liberation' of some sort.

To be free is *not* a 'natural' condition; it is an achieved condition. Wine is a notable 'liberator'; but is there not a more significant 'liberation' than this?

This question takes us straight back to the Greek's view of the world and his place in the world. It is a twofold world composed of the necessary processes of nature and the emancipating processes of human artifice – men making something *out of* the things of the world.

The emblem of human freedom is, then, this power of artifice in which men are emancipated from natural necessity. In designing and making things, and in deliberation, choice and action, men are 'free'. This is the freedom which distinguishes *men* from *beasts* and which makes them akin to gods.

But if all men are, in this sense, potentially 'free', able to impress themselves upon the world, are there not some men who enjoy this freedom more fully than others? And are there not some circumstances which offer it in greater measure than others?

Who is the 'free man'? And what are the specific circumstances of 'freedom'?

First, it was clear to the Greek that a slave was not free, and for two reasons. First, he has a 'master' who rules him 'despotically' and secondly, a slave is wholly engaged, within the 'household', in producing the necessities of life; that is, in serving the necessary 'life-process'. He is too close to the earth to be 'free'.

Secondly, the only 'freedom' which can be enjoyed within the family – 'household' – life is the limited freedom of fabrication. And this is true also of the peasant, and the artisan. They enjoy the very limited freedom of being able to make things.

It follows, then, that the genuinely 'free man' is he who by circumstances or education is able to live at least a part of his life outside the 'household', and actually does so.

In short, the 'free man' is the man of the *agora*; for it is only there, in political activity, that the kind of deliberation and action which constitutes being free from natural necessity is possible. *Polis*-life is 'free' life. A man is *free in virtue*, not of being a 'worker', but in view of being a *citizen*.

Every man, says Aristotle, belongs to two worlds. He belongs to the world of 'nature', the private world of the *oikia* where relationships are biological, and activity is governed by natural necessity. And he belongs to the public world of the *agora*. And it is this second life, the *bios politikos*, which offers him the opportunity of being 'free'.

Moreover, this 'freedom' is the product of a 'liberation'. You become a man of the *agora* when you reach the age when you take the oath of citizenship, when you are grown up.

Then, and not until then, is a boy liberated from the tutelage of his father and his exclusive engagement in the private affairs of his 'household'. Then, and not until then, can he (while remaining a member of his family) step out into the public world of the *agora* and have his name registered on the roll of citizens.

And there may be further heights of freedom to reach. For example, at the age of thirty, in Athens, he is eligible to become a member of the *Heliaea*. But 'coming of age,' becoming a citizen, is the moment of emancipation and consequently becoming a 'free man'.

On this reading of things, it would appear that the Greek would connect 'freedom', not exclusively, but unmistakably, with a democratic *polis*. And this I think was so.

In a 'democracy' every citizen has the opportunity of engaging in the 'free' activity of deliberation and choice in respect of the public affairs of his *polis*. But, whatever its constitution, a *polis* was recognized to provide a condition of 'freedom' which could never be enjoyed by those who, like Persians and Egyptians, were ignorant of *polis*-life.

There was, then, in the Greek view of things, no opposition between being 'governed' and being 'free'. *Arche* and *eleutheria* were counterparts of one another.

The opposition, as they understood it, was between being 'free' and being under the command of a 'despot', or being in the position of a slave in a household.

In short, whereas we are apt to regard the 'private' life of a man as the realm in which he is 'free', the Greeks regarded the private life of the *oikia* as a realm of 'necessity', and the 'public' life of the *agora* as the realm of 'freedom'.

5

Now, among the many other beliefs in terms of which the Greeks gave an intellectual organization to *polis*-life, there is one which deserves special consideration.

As we have seen, it was commonly recognized that a new sort of human being had emerged with the *polis*, the human being denoted by the word 'citizen'. And the relation of citizen to citizen was identified as almost unique among human relationships because it was a relationship of 'equals'. The only proper counterpart to this relationship was that which exists between 'friends'.

This, it was believed, was one of the chief differences between the *oikia* or the tribe, and the *polis*. In *agora*-life the 'natural' unequals of the 'household' – women, children, and slaves – never appeared.

The idea of *isotes,* 'equality', then, as it appeared in the Greek political vocabulary, was understood as the counterpart of *polis*-life.

Equality, in some sense, and a *polis*, go together; just as 'freedom' and a *polis* go together.

Now, this notion of 'equality' had nothing directly to do with a 'democratic' constitution. It was not applied to human beings as such. It did not refer to the 'natural' qualities of men, or to their property. Men were not thought of as having been in any sense 'created equal'. It was 'citizens' who by legal definition were equal, and who, by circumstance, in the *agora*, were equal.

Moreover, there was much in the Greek notion of *politike*, and in their notion of *arche*, which recognized and had a place for this notion of 'equality'.

For example, where political activity is understood to be an activity of 'persuasion', it assumes or entails a certain sort of egalitarianism. It is only 'equals' whom you try to 'persuade'. Command implies 'unequals', subordinates.

And where the 'ruler,' the *archon*, is *not* thought of on the analogy of the father of a family or of the owner of an estate and slaves, where he is *not* thought of as a 'god', but *is* thought of as a man who initiates a debate, gathers the consensus of opinion, and sets things going in a certain direction – where this is the notion of 'ruling', the main 'inegalitarian' analogies have disappeared.

But besides appearing in this general way in the Greek political vocabulary, the word *isotes* appeared in two specific connections.

(1) In the word *isonomia* (equal laws).

This word started life as indicating the quality of 'balance' which belongs to a healthy organism in which each part properly performs its functions in relation to the other parts.

But it entered the Greek political vocabulary to express the condition of things in a *polis* where rule was 'by law' and where every citizen was equal before the law.

Isonomia (literally, 'the same laws administered in the same way for all conditions of citizens') was said by

Herodotus (III. 80) to be the 'most beautiful word' in the Greek political vocabulary.

It had, however, nothing expressly to do with a democratic constitution. Thucydides, for example, speaks of an 'isonomic oligarchy'. It was something which could subsist wherever there was *arche* in the proper sense.

Indeed, it was often observed that *isonomia* and democracy were apt *not* to go together. The partiality and the prejudice of an assembly of the *demos* was notorious; it was apt to rule, not according to the law, but according to the whims of the moment. And what was characteristic of a 'democracy' was, not *isonomia*, but something quite different – an equalizing of property or wealth.

(2) The second word in the Greek political vocabulary which took up this notion of 'equality' was the word *isogoria*, which meant the equal right of speech.

This was more genuinely connected with *demokratia* than *isonomia*; but it did not originate with a democratic constitution.

Isogoria was the practice which prevailed in the council of 'notables' which was the partner of the 'king' in the monarchical *polis*. What a 'democratic' constitution did was to extend *isogoria* to the assembly of the *demos*. But it belonged to the Greek notion of *politike*.

Politics, that is, citizens speaking and listening to the utterances of other citizens, was impossible without *isogoria*.

6

Now, these beliefs about law, justice, government, freedom, equality, and so on, are not, I think, to be regarded as abstract ideas upon which the Greeks modelled, or tried to model, their conduct of affairs and their institutions.

They are, rather, the reflections of the feelings, emotions, and events which composed their political experience and which they used to give an intellectual organization to that experience.

The experience which overshadowed all others in generating these beliefs was the emergence of *polis*-life – a life that was neither tribal, nor home life, and which it was recognized that human beings (with the help of the gods, perhaps) had created for themselves and which reflected the unique qualities of human beings.

The *polis* emerged as the product of contingent circumstances. And a certain ancient, tribal way of thinking about 'law' (*themis*) was superseded by other and more appropriate ways of thinking – *thesmos* and *nomos*.

With the *polis* appeared the 'citizen'. And reflection disclosed that the distinguishing feature of the citizen-to-citizen relationship was properly to be described as *isotes*, a relationship of 'equality'. The *idea* of 'equality' emerged from the *event* of citizenship.

The *agora* and *agora*-life appeared. And the word *eleutheria* ('freedom') was available and seemed appropriate to describe that sort of life and activity – a life of speech, choice, decision, and action, 'free' from the natural necessity characteristic of the *oikia*.

The most unmistakable feature of *polis*-life was the singleness which it imposed upon tribal diversity. And the word 'justice' was available to describe the quality of this unity and to describe the process in which it had been achieved – a deliberative process.

And so on. Each of these words, as it was incorporated into the Greek political vocabulary, took on a new 'political' meaning.

But there is something to add to all this, and something very important.

A *polis* emerged out of a union of tribes. And in these circumstances it might be expected that the Greeks should think of political activity as the art of reconciling diverse interests, and of a *polis* as a limited liability company for the peaceful exchange of goods and services.

But, in fact, a *polis* became something very much more than this.

Each of these cities gathered to itself the exclusive loyalty of its citizens. Each had a fanatical feeling for its own independence; a passion for autonomy and self-sufficiency. Each was a religious community, with gods exclusively its own.

And in these circumstances, it became impossible for the Greeks to think of the law of a *polis* as merely the rules which arbitrated between diverse interests.

A *polis* was something more than a convenience. And the Greeks gave a great deal of thought to formulating the difference between a mere alliance of tribes for the peaceful exchange of goods and services, and a *polis*.

This difference was often appealed to in political speech. Pericles often referred to the unity and harmony which distinguished Athens; and Sparta had an even stricter sense of itself as something very much more than a mere association.

But all this remained on the edge of things. It needed a philosopher to formulate this feature of *polis*-life.

Aristotle had a characteristic way of tackling this problem.

A *polis*, he said, is certainly an association of families, living on a common site, designed and organized in such a way as to guard against being unjust to one another, and so live in peace.

But, he goes on, *if* it were merely this, there would be nothing to distinguish it from an alliance of families, or to distinguish its law from the agreed rules of an alliance, and very little to distinguish it from a well-organized market.

The difference, as Aristotle understood it, lay in the fact that a *polis* was *not* merely an association for the sake of protection and a more prosperous and more peaceable life. It was an association for the sake of a 'good' human life.

What distinguished *polis*-life from all other forms of human life was that it supplied the conditions for the exercise of the uniquely human qualities of human beings.

Animals are capable of co-operation; tribal societies seek the most prosperous life which their circumstances allow. But a *polis* is to be understood as an association of human beings, brought together and held together, not by 'nature' or 'natural ties', but by choice; and an association of human beings devoted to living a life which fully engaged their unique powers of rational deliberation, choice, and action.

In short, what distinguished a *polis* was *politike* and *arche*: it was a society in which human beings could enjoy their unique capacity for freeing themselves from the bonds of natural necessity, and a society whose unity was sustained not by 'nature' but by *arche*, 'government'.

Editorial Note

LSE 1/1/21, file 2, fos. 63–74. Photocopy of a typescript with autograph corrections.

Six

Aristotle (1)

1

I do not think there is anything to be gained by denying the name 'political thought' to any of the mental activities which are apt to go on in politics and government.

A speech in the House of Commons, the advice given by a civil servant to a minister, a pamphlet advocating the reform of the betting laws, are no less examples of 'political thought' than the constitution of the United States, Hooker's defence of the Elizabethan church settlement, or Plato's *Republic*.

Nevertheless, I think we shall go seriously wrong unless we recognize that there are different levels of political thinking, and that we shall not expect quite the same thing from a speech of Pericles as we shall expect from Plato's *Republic*: nor should we judge them in the same manner.

So far, we have been concerned with a fairly well-defined level of Greek thinking about politics: the sentiments, beliefs, and ideas which composed what may be called the practical political vocabulary of the ancient Greeks.

These beliefs gave an intellectual organization to their politics, and made them more fully aware of what they were doing. But, like most beliefs of this sort, they were imperfectly thought out, they were ragged at the edges, and they often suggested questions for which they had no answer. The most notorious example of this was the confused popular belief about the connection between 'laws' and 'nature'.

I want now to go on to consider some of the other levels of political thought among the ancient Greeks: the levels where thought acquired a 'scientific' or a 'philosophical' refinement appropriate for answering some of the questions suggested but left unanswered in their practical political beliefs.

Some peoples seem to have got on well enough without anything very much in the way of political philosophy; but it

is only to be expected that so curious and so enquiring a people as the Greeks should have been intrepid explorers of
their political experience at these 'scientific' and philosophical levels – although it has to be admitted that what may be
called 'scientific' and 'philosophical' thinking about politics
was, for the most part, confined to Athens, although others
besides Athenians took part.

Of the many writers who pursued this enterprise, Plato
and Aristotle are incomparably the most famous. And
although Plato was born some eighty years before Aristotle,
it is with Aristotle I propose to begin.

2

Aristotle was born in 384 B.C. in northern Greece, where his
father was court physician to the king of Macedonia. He was
destined for a medical career, but instead of starting on his
medical education he went, at the age of eighteen, to Athens
to study in the Academy of Plato.

This Academy was in the nature of a university designed
to give a general education in what may be called the explanatory sciences rather than the practical arts: the curriculum
centred round mathematical and philosophical studies.

After studying and teaching there for twenty years, and on
the death of Plato, Aristotle migrated to a city named Assos,
on the coast of Asia Minor, where a branch of the Platonic
Academy had been established; and later he went to the
island of Lesbos.

When he was forty years old he was invited by King Philip
of Macedonia to be tutor to his son Alexander. After a period
of about five years in his native Macedonia he returned to
Athens, founded a school of philosophy of his own, called
the Lyceum, and remained there for the rest of his life.

The works of Aristotle as they have come down to us, some
of them after a long period during which they were lost and
forgotten, are mostly in the nature of textbooks or treatises.
They cover almost every aspect of Greek thought: physics,
biology, astronomy, logic, metaphysics, ethics, art, economics, rhetoric, and politics.

Many of them have reached us in an incomplete form, not
because a few pages are missing, but because they were left
in the form of lecture notes; and some of them have been
reconstructed from notes taken by his pupils.

This is the character of the *Politics*. It is disjointed and disordered; in it arguments are begun which are never finished; casual, disconnected observations abound; it is divided into eight books, but the divisions are often arbitrary. Nevertheless, it remains incomparably the most read and the most influential work on politics ever written.

What holds it together and gives it a unity is: (1) its exclusive concern with the Greek *polis*, and (2) the organization which these reflections on *polis*-life derive from having been connected with Aristotle's more general understanding of the *cosmos* and the place of human beings and political activity within this *cosmos*. This, indeed, is what gives the book its philosophical character.

A large part of this book is concerned with establishing the place of politics on a kind of intellectual map of the *cosmos*.

Consequently, I propose to begin by saying something about Aristotle's map of the universe, which constitutes both the context into which Aristotle is putting 'politics' and the apparatus of inquiry he is using to answer the question: What is politics?

3

As a Greek, Aristotle recognized the *cosmos*, or universe, as a totality of connected, living things, each of which has a 'nature' of its own which it exhibits in the way in which it moves, or behaves. The 'nature' of a thing is *not* to be discovered by asking: What is it made of? but by asking, What is the 'principle', or cause, of its behaving in the way in which it did behave?

To understand the *cosmos*, then, is to have reliable knowledge about the processes of movement, of change, or behaviour which are characteristic of the components of this *cosmos*. To understand politics is to understand it in its place in this *cosmos*.

The first principle of Aristotle's understanding of this *cosmos* is that it is made up of a number of different things each of which has a characteristic way of moving, behaving, or 'living'. And its characteristic way of moving *is* what the thing is; its 'nature'.

Thus, to be a stone is to behave in a manner which exhibits the 'nature' of a stone. And to be a man is to behave in a human manner – that is, to exhibit 'human nature'.

But, as Aristotle understood it, to behave as a stone, or as a human being, is not merely to exhibit the 'nature' of a stone, or a human being; it is a constant striving to become more and more completely stone-like, or 'human' (as the case may be).

Thus, all the movement that goes on in the universe, all the change that takes place is:

- Things exhibiting their 'natures'; stones falling, water running downhill, dogs yapping, clowns making jokes etc. Each thing acting according to its nature, or being 'just' to itself.
- Things exploring their 'natures' in an attempt to achieve a more and more exact and unqualified exhibition of their 'natures'.

Or, as one might say, all movement (and there is nothing but movement in the universe) is, at the same time:

- Diurnal movement: a thing responding to its contingent environment in its characteristic way.
- Secular movement: a thing endeavouring over time to do this ever more perfectly. Or it might be said that a thing not only is identified in terms of the way in which it behaves, but also every item of its behaviour is both exhibiting its nature and learning more about its nature.

Now, in the language of the philosophers, this idea of movement is called teleological movement or change.

This means:

- Movement which is directed towards a *telos*, or an end or a fulfillment, as distinct from fortuitous or purposeless change.
- Movement directed towards an end or a fulfillment which is potential within the thing that moves, as distinct from an end or a fulfillment imposed on it from outside.

Or as it might be said, all movement is growth, but growth in which the being concerned is becoming what it is in its 'nature' to be.

Perhaps, the simplest way of understanding what Aristotle thought about the world is to say that he thought of all the movement or behaviour of things on the analogy of biological growth: that is, movement directed towards a condition of 'maturity' or of being 'full-grown'. And this condition of being 'full-grown' is a condition in which the 'nature' of a thing is fully realized.

For example:

- An acorn grows up into a sapling, the sapling into a full-grown oak tree, and the process goes on until the tree reaches its 'natural' size. It is the 'nature' of an acorn to become an oak tree.
- A boy grows up into a man, and reaches the condition of being an adult man. And everything he does is not only an exhibition of 'human nature' but a striving to realize adult 'human nature'. Boys don't become 'gods' or 'elephants' because their only potentiality is to become men.

But, in all cases, this process of 'becoming' is followed by what Aristotle calls a process of 'passing away', which is equally characteristic of the thing concerned. It belongs to a man, for example, to have a certain span of life.

The movements, changes, manners of behaviour, then, of the things that compose the universe are continuous processes of coming into being and passing away, governed by the different natures of the different things concerned.

The *cosmos*, then, for Aristotle, was a continuous process of teleological change.

Now, this conception of the natural processes which go on in the universe – at any rate the sublunary part of the universe – needs to be qualified. It is not impossible for a natural process to be obstructed.

A tree, because its seed has fallen upon poor soil, or from some other cause, may never in fact reach maturity. It may be pushed off the line of its 'natural' or 'normal' development.

A boy, because he has not received the appropriate nourishment or education, may pass away without ever having realized 'human nature' to the full.

And this may happen to anything in the sublunary world.

These obstructions of normal processes Aristotle calls 'accidents', divergences from the normal. But what is an 'accident'?

If the growth of a tree is obstructed by the seed falling upon stony ground, that growth is being obstructed by the 'natural' behaviour of the stone: it is the 'nature' of a stone to be hard, resistant, not to provide nourishment. The tree never becomes a full-grown tree because the stone insists on being and behaving like a stone.

Thus, 'accident' is not really a break in the teleological processes of the world; it is the product of a fortuitous clash between two different 'natures', each seeking its own end or fulfillment, and one succeeding and the other failing.

Nothing that is, nothing that happens in the world, can be regarded as 'unnatural', but the sublunary world holds examples of 'normal' and of 'abnormal' behaviour in particular things.

Now, there is a particular and very important example of this clash of 'natures'. Aristotle calls it artifice.

Artifice is the designed clash of two natures; and human beings alone are capable of injecting it into the world.

When a man fells and cuts up a tree and makes it into a table he is doing violence to the 'nature' of the tree: it is not potential in a tree to become a table. Nevertheless, in making the table out of the tree, the man is exercising one of *his* 'natural' powers: it is 'natural' to men, it is a potentiality in human 'nature', to be a maker of artifacts. To make an artifact is, then, to impose the teleology of 'human nature' upon the teleology of the 'nature' of something else.

Human beings, then, are recognized to have this unique power of imposing their own 'natures' upon the rest of the world by design; the power of choosing to make the other things of the natural world serve human purposes.

Other things impose their 'natures' upon one another 'by accident'. Man alone does this by design. And it is in virtue of his power, the power of acting in pursuit of a conscious purpose, that Aristotle calls men 'rational' beings.

And, as we shall see, this involves attributing to human beings a 'nature' quite unlike the 'natures' of the other things which compose the *cosmos*. It is the 'nature' of a man, it is potential within human nature, to *choose* for himself what he shall aim at; or to arrive at his own perfection in a series of choices, and not merely in a series of determined events.

'Rationality', in Aristotle's vocabulary, means the power of realizing one's 'nature', fulfilling one's potentiality, in conduct which springs not from natural necessity but from conscious choice or design.

There are, then, three permanent characteristics of the world in which we live:

- Natural necessity – movements which go on according to the law of the 'natures' of the things which compose the world.
- Accident or chance happenings.
- Artifacts – things made by men by their imposing their own purposes on natural processes.

Now, of all the entailments of this view of things two are specially important for us.

- Understanding or explaining anything in the world is discovering its 'nature', discovering what 'causes' it to behave as it does and be what it is.
- The only way to make this discovery is by observing how a thing moves or behaves when it is *not* being obstructed by the behaviour or movement of some other thing.

'Science', systematic inquiry, then, the attempt to acquire reliable knowledge about the world, is an inquiry which concerns itself with the two major aspects of this world.

- It is inquiry into what 'causes' a thing to behave as it does and be what it is; an inquiry into the 'natures' of things.
- It is an inquiry into what may cause a thing to behave in a manner eccentric to its own 'nature' – that is, an inquiry into the circumstantial or contingent relations between different things; the accidents which happen to them, or (in the case of men) the designs they may have and carry out.

The first is a philosophical inquiry; the second is an 'historical' inquiry.

This, then, is the understanding of the *cosmos*, and of the place of human beings within it, which supplies the organizing ideas of all Aristotle's reflections on the *polis* and political activity.

And, before we go any further, we may notice at once how this set of ideas about the world enables Aristotle to recognize a *polis* both as an artificial creation of human beings, a human invention, *and* as something that is 'natural' to human beings.

It is 'artificial' because it is chosen, and is *not* (like the family) a product of natural necessity.

It is 'natural' because it belongs to the nature of human beings to determine their conduct 'rationally' – by making conscious choices. And this is precisely what Aristotle understands *polis*-life to be.

And in order to understand and explain *polis*-life, what has to be shown is that it is a way of living which belongs to the 'nature' of human beings and necessary to the fulfillment or achievement of that 'nature'. ||

4

The *Politics* of Aristotle is concerned with seven main themes or inquiries. Each of them is suggested by the political experience of the Greeks and each of them is formulated in terms of this understanding of the *cosmos* and of human 'nature'.

- The 'nature' of the *polis* and of the citizen to citizen relationship as it may be gathered from a study of the *polis* coming into being or emerging, from a study of its unobstructed growth.
- The 'nature' of the *polis* as it may be gathered from a study of some imaginary cities constructed by theorists and held to be well-constructed, and from the study of some actual cities held to be well-governed, i.e., those which exhibit, or purport to exhibit, the end potential in a *polis*.
- The 'nature' of citizenship and of a constitution determined by considering in abstract terms the end or purpose of a *polis*.
- An inquiry into the 'nature' of the *polis* pursued by a method of ideal types.
- An inquiry into cities whose 'natural' or normal development has been obstructed. That is, a study of political 'monstrosities', stunted growths, the results of political 'accidents'. This may be understood as a study of the pathology of the *polis*.
- An inquiry into the causes of political 'accidents' (here called 'revolutions'), and into the means of preventing them.
- Reflections on the sort of constitution which most nearly represents the 'nature' of a *polis*.

What Aristotle has to say on some of these themes is collected together in one place in the *Politics*; what he has to say on others is scattered throughout the work.

5

I propose now to say a little about how Aristotle pursues some of these themes.

(1) Nobody can get far into Book I of the *Politics* without perceiving that Aristotle is telling us something about the history, and particularly about the early history and emergence, of the Greek *polis*. Here, indeed, is a masterly account of what I have called the legend of Greek politics, and Aristotle himself was one of the great constructors of this legend.

Nevertheless, the 'history' of the *polis* as it appears in Book I of the *Politics* is a strange sort of history. No particular *polis* is mentioned; the events recorded are all of a very general character. It is, in fact, what the eighteenth century called 'philosophical history' or 'conjectural' history.

The *polis*, here, is not so much a historical phenomenon as a 'natural' phenomenon. Aristotle is treating it as if it were a species of animal or tree, and he is asking himself the question: What is the characteristic process in which a *polis* emerges and develops?

And he is asking this question because he believes that the best way of getting to know the 'nature' of anything is by studying it 'coming into being', as he says. The 'nature' of a thing is to be discerned in its behaviour. Its behaviour *is* its 'growth'.

This, then, is the 'natural history' of the *polis*, as Aristotle understands it.

The 'seed', so to speak, from which the *polis* grows is a potentiality in human beings: the power of rational deliberation and of speech. Human beings are, thus, 'by nature' political creatures, and *polis*-life is the 'natural' life of a man because it has its roots in human nature itself.

Certainly the *polis* is the product of human choices, it is an invention of human beings; but it is a condition of life in which alone the peculiar 'excellence' or 'nature' which belongs to human beings can be achieved; their peculiar 'excellence' being the ability to deliberate and to speak and to choose.

Polis-life is a highly specific sort of life – it is not merely a 'social' life (sociability is *not* peculiar to human beings) – it is a life in which human beings are engaged in political activity; that is, the activity of deciding things by deliberating and talking about them.

But, if this is the 'seed' in human 'nature' from which the *polis* springs, the *polis* itself emerges (often provoked by a contingent need for defence) as a union of families and tribes.

And it is set on its course of development by an activity called 'justice' – a human, deliberative activity of giving their due to the laws and religious beliefs of each of the tribes which compose it: *Dike* belongs to the 'nature' of the *polis*.

But this is only the beginning of a long process of development in which this 'nature' is gradually explored and realized: the process in which a *polis*, like a man or a tree, grows up and becomes adult.

When it first emerges the *polis* has a king; but kingship gives place to aristocracy, aristocracy to oligarchy, oligarchy to tyranny, and tyranny to democracy. And here, or hereabouts, the process stops. Why?

Not because Aristotle regards a democratic constitution, like that of Athens in his own time, for example, as a perfect constitution, but because he believes that the adult or grown-up *polis* will have a constitution which has 'democratic' elements; and until a 'democratic' constitution has emerged these essential elements of the 'nature' of a *polis* will remain merely 'potential'.

When Aristotle says that the adult *polis* is a 'democracy of some sort', we know that he means that some kind of democratic structure is potential in the *polis* from the moment of its emergence – as a full-grown oak tree is potential in the acorn. And we know, further, that he believes that this entire process of change is the *polis* striving to attain its adult form.

The *polis*, then, emerges in an activity of doing 'justice', and the whole process of its growth is a striving after a more complete and a more exact 'justice'.

Now, I have spoken as if Aristotle thought of a *polis* as if it were, itself, a tree or a plant. And this is how Aristotle speaks of it. But he can only do so because, all the time, he is understanding a *polis* as human beings behaving in a certain manner. A *polis* is an artifact; but all artifacts are to be recognized as forms of human conduct. And the peculiarity of a *polis* is that it is an artifact entirely made out of human conduct. It is not like a vase made out of clay; both it and its materials are human conduct.

(2) But, besides this study of the *polis* coming into being, Aristotle has another inquiry to make. He is interested in the different constitutional forms, not only as stages in a normal development in which 'justice' is generated, but also in themselves. And he now turns to consider them as structures which can be classified.

Now, classification is an ambiguous and somewhat arbitrary activity. It entails the choice of a principle.

Some principles of classification reveal more than others and therefore are more useful. But before classification can begin a principle of classification must be chosen.

For example, there have been various principles used in biology for classifying animals:

- number of legs – bipeds, quadrupeds, etc. 'insect' – six legs;
- habitat – land, air, water – amphibious;
- mode of generation – mammals, oviparous, etc.
- presence or absence of backbone – vertebrate or invertebrate.
- the sort of food they eat – herbivores.

And each of these principles, in operation, reveals a different classification of animals; and each may be enlightening.

Aristotle's classification of constitutions is based upon *two* principles:

In every *polis* the activity of governing, *arche*, is in the hands of *one* man, a *few* men, or *many* men. And, as an empirical corollary to this: the few are always wealthy and the many are always poor.

In every *polis* governing is carried on either solely for the benefit of the rulers themselves, or solely for the benefit of the ruled. And as a corollary to this: the first is always unjust, the second always has some semblance of justice.

When these principles are applied the following classification of constitutions emerges.

Number of Rulers	Just Constitutions	Unjust Constitutions
One Man	Kingship or monarchy	Tyranny
A few men (wealthy)	Aristocracy	Oligarchy
Many men (poor)	Polity (*politeia*)	Democracy

In the *Politics* Aristotle elaborates these broad classifications. There are at least two different kinds of 'democracy'
and there are several different kinds of both monarchy and
oligarchy – but we need not concern ourselves with these
refinements.

Now, there are some important things to notice about
these principles of classification and the scheme of constitutions which emerges from them; they are not always properly understood.

Aristotle is reputed to be very much an empiricist, concerning himself with observations and with conclusions
which may legitimately be drawn from putting observations
together. And he often deserves this reputation. He was a
tireless observer, both of the natural and of the political
world, and he had an immense appetite for information.

But neither these principles of classification, nor this
scheme of constitutions, are based upon observations in this
sense.

To say, for example, that every *polis* is ruled by one, or by a
few rich, or by many poor, and to represent these as not only
exclusive categories (which they are) but also as categories
into which all the cities of the Greek world could be put without remainder, is certainly not true.

Or, to say that all cities are ruled either for the benefit of the
rulers, or the benefit of the ruled, is to propose a dichotomy
which does not correspond to any facts in Greek history.

Of course, there were some notorious examples of cities
ruled in a violently oppressive manner, and most of them
were 'democracies' in the accepted Greek sense of the word;
but most cities were, in fact, governed partly in the interests
of the rulers and partly in the interests of the ruled.

The scheme of constitutions which springs from these
principles of classification has no direct connection with any
particular cities of the world of the Greek *polis*. It is, in fact,
not a classification of known cities in terms of their constitutions, but a scheme of ideal types, none of which is exactly to
be found anywhere.

This becomes clearer when we observe that Aristotle in
using these common words of the Greek political vocabulary
– 'kingship', 'aristocracy', 'oligarchy', 'tyranny', 'democracy', etc., has given each of them a new meaning.

Monarchy in Aristotle's scheme means 'just government by
one man'. But government by one man was never character-

istic of any Greek *polis* – it was characteristic only of the oriental despotisms or, for example, of the hereditary kingdom
of Macedon.

The Homeric *basileus* ruled always in consultation with his
council of 'notables'. And there was nothing in 'kingly' government, as the expression was normally used, to signify that
it was inherently 'just'.

Aristocracy and *oligarchy* are distinguished by Aristotle as
'just' or 'unjust' forms of minority government. But, before
Aristotle, they had no such meanings.

'Aristocracy' normally stood for the exercise of *archê* by
some fraction of the whole number of citizens distinguished
on account of noble blood; and 'oligarchy' meant rule by a
minority distinguished by anything except noble blood. Both
could be, and were in Greece, either 'good' government in
Aristotle's sense, or 'bad' government.

Tyranny, in Aristotle's use, is the rule of one man for his
own sole benefit; but what distinguished 'tyranny' in Greece
was that the ruler was a usurper: he might rule well or ill.

Democracy for Aristotle means 'government by the many
poor in the sole interests of the many poor', whereas its normal meaning was government by an assembly of *all* citizens
(in which it is true the poor were usually the majority); all citizens above a certain age being eligible to hold office as
archons and the archonships were usually filled by lot.

And *polity*: this word was not invented by Aristotle, but
again he uses it in a restricted sense.

Its normal meaning was a constitution in which there was
a mixture of oligarchic and democratic institutions and in
which the office holders were men of some substance. But
with Aristotle it means a constitution in which 'free birth'
and 'wealth' are the qualifications for office.

Now, it cannot be supposed that Aristotle intended us to
understand that he believed that, for example, all the 'democratic' constitutions of Greek cities conformed to his definition of *demokratia* and that all oligarchies were ruled solely in
the interests of the oligarchs: this is a gross and unmistakable
error.

What, I think, we have to suppose is that in his scheme of
constitutions the names do not stand for boxes into which
actual constitutions could be distributed without remainder;
they stand for ideal types.

His procedure is not that of an observer, but that of a logician. And this is a procedure to be met elsewhere in Aristotle's works.

For example, in his *Metaphysics* he distinguishes seven meanings for the word *phusis*, but at least three of them are not actual meanings at all (nobody ever used the word in these manners), but 'possible' meanings, put in by Aristotle to make his review *logically* complete.

These 'constitutions' of Aristotle are not 'actual' but 'possible' or 'ideal' constitutions defined so that each has a simple and exclusive character. And this, indeed, is the character of *all* classifications.

What, then, is the point of this Aristotelian scheme of ideal types? What use does he make of it?

And before trying to answer these questions it is worthwhile to remember that other political thinkers, often under the influence of Aristotle's *Politics*, have considered the structures and operation of different sorts of government in relation to ideal types or models – Montesquieu, for example, and Max Weber.

So far as Aristotle is concerned, this procedure enabled him to do two things.

First, to discern the constituents of the constitutions of actual cities, and to determine the tendency a constitution has towards 'justice' or 'injustice' and (a very important consideration for Aristotle) its tendency towards stability or instability.

Most cities were, in fact, mixtures of varying proportions of the characteristics represented by these ideal types.

Secondly, it enabled him to construct what he describes as the most viable constitution for 'most' cities by combining in different proportions the ideal elements which his scheme of types gave him.

And he does this in much the same manner as a metallurgist, wanting a product with certain qualities of hardness, for example, tensile strength and malleability, makes an alloy out of a number of different metals combined in different proportions.

And it is characteristic of Aristotle to want to make a construction of this sort and to do it in this way instead of doing it in the very different manner that Plato, as we shall see, employed.

We will have to consider later what Aristotle believed to be the mixture of these ideal characteristics which would constitute the best sort of constitution for a *polis*. But we may expect it to be a mixture, in certain proportions, of monarchy, aristocracy, and democracy.

(3) From Aristotle's inquiries in the *Politics* there emerges a vision of three possible political sciences or bodies of knowledge relevant to the understanding of *polis*-life and the practice of *politike*, the art of politics.

There is, first, the study of what Aristotle thinks of as the normal development of a *polis*, a development in the strict sense in which the potentialities present in the emergent *polis* are realized and in which the *polis* grows up to be an adult *polis*.

This might be called the 'biology' of the *polis*; and it begins with the identification of the *polis* as belonging to 'the class of things that exist by nature'.

This raises some important questions. What is the difference between a 'household' and a *polis*, and how out of a union of 'households' can something that is not itself a 'household' emerge?

What is the difference between an alliance of 'households' and a union of 'households'?

What is the difference between a member of a 'household', and even the head of a 'household', and a 'citizen'?

How are we to account for the different species of *polis*? For, Aristotle does not take the simple view that variety here is simply divergence from a norm. There may be good and bad dogs, but different species of dog are not to be understood as simply better and worse dogs.

And, the most important question: By what analogy, Aristotle asks, are we to understand governing in a *polis*? Not the analogy of a master's rule over his slaves; that is a relationship of owner and owned. Not the analogy of a father's rule over his children, that is, an educational relationship. But, Aristotle thinks, the relation of husband and wife is, perhaps, not so remote from that of ruler and ruled in a *polis* – although it is nothing like an exact parallel.

This sets Aristotle on to thinking that there may be persons who are to be recognized as 'naturally' rulers and others who are 'naturally' subjects. Male, he thinks, has a 'natural' authority over female, the elder over the younger, the wiser or more intelligent over the less wise or less intelligent.

And if there are 'natural' rulers, what effects will this have on our beliefs about the government of a *polis*?

There is, then, a science of politics which may be called the 'biology' of the *polis*: it is concerned with the 'normal' and with the operation of normal processes.

There is, secondly, the possibility of a science of political abnormalities, the results of political error or 'accident'. This may be described as the 'pathology' of the *polis*.

It is a study of political disease and the causes of political disease; and it springs easily from Aristotle's belief that every natural thing has a normal mode of behaviour in which it is striving to realize its own specific 'nature', but that this normal mode of behaviour may be interrupted or obstructed.

For Aristotle the major form of diseased *polis* is one in which government is carried on solely for the benefit of the rulers and not the ruled, for this is 'injustice' and it is a political disease because 'justice' belongs to the 'nature' of the *polis*.

The symptoms of this disease are discontent, disunity, the absence of *eunomia*, and often revolution.

But each species of *polis* is prone to diseases peculiar to itself, and some are more liable to disease than others.

A *polis* which has a constitution naturally resistant to disease must be considered superior to those which are liable to catch anything that is going.

And thirdly, there is the possibility of a 'remedial' science of politics, the aim of which, like that of the science of medicine, is to devise cures for political disease.

But to cure is not to transform, it is not to turn the patient into a different sort of being: it is to restore to him such health as he is naturally capable of enjoying.

Therefore, in this remedial science of politics, Aristotle's attention is directed, not towards the imaginative construction of a perfect *polis*, but towards the discovery of the conditions in which each species of *polis* may be as healthy as its constitution allows it to be – that is, to restore its own constitution to working order.

Now, when I say that from the *Politics* of Aristotle there emerges a vision of these three political sciences I mean that this is the way in which Aristotle thought, and that the *Poli-*

tics makes a contribution to these three ways of considering the political experience of the ancient Greeks.

6

I have left until next week a consideration of Aristotle's beliefs about the relation of *polis*-life to human 'nature' – what may be called his philosophical exploration of *polis*-life.

But, so far as we have got, you will recognize this book, the *Politics*, as a mixture of several different modes of thinking about political matters. There is something like 'history' in it; there is something like 'science'; there is philosophical explanation; and there is practical advice and recommendation.

We must get used to this sort of mixture, because it is common enough in the literature of European political reflection. But getting used to it does not mean failing to recognize the important differences between these modes of thought.

Editorial Note

LSE 19/1. The first two sheets are photocopies of autograph sheets numbered '1', '2', '3', '3a' in Oakeshott's hand, and replace the first two sheets of the sixteen-page lecture, a photocopy of a typescript with autograph corrections. This version is more legible than the copy at LSE 1/1/21, file 2, of which fos. 76–9 are photocopies of autograph sheets replacing fos. 80–2, and fos. 83–9 are photocopies of a typescript with autograph corrections.

Seven

Aristotle (2)

1

The book called the *Politics* is a work in which Aristotle is reflecting upon the experience of the ancient Greeks, and particularly upon what they regarded as their greatest achievement, namely, *polis*-life.

The context of this examination of *polis*-life is an elaborate view of what goes on in the world in general.

It is a world in which everything has its own distinctive 'nature'; and this 'nature' is, at once, (1) the principle of its normal behaviour, and (2) the 'end', or 'excellence', which this normal behaviour is striving to achieve.

The normal behaviour of anything is sometimes frustrated by accidents; and an accident is a conflict between two or more normalities.

Understanding anything in the world is a matter of discussing its 'nature' – its normal behaviour – and knowing something about the accidents which may befall it.

From this there emerges, for Aristotle, a vision of four possible political 'sciences', or bodies of knowledge relevant to the understanding of *polis*-life.

- A science of the normal development of *polis*-life; a development in which the potentialities of the emergent forms are realized.
- A science of political abnormalities, the outcomes of political error or accident: *polis*-life thrown of its normal course: political pathology.
- A remedial science of politics, in which cures for these 'diseases' abnormalities, 'accidents' etc. are devised.
- A science in which a 'constitution' for *polis*-life might be designed which is most resistant to the sort of 'diseases' which it is most liable to. This is the science of the most generally reliable kind of *polis*-life: the best all-round constitution.

And you will find in the *Politics* passages, moments, and sometimes whole chapters, in which one or other of these themes are being pursued.

Instead of saying anything more about these, I want this evening to follow Aristotle in another direction of his thought; what may be called his political philosophy. And in looking at this we will get our first glimpse of what it is to reflect philosophically about politics.

2

Throughout the *Politics* Aristotle is always returning to a brief characterisation of *polis*-life.

It is a manner of living in which human beings deliberate together about their common affairs and choose the courses of action to be followed.

And what Aristotle, as a philosopher, wants to show us is that this manner of living is an exhibition of the 'nature' of human beings; and that, therefore, living this sort of life may be understood as human beings striving to achieve the 'end' or 'excellence' potential in a human being.

At the outset there is an apparent difficulty to be overcome. As a union of families or tribes, *polis*-life is not a primordial condition of human life, nor is it a universal condition. It appeared first at a certain point in the history of Greek peoples; and there are large parts of the world where it has never emerged. Can it be true that a large part of the human race does *not* live in the manner which displays human nature?

How Aristotle overcomes this difficulty will appear as we go along.

Now, there are three questions which may be asked about *polis*-life, each of them (as Aristotle understands it) carrying his inquiry a step further; and only when he has found the answer to the third of them does Aristotle think he has shown us *polis*-life as human beings exhibiting their 'nature' and pursuing 'human' excellence.

(1) *Polis*-life is an emergence in human history, and we may inquire, first: How *did* it emerge? We may seek, that is, in the contingencies of human circumstances, for some 'historical' reasons for its emergence.

Aristotle's answer to this question is easy, but it does not carry us very far.

He believes that *polis*-life emerged among sets of neighboring families or tribes because they needed some defence against common enemies which a more temporary alliance of tribes would not provide.

This, in Aristotle's view, accounts circumstantially for the emergence of *polis*-life.

And all that we may note is: (a) That it is a very generalized account which attributes the emergence of *polis*-life to a single, universal, cause, and is therefore not very satisfactory history. (b) That it is a very incomplete account; what needs to be added to it is some recognition of city-states which were founded (as many of the city-states of Hellas were founded) by emigrants from already existing city-states.

In short, all we have is a suggestion about the conditions in which some of the city-states of Greece actually emerged.

(2) The second question is: How *could polis*-life emerge? In other words, *polis*-life (which is admitted not to be primordial in human life) still remains only partially intelligible unless we can recognize it, not only as a brute fact with some contingent 'historical' reason for it having appeared, but also recognize it as something that is *possible*.

If it, in fact, *exists*, it must be *possible*; but the grounds of its possibility have to be understood.

Now, this is a very important question. It is a question which we shall observe people asking again and again in the history of European reflection about political society, and which has received many different answers. It is a question which *must* be answered if we are to have an adequate explanation of political life.

What, then, makes *possible* this association of families in which common affairs are arranged by deliberating about them?

In considering this question Aristotle rejects one answer which, if it pointed to something relevant might be considered to be a convincing answer. He says, the *possibility* of *polis*-life is not to be found in the natural sociability of human beings.

Why is this answer insufficient? Aristotle thinks there are two very good reasons for its insufficiency.

Polis-life is something peculiar to human beings, and while it is true that human beings are sociable, gregarious creatures, they are not the only sociable creatures in the world. In other words, what has to be accounted for, *polis*-life, is something exclusively human, and it cannot be accounted for by pointing to a characteristic which is not exclusively human. If 'sociability' made the *polis* possible, why do not other notoriously sociable creatures, like bees and ants and wolves, live a *polis*-life?

And, secondly, *polis*-life is something very much more than a merely 'sociable' life; it is a life of 'political' activity. And, even if human beings were the only 'sociable' creatures in the world, their sociability would not account for something different from a merely sociable life; namely, a *polis*-life.

Having disposed of this insufficient answer Aristotle is left with the question: What power, capability, or aptitude is common to all human beings, exclusive to human beings, and contains within it the possibility of *polis*-life? – that is, a life in which human beings deliberate with one another about what shall be done.

The answer he gives is: the capability which makes *polis*-life possible is that of speech, of communicating with one another in words. 'Man alone of the animals is furnished with the faculty of language,' he says; and we need to look no further than this in order to see the possibility for human beings of a life in which common affairs are decided by deliberating and talking about them – the possibility, namely, of *polis*-life.

What Aristotle has done here is to seek and find universal in human nature something which makes *polis*-life *possible*. And *polis*-life, on account of this discovery, is no longer a brute fact to be observed in the world, but has become an intelligible fact. Here is an explanation, which is fuller and deeper than the explanation which pointed to the merely contingent circumstances of the need for defence against enemies. It shows how, from this need for defence, *polis*-life, and something else, could emerge.

(3) But it is still an incomplete explanation.

For something to be wholly intelligible we need to be able not only to know that it exists, and to understand that it is *possible*, but also to understand that it is *necessary* and to discern the ground of that necessity.

The third question is, then: Why, given human beings, *must* there be *polis*-life? This is a genuinely philosophical question; answering it is an attempt to explain what *is* by showing its *necessity*.

Now, as it stands, it is an ambiguous question; and Aristotle himself removes the ambiguity by telling us what he means and what he does not mean by it.

'Necessity' might mean natural necessity. And if this is what it were to mean here, a demonstration that *polis*-life was a necessary condition of the survival of the human species might be taken as a proof of its necessity.

But Aristotle tells us that he is *not* undertaking to show us that *polis*-life is necessary to the survival of the human race. Indeed, he does not believe this to be the case.

Polis-life may help to preserve the human species; but, so far as Aristotle is concerned, the only manner of living which is necessary for the survival of the species is 'household' or 'family' life – a life, namely, in which men get their living and procreate. And 'family' life, we know, is possible in the absence of *polis*-life. Moreover, the human race does not show any signs of coming to an end in such places as Persia or Egypt where the experience of *polis*-life is unknown.

With this put out of the way, Aristotle makes clear that what he is undertaking to show is that *polis*-life is *necessary* to human 'nature', to the achievement of human beings of the potentialities of their 'nature'. To show, in short, that men who have no experience of *polis*-life lack something that is necessary to the achievement of that particular excellence which is characteristic of human beings, and do not merely lack something necessary to survival.

And Aristotle announces this undertaking by saying that he is concerned to show *polis*-life as the necessary condition of the *good* human life. For the 'good' of anything is the complete realization of its 'nature'.

The question: Why *must* there be a *polis*? may, then, for Aristotle, be reformulated in the following alternative ways:

- What do we know about human 'nature' which will reveal to us, not only that human beings are capable of *polis*-life, but that in the absence of *polis*-life that 'nature' *must* remain imperfectly realized?
- How can it be shown that human beings in inventing *polis*-life are acting teleologically – that is, acting in such a way as to achieve what is potential in human 'nature'? How can it be shown that this particular piece of human

conduct (the invention of *polis*-life) is 'natural' to human beings?

In short, in order to understand *polis*-life fully – that is, to exhibit its necessity – we must get to know something more about human 'nature' and the human 'good' in which that 'nature' is realized and fulfilled. What is the 'human good'? What is the 'end' which all 'human' conduct is designed to achieve?

3

Now, Aristotle's answer to this question is to be found in the work of his called the *Ethics*, and all that he says on the matter in the *Politics* assumes the conclusions of the *Ethics*. The last page of the *Ethics* leads on to the *Politics*.

I propose, therefore, in order to help you to understand the *Politics*, to put before you the main line of the argument of the *Ethics*, and to do so in the form of five questions and the answers Aristotle gives to them.

(1) The first question is: What specific 'end' is the activity we call 'human conduct' in process of realizing? What does *human* activity naturally aim at?

To this question Aristotle first gives an answer which is not in fact an answer at all, but a restatement of the question.

The answer, he says, is *eudaimonia*. Now this word *eudaimonia* is usually translated 'happiness'; and when it is translated in this way, the answer to Aristotle's question is: Human activity is a process in which human beings strive to achieve happiness; the happy man is the man in whom human 'nature' is fully realized.

But *eudaimonia* really means something much less specific than 'happiness': it means something much more like 'satisfaction' or 'fulfilment'. But to strive after the 'satisfaction' of their own natures is *not* peculiar to human beings; it is the common characteristic of the behavior of all natural things.

A horse, an elm tree, and a sunflower are each behaving in such as way as to 'realize' or to 'satisfy' their 'natures': each of them aims at its own specific *eudaimonia*.

All that Aristotle has done by answering this question in this way is to impress upon us the initial fact that he understands the behavior of human beings, like that of every other species of natural thing, to be *teleological*: to be aimed at the achievement of a specific end potential in human nature. So we must start again.

(2) The question we want to find an answer to is: What specific 'satisfaction' or fulfilment does *human* conduct aim at? What is the peculiar *human eudaimonia*? And Aristotle answers this question by saying that human activity has *two* special characteristics which between them determine the *eudaimonia* of human beings and distinguish it from that of all other things.

First, human activity is motivated by 'desire'. And by 'desire' Aristotle means 'conscious attachment to purposes pursued'.

Stones, trees, animals move and change, grow and behave in response to their 'natures', and in pursuit of the realization of their 'natures.' But they follow and seek their 'natures' ignorantly and blindly. An acorn does not 'desire' to become an oak tree; it blindly fulfills its destiny, unless it is frustrated by 'accident', for example, action by a pig.

Human beings, on the other hand, move on their way towards the realization of their particular inherent excellence 'self-consciously', in response to specific 'desires'.

Desires are not merely 'wants', 'urges', 'impulses', or 'inclinations'; they are 'urges', 'impulses', or 'inclinations' which have been selected, or singled out to be pursued in preference to other 'urges' and 'impulses'.

Secondly, *human* conduct is capable of being governed and directed by 'reason'.

Aristotle uses the word 'reason' in several different senses, but in this connection it is the counterpart of 'desire' and it means the power of deliberating and making certain choices about what to do.

To be rational means to be able to choose between the many impulses, the many courses of conduct, which may present themselves to a man on any occasion; and it means choosing that course of conduct which will lead to the realization of the particular 'excellence' which is inherent in human 'nature'.

In other words: desire is the power of choosing between different impulses; and reason is the power to choose to pursue those impulses the satisfaction of which will contribute to the human *eudaimonia*. And desire and reason are exclusively human powers.

Now from these two observations about human conduct
Aristotle formulates his answer to the question: What is the
specifically human *eudaimonia*? He says: The *eudaimonia* of a
man is to follow his 'nature' and to achieve the excellence
that belongs to that 'nature' by the exercise of rational choice.
This is what distinguishes human beings from all other creatures.

This may be restated in another way. What Aristotle has
said is that the particular virtue of excellence of being a man
is to regulate 'desire' by 'reason'; to act in such a way that
'desire' impels us towards what 'reason' has chosen. 'Reason' being the faculty by which a man knows what his 'nature' needs, knows where human excellence lies.

(3) But, Aristotle continues, how is this adjustment in the
components of human soul (desire and reason) to be brought
about? How do desires come to be controlled by rational
choices?

He answers: by practice and by acquiring a habit of living
according to a rule. Human excellence is to be achieved, and
rational choices followed, *only* when choice is governed by a
rule or principle.

(4) This gives Aristotle his fourth question, the most important of all: namely, What is the rule which 'reason' gives as a
guide to conduct? What is rational choice? 中庸 ...... ——|

It is, answers Aristotle, choosing, in conduct, a *mean*, or
middle way, and of avoiding extremes. The rule of 'reason' is
to avoid excess.

The human *eudaimonia* is achieved when human conduct
exemplifies the principle of the mean. Or, since the achievement of the human *eudaimonia* is the same thing as realizing
the peculiar excellence which belongs to human 'nature',
aiming at the mean may be described as 'good' human conduct, the 'good' life for man.

Aristotle's doctrine, then, is that human conduct is distinguished from animal conduct by the conscious pursuit of
chosen purposes; and that *good* human conduct is distinguished from *bad* human conduct by choosing a mean
between extremes and rejecting excess.

Here, as you will at once perceive, Aristotle is catching up
into his moral philosophy the moral sentiments we have
already seen belonged to the Greek people.

It was the message of the Delphic oracle that human beings were neither gods nor beasts and that the appropriate conduct for human beings was *meden agan*: 'nothing in excess.'

But we must be clear about what Aristotle is doing. He is not telling human beings what virtuous human conduct is; he assumes that they know this already. He is saying:

You and I agree that certain forms of conduct are virtuous and others are vicious, and by virtuous conduct we understand conduct which is conducive to the achievement of the excellence inherent in human 'nature'.

But you are accustomed to thinking of virtuous conduct in terms of a list of virtuous acts, you don't see what is the common principle which runs through all these virtuous acts.

I, however, am a philosopher, and my business is to *explain* the variety of virtuous acts by discerning their common principle. That common principle is the principle of the mean. Hence, it may be said that a virtuous disposition in a man will be a disposition to aim at a mean and to avoid extremes.

In short, he is not telling his audience how they ought to behave; he is merely *explaining* to them the general character of all good behavior. 'Moderation' is not one virtue among others, it is the 'nature' of all virtue; it is what makes good behavior *good*. NB

(5) But there remains a last question to be answered; namely, by what test shall a man know that he has a virtuous disposition? How shall we know when we have properly acquired the habit of behavior signified in the expression 'desire governed by reason'?

And to this Aristotle answers: You may be sure that you have properly acquired this habit when aiming at the mean is easy for you, when it is a pleasure and not a pain, when you feel it as a release and not a frustration. The human *eudaimonia* is to choose always a mean in conduct and to take pleasure in making this choice.

4

Now, you will recollect that we embarked upon this exploration of Aristotle's ideas about *good* human conduct because it is by means of these ideas that he proposes to explain: (1) the *necessity* to human beings of *polis*-life; and (2) the appropriateness to human beings of a *polis* with a certain sort of constitution.

Let us return to this theme.

(1) Now, it is *not* Aristotle's view that *polis*-life, as such, supplies *all* that is needed by human beings in order for them to be what their 'nature' requires them to be. He believes that 'household' and family life are essential to human 'nature', and he is critical of Plato for not seeming to recognize this.

But he believes, also, that *polis*-life supplies something that 'household'-life does *not* supply and something equally necessary to human 'nature'.

And, briefly, what Aristotle understands the *polis* to supply is a life in which conduct is determined by choice, a life in which 'desire' may be controlled by 'reason' – in short, a life which we have seen is preeminently necessary to what is characteristically *human* in human 'nature'. Without it a humanly 'good' life is impossible.

Now, what is Aristotle thinking of when he tells us that *polis*-life, unlike 'household' life, is conduct determined by choice?

He is, I think, pointing to the fact that family life is not *NB* something that you *make* for yourself. You are born into a family, and the relationships of a family – brother and sister, father and mother, and even owner and slave – are not 'chosen' relationships; they are the sort of relationships which men share with animals.

A *polis*, on the other hand, is something entered into by an act of choice; those who join to make a *polis* have made a decision to do what they are doing. The relationship between citizens is described by Aristotle as a relationship of 'equals' and of 'friends' – a relationship of choice, *not* blood or birth. Moreover, the common activity of men in *polis*-life is one making free choices about what to do. It is public affairs *made* human.

In short, *polis*-life is *artifice* and therefore it reflects this uniquely human aptitude for artifice, in a way in which family life does not.

Thus, Aristotle can say: 'there is an immanent impulse in all men towards *polis*-life, but the man who first constructed a *polis* is the greatest of benefactors.'

These, then, are the arguments by which Aristotle designs to show that *polis*-life is *necessary* to human beings. And to show the *necessity* of something is to have explained it fully.

In this explanation *polis*-life appears no longer as a merely contingent happening in human history, nor as a merely possible emergence, but as a necessary feature of a human life which can be a 'good' life. Of course all of this leaves much that is unexplained; Aristotle cannot 'explain' *why* human beings are what they are. The 'rationality' of man remains a brute fact, the unexplained principle by means of which *polis*-life is accounted for. But this is the common feature of all explanations of this sort – they all go back to something unexplained and perhaps inexplicable.

(2) But the argument does not stop there. Aristotle not only thinks *polis*-life, this 'second' life which men make for themselves in order to satisfy an immanent impulse in their 'nature', is necessary; he thinks also that only a *polis* with a certain sort of constitution will satisfy this immanent impulse. What sort?

Or, to put the question in another way, *politike*, the activity which creates and sustains *polis*-life, is characteristically and exclusively human activity. Consequently, 'good' political activity (and its product, a 'good' *polis*) will display the characteristics of 'good' human conduct in general. What are those characteristics?

Having read Aristotle's *Ethics* we know the answer to this question already: the principle of all 'good' human conduct is aiming at a mean and avoiding excess. And this will also be the principle of 'good' political conduct, and its product a good constitution for a *polis*.

Or, to look at the matter from the other side, the product of 'good' political activity (namely, the structure and constitution of a *polis*) will be good (that is, appropriate to human 'nature') if it reflects the principle of moderation and the avoidance of excess.

This is the principle; but what of the detail?

(a) First, this constitution will be a 'mixed' constitution – a constitution from which the propensity to run to extremes has been excluded.

The rulers will be neither exclusively the rich, nor exclusively the poor; neither exclusively the noble, nor exclusively the ignoble; they will be drawn from a 'middle' class, neither rich enough to be indifferent to the claims of the poor, nor poor enough to be indifferent to the claims of property.

This constitution will be a mixture of a sort of aristocracy and a sort of democracy. And this moderate 'constitution' will have also the virtue which goes with moderation, namely, stability; of all constitutions it will be the one least liable to sudden disintegration or revolutionary upheaval. It is called by Aristotle *polity.*

(b) Secondly, the principle of the mean will determine the citizen population of this *polis* and the extent of its territory: both will be 'middle-sized'.

In population, it will be large enough to provide the variety of skills necessary to meet its own needs and the diversity of activities necessary to provide a stimulating life, but not so large as to prejudice its unity or to make it impossible for it to be addressed by a single speaker: politics is talk.

In territory it will be large enough to be self-sufficient, but not so large as to be indefensible against external enemies. Like a ship – if it is too small it will be easily swamped, if it is too large it will be unmanageable.

(c) The 'good' human life, we have seen, is a life lived according to a rule – the rule of aiming at a mean in human conduct.

The *polis* appropriate to such a 'good' human life will, therefore, be one ruled by a law and not by the arbitrary command of a despot – whether that despot be a single tyrant or a tyrannous assembly. The rule of law, indeed, is itself the rule of moderation and 'reason'; the law demands from its subjects neither the excess of heroic behavior nor the defect of 'beatnik' indifference and inconsequence, but a steady, moderate, undramatic consideration for others.

(d) The 'good' human life is a life in which 'reason' directs 'desire' to choose the avoidance of excess.

In the *polis* this is recognized as 'justice.' 'Justice' is a mean between extremes; it is giving each man neither more nor less than his due.

(e) And further, the 'equality' characteristic of this *polis* will be neither an absolute equality which recognizes no differences, nor the minimum equality of equality before the law, but an equality of breeding, education, and judgment in which citizens recognize their affiliation with one another and share a common political education which teaches them those habits of moderation which are appropriate to human conduct.

Aristotle, then, has shown us (1) that *polis*-life is not only a fact and a possibility but a necessity for human beings; and in doing so he has given us this 'philosophical' explanation of *politike*.

Politike, he tells us, is the preeminently human activity; it employs precisely those powers and aptitudes which are exclusively and characteristically human, and without a *polis* these powers and aptitudes would be unemployed and human 'nature' would be frustrated in its striving after the excellence that belongs to it. In short, *polis*-life is the necessary condition for the attainment of human 'nature'.

And (2) he has shown us what sort of constitution provides most appropriately for human excellence; namely, a constitution which exhibits, at large and in every detail, the characteristic of 'moderation'.

5

But before we leave Aristotle, there is something else important to notice.

If we understand him to have succeeded, within his own world of ideas, in showing the necessity of *polis*-life to human 'nature', and thus to have found a place for *politike* on the map of human activity, we are not to understand that Aristotle believed political activity to supply *all* that human beings need to realize their 'natures'. Simply to bring the common affairs of a *polis* under the control of reasoned choice is *not* itself the sum of human excellence.

Below, and inferior to, political activity, is family life, the life of the 'household', which supplies human beings with something (not supplied by the *polis*) which they also need: the conditions of racial survival.

But, also, there is another mode of activity in which human beings employ an aptitude which Aristotle understands to be the supreme aptitude of their 'nature', an aptitude even more fundamental than that of a life governed by rational choice of what to do and what not to do.

In *polis*-life human beings are making rational choices about how they shall behave towards one another; they are doing what only human beings can do and they are doing what human beings *must* do if they are to fulfill their human 'natures'. And in doing this they are employing what Aristotle calls their 'practical reason', the 'reason' which may control desire and action and direct it to the achievement of human excellence.

But human beings have another aptitude which he calls 'theoretical reason' – the ability not merely to choose the courses of action in which their human 'nature' is realized, but the ability to understand and to explain what they are doing. And it is in this 'theoretical' or 'contemplative' activity that human beings are distinguished from animals even more securely and more completely than in political activity. Human beings are not only *praktikos*, but also *theoretikos*.

In this sort of activity human beings are employing the aptitude of human nature which not only puts them far above animals but which affiliates them to the gods.

Here, then, is Aristotle's final word on the place of political activity on the map of human activity.

Politike, because it is an activity of rational choice, is a more characteristically 'human' activity than the activities men share with animals – the activities of getting a living, procreation, and carrying on the human race.

Nevertheless it is *not* the highest activity of which human beings are capable. This highest activity – in which men reveal their godlike capacity – is an activity of contemplative understanding.

Thus, in Aristotle's map of human activity there is a place for getting a living and carrying on the human species; there is a place for *politike* (the activity of making and sustaining a *polis*), and there is a place for the activity of understanding and explaining.

On this map these activities are arranged in a hierarchical order: *all* are necessary to the fulfillment of human 'nature', but the last is more exclusively and characteristically human than the other two.

This Aristotelian map, with a few amendments scribbled on it by later thinkers, was the context of all European political thought for 2,000 years.

Editorial Note

LSE 19/1. The first sheet is a photocopy of autograph sheets numbered '1', '1a' in Oakeshott's hand, and replaces the first one-and-a-half sheets of the fourteen-page lecture, a photocopy of a typescript with autograph corrections. This version is more legible than the copy at LSE 1/1/21, file 21/1/21, file 2, of which fos. 90–1 are photocopies of autograph sheets and fos. 92–110 are photocopies of a typescript with autograph corrections.

Eight

Plato (1)

1

Aristotle's attempts to understand *polis*-life led him in a variety of directions. The *Politics* is a supremely miscellaneous work.

Sometimes he takes the path of history, and illuminates *polis*-life by explaining the circumstances in which it emerged. On other occasions he is more like a scientist, concerned to understand the features of *polis*-life as examples of the operation of general laws. And beyond this, he is a philosopher, seeking to identify the place of *polis*-life in his map of human activity, and considering the *polis* in relation to 'human nature'.

And each of these explanatory enterprises is apt to flow over into some practical reflections about the best sort of constitution for a *polis*, or about the best way to avoid, or to repair, political disasters, like revolution or the dissolution of a *polis*.

Aristotle's *Politics* is one of the masterpieces of political reflection that has come to us from the ancient Greeks. And this morning I want to begin to consider another of these masterpieces, namely the work we know as Plato's *Republic*.

Plato wrote other works on political themes, but I shall confine what I have to say to the *Republic*. It is a book which you should all read, and what I have to say is designed to make it more intelligible to you when you do read it.

But, first, I must say something about Plato himself, and how he came to write the *Republic*.

Plato was born towards the end of the fifth century B.C., roughly two generations before Aristotle; and unlike Aristotle he was a native-born Athenian and a member of one of the leading families of the city.

During his early years, Athens suffered disastrous defeats in the war with Sparta and was the scene of several violent revolutions. It was, moreover, a time of intellectual ferment when ancient beliefs were being questioned by some and scorned and ridiculed by many; it was the golden age of the 'Sophists'.

The 'Sophists' were not a school of thinkers; they had no common doctrine. They were independent public lecturers who entertained the always curious and intellectually excitable Athenians with their often disruptive and critical discussions.

Among these public talkers was one, named Socrates, who became more famous than all the rest, partly on account of what distinguished him from the others.

The difference between him and the other public disputers of his day was, first, that he did not talk for pay, listening to him was a free entertainment; and secondly, he always asserted that he didn't know anything but was trying to find out, whereas the typical 'sophist' posed as a know-all who could tell his listeners what the truth was.

Notable among the admirers of Socrates was Plato. But in 399 B.C. Socrates was accused of not believing in the gods and of demoralizing the young by his teaching; after a trial he was condemned to death and executed by being given a cup of poison to drink.

In his early days, Plato may have had political ambitions, but in disgust at the execution of Socrates, whom he regarded as the one intellectually honest man in Athens, his thoughts turned in other directions. For Plato, the condemnation of Socrates was the condemnation of Athens.

He withdrew to Megara and later to Sicily, and during an absence of nearly twenty years from Athens he composed a number of philosophical conversation-pieces in which Socrates is the central character and speaker.

When he was about forty years old he returned to Athens and opened a school, called the Academy, which offered an education in the explanatory sciences rather than the political arts.

The book we know as the *Republic* was written in the early years after his return to Athens. And like other of Plato's works it is a conversation in which Socrates is made the chief speaker.

It is a work quite unlike Aristotle's *Politics*. It is a sustained philosophical argument devoted to a single theme, namely, justice. Indeed its original title was, simply, *Concerning Justice.*

The question being asked throughout is, What is justice? And, at one point in the argument Plato has a good deal to say about the structure and the organization of a *polis*.

It is no puzzle why Plato should have thought that the questions What is justice? and What is a *polis*? overlap one another: justice and the *polis*, as we have seen, had always gone together in Athenian thought.

But, in order to understand Plato's answer to this question, What is justice? one must *first* understand *what* sort of a question Plato thought this question to be, and *how* he thought it must be answered.

This, no doubt, is annoying. But it is one of the things we have to tolerate from philosophers, who will never allow any question to be a straight question with a straight answer.

And I want this morning to say something about Plato's method of inquiry; and in my next lecture to say something about the conclusions about the nature of justice it led him to.

2

And the reason why we must consider Plato's method of inquiry first is because we shall be discovering what Plato thinks we must attend to if we are to understand or explain anything whatever that falls within our experience, or, indeed, if we wish to engage in any sort of practical activity.

The first thing we have to consider is, then, what the books call 'Plato's doctrine of ideas'.

3

We are accustomed to use this word 'idea' in a loose and general sense. We say, 'What's the idea?' or 'What's the big idea?' Or we say, 'the idea of the play is . . .'; and, 'the idea of democratic government is . . .'; and, 'this is Darwin's idea of evolution'; or, 'this is Karl Marx's idea of social change'. And at least we know roughly what we mean.

For us, the word 'idea' stands for 'something' in somebody's head; and it stands for a general 'something', which is often obscured by a lot of irrelevant detail.

Now, when Plato uses this word 'idea' his meaning is not entirely remote from ours, but it is much more precise and it has entailments which our use of the word usually does not have.

And the best way of getting at what he means by the word is, I think, by considering, not how we use it, but some other ways of speaking we have, and some other words we use, which correspond more closely to Plato's way of thinking when he uses the word 'idea'.

In our attempts to make the world intelligible to ourselves we are accustomed to make various distinctions, and one of the commonest and most important of these distinctions is that between the *essence* of a thing and its accidental, circumstantial, contingent details or accompaniments.

By the 'essence' of a thing we mean that without which the thing would not be what it is. We say: 'this is essential', meaning that it can't be dispensed with, and that, normally, there is something else in the situation, called 'inessential', which can be dispensed with without loss. The circumstantial characteristics of something are characteristics which may or may not be present and which, if they are present, are nevertheless recognized as having no inherent or necessary connection with it.

Let us, like Plato himself, take an example from geometry. If we were to use the expression, 'the essence of a triangle', our train of thought runs something like this.

We are aware that there are many different sorts and sizes of triangle, but we think we can detect something which is common to all triangles, which belongs to nothing but triangles and in virtue of which a figure is properly called a triangle. And we have an abstract word for this: we call it 'triangularity'.

The essence of a triangle is 'a three sided plane figure'. We know that the lengths of its sides do not matter; we know that some triangles have sides of equal length but that this does not belong to the essence of a triangle; we know that some triangles are drawn in pencil, others in ink, others in yellow chalk; we know that they may be drawn on paper or in sand – but none of this has anything whatever to do with triangularity.

Now, the Greeks were pioneers in making distinctions of this sort; they invented many of the logical tools we use in making the world intelligible to ourselves. And you will see at once, from what we have already observed about their ways of thinking, that their word *phusis* – 'nature' – had a meaning which corresponds pretty closely to our meaning when we use the word 'essence'.

The 'nature' of a thing was that in virtue of which the thing is what it is and not another thing: the 'principle' of its character.

When Aristotle said that a *polis* is a self-sufficient association of 'households' for the purpose of a good human life he imagined himself to be telling us what the 'nature', or as we might say, the 'essence' of a *polis* is. He is saying something which he believes to be true of all 'cities' and of nothing but 'cities'.

Or again, it is by means of observing a distinction of this sort – a distinction between what is 'essential' and what is 'inessential' – that we come upon the conception we denote by the word 'change'.

The things we observe in the world often alter – they alter their place, their shape, their chemical composition, their appearance; they grow, they decay.

But when we use the word 'change' we are referring to a process in which there is, at once, an alteration and a remaining the same. If there were no alteration there would be no change; if there were no remaining the same there would be no 'change', but the replacement of one thing by another quite different thing. And this process is intelligible to us when we understand that what is altered is the 'inessential' and what remains the same is the 'essential'.

When one asks for 'change' for half-a-crown and is given a shilling, a sixpence, two threepenny bits and six pennies, it is a genuine 'change' because although there are now ten coins instead of one, the 'value' is unchanged: the 'essence' of a half-crown is not its weight, color, size, etc., but, from this point of view, its 'value'.

And here again, what the Greek would say is that the 'nature' of a half-crown is to be 'worth' so much. The 'nature' of a thing is its permanent and unchanging character, that which if it were different it would be another thing, that which 'causes' the thing to be what it is.

Now, what Greek thinkers (in a general way) were accustomed to regard as the 'nature' of a thing, and what we often call the 'essence' of a thing, Plato spoke of as the 'idea' of a thing.

Triangularity – the essential character of all triangles – is the 'idea' triangle.

Thus, for Plato, every actual thing in the world has an 'idea' or an unchanging and essential character, and has also accidental, contingent, inessential, and changing characteristics.

There is an 'idea' man, table, *polis*, justice, courage; and there are men, tables, cities, just judgments, courageous actions, each of which is composed of an 'idea' or essence and some accidental, changeable characteristics.

Now, if we understand Plato to be using the word 'idea' in very much the same way as we are accustomed to use the word 'essence' (only perhaps a little more precisely), we can see at once that it entails a distinction between 'ideas' and the actual, particular, things which fall within our experience.

The characteristics of these actual 'things' (particular men, actions, cities, triangles, chairs, and tables) is (1) that we are able to see, touch, hear, and otherwise observe them. They belong to the world of space and time; (2) that each of them is liable to change; they begin and cohere, they grow and decay, they are here and not there, they are now and not then.

On the other hand the characteristic of 'ideas' (like humanity, courage, justice, triangularity) are (1) that we cannot see, touch or hear them. They do not belong to the world of space and time; (2) that they are not liable to change.

You could listen to a just judgment being delivered; but you could not hear 'justice' itself. You might do a courageous action, but you could not do 'courage' ; you could have a generous feeling, but you could not *feel* generosity. You might draw a triangle, but you could not draw 'triangularity'. Triangularity is not a perfect example of a triangle, because it is *not* an example of a triangle at all.

In short, 'ideas' or 'essences' are not 'other things', like but in some respects different from the things we can see and touch; they are nothing like these 'things' at all.

They are timeless, changeless, and are devoid of accidental characteristics.

Now, it is specially important to recognize this difference between 'ideas' or 'essences' and particular things when the adjective 'ideal' is used in place of the noun 'idea'.

We are accustomed to use this word 'ideal' to stand for a particular example of a thing which we think especially desirable or, as we say, a 'perfect' example. We might think that it would be difficult to establish an 'ideal state' in the world, but we would not think it inherently impossible because we use 'ideal' as an adjective to qualify a particular thing.

But in Plato's usage the adjective 'ideal' cannot be attached to a particular thing because 'ideal' means 'essential', and an 'essence' can never be a particular thing.

Thus, *if* you think of Plato's enterprise in the *Republic* as telling us something about the 'idea' *polis* and at the same time understand what he is doing as giving us a sketch of a particular, very desirable, and in that sense 'ideal' *polis*, you are misunderstanding him altogether.

For him, the 'ideal' *polis* could not exist in the world, could not possibly be established in Attica or anywhere else, not because it would be too difficult, but because it would involve a logical contradiction.

The 'ideal' *polis* for him is simply the 'idea' *polis*, or the 'essential' character of all cities and therefore not itself the concrete character of any particular city.

4

So much, then, for the words 'idea' and 'ideal' in Plato's vocabulary, and for the *distinction* between 'ideas' and particular things.

But what is the relation between 'ideas' and particular things? There must be a relation of some sort between a particular triangle and triangularity, between a particular man and the 'idea' humanity, between a particular courageous action and the 'idea' courage. What is it?

Now, as Plato understood it, the particular things of the world, the things we can touch and see and hear and taste, are, each of them, *copies* of their 'ideas'. That is to say 'ideas' are *models* or *archetypes*, and particular things are copies of these models.

The relationship, then, between actual triangles and 'triangularity', or between courageous actions and 'courage', is that of copy to model. And following out this analogy of model and copy, Plato believed that the models come first and the particular things of the world, the copies made from these models, come after.

It is difficult to find an exact analogy to illustrate this view of things, but what Plato is thinking of is a relationship something like that of the full orchestral score of a piece of music and a particular performance of that piece of music: the performance might be said to be one particular copy of the score.

Or, it is something like the relationship between an engineer's drawing and a particular motor-car. The drawing comes first; the drawing (that is, the 'idea') is not itself a car, you couldn't drive it on the road; and a particular car is a copy of this drawing, made in different materials – steel instead of paper and ink.

This parallel of course is not exact; it breaks down because the drawing (although it is not itself a motor-car) is itself a particular thing, and the score (although it is *not* a performance) is itself a particular thing, but an 'idea' is not a particular thing; it is the 'essence' of a particular thing. And the relation between a just action and the 'idea' justice is the relation between a copy and a model copied.

As Plato understood it there were three sorts of things in the world, and all of them are to be recognized as copies or models or archetypes. There are (1) natural things; (2) things made by men which are copies of natural things; (3) things made by men which are not copies of natural things.

(1) Natural things: horses, trees, men, mountains, etc. These Plato imagined to have been made by a craftsman god. And the manner in which they had been made was by this divine craftsman making copies of ideal models. Ben Nevis and Mount Kenya are both copies of the 'idea' mountain. You and Napoleon are both copies of the 'idea' man.

The divine craftsman lives in 'heaven', and he is supplied with models or archetypes for each kind of thing he is going to make, and a mass of formless material out of which he makes his copies from these models.

(2) Things made by men as copies of natural things: pictures of horses in paint, drawings of mountains, statues in stone of human beings. Like a tailor who has a roll of cloth out of which he makes a pair of trousers; and the ideal model which he copies, since it is not itself a pair of trousers, must be supposed to be something in his head: the *idea* 'trousers'.

Here the process is similar, but the craftsman is human instead of being divine and what is copied are not 'ideas' but particular things.

These things, pictures, statues, etc., made by men as copies of particular things in the natural world are, you will see at once, two removes from the original 'idea' or model. A sculptured man is a copy of a copy of the 'idea' man. And on this account Plato had a low opinion of human works of art, which he regarded as mere copies of copies. _ _ !

(3) Things made by men which are *not* copies of things in the natural world: tables, chairs, houses, cities, courageous actions, etc.

How do these come to be made or done? They must be copies of models because that is the only activity Plato will recognize; and since there are no models of them in the natural world, they must be copies of original models.

This sort of human activity is, then, like the divine activity in which the things of the natural world were made. A table is a copy made by a carpenter of the 'idea' table; a courageous action is a copy made by a man who performs it of the 'idea' courage.

Everything in the world, natural or artificial, is a copy, direct or indirect, of its 'idea' or ideal model. But what about this activity of copying? It is an activity in which imperfection or misrepresentation is unavoidable.

Copies may be more or less exact. And it is very difficult to make an exact copy. Even the craftsman god does not always succeed and the result is a three-legged chicken or an idiot boy: idiocy is eccentric to the idea 'boy'.

The copy must always misrepresent the model because it is made in different material from that of the model. The copy is made in impermanent, changing, and unstable material; the 'idea' or model is permanent and unchanging. Every performance, in some degree, misrepresents the full orchestral score, simply because it is a performance and not itself the score.

A copy made in this unstable, changeable material is itself unstable, and in the course of time it *must* become a less exact copy. A man gets senile, the stone of a statue decays, a pair of shoes wears out.

The conclusion of all this is that the world of things we live in, this world of copies of ideal models, is pretty remote from the ideal models themselves. The copies, many of them, were never very exact; they are inevitable misrepresentations; and time can only make them less exact.

5

Now, this vision of the world as composed of changing, insubstantial, accidental things, each of which is to be understood as a copy, direct or remote, of an eternal unchanging essence or 'idea,' leads Plato to two different and important conclusions.

(1) The first conclusion is about the nature of genuine *knowledge*.

These impermanent, unstable things of the world which appears before us when we open our eyes, these particular things, in which essence and accident are mixed, accident obscuring essence, are incapable of being '*known*' in any important sense of the word 'know'.

The most we can have about them is 'opinions' (*doxa*). They are mere descriptive 'images' (*eidolon*), insubstantial shadows (*skia*); and the connection we make with them through our senses is a connection which must fall far short of 'knowing' or 'understanding'.

If, then, we want to understand the world in which we live we must recognize that the things which compose it are 'copies'. And we can only recognize this by knowing the 'ideas' or archetypes of which they are copies.

Genuine knowledge is knowledge of the permanent 'ideas' of things. To know anything is to know its essential character.

This is Plato's first conclusion. To understand and to explain are intellectual activities in which the permanent essences or 'ideas' of things are separated from the accidental and temporary characteristics of things.

Those who aspire to understand and to explain the world must 'turn away' (*periagoge*) from the particularity of things and attend only to permanent essences or 'ideas'.

And this, as Plato understands it, is precisely the philosophic enterprise. Where true knowledge is sought, the question to be asked is: 'What is the "idea" or essence?' Consequently, if you want to understand 'just conduct', or *polis*-life, what you must enquire is, What is the idea justice? What is the idea *polis*?

(2) But, from his vision of the world as composed of unstable things in which essence and accident are mixed, accident obscuring essence, Plato draws a second conclusion.

This time it is not a doctrine about human understanding and explanation, but a doctrine about human fabrication and action.

When Plato said that the particular things of the world are related to their 'ideas' or 'essences' as copies are related to 'ideal' models he understood this to indicate: (1) that particular things could be understood and explained only in terms of their 'essences' or 'ideas': you cannot understand a copy unless you know its archetype; (2) but also, that particular things can appear, or come into being, only in an activity of copying their 'ideas' or 'essences': you cannot make anything unless you know the model you are copying.

The craftsman god makes the things of the natural world by copying models which he has before him. And human beings make things they are capable of making by copying models. We may recognize in this the preeminent place which the activity of fabrication occupied in Plato's thought. The natural and the human world is the product of fabrication, making by copying.

Now, the entailment of this is that whether you are a god or a man, in order to make anything you must know the 'idea' you are to copy.

A god could not make a man unless he had the 'idea' man before him from which to copy; and a man could not build a ship, or make a table, or write a play or a poem, unless he knew the 'idea' ship, table, play, poem.

There is, then, no place in Plato's world for an activity of 'free creation': all is copying, and you cannot copy without a known model.

Moreover, as Plato understood it, this applied not only to 'fabrication' in the strict sense, to *making* things, particularly things, like cities or constitutions, which have no model in the natural world; it applied, also, to the performance of actions.

Thus, as he understood it, a 'just' or a 'courageous' action was a copy of the 'idea' justice and the 'idea' courage. And no man could make a just judgment or perform a just action or do a courageous deed unless he knew the 'idea' justice and the 'idea' courage.

But we have seen that Plato identified a concern to understand things, a concern with the 'ideas' of things, with philosophy.

If, however, it is true that a philosopher is a man who, because he is concerned to understand and explain things, must know the 'ideas' of things, it must now be equally true that one requires to be a philosopher in order to make anything or to perform any action.

In short, a knowledge of the 'ideas' of things is the necessary qualification for *both* understanding and doing. One must be a 'philosopher', *both* if one wants to understand the world, *and* if one wants to make or do anything in the world – other, of course, than merely enjoying something that exists in the natural world.

Thus, in Plato's view of things, knowing and explaining are joined with making and doing. And in his philosophy a theory of knowing and explaining is joined with a theory of making and doing.

What joins them is this belief that both knowing and doing are impossible without reference to the 'idea' of what is to be known and the 'idea' of what is to be done.

Here, then, is the heart of the doctrine which Plato is to apply to the politics and government of a *polis*.

Polis-life is the pursuit of human excellence or 'justice'. *definition*

It is impossible to understand what this really means unless we acquire a knowledge of the 'idea' justice; and it is equally impossible to participate in this pursuit of justice, to engage in political activity, unless we know the 'idea' justice.

The *Republic* is designed to reveal this to us.

There is, perhaps, something puzzling about this assimilation of action to understanding and explaining; something a little odd and unfamiliar about this notion that action is making a copy of the 'idea' of the action; something a little strange about the notion that a man who cannot answer the question: What is courage? is incapable of doing a courageous action, because he doesn't know the model he is to copy.

These are notions which Aristotle, in a large measure, rejected. Nevertheless, they are at the heart of Platonism, and they have never been far below the surface of Western European thought.

6

We shall have to consider later in detail the conclusions Plato drew from this view of the world and of human activity, but I would like now to draw together all I have been saying by introducing you to Plato's own account of it in what is, perhaps, the most famous passage in the *Republic*: what is known as the parable of the cave.

The argument of the *Republic* is graced, at frequent intervals, by brilliant poetic allegories. At the beginning of Book VII Plato introduces one of these allegories. You should read it with care: every word counts.

In it he likens the common world in which we live to an underground cavern, like a long passage with one end open to the light.

The inhabitants of this cave (that is, human beings) have lived there all their lives, at the far end, remote from the entrance. Moreover, their legs and necks are shackled in such a way that their backs are turned to the distant entrance of the cave and they are forced, as if in blinkers, to gaze steadily at the end wall. They can talk to one another but they cannot see each other; they can see only what may appear on the end wall of the cave.

Some way down this passage-like cavern, towards the entrance, there is a parapet, or half-wall, and behind the parapet is a fire. From time to time, people crouching behind the parapet hold up artificial objects, made of wood, etc., which include figures of men and animals.

These objects, on account of the fire behind them, cast flickering shadows on the end wall of the cave at which the prisoners are forced to look. They are like an audience in a cinema.

And because the flickering shadows of these artificial objects are *all* that the prisoners in the cave can see, or have ever seen, they are taken for real things. The prisoners talk to one another about these shadows and even run a sweepstake on which shadow will appear next, because in the course of years they have become familiar with the pantomime, and have names for the different shadowy appearances.

But, says Plato, suppose one of these prisoners were, somehow, to release himself from his shackles and were to stand up and to turn towards the distant entrance of the cave.

And suppose, further, that he were to walk towards the entrance, passing the pantomime at the parapet and seeing the artificial objects which had cast the shadows, and so, out into the sunlight world outside – what would he feel and think?

At first he would be dazzled and bewildered. But he would gradually become accustomed to the new world of light and in the end would come to contemplate the sun, recognizing it as the cause of all light and therefore as the final cause of the shadows in the cave.

In short, he would become himself enlightened; he would understand the shadows in the cave and would be able to explain them to himself as various images emanating from a single source.

Now, says Plato, imagine, further, that this man returned to his former seat in the cave. It would take him some time to get used to the darkness.

But, in talking with his fellows, he would be able to enlighten them and to explain their world of shadows to them, telling them what these shadows really were – that they were only copies, and that they were living in a world of illusion. At first, says Plato, the prisoners in the cave would not believe what they were told. Then, they would be angry at being told that they lived in a world of mere shadows, and, says Plato, if they could lay hands on him they would want to kill him. A reminiscence, no doubt, of what had happened to Socrates.

That is the story, or the main part of it. //

Plato wishes us to understand that, in so far as we live in the world of particular things we are prisoners of the illusion that they are real things. We live in a world of unstable, flickering, experiences which we mistake for the real world.

The escaped prisoner, on the other hand, is a man who has acquired a knowledge of the 'ideal' cause of these images, and this enables him to *understand* them: they are mere copies of ideal models. And it enables him to enlighten the prisoners in the cave, thought they can't be expected to welcome this enlightenment.

He is the philosopher. In virtue of his inquiry into the ideas of things he can understand and explain.

But Plato goes further.

Of course, among these particulars there will be, not only the things we can touch and see, there will be *also* the particular *actions* performed by shadowy human beings and denoted by adjectives such as just, courageous, good, etc.

And these, of course, can only be understood if we know the 'ideas' or models of which they are copies.

But these actions not only cannot be *understood* unless we have a knowledge of the ideas of which they are copies, they cannot be performed unless we have this knowledge. A courageous action is a copy of the idea courage, and we *must* know the model we are copying in order to make this copy.

Thus, among the prisoners in the cave, the returned 'philosopher' is, not only the only man who can understand, for example, what a just action really is, he is the only man who can *do* a just action.

He alone can *be* 'just', because he alone knows what 'justice' itself is.

And if, as Plato supposes, the ability to act justly is the chief quality we require in a *ruler*, the philosopher alone will have the ability which gives him the authority to rule.

We will consider next week where this remarkable doctrine led him.

Editorial Note

LSE 1/1/21, file 2, fos. 113–30. Fos. 114–15, 127–8 are photocopies of autograph sheets; fos. 113, 116–26, 129–30 are photocopies of a typescript with autograph corrections. Fo. 129 has been placed out of sequence in the MS but should follow fo. 113.

Plato (2)

1

Plato's *Republic* is a long and elaborate conversation designed to answer the question: What is justice?

Last week we were concerned with what may be called the intellectual apparatus which Plato uses in trying to answer this question: what is called in the books 'Plato's doctrine of ideas'.

From this point of view, the four main principles of Platonism are:

(1)   That the world to which we open our eyes contains natural things (made by God), and things made or done by human beings – artifacts and actions. And each of these things and actions is an imperfect copy or representation of an 'idea' or 'ideal model'.

(2)   Understanding any of these things made or actions performed is a matter of knowing the 'idea' or 'ideal model' of which it is a copy.

(3)   Further, for a human being to make an artifact, or to perform an action, is for him to make a copy of the 'ideal model' to which it corresponds, and therefore making and doing entails a knowledge of the 'ideal model'.

(4)   Since to know the 'ideas' of things and of actions is the peculiar enterprise of 'philosophy', *all* understanding, making or doing are, in this respect, 'philosophic' activities.

You cannot understand or make a ship without knowing the 'ideal model' of which the ship is a copy – that is, without being a philosopher.

You cannot understand or do a just action without knowing the 'idea' justice of which all just actions are copies – that is, without being a philosopher.

The only man who need not be a philosopher is a sculptor or a painter, because his models are *not* 'ideal' but merely things in the natural world.

This doctrine is composed of beliefs about the appearances and the realities of the world in which we live, and about the logic of any inquiry designed to reveal the true nature of experiences like just conduct.

And I spent some time on it because I think the significance of the *Republic* will escape us unless we understand these beliefs which underlie its argument.

This morning I want to say something about the course and substance of the argument in the *Republic*, and the conclusions Plato reaches in this inquiry into the idea of justice: the 'idea' of justice being the 'ideal model' of which anything which is properly qualified by the adjective 'just' is a copy.

2

Now, for Plato, this is preeminently an intellectual inquiry.

We may observe just actions, we may hear a man deliver a just judgment, but we cannot either see or hear 'justice' itself.

It is true that Plato has an exceedingly graphic way of writing, and he often represents this intellectual comprehension of an 'idea' as a 'vision'; but we should not be misled into thinking that the 'idea' of anything can be 'seen'.

The 'idea' justice is the unseen principle in virtue of which an action or disposition may properly be called 'just'. And it can be understood and used to explain human actions and dispositions precisely because it is not a particular example of justice. It is the unchanging 'law' the operation of which 'just' actions are examples or copies.

Now, this inquiry into the 'idea' justice, like all other intellectual inquiries, must be taken in two stages.

(1) We must, first, make up our minds where to look for what we want to discover: the analogy of a 'hunt' or the game of 'hide and seek' is a favourite of Plato's when describing an intellectual inquiry.

We live, like the prisoners in the cavern, in a world of shadowy images; hidden in each of these images is an 'idea'; consequently, we have first to identify the 'images' which, however inaccurately, are copies of the particular 'idea' we are seeking to understand.

(2) Secondly, having made up our minds about the direction in which it is most profitable to look, we must bring to bear our reflective intelligence in order to elicit *in* these particular shadowy images the 'idea' of which *they* are copies.

Book I of the *Republic* is mostly taken up with the first stage of this inquiry. 'Images' of justice are being looked for and identified.

Different participants in the conversation make different suggestions about the sort of things or the sort of conduct which it is proper to qualify by the adjectives 'just' or 'unjust'.

The preliminary question Plato wants to answer is: If we are looking for an 'image' of justice, where shall we look? What sort of 'images' or things in the world does the 'idea' justice inhabit?

The unmistakable answer to this question seems to be: 'Justice inhabits human conduct: we must look for it in human conduct'.

It is true, of course, that in its earlier use in Greek writing the word 'just' stood for something much less specific than this. It stood for the reciprocal relationships between the parts of any complex whole in virtue of which it 'worked' as a whole. But by Plato's time this was a remote metaphor: the words 'just' and 'unjust' had come to specify a quality in *human* conduct and not, for example, in the behavior of elephants or electrons.

This preliminary conclusion, then, is stated by Plato in the proposition: 'Justice is a quality of the human soul'. And what he means is that the only place to look for 'images' or copies of the idea 'justice' is in human dispositions, human conduct, and the products of human activity.

But, besides reaching the conclusion that only human conduct and the products of human activity can properly be called either 'just' or 'unjust', Socrates, in this conversation, insists that justice and injustice are qualities, not of some kinds of human activity, but of all kinds.

A man, he says, may properly be called 'just' or 'unjust' in everything that he does.

By the end of Book I of the *Republic*, then, one important point has been settled; namely, how the words 'just' and 'unjust' are going to be used in the rest of the conversation.

And we may notice that a much more comprehensive meaning is given to these words than we usually give. The conversationists agree that to say that a man is 'acting justly' is to say that he is doing what is right and is behaving as he ought to behave. Justice and virtue or goodness are identified with one another. The 'just' man is a man as he ought to be; or to be 'just' belongs to the 'idea' man.

Now, our normal use of the word 'just' is different from this use in *two* respects.

(1) We think, perhaps, that to be 'just' is to exhibit *a* virtue; but we sometimes think that what the situation calls for is not *this* virtue but some other. We may say, for example: 'The "right" thing here is not justice but mercy'.

But Socrates and his companions are agreed that in their debate 'justice' is to stand for what is right in human conduct on all occasions. Thus, in their way of talking, if 'mercy' is the right thing, then it would be 'unjust' *not* to be merciful. In short, what is being discussed is 'right' human conduct.

(2) *We* ordinarily think of 'just' and 'unjust' as words which apply to the relationship of one man to another. We think of being 'just' as a '*social*' virtue; and it is only metaphorically that we speak of a man being 'unjust' to himself.

But in the *Republic* justice is *not* preeminently a 'social' virtue; indeed, it is a 'social' virtue only derivatively. Justice and injustice are qualities of a human personality which do not *need* a relationship with others in order to bring them into play.

In the *Republic* the conduct of a man alone on an island could be 'just' or 'unjust'; and a man is 'just' or 'unjust' to other people *only* by virtue of being himself a 'just' or 'unjust' man.

The words 'just' and 'unjust,' then, are to stand for qualities to be found in human conduct or the products of human activity. A man may be 'just' or 'unjust' in everything that he does, when he is alone or when he is with others; and to speak of an action as 'just' is to say that it is right.

But the conversation cannot proceed until this view of things is refined and made a little more exact.

'Even if it is true,' says Socrates in his plausible way, 'may we not suppose that justice and injustice will be exhibited more obviously in *some* kinds of activity and in *some* situations than in others?'

And so the question is: Shall we not be wise to look for 'images' of justice and injustice in some human activities rather than others, and if so in what activities?

Is there an 'image' of justice to be found, for example, in a carpenter making a chair? or, in a farmer harvesting a field of wheat? or, in a general planning a battle? Certainly; but is there not some better or more obvious place to look for it?

Now, if *we* were considering this question, it would not be surprising if somebody were to say that the best place to look for 'images' of justice and injustice was round the corner, in the Royal Courts of Justice. After all, 'justice' is the business of the place.

At least, to *our* way of thinking, this would be a more sensible suggestion than, for example, the suggestion that we would do specially well to look for these qualities in the stock exchange or in Covent Garden market. We might look there if we were discussing 'honesty' and 'dishonesty', but not 'justice' and 'injustice'.

But in the *Republic* the conversationists are Greeks, they are Athenians, and consequently it does not surprise us that, before long (in the middle of Book II), somebody says: 'Why, the supremely obvious place to look for an "image" of justice is in the activity of a statesman and in the structure and constitution of a *polis*'.

And we are not surprised by this because we know that according to popular belief it was 'justice' – *dike* – which *made* the *polis*. The *polis* was constituted in a judicial activity of dealing out 'justice' to the various tribes and families which came together to compose it.

'Justice', according to the legend of Greek politics, was the midwife of the *polis*. It was *dike* which transformed the *themis* of the tribe into the *thesmos* of the *polis*.

'Justice' and 'injustice' were recognized to be uniquely characteristic of a *polis*: the 'household' and the tribe are not the scene of just and unjust actions.

No Greek, then, could fail to think first that the 'image' of 'justice' or 'injustice' was most profitably to be looked for in the structure of a *polis*.

But the suggestion that the image of justice shall be looked for there gives a momentous change of direction to the whole argument of the *Republic*. A very large part of the rest of the work is concerned with the question: What is the *polis*? What is the 'idea' *polis*? because this seems to be an appropriate way of answering the question: What is justice? To be 'just' belongs to the 'idea' *polis* no less than it belongs to the idea 'man'.

3

This change of direction in the inquiry is, at the time, defended dialectically by Socrates. He says:

nb.

> What we are looking for, this 'idea' justice, is a quality which can be reflected both in the conduct of an individual man and in the structure of a *polis*. We are interested in it wherever it appears, though we are chiefly interested in it as a quality of the human soul because it belongs to a *polis* only because a *polis* is the work of human beings.

But, since a *polis* is larger than an individual man, we may expect the 'image' of justice (and of course injustice) to appear on a larger scale in the structure of a city, and consequently to be more easily discernible there than in the conduct of individual men.

Let us, then, look first for the reflection of justice in the structure of a *polis*. But whatever conclusions we may reach about the 'idea' justice from seeing it reflected in the *polis* will hold good for justice in the individual soul, because 'justice' is one and the same quality wherever it is reflected.[1]

In short, the structure of a *polis* may be expected to provide a clearer, because a larger, 'image' of the 'idea' justice that is to be found in the conduct of individual men.

Now, this is something very much more important than a way of pushing the conversation in the direction Socrates wants it to take.

It indicates Plato's conception of the relationship between the individual man, the citizen, and the *polis* – and it is both a remarkable and a highly characteristic conception.

According to *our* commonplace way of thinking, a society is composed of individual men and women. But here Plato is not thinking in those commonplace terms at all. For him, the *polis* is not composed of individual human beings; its structure represents the structure of an individual human soul.

A *polis* and an individual soul are organizations of exactly the same character but of different dimensions; the one is merely larger than the other.

---

[1] A note in Oakeshott's hand suggests he included a quotation from the *Republic* 368d-369a at this point.

And the government of a *polis* is an exact counterpart of the mastery a man may be said to have over himself. A man 'governs' himself, well or ill, or fails to govern himself, in exactly the same sense as a king governs, well or ill, or fails to govern, a kingdom.

Consequently, for Plato, a 'just' *polis* will structurally represent or reproduce a 'just' man.

Indeed, Plato takes the view that there is a correspondence between citizen and *polis*, so that the adjectives we apply to constitutions are applicable also to types of human character: thus there is a kingly, an aristocratic, an oligarchic, a tyrannous, and a democratic *polis*, and a kingly, aristocratic, oligarchic, democratic type of man.

In short the *polis* and the individual man are replicas of one another; to understand the one is to understand the other. To understand what it is to be a just man is to understand what it is to be a just *polis*.

Now, it is worthwhile dwelling for a moment on this rather strange notion, because it is the spring of Plato's whole political philosophy.

It has to be distinguished from *two* other beliefs, which do not go anything like so far.

(1) Plato might have said that the constitution of a city is something which is made by men, and that it takes 'just' men to make a 'just' constitution.

But he says more than this: he says that the 'idea' of a 'just' man is identical with the idea of a 'just' city. There is only one idea 'justice', and every possible example of 'justice' is an example of this one idea.

(2) Secondly, Plato is sometimes said to have believed that a society is, in some mystical way, more than the people who comprise it: the whole is greater than the sum of its parts.

But, in fact, he is saying something quite different from this. He is saying that the relationship between a man and a city is that of microcosm to macrocosm.

Now, the macrocosm is larger than the microcosm, and is therefore easier to perceive.

But the qualities of the macrocosm are derived from the qualities of the microcosm: a 'just' constitution of a *polis* is a *reflection* of a 'just' constitution of a human soul.

And, it may be noticed, Plato here is harking back to the original meaning of the Greek word 'justice': long before it became a 'moral' or a 'political' or a 'legal' word, it meant simply the condition of any complex whole when its parts all fulfil their own particular function.

The question is, then, what do we know about the structure and components of the complex whole we call a human personality which will help us to identify a 'just' condition of it, and distinguish it from an 'unjust' condition of it?

4

Plato's answer to this question runs something like this:

(1) A human personality or soul is composed of three faculties or 'powers'; namely, reason, courage (or spirit), and 'want': a deliberative faculty, an executive faculty, and an appetitive faculty.

Every man in the world has these three powers or manners of being active. They are the universal components of human personality.

But different men enjoy these three powers in different proportions. Consequently, different souls may be said to be composed of different mixtures of these three powers.

Indeed, what distinguishes one man from another is, precisely, the proportions in which these three powers are mixed in his soul.

Each of these powers is an ability to behave in a certain manner and an ability to perform certain sorts of actions.

Reason is the ability to behave reasonably and with judgment. Courage is the ability to behave courageously. 'Want' is the ability to seek and to acquire.

Therefore, none of these three powers can take the place of (or, as Plato says, 'do the work of') either of the others. A man cannot in virtue of reason act courageously; and exhibiting courage or want in our conduct is different from exhibiting reason.

But, although none of these powers can do the work of either of the others, although each is in this sense autonomous, they are not all of equal significance. Indeed, there is a hierarchy of importance among them.

Reason, although it cannot take the place of either courage or 'want', is, nevertheless, superior to both courage and 'want'. Courage comes second in this hierarchy of importance, and 'want' last.

The main thing which determines this hierarchy is the relative self-sufficiently (or ability to exist on its own) of the three powers: reason is absolutely self-sufficient; courage has some degree of self-sufficiency; 'want' has none at all – it is absolutely dependent.

Thus, the ground for saying that one of these powers is superior to another is not its ability to do better (or even to do at all) the work of the other, but its 'natural' authority over that other.

For example, an ability to have wants is, by itself, unusable. Before 'want' can operate there must be added to it, as a guide and director, the ability to choose between wants. And this ability to choose is one of the characteristics of the faculty called reason. Choosing is not the same thing as wanting and cannot take its place; but wanting without the ability to choose is sterile.

(2) Now, to this analysis of the parts of the human soul and their relations with one another, Plato adds two other principles.

(a) That these different faculties or powers exist in different mixtures or proportions in different men *by nature.* In respect of the compositions of their souls men are *born* different from one another.

Some men are born with more reason than courage and want, others with more want, others again with a preponderance of courage.

These differences are 'natural' in the sense that they are differences in the accuracy of the copy of the 'idea' man which each man represents. And, as we shall see, since, in Plato's view, reason is preeminent in the 'idea' man, those who have a preponderance of courage or want in their souls are less accurate, or more degenerate, copies of the ideal model 'man'.

(b) Nevertheless, by a process called 'education' it is possible to modify the structure of a man's soul. A soul born with a preponderance of courage or of want may become a soul in which reason predominates.

There are, of course, limits to what can be expected from 'education'; but no man is necessarily fixed forever in the character with which he was born.

Thus Plato reaches two important conclusions:

- that 'no two persons are born exactly alike'. But there are three general types of human being, each distinguished by a predominant faculty – reason, courage, or want.
- that since to have a predominant power means to have a special aptitude for behaving in a particular way – reasonably, courageously, or desirously – each man may be said to be specially fitted to do one thing rather than another: 'there is no twofold or manifold in man; everyone has a predominant aptitude'.

5

Now, it is these observations about the human soul which suggest to Plato his doctrine about the conduct proper to a human being – that is to say, his doctrine about 'justice' in the human soul.

Every human soul is a complicated structure, displaying three dispositions in differing strengths, *one* of which will naturally be predominant.

And since to say that a man is 'just' is to say something about the condition of his soul, 'justice' may be thought of as a particular relationship between the component dispositions of the soul.

Plato's doctrine may, perhaps, be summed up by saying that there is, so to speak, a beginning, a middle, and an end in human justice: an intimation of justice, a substantial justice, and a condition of absolute justice.

(1) It is the beginning of justice for each human being to exercise his predominant faculty (whatever it is) and behave in the manner it demands. 'Every man ought, in accordance with his particular nature, to do the one work for which he has a particular aptitude'.

We are not, at the moment, considering a 'just' order of society; we are considering only the just condition of a human soul. And Plato holds that a man is 'unjust' in the simplest and most elementary way, if he refuses or is denied his own particular opportunity of excellence. And excellence is simply what one can do best.

He may, by 'education,' try to change his predominant aptitude; but whatever that aptitude is, he should submit to it and exercise it. Not to do this is being unjust to himself.

The first precept of 'justice', then, is 'Be true to yourself, whatever that self may be'. This is minimum justice; the least intimation of a condition of 'justice' in a human soul. And this minimum condition of 'justice' is within the reach of every man if he is not denied it.

(2) But justice depends not only on being true to whatever your particular aptitude is, but also on the recognition that some aptitudes are superior to others.

The 'just' man will be the man in whom each of these powers – and he has all of them in some degree – performs its own particular function properly. In other words, the 'just' soul is that which reflects the hierarchy of the faculties.

It is the function of reason to rule over courage and want; therefore, in the 'just' soul reason (however little of it there may be) rules. A soul in which want is not only the strongest faculty but is also the ruling faculty and reason is subordinate to it, is a disordered soul and 'unjust'. 'Want', in fact, is incapable of ruling even itself.

To be a well-ordered soul is, then, what may be called substantial 'justice'. Of course, you will have a better opportunity to be a well-ordered soul if reason is the predominant faculty; but even if reason is the smallest of one's gifts it may still be the ruling power and in the just soul it must be.

(3) But what is the summit of justice? What 'image' or condition of justice in a human soul is closest to the 'idea' or 'ideal model' justice?

In answering this question Plato propounds a difficult, but I think intelligible doctrine. He tells us that the entirely just soul is one in which reason is, not merely the predominant and the ruling aptitude, but is the *only* aptitude. It is the soul which is, so to speak, filled with reason so that there is no room for any other faculty.

Of course, in such a soul, reason could never take the place of courage or want, doing their work for them. The characteristic of this soul is that the necessity, as well as the opportunity, of behaving in either a courageous or a desirous manner has been entirely removed.

Now this seems, at first sight, an odd doctrine. What has become of Plato's insistence that *every* soul has, in some degree or another, *all three* of these powers, and that men differ from one another, and are superior to one another, only in respect of the faculty which is predominant?

I think there are two considerations which make sense of this Platonic conception of the wholly rational man.

(a) We must remember that Plato is concerned with the 'idea' justice, the 'ideal model' of which no actual man could be anything more than an imperfect copy.

And, although a wholly rational man is an impossibility, it is an impossibility only in the same sense as it is impossible for the 'idea' to be itself an actual copy or example.

It is impossible that any actual man should be wholly rational; but the 'idea' man is that of a wholly rational being.

(b) The conception of a wholly rational man is reached by removing from the human soul its two other aptitudes – courage and want. And the suggestion is that this is a valid procedure. Why?

Because *both* courage and want are aptitudes which are, so to speak, accidental to the 'idea' man. They belong to the copy and have no counterpart in the ideal model.

Courage and want are aptitudes which, unlike reason, require for their exercise the world of time and space. Both involve *doing* something. But in respect of its rationality, the soul is timeless; it exhibits the 'idea' man without the alloy of the material which belongs to the copy.

Here, then, is Plato's conclusion.

Justice is a condition of the human soul.

The 'idea' justice is that of a wholly rational soul: this is the definition of justice.

But the most perfect 'image' or 'copy' of the 'idea' which can actually appear in the world is that of the soul in which reason is predominant and rules courage and want.

6

Now, let us remind ourselves of Plato's design when he is engaged in this elucidation of the 'idea' justice in the human soul.

He embarked upon it as a consequence of reaching the conclusion that the proper place to look for an image of justice was in human dispositions and human conduct. But he also believed that an image of justice could properly be looked for in the products of human activity, and among such products the *polis* is supreme – the greatest work of human beings and the work most completely expressive of human 'nature'.

Moreover, he believed that a *polis* was a replica of a human soul. Consequently, his conclusions about justice in the human soul carry with them some very important conclusions about the character of a *polis* as an image of justice.

What of the just *polis*? It is a *polis* which is the counterpart of a just human soul; it is a *polis* which, in its structure and organization, reproduces the structure and organization of a just human soul. Let us consider this in a little more detail.

Every *polis*, so the argument will run, is a replica of the human soul.

As the human soul is composed of aptitudes for rational, for courageous, and for desirous conduct, a *polis* will be found to be composed of three kinds of men – men in whom each of these aptitudes is predominant: that rational kind of man, the courageous kind of man, and the kind of man whose special aptitude is to want.

Let us apply to this *polis* the principles of justice we have already learned from studying the individual soul.

A *polis* will be 'just' if each of its citizens is permitted to exercise the special aptitude which belongs to him. A *polis* will be 'just' if those whose predominant aptitude is for courageous behavior fight for and defend it; and if those whose predominant aptitude is for desiring produce the necessities of life in it; and if those whose predominant aptitude is for rational conduct, *rule* it.

This is the 'well-ordered' *polis*, the *polis* in which not only is each man doing what his special aptitude fits him to do, but in which, also, the proper hierarchy of the faculties of the soul is preserved.

Or, we may put the situation the other way round, by asking the question: What are the marks of an 'unjust' *polis*?

(1) A *polis* will be unjust which demands from each citizen 'manifold' activity, which requires or allows each of its citizens *not* to do that 'one work' for which his predominant aptitude fits him, but to do *other* work as well.

This is an 'unjust' *polis* because it is a *polis* which requires or allows its citizens to have 'unjust' souls, in the simplest and most elementary sense. It does not allow its citizens to be 'true to themselves'.

If the man of courage or of want is made to rule (which is properly the unique function of reason), then the man of courage and of want is being denied the justice which belongs to him, and the *polis* has had imposed upon it an 'unjust' constitution.

And with this Plato sweeps away not everything, but a very great deal of what the Athenian understood by 'democracy'. 'Democracy' requires *all* citizens, regardless of the special aptitudes which belong to their different characters, to take their turn at ruling and being ruled.

The 'happy versatility,' as Thucydides called it, of the Athenian character, in which every citizen was considered to be qualified to hold any office and which exhibited itself in the rule of the popular assembly, is recognized by Plato to be the exact opposite of a 'just' condition of a *polis*.

(2) A *polis* governed by those of its citizens whose predominant aptitude is either courage or want will be an 'unjust' *polis*; and it will be unjust because it makes a ruler out of aptitudes which (because they require to be ruled) cannot themselves rule.

A *polis* governed by those whose aptitude is to fight, one which is ruled by its army, is a merely warlike *polis*, beckoned by every call to fight and incapable of discrimination. It is a disordered or 'unjust' *polis*. Perhaps it might be called a merely expansionist *polis*.

A *polis* governed by those whose aptitude is to 'want' and to acquire is a merely 'productivist' *polis* in which every plausible opportunity of betterment is grasped at. In such a *polis* there is no deliberation or choice, no rejection of one want in favour of another, because want itself is incapable of deliberation or choice. It is a disordered or 'unjust' *polis*.

Plato's understanding of the 'idea' justice leads him, then, to the doctrine of the authority of reason to rule; or, as he puts it, the authority of those who by nature or by education have souls whose predominant aptitude is for rational conduct.

And who are these men? Are they not those who, dissatisfied with the shadowy world of the cave, turned their backs upon the meaningless pantomime of changing images and sought to understand it by inquiring into the 'ideas' of which these images were mere copies? Those who, having attained to a knowledge of the 'idea' justice are able to act justly? Are they not, in short, those whom Plato calls 'philosophers'?

In this long and elaborate argument (which I have only scratched the surface of) Plato has moved from a doctrine about knowledge and about human activity, to this doctrine that a *polis* is properly constituted and ruled only when it is constituted and ruled by men whose special aptitude and engagement is knowledge of the 'idea' justice. For it is this aptitude, and this engagement, which enables them to act justly.

7

Now, Plato recognized that this rule of reason, or the rule of a *polis* by those whose predominant aptitude is for rational activity – rule by 'philosophers' – brought with it some difficult problems.

How, for example, can citizens, whose predominant faculty is not reason, be persuaded to submit themselves to the rule of those whose predominant faculty is reason? How to establish and make acceptable the rule of 'philosophers' to those who are not philosophers?

What course of education can be devised to reinforce the faculty of reason in those who have it naturally predominant in their souls?

What manner of life must be imposed upon these rational rulers to make certain that their lesser aptitudes for want and courage shall not usurp the authority to govern and turn their rule into misrule?

How can philosophers, whose essential attribute is an aptitude for the contemplative life passed in the inquiry into the 'ideas' of things, be persuaded to leave this for the distracting life of ruling a *polis*?

What sort of deliberation is required to decide about responses to political situations?

Much of the *Republic* is concerned with questions of this sort, and Plato has some remarkable answers for them. But they are questions which follow from and depend upon this central doctrine: that the image of a just man is a man in whom reason rules his other faculties; and that the image of a just *polis* is a *polis* whose constitution provides that every man shall do that one work for which he has a special aptitude, and that those whose special aptitude is reason shall rule.

Editorial Note

LSE 1/1/21, file 2, fos. 131–9, 141, 143–51. Fos. 132, 139 are photocopies of autograph sheets; fos. 131–8, 141, 143–51 are photocopies of a typescript with autograph corrections. Fo. 140 is a photocopy of an autograph sheet that has been crossed through; fo. 142 is an alternative draft of fo. 141.

Ten

Stoics and Epicureans

1

Our study of political thought, so far, has been a study of the intellectual responses evoked by the political experience of the ancient Greek *polis*.

We have been concerned with thinking about political activity at two levels:

The practical level, in which the ancient Greeks gave a rough and ready intellectual organization to their political habits and customs.

The philosophical level, at which writers like Plato and Aristotle took up and sorted out the popular political beliefs and attempted to remove some of the ambiguities and incoherence of those beliefs.

This political experience of the *polis*, fascinating in itself, lively, various, and changeful, is made doubly fascinating by the reflections it provoked among those who lived through it during the seven hundred years of its history.

But this experience came to an end, and in a manner which is almost unique among political experiences.

On the face of it, it was a dramatic end at the close of the year 338 B.C. This is the date of the battle of Chaeronea in which Philip of Macedon subjugated the free and independent cities of the Greek mainland, turning them into dependencies of an imperial power.

But we must not exaggerate either the drama and the unexpectedness of this end, nor its suddenness. In many of these cities politics had taken a turn which allied itself to what entered from the outside to overwhelm them. If you read the speeches of Demosthenes, you will get some idea of what was happening in Athens.

The old pride of citizenship had declined: there were beginning to be men (mostly engaged in trade) who were citizens of more than one *polis* and had no single allegiance; the feeling for autonomy and self-sufficiency were disappearing in a mixture of races. Indifference and the pursuit of private fortune took the place of the old passionate interest in public affairs.

Democratic constitutions of one sort or another gave way to oligarchies, and the oligarchs were superseded by a new sort of tyrant – one who modeled himself upon an oriental despot. Revolution and violence bred dictators who sought, *not* to 'govern' as the Greeks had understood it, but to exercise dominion.

And where these tyrannies emerged, the hopes of citizens centred no longer upon a recovery of their political initiative, but merely upon a tyrant who would be benevolent rather than rapacious.

What supervened upon the Greek world of independent city-states was, then, the product of changes which were taking place within the cities, combined with the conquest of the armies of Philip and Alexander of Macedon.

And what supervened was a vast military empire, the language of which was Greek, and which carried the arts and the technology (but not the politics) of the Greeks to Africa and to Asia, but which was oriental rather than Greek in character.

Kingship took the place of constitutional rule. The laws of a Greek *polis* became subject to the decrees of a conqueror made known by a local governor. The centre of government moved outside the city to some distant court or camp. Politics which had been the activity of friends and acquaintances became world-wide and evaporated. What took its place was military rule.

Some small attempt was made by political thinkers to embrace this new experience.

No proper theory of the Hellenistic empire ever appeared. But it was made more intelligible, and perhaps for some more tolerable, by finding an analogy between the new kings and the old 'heroes' and 'demigods' of Greece – Alexander was likened to Heracles. The kings were credited with divine powers and a divine mission; divine honours were accorded to them. It was all dreadfully unsophisticated.

But, if the Hellenistic empire itself found only a sketchy intellectual recognition, the situation which it imposed upon the Greek world of hitherto independent and self-governing

cities was deeply reflected upon. And even in this disintegrated world (or, perhaps because of it) Greek thinkers
found the energy to compose some kind of coherent intellectual response.

Indeed, the situation called forth many such responses;
but two of them proved more effective and more enduring
than the others, namely, Stoicism and Epicureanism.

The teachings of Zeno, the Stoic, and of Epicurus were concerned with much that has nothing to do with politics, but
they each contained something that may be called a political
doctrine or message. One hesitates to call them political
philosophies.

It is true that the urge to explain is present in both, and neither merely scratched the surface of things. But whatever
explanatory enterprise they may contain was deeply over-
laid by the much more immediately appropriate enterprise
of reassurance and consolation.

In fact what both Stoicism and Epicureanism offered was
what may be described as a profoundly thought out (and in
that sense philosophical) reassurance to those who had lost
their status as free citizens of a free *polis* that they had not lost
everything. The good human life had for so long been identified with *polis*-life that when the *polis* disintegrated the one
thing people wanted to be told was that the good human life
was still possible. And this was the message, differently
worded, of both Zeno and Epicurus.

2

The doctrines of Stoicism and Epicureanism were first propagated in Athens during the fourth century B.C. But, by way
of introduction, let us jump the centuries to the year 155 B.C.,
an interval during which most of the Greek-speaking world
had been conquered by the armies of Rome.

In that year, Carneades, a citizen of Athens, came to Rome
as the leader of a diplomatic mission. In the intervals of business he was asked to address the intelligentsia of Rome, and
for their entertainment he delivered two lectures on the principles of political order.

(1) The first was a discourse designed to show that there was
an 'order' in the *cosmos* and that the order of a civil society
could be understood as a copy or replica of this 'natural
order'.

He propounded the doctrine that the *cosmos* was governed by a 'natural law', and that human beings, in virtue of a faculty of reason, which they alone enjoy, can perceive this 'natural' law and are, consequently, able to construct human societies whose law and organization are a reflection of this 'natural' law – though, of course, they do not always succeed in doing so.

'Justice' in human conduct and in human societies is conformity to the 'just' and rational order of the *cosmos*.

In short, the *polis* had gone, but a model upon which a good human life could be constructed still remained: an ideal model.

(2) On the next day, however, Carneades delivered a second lecture in which he propounded a very different doctrine.

The *cosmos*, he said, has no law and no order, and therefore exhibits nothing recognizable as 'justice'. It contains no authority which gives each thing its 'due'.

Indeed, the *cosmos* is nothing but a fortuitous concourse of 'atoms', and provides no model whatever for an ordered human society, nor any analogy by which an ordered human society may be understood.

Nevertheless, civil order does exist in the world, and since the *cosmos* provides neither a model nor an analogy for it, it must be understood as a purely human creation, a work of human artifice.

And to understand a civil order all we need is to recognize that it has utility to human beings, that it is within the known powers of human beings to fabricate it, and that it need not be a *polis* of the old kind.

The human aptitude which makes it possible is the ability of making agreements with one another, which, in turn, springs from the power of communicating with one another by speech.

The 'reason' that enters into the situation is not the power of perceiving the order of the *cosmos*, because there is no such order; it is only the power of detecting what is useful. Justice among human beings is what they agree to regard as just; and this agreement is both possible and useful.

Carneades was a retired professional boxer, a man of cynical disposition and a loud voice. No doubt he intended to confuse, and had a certain Athenian contempt for these unlettered Romans. It is reported that he succeeded in annoying Cato (the most famous Roman senator of his day) and in this year a decree was issued banishing Greek philosophers from Rome.

Now, I have jumped the centuries to Carneades, because his two lectures were expositions (rough and ready it must be admitted) of the two doctrines about civil order which Greek thinkers had propounded in the fourth century B.C.

These doctrines were designed to commend civil society to men who had been deprived (or were being deprived) of the traditions of the Greek *polis*, and to reassure them that having lost all, or nearly all, that they understood by politics they had, nevertheless, not lost everything.

The first lecture was on Stoicism, the second on Epicureanism. And I want now to say something about each of these doctrines.

3

The founder of the Stoic teaching was a man named Zeno (*c.* 300 B.C.). He was not an Athenian, but a Cypriot. But he came to Athens and, after studying in the Platonic Academy (Plato himself was, of course, long since dead), set up a school of his own in a place called the Porch (*stoa*) – hence, Stoicism.

(1) There are, of course, many reminiscences of Platonism and of Aristotelianism in this teaching. Its foundation was the belief that there are two permanent and indestructible features of the *cosmos*:

- Instability, change, movement, the coming into being and the disintegration of all the individual things which compose it.
- A universal law or order which governs and determines this change and movement. Change, happening, movement are not fortuitous; they are to be understood as the operation of an unchanging law.

This law of the *cosmos* was thought of by Zeno in various ways.

From the religious point of view, it was a providential order; an order imposed upon the *cosmos* by divine wisdom.

From the scientific point of view, it was a 'natural' order, according to which each component of the *cosmos* obeys the 'law' of its own nature.

From a philosophical point of view, it was a 'rational' order – an order not imposed upon the *cosmos* by the caprice of a creating god (and therefore inscrutable), but a self-explanatory order.

The prime observation of the Stoic teaching is, then, that of a *cosmos* ruled by a permanent, inflexible law, divine, natural and rational – a *cosmos*, therefore, which afforded a model or an analogy for an ordered human society.

(2) Within this *cosmos* human beings are distinguished as 'rational beings'. This means that they are capable of apprehending its law and capable of obeying it, not blindly, like animals and vegetables, but consciously, and by choosing to do so.

Here you will observe a strong reminiscence of the teaching of Aristotle.

The characteristic virtue of human beings, then, is this voluntary conformity to the law of nature. All evil, misery, and injustice springs from the violation of this law – that is, from 'irrational' conduct.

Human beings, however, have a propensity for going their own capricious ways regardless of the law of nature, and this propensity is called 'passion'. It signifies thinking and behaving, not in accordance with their own 'rational' natures, but at the dictation of external, contingent circumstances.

The thoughts and actions which human beings think and perform in this manner are 'passions' because they are 'suffered' rather than 'done', and they signify the absence of *self*-command. Men are said to be 'slaves' to their 'passions'. Human beings, with both 'passionate' and rational dispositions, find their *eudaimonia* in subjecting their passions to their reason and voluntarily obeying the law of the *cosmos*. In short, men deprived of the law of a *polis* directing them to the good human life, still have a law to direct them, and are still capable of a good human life.

From this image of human 'nature', Zeno derived the precept, injunction or law of human virtue: 'Follow nature.' It is a precept already familiar to us from our study of Plato and Aristotle, but in Zeno's teaching it is given a fresh turn appropriate to the circumstances of his time.

Plato had said that good conduct for human beings was conduct modelled upon the 'idea' good.

Aristotle had said that human *eudaimonia* was the realization of what was potential in a human 'nature' characterized by 'rationality'.

But for Zeno, what in Plato and Aristotle were, fundamentally, elucidations of human virtue, 'Follow nature' becomes unmistakably a precept for human conduct; and moreover, it is a simple and dogmatic precept, appropriate for men who were lost and were seeking a guide to the good life.

For Zeno, 'Follow nature' meant, '*Obey* the law of nature' – 'Let your passions be governed by your reason'. You may think this is a commonplace way of understanding the human condition. So it is; we have it at the back of our minds all the time. But it was the Stoics who formulated it.

(3) But Zeno's teaching contained something else supremely appropriate for the circumstances of his time: in this pursuit of a good human life, each man is not a solitary traveler. Zeno held that, in virtue of their common character as 'rational' beings, all men may be considered to be citizens of a single, ideal community, called the *cosmopolis* – this *polis* of the *cosmos* – whose law is the rational law of 'nature'.

The audiences of Plato and Aristotle had been men who were conscious of belonging to a particular *polis* which gave them a place and a home in the world; a *polis* which, in principle, was a morally self-sufficient as well as an independent community.

Zeno was talking to men who had been deprived of this consciousness, men whose ostensible allegiance was to the distant ruler of a vast, formless, irrational empire which had an empirical quality but no moral quality.

For these men to be told that they were citizens of a universal *polis* whose law was the law of reason and nature, came as an immense reassurance and consolation.

It was from their citizenship in this *cosmopolis*, and from their common subjection to the law of reason, that men derived their moral rights and duties – moral rights and duties which seemed to have disappeared from the world with the destruction of the *polis* as a moral community. 'It is true', says Zeno, 'you have lost your *polis*; but the *cosmos* is, as it were, a *polis*'.

(4) But further: Zeno did not deny the obvious fact that, in addition to being a citizen of the *cosmopolis* – a citizen of the

world – every man was also a citizen of some narrower, particular, civil society.

Nor did he deny that, in addition to having a duty to obey the law of the *cosmopolis* – the law of nature – every man found himself the subject of rights and duties under the local, man-made, laws of his particular state.

But what the doctrine of the *cosmopolis* and the law of nature provided was a criterion by which to determine the 'justice' or 'injustice' of human arrangements.

In short, the *cosmopolis* and its law provided an ideal model for all lesser, man-made cities, kingdoms, and empires, which were to be considered 'just' in virtue of their being true copies of the *cosmopolis*.

Together with this doctrine about the character of civil societies went, of course, an interpretation of political activity, of the activity of governing, and of the qualities required in rulers.

Properly speaking, political activity was understood to be an activity in which the laws and arrangements of local societies were made and kept in conformity with the ideal laws and arrangements of the *cosmopolis*.

And the qualities to be desired in government were perceived to be qualities of 'reason' and 'wisdom', which would enable a ruler to rule in accordance with the law of the *cosmos*.

In short, the good man, the good citizen, and the good ruler were men all of the same kind – men whose passions were in control of their reason and who 'followed nature'.

Stoicism did not place a high value upon political activity. To his audience Zeno suggested that *politike* was not an activity necessary for the achievement of the human *eudaimonia*, as Aristotle had thought it to be.

But where, in other circumstances, political activity was not so peripheral and unpromising an activity as it was in fourth-century Athens – in republican and imperial Rome, for example, which was deeply influenced by the Stoic teaching – the doctrine of Zeno was readily modified in this respect, and the good man was thought to have a duty to be an active citizen.

(5) In the political doctrines of Stoicism, then, there are many reminiscences of earlier Greek thoughts about politics,

law, government, and justice. But these thoughts have become formalized, perhaps vulgarized.

The *cosmopolis* was a kind of poor man's version of the Platonic ideal model of which every *polis* was an imperfect copy. Aristotle's idea of the human *eudaimonia* as the realization of the potentialities of a specifically human 'nature' is turned into obedience to an ideal law of nature. And even 'reason' itself becomes a law to be obeyed rather than an aptitude to be used and enjoyed.

But this vulgarization gave Stoicism a simplicity, a strength required by the current circumstances. It was a doctrine appropriate to men who could no longer live in the confidence of being citizens of a *polis* capable of providing them (in the activity of the *agora*) with an opportunity of exercising the human aptitudes of decision and action, and (in its laws) a focus for loyalty.

Stoicism is a severe and unsmiling doctrine for severe and unsmiling times; a consolation prize rather than a prize to match the confidence and the elation of a *victor ludorum*.

And this is what it has always remained. In the subsequent history of Europe there have been not a few occasions when the circumstances of third-century Greece have been reproduced – circumstances when a traditional morality and a traditional politics have disappeared. When this has happened, there has often been a recourse to the teachings of Zeno, in which an ideal citizenship replaced a lost actual citizenship, and an ideal law of lature replaced a lost actual legal system.

4

Now, at the end of the fourth century B.C., perhaps a generation after Zeno had stood in his porch instructing his pupils, another man in Athens was teaching a doctrine which composed the other main response of Greek thought to the circumstances of the time. It is a less severe, more light-hearted response; and like Stoicism it has become one of the great traditions of European thought about the human condition.

This man was Epicurus. He was an Athenian by birth, and he gathered round him a community of pupils who met in his garden.

Like Zeno, he was a philosopher who had an explanation for what went on in the *cosmos*, and it was an explanation which owed much to earlier Greek thought, but to Democritus rather than to Plato or Aristotle.

And like Zeno, Epicurus had a practical message of consolation and reassurance for his generation. Embedded in his teaching is a doctrine about the utility of a civil order.

He wrote little that has survived – a hundred pages of fragments and a few letters to his friends. But nearly two hundred years after his death the Epicurean philosophy was expounded in Latin by a Roman poet named Lucretius in a long didactic poem called *De rerum natura* – 'Concerning the Nature of Things.'

(1) The principles with which Epicurus began were almost the direct opposite of those of Zeno.

The world in which we live, the world before us when we open our eyes, he recognized to be composed of unstable, moving, changing things, things coming into being and disintegrating. But, while Zeno perceived in this change and movement the operation of a universal law, Epicurus perceived simple chaos.

The constituents of the *cosmos*, he said, are 'atoms and the void' – an infinite number of invisible particles, moving perpetually and fortuitously in infinite space, bumping into one another occasionally, and sometimes clustering together for short periods of time to compose the visible things of the world.

From this somewhat unpromising beginning, Epicurus deduced and made intelligible the main components of the *cosmos* as the Greeks understood it, namely, gods, things, and human beings.

The gods, he said, are creatures who live blessed and untroubled lives and are the amused and disinterested spectators of what goes on in the world.

They are totally indifferent to how human beings behave, and have no feelings or ideas about how men ought to behave. They are, therefore, neither to be loved nor feared by men, but only to be envied for their untroubled existence.

There is no 'providence' to help men in difficulties and to reward those who behave well; and there is no 'nemesis', or divine punishment, for ill-doing. There is no 'fate'.

This doctrine about the gods was, itself, intended as a reassurance to men who, in this evening of Greek religious belief, had been overtaken by a great fear of their gods. Epicurus believed that this 'theology' would release men from their fear of divine anger and divine punishment.

The natural world of things is a world of change and movement which has no order in it and obeys no law. Things are temporary clusters of atoms which come into being and pass out of existence fortuitously – both necessity and purpose are absent from the *cosmos*; there is nothing but chance.

Similarly, human beings are composed of temporary conglomerations of atoms. But they are creatures of a peculiar sort.

During their temporary existence, they have an ability to choose and originate their own movements, they have some power of perceiving what is friendly and what is hostile to their happiness and self-preservation; and they have the power of communicating with one another in speech.

They are at liberty to please themselves; they have no obligation to one another, and no obligation to please the gods, they belong to no divine, rational, or natural order.

(2) There is, however one fundamental natural impulse common to all human beings: all men desire pleasure and have an aversion to pain. Consequently, all human activity is to be understood to be directed towards the enjoyment of pleasure and the avoidance of pain.

But since, as Epicurus understands it, to seek pleasure and to avoid pain belongs to the 'nature' of human beings, he is able to formulate his precept for human conduct in the well-known expression: 'Follow nature.'

For the Stoic this expression meant: 'Obey the law of nature; let reason rule passion'. For Epicurus it meant: 'Have confidence in your natural impulses; pursue pleasure'. 'Divine pleasure is the guide to life'. An agreeable and reassuring doctrine.

(3) The good life, then, for human beings, their *eudaimonia*, is for each man to pursue his own pleasure – but with judgment.

The Epicurean life was nothing like what the vulgar imagination made of it; it was nothing like an orgy. Epicurus believed that, after the few essential desires had been satisfied, pleasure was a kind of equilibrium to be maintained chiefly by the avoidance of desires and so of the pain of unsatisfied desires.

In short, the greatest pain is frustration and, the world being what it is, this is most surely avoided by *not* having desires. It is, fundamentally, an ascetic doctrine.

But, whatever element of judgment there must be in the pursuit of pleasure, the good human life was *not* at all concerned with 'right' and 'wrong', or with doing your 'duty', or with observing obligations to other people.

Indeed, it was *not* lived in relation to other people; it not only could be lived alone, but it was 'naturally' lived alone. Each man is alone in an indifferent *cosmos*.

It could be achieved without a *polis*, by an independent individual man pursuing his own pleasure with judgment, and preferably unencumbered by relationships with other people.

And to a man who had lost his *polis*, which had formerly given him his standards of good conduct, to a man who had found himself deprived of any significant *agora*-life, it was a consolation and a reassurance to be told that these things were not necessary, and that he still had within himself *all* that was needed for a good human life.

If the Stoic found a place to be at home in the *cosmopolis*, the Epicurean found it in himself. Both, it would seem, were well equipped to live in the empire which had taken the place of the *polis*.

(4) Now, it would appear from all this that the Epicurean doctrine would have no place for a theory of civil order. It is made to look as if civil society, its laws and obligations, was something a man could very well do without. If any explanation of civil society were in place in the Epicurean doctrine it would seem to be a slightly more detailed demonstration of its superfluousness.

But Epicurus recognized that civil societies existed, and he found a place for them and an explanation of their existence in this scheme of things.

His questions were: What *must* be the nature of civil order if human beings are what I have said they are? And, What is the utility of a civil order to human beings of this sort? How can it contribute to pleasure?

A civil order entails laws and public arrangements; it entails the observance of rights and duties; it entails notions of what is just and unjust; and it entails government.

But none of these things are inherent in human 'nature'; human beings are neither naturally 'social' nor naturally 'political' creatures. And, moreover, there is no suggestion of an order in any corner of the *cosmos* which might be used as a model for a civil order. How then can we conceive of a civil order emerging among human beings? And what is its use?

And to this difficult question Epicurus answers that we can only suppose that civil orders (which certainly exist) are the voluntary creation of human beings and that the manner in which they are created is by human beings agreeing among themselves. At least, they are equipped to come to such an agreement in virtue of their natural ability to communicate with one another in words. Indeed, speech is the sole social quality of human beings.

The agreement itself will be an agreement to regard some sorts of conduct as 'just' and other sorts as 'unjust', to make laws for themselves and to set up a common authority to punish offenders against these laws.

In short, a civil order *must* be the result of an agreement, a treaty, or a contract between human beings who find themselves living next to one another; and it must be this because, men being what they are, no other generation for a civil order is imaginable.

But for what purpose should human beings enter into such agreements? What is the utility of all this paraphernalia of laws and obligations, of rights and duties, of justice and injustice, of government and the enforcement of law?

And when Epicurus asks the question, What is the utility of it all? it must be interpreted to mean: What useful contribution does it make to the human *eudaimonia* – that is, to the well-judged pursuit of pleasure?

The answer Epicurus gives is that, of course, human beings would never have been so foolish to enter into such agreements and to set up civil orders – all of which *must* constitute a *prima facie* hindrance to the pursuit of pleasure – unless they feared that in their absence the pursuit of pleasure would be even more greatly hindered.

The sad fact about human life, as Epicurus observed it, is that every man has a next-door neighbor who is capable of frustrating his pursuit of pleasure.

Men fear one another because they are apt to hinder one another's pursuit of pleasure. The utility of a civil order lies in its propensity to reduce this fear by limiting the occasions of it.

But how does the creation of a civil order mitigate this fear and reduce this liability to mutual frustration? It does so, says Epicurus, by narrowing the field of human conflict.

In constituting a civil order we, admittedly, limit our individual freedom to do what we judge to be most likely to bring us pleasure, but we get out of this civil order a security from the petty and continuous frustrations we are otherwise apt to suffer from our neighbors. We are protected against one another.

To agree upon what shall be regarded 'just' conduct and to make people behave justly towards one another establishes no more than a common minimum of non-frustration, but that minimum is better than being continuously at the mercy of other men, depending for our unhindered pursuit of pleasure upon a good will in others which we have no reason to believe exists.

There is, however, one serious gap in this theory of a civil order, which Epicurus proceeded to fill.

It will be seen at once that for each man it will be an advantage to be 'unjust' – that is, to go his own way in the pursuit of pleasure regardless of the rules of noninterference which belong to a civil order – so long as everybody else behaves 'justly'.

The best situation for a man is not to keep the rules in a civil society in which everyone else is very punctilious in keeping the rules. The best situation will be that of an anarchist protected by a policeman, or of the queue-jumper among people all of whom are punctilious about keeping their proper places.

What is there to prevent or to discourage any man from trying to get into this position? The answer Epicurus gives to this question is: what discourages this sort of behavior in a civil society is fear of the pain of punishment.

If one could behave 'unjustly' and be certain of never being found out, or, if found out, be certain of avoiding punishment, then the lawbreaker among those who keep the law would clearly be in a superior position for the pursuit of pleasure than anyone else.

But in any well-established civil order (and a sketchy or uncertain civil order would have no utility to anyone) we can never be *certain* of getting away with it, and not to be certain of escaping punishment is to suffer the fear of punishment even if, by chance, one manages on any occasion to avoid punishment – and the fear of punishment is pain.

Consequently, for a man who is, as Epicurus assumes all men to be, 'concerned for himself alone', it is better to accept the common advantage of a civil order and to observe its rules than to suffer either the continuous and unlimited interference of other people or the pain that goes with the fear of punishment. Q.E.D.

An elegant if a not entirely convincing proof. And a line of thought which later political philosophers were to pursue, notably Hobbes.

5

The explanations of civil order, of law, and of government which are contained in the Stoic and the Epicurean doctrines, and the practical precepts which each of these doctrines suggests, were offered, in the first place, to the Athenians of the fourth and third centuries B.C. who, like the rest of the Greeks, had lost the *polis*-life which earlier generations had created and had enjoyed.

The question which these doctrines answer was evidently the question which had emerged with this new circumstance, the question, namely: What is there to replace what I have lost? I live subject to a civil order, imposed by a remote, foreign ruler, a civil order which commands my conduct but which has no moral authority such as the *polis* had: What am I to think?

(1) To those who asked this question, Zeno announced that they should think of themselves as belonging to a moral order more magnificent than that of the ancient *polis* – as citizens of the *cosmopolis*.

This universal city (of which all men are citizens in virtue of their common rational character) had a law – the universal law of nature. It was a law not made by men, but it proclaimed the moral rights and duties of all men.

The moral allegiance which the current civil order could not claim, or could claim only in so far as it reflected the order of nature, was owed to the *cosmopolis* itself.

(2) The teaching of Epicurus, though different from that of Zeno, was a not less appropriate answer to the question.

Epicurus announced that there is no moral order and that human beings need no moral order: the good life is something each man may achieve for himself – the life of the prudent pursuit of pleasure.

What men need is a civil order; and a civil order may perform its function in human life without its being at the same time a moral order. The fact that there is no 'justice' in the universe does not prevent human beings from making a 'justice' for themselves – that is, making a purely conventional civil order.

Perhaps it is imposed by some remote, foreign ruler; but even if this be so, its utility is not destroyed. And nothing is of any consequence in the civil order but its utility.

Editorial Note

LSE 1/1/21, file 2, fos. 152–66. Photocopy of a typescript with autograph corrections.

The Political Experience of the Ancient Romans (1)

1

Political thought, as I am trying to put it before you, is a reflective activity in which a political experience acquires an organization of sentiments, beliefs, and general ideas.

In its most practical aspect, it is commonly concerned with deliberation about policy and about the institutions and instruments of government.

But it may branch out into an imaginative construction of a legend of political life which endows the aspirations and fortunes of a political society with a heightened self-consciousness; or into a philosophical examination of the conditions of political life.

We have seen something of what this amounted to among the ancient Greeks.

I want now to turn to the second of the great political experiences we have to consider – that of the Romans.

I hope I shall be able to interest you in the Romans. They were a remarkable people, and their political experience is one of the most memorable of all the political experiences of European peoples.

I think it is hardly an exaggeration to say that the Romans are the only European people to show a genuine genius for government and politics. This may appear to be a second-rate kind of genius, but when it acquired the dimensions it did among the Romans it is pretty impressive.

In most respects the political experience of the Romans is utterly unlike that of ancient Greece. The expression 'the ancient world', which puts Greeks and Romans together, is one of the most misleading generalizations ever made.

Greek politics was the politics of a world of independent city-states, each with a character and history of its own. In

Athens, it was the politics of perpetual revolution, the product of an all too lively political imagination; illuminated, in the end, by astonishing achievements in philosophic reflection and understanding.

Roman politics was the politics of a single city-state which, in the course of a thousand years, grew to embrace in a single empire the greater part of the known world.

It was the politics of a people whose inventive powers were devoted, *not* to risky political experiments or to dazzling speculative adventures, but to interpreting and responding to the situations into which their impulses or their fortunes led them. The 'rationalistic' disposition of the Greeks (or, at least, of the Athenians) was almost wholly absent from Roman politics.

I propose to begin by saying something about the events which compose this political experience – the events and the immediate interpretations which the Romans put upon them. It is a story in which fact and legend are mixed, and in which legend is more important than fact.

The books on your list which you should be reading in this connection are:

R.H. Barlow, *The Romans*
L. Homo, *Roman Political Institutions*
F.E. Adcock, *Roman Political Ideas and Practice*
F.R. Cowell, *Cicero and the Roman Republic*
H.J. Rose, *Ancient Roman Religion*
D. Earl, *The Moral and Political Tradition of Rome*

And if any of you care to venture further into the histories of Livy and Tacitus, so much the better.

2

In considering this political experience, we are met, at the outset, by a legend: the legend of Roman politics as it appears in the writings of Livy, Tacitus, Polybius, Cicero, and Virgil – not philosophers (like Plato and Aristotle), but historians and lawyers and poets.

This legend is composed of the beliefs the Romans had about their beginnings, and the interpretations they imposed upon their fortunes. It constitutes the political self-consciousness of the Romans.

This legend is the story of a hero and the vicissitudes of his life in the world. The hero of this legend is the Roman people, the *populus Romanus*.

No people of modern times has exceeded the Romans in their self-consciousness. They 'saw' themselves, as an actor might 'see' himself, playing a part on the stage; and they were fascinated in the part they understood themselves to be playing. Sometimes it seems as if this severe and practical people lived in a dream world, so great is their self-absorption.

In modern times, the only thing comparable to this is, perhaps, the self-absorption of the French in their period of revolution, or that of the British people in their imperial dream. Both dreams were short-lived.

The Athenians had moments of thinking they had a mission to be the 'teachers' of Hellas, as Thucydides says; but the Romans believed they had a mission to rule and civilize the world.

Moreover, the self-absorption of the Romans was that of a profoundly religious people. You may think it odd to speak of the Romans as 'religious', but they were; and if they had not been, Christianity would have had a very different history.

In the nineteenth century – in the era of the emergent so-called democracies – the politics of ancient Greece was a fashionable subject of reflection; but at all other times ancient Rome has supplied the models and the vocabulary of European politics.

This legend, however, was an imaginative interpretation of events and circumstances; and it is about this other formulation of the political experience of the ancient Romans – namely, what actually happened, so far as a modern historian of ancient Rome can discern – that I must say something first. There was a time when Roman political history was familiar to any student of history, but since this is no longer the case, you must forgive me for spending some time on it.

3

The Italian peninsula, the scene of this experience, is a land of mountains and hills, valleys and plains. But, unlike Greece, its mountains form no impassable, or even difficult, barriers; and at least two of its plains are extensive. It has a long coast-

line; but natural harbors are few and there are no significant
coastal islands: there is nothing to provoke its inhabitants to
a notably seafaring life.

Unlike that of Greece, the soil is fertile; its rivers are many,
and only in the south is the countryside significantly arid. In
short, it is a land fit for the farmers who were to inhabit it –
farmers whose relationship to their land was a mixture of
love and submission. The Romans began by being a people
of farmers and soldiers, and this is what they remained to the
end of their history.

(1) In very early times this peninsula was invaded from the
north by a variety of peoples whose names are known to us.
They spoke different languages, they were at times friendly
and at times hostile to one another, but in many respects
were not dissimilar.

Each of these peoples was composed of tribes or clans, kinship groups of one dimension or another. They were pastoral
peoples, who brought their cattle with them; but they were
not mere nomads and were already learned in the arts of
agriculture.

The most important of these peoples, from the point of
view of later history, were those who were called, respectively, the Latins and the Sabines. These settled in and about
the Alban hills which lie immediately to the southeast of the
river Tiber, and now look down upon the airport of Rome.

If you have ever been there you will not wonder why a
wandering people should have come to settle there: it is irresistible. The fertile land, the wooded slopes, the lakes (like
Lake Nemi), and the rivers. They settled, they cultivated the
land, and they built towns which were at once strongholds,
granaries, and places to live in.

The religion of these people was a family religion, the worship of ancestor-gods, the head of each family being a priest
in his own household, celebrating the rites in which the gods
of the hearth and the home were worshiped; and the law was
a tribal law.

But, in each of these independent fortress towns, social ties
were added to the ties of blood. The family gods and the
tribal laws gave place to gods, religious ceremonies, and
laws of territorial communities.

So these people lived, governed by their chiefs, often at
war with one another – lives, centred upon urban strong-

holds, which, if they were not yet properly political, were not merely tribal.

The most famous of these fortress towns was a Latin settlement called *Alba Longa*.

There was a legend (of much later construction) about its foundation. It was reputed to be composed of a union of Latins and Trojans, the Trojans having arrived in that part of the world under the leadership of Aeneas after he escaped from the burning city of Troy. And according to the legend Aeneas was the first 'king' of the settlement known as *Alba Longa*.

(2) Following these peoples, coming we do not know from where, there appeared in the Italian peninsula another people of a different sort from the Latins, the Sabines, and their companions.

This people we know as Etruscans. They settled the whole of west-central Italy north of the Tiber, in what is now Tuscany, pushing earlier immigrants south and occupying an area which reached down to the Latin and Sabine settlements in the Alban hills.

The Etruscans were a severe, masterful, and warlike people, more advanced in military skill, in artistic achievement, and in manner of life than their neighbors. Their arrival and hostility did something to unite the settlers in the Alban hills.

At a point where a stream, called the Anio, which descends from these hills, joins the river Tiber, about fifteen miles from the sea, and where there is an island in the Tiber making the crossing less difficult, there lie seven small hills.

Here the territory of the Etruscans and that of the Latins met. And about the year 750 B.C. (traditionally, 753 B.C.) this area began to be occupied, as a frontier post, by a community of Latin people from *Alba Longa*.

4

The first of the seven hills to be settled was the Palatine; and the Latins who settled it were, according to the legend, led by a man named Romulus, the reputed son of Mars (then the god of agriculture) and a niece of a 'king' of *Alba Longa*. Later legend equipped Romulus with a romantic and extraordinary upbringing appropriate for one who was to be recognized as the progenitor of the Roman people and the father of the Roman state.

Not long after this first settlement, other of these hills were similarly occupied by Latin and Sabine communities; and in the course of time each of the seven hills was settled – one of them, reputedly, by an Etruscan community.

Walls were built, treaties were entered into; alliances were made. One hundred and fifty years later there was a wall which enclosed a large part of the area of the seven hills; and the communities of these hills had somehow come to recognize themselves as a single *civitas* – that is, a *political* community, a *polis*. Thus was the city of Rome made, the *civitas Romana* founded, and thus the *populus Romanus* emerged.

In the legend of Roman politics this was, and remained, the most momentous event. The Romans might, at some periods in their history, look forward, but they never failed to look back with wonder and pride to the foundation of their *civitas*, and every event of their subsequent history was dated from the year of its foundation. What we call 753 B.C. the Romans called *anno urbis constitutio* – the year of the foundation of the *civitas*, year 1. The only comparable event in modern times which has generated similar emotion has been the founding of the United States of America.

5

The *civitas Romana* was, then, composed of a number of hitherto independent, territorial communities of settlers. These communities spoke the same language; but they were not the same 'people' – at least two peoples (Latins and Sabines) were represented – and to unite them into a single community was not easy.

Traditionally, the means by which this unity was achieved was, in the first place, by a *treaty*. And this word 'treaty' (*foedus*) became the characteristic Roman idea in connection with the formation of a 'state' or with any great constitutional settlement. In Livy this idea of a community emerging from a treaty is even pushed back into the legendary past when he writes of *Alba Longa* as having emerged from a 'treaty' between the Trojans led by Aeneas and the 'Latin' people of the locality which created a single 'polity'.

There is a characteristic formality about the founding of Rome, which contrasts with the informality of strangers meeting, getting to know one another, and settling down together which Aristotle imagined to be the origin of a *polis*. No Greek city ever looked back to the moment of its foundation as the Romans did.

Somehow or other, then, in a manner that remains obscure, these original communities of the seven hills became a single *civitas*. And this unity was based upon a reorganization (attributed to Romulus but which must have taken several generations to achieve) in which the old components were superseded by social and territorial units which had nothing to do with the seven hills themselves.

The materials, so to speak, available for organization into a community of a new style consisted of the traditions of government which the settlers brought with them, and the Latin and Sabine families who had composed the original settlements.

There are two things to note about these families.

(1) They were 'households' consisting of a man, his wife, children, the freemen attached to the household (*clientes*), and slaves; and over all these the head of the household had absolute authority. In his household, the head was both king and priest.

The Roman family in its earliest appearance is in the hands of a 'despot', in whom is vested not only the property but also the lives of this family and dependents. This despotic family rule, though in later centuries it was greatly modified by Roman law, remained always a kind of emblem of government for the Romans, who recognized a kind of parallel between household rule and the rule of a king or an emperor. But it was by no means the only source of Roman traditions of government.

(2) Long before the settlement of the seven hills was achieved, a distinction between families had established itself. This was *not*, fundamentally, a distinction of wealth, but of social prestige derived from ancient lineage and also the long enjoyment of wealth.

There were, in this sense, noble families (later called 'patrician' families), and what were later called 'plebeian' families. These two kinds of families were long kept distinct from one another, not only by the different parts they were to play in the political life of the Roman *civitas*, but also by the prohibition of intermarriage between them.

But it is a mistake to suppose that either in these early years, or later, that the 'plebeian' families were necessarily poor: they were simply the families which could not claim 'nobility' and which were excluded from the precise privileges and the duties of the nobility.

This distinction is of the first importance because from it sprang the characteristic Roman political notions of *dignitas* (which went with *auctoritas*) and *libertas*. *Dignitas* belonged to the 'noble', *libertas* to the plebeian.

The reorganization which constituted the *civitas Romana* consisted of the replacement of the sub-communities of the seven hills by a new set of sub-communities called *curiae*. Each family found itself joined to neighboring families in a *curia*.

Now a *curia* was a territorial unit, and at the same time it contained relics of older 'tribal' divisions. It became an association of families, living in a defined area, who participated in common religious festivals, who had a meeting place and a place of worship of its own, and a public life of its own.

In this early stage it is important to us because the 'Roman people' – the *populus Romanus* – was held to consist of those who were members of a *curia*. And it is also important to notice that each of these *curiae* included both noble and plebeian families; it was an organization which cut across the social classes, just as an English parish does.[1]

6

This, then, was the Roman people from its first appearance: a people who, by devious ways, had graduated from a tribal to a political character, and from being a collection of settlements to being a single *civitas*. How were these people governed?

(1) Rome, in these early days, was ruled by kings, the first of whom was Romulus. The office of *rex* was to exercise on behalf of the community the comprehensive authority which the Roman understood by the word *imperium* – government.

This is a word the meaning of which we shall have to consider later in detail: but it may be taken now as it is the Latin word for 'government'. For the moment we will concern ourselves with its meaning in connection with the early kings of Rome.

Kingship was not a hereditary office, nor did a *rex* hold his position either by popular or by divine appointment. The

---

[1] Oakeshott's marginal note: 'Athenian citizen = one who belonged to one of the original tribes.'

noble families had something to do with his appointment and so also did the plebeian, but when once he was installed he was an autocrat and held his office for life.

His office had three main duties.

- He possessed the *auspicium*, the ability and the sole authority to ascertain the will of the gods; and he had the duty to secure the *pax deorum*, the peace between the community and its gods, without which, it was believed, no community could prosper or even survive.
- He was the commander in battle.
- He was the custodian of the law and the administrator of justice between his subjects. The three normal functions in primitive government: the gods; war; and peace.

(2) Beneath the *rex*, the heads of the noble families (the 'fathers', *patres*, who were the heads of the aristocratic families) had an important part to play. They could be summoned by the king to give him counsel.

Later these 'patricians' came to compose a more exactly official body called the senate (the council of elders); but, in the early years of Rome, they were simply the 'magnates' of the kingdom whom the king might consult if he chose: their business was to discuss and to advise when called upon to do so.

They had, however, a position of great importance on the death of a king. It was into their keeping, on such occasions, that the *auspicium* and the whole *imperium* reverted, to be held and exercised until the appointment of a new king.

On these occasions the *patres* were the custodians of the *arcana*, the secrets and the mysteries, of government. In this manner it was believed, so Livy tells us, that the authority of the semi-divine Romulus, the first king, was handed on in an uninterrupted transmission.

The notion of an authority, legitimate because of its uninterrupted transmission from an original authority, is a very important and characteristically Roman idea. It was, much later, reflected in the notion of papal authority.

(3) The third feature of this manner of government was an assembly of the *curiae*: the *comitia curiata*.

This assembly could be called together by the king, and was called mainly for the purposes of proclamation and for witnessing certain important religious ceremonies. It was in no sense an assembly for debate, but on rare occasions it was asked to signify assent, and when it did so its members voted by *curiae* and not as individuals.

This was, and was recognized to be, the assembly of the whole *populus Romanus*: and, as such, it of course included both noble and plebeian persons. That is to say, while plebeian persons were excluded from the senate, patrician persons were members of the *comitia curiata*.

Thus, in this system of government, there was room for deliberation and advice (the senate), for public proclamation and approval (the assembly of the *curiae*), and for executive decision (a king).

And the autocratic position of the *rex* was not only made intelligible by the parallel autocratic position of the head of a Roman family, but was maintained by the fact that these were years of constant emergency and filled with warlike operations.

7

The Roman people were ruled in this manner, by kings, for a period of about 250 years.

The most famous of these early kings was Numa; to us a misty, priest-like figure, but one who during his long and relatively peaceful reign was reputed to have been deeply learned in the laws of gods and men and to have given a religious formality to the public life of his people.

At some point during this period, it would appear that Rome came under the rule of alien kings of Etruscan origin. And whatever other mark these Etruscan lords may have left upon Roman life, their rule was the occasion of two important happenings:

- A reorganization of the Roman people, originally for the purpose of conducting military operations, but later having a very great political significance.
- And a revolution which, after the foundation of the *civitas Romana* itself, was to be regarded as the most momentous event in the Roman political experience.

(1) The first of the Etruscan kings, Tarquinius Priscus, for the purpose of increasing the military force at his disposal, set on foot a change in the manner of raising levies which was completed by his successor Servius Tullius.

The old military organization corresponded to the 'curial' structure of the population, each *curia* being responsible for its quota of soldiers.

But under these so-called Servian reforms the military organization was divorced from the *curia* and based upon an arbitrary division of the free landholders of Rome into companies of a hundred ('centuries'). These companies were of different 'classes', each with its military function to perform: the 'centuries' of horsemen, for example, being composed of the wealthier landholders who could afford the necessary equipment.

Military enterprise being so important a part of Roman life, these 'centuries' came to supersede the *curiae* as the political constituents of the Roman state. In the course of time they came to meet in an assembly, called the *comitia centuriata*, which, for many important purposes, took the place of the assembly of the *curiae* and was recognized as the assembly of the Roman people.

Thus the Roman state, from being composed, politically, of *curiae*, half-religious and half-political, socially mixed, communities of neighbors which met and voted in the *comitia curiata*, was transformed into a collection of socially homogeneous sets of a hundred landowners, under military discipline, from which all relic of ancient tribal allegiances had been excluded, and which met in a new assembly of their own.

(2) The third Etruscan king of Rome, Tarquinius Superbus, was not only the last of his line but also the last of the kings of Rome.

In a revolution, in the year 509 B.C., he was deposed and exiled. The revolution was inspired by the aristocracy, and was led by a patrician, Lucius Junius Brutus.

But it was hailed by the Roman people as an emancipation from tyranny. In the legend of Roman politics it was celebrated as the 'beginning of liberty'. It was the foundation of the Roman republic.

But this *is* legend; for, as in many other revolutions, the regime which succeeded to that of the early kings of Rome, namely, the Roman republic, inherited relatively unchanged all the political institutions (except kingship) of those early centuries, and all the important beliefs and ideas which went with them.

The *rex* did not disappear altogether. He became a *rex sacrorum*, a person who performed some, but not all, of the religious duties of the defunct kings.

Having got rid of a king whose authority had become tyrannous, the *imperium* (the authority to rule) reverted to the assembly of patricians, the senate, as it would have done if the last king had died and not been expelled.

It would seem that the senate were determined upon two things – first, that this *imperium* should never again be normally exercised in its entirety by one man; and secondly, that whoever exercised it should not do so for more than a limited period of time.

Thus, there was set up, as the successor to the *rex*, a magistracy of two independent persons, neither having authority to prevail over the other, the duration of their office being a single year.

These magistrates were called *praetores* or *praetores consules* (joint rulers): consuls.

These consuls were appointed in a manner that conformed to all the old traditions and current arrangements. They came from the patrician nobility; the participation of the senate in their election preserved the constitutional fiction that their authority to 'take the auspices' and preserve the *pax deorum* descended to them in an unbroken transmission from Romulus himself.

The participation of the new assembly of *curiae* recognized and confirmed a recent change in the distribution of power.

And the participation of the assembly of *curiae* was a bow to ancient tradition.

(3) But if this device solved, at least temporarily, the problem of tyranny, it left a situation common enough in Roman history unprovided for.

A dyarchy of two consular magistrates may be supremely appropriate in circumstances of peace and quiet when the chief concern of the subjects of a government is to be allowed to enjoy their rights and to be assured of impartial justice; but is it appropriate in an emergency, when an enemy is at the gates and rapid decision and unified command are what the situation calls for?

So, having provided for 'liberty', the Romans proceeded to provide constitutionally for 'security'. In an emergency it was within the authority of the consuls to appoint, for a period of not more than six months, a 'dictator', a *magister populi* (master of the people) who would himself exercise the *imperium* entire.

(4) The Roman republic, then, was the Roman *civitas* in which the executive officers of government were two equal magistrates appointed for a year a time. No new notion of 'government' was entailed in this arrangement.

Together these magistrates performed the duties which kings had hitherto performed. They were endowed with the *imperium*; they had the duty of preserving the *pax deorum* (perhaps the most important duty of a Roman ruler); they commanded the Roman army in war; as judges they administered the customary, unwritten law.

In the early years of the republic these magistrates, although their election was a matter in which both the senate and the *comitia centuriata* participated, were always drawn from the patrician families, and were the nominees of those families.

8: The Rule of the Patrician Consuls

But these early republican arrangements, if they closed one chapter in the political experience of the Roman people, also opened another.

The distinction between the 'noble' or patrician families and the plebeian families was very ancient. It was an historic distinction, and while it may have reflected a difference of wealth, it did not in the early years of the republic reflect the current distribution of wealth. It was a social distinction, and one which was maintained chiefly by marriage laws.

According to the legend, Romulus had originally 'created' the senatorial class by designating a hundred of the heads of noble families to be 'senators', and these had handed on their social position and political rights to their descendants.

Whatever historic truth this may reflect, the fact was that by the beginning of the fifth century B.C., the patricians had closed their ranks against new entrants, and had protected themselves by a law which prevented a plebeian from marrying into a patrician family.

Nevertheless, plebeians are *not* to be thought of as a poor or a propertyless class. They consisted of wealthy families and poor families, of landowners and craftsmen, of men who had commended themselves as 'clients' to noble families and

formed part of a noble household, and men who were independent. They were all 'free' men and were, alike with patricians, *cives*, citizens of the Roman *civitas*.

Now, this distinction between *patres* and *plebei* had, in the
early monarchy, had no very great political significance.
Together both classes were represented in the *curiae* and (less
completely) in the *comitia curiata*.

In the organization of 'centuries' they had become separated from one another, but they were both represented in
the *comitia centuriata*, the assembly of the *populus Romanus*.

Under the kings, if the patricians had a special position
denied to the plebeians, they were *both* subordinate to the
rex.

With the republic this situation was inevitably modified. If
the rule of patrician consuls gave the patrician class a 'freedom' it had not enjoyed under the monarchy, it did not do
exactly the same for the plebeians.

If the *populus Romanus* (patricians and plebs alike) might
complain of the tyranny of an autocratic king, and might be
discontented with the 'justice' he imposed, under the republic the rule of the patrician consuls was the subject of similar
complaint and discontent among the plebeians.

In short, the republican constitution could be suspected of
government not only by the patricians, but in the interests of
the patricians at the expense of those of the plebeians.

This suspicion came to the surface in relation to the administration of the law with regard to debtors. The consequence
of indebtedness has always been a fertile source of political
change: in Greece, Solon's main problem was to reform the
law about debtors, and the same situation has appeared in
many more modern contexts.

The law of Rome, as it stood, prescribed the loss of liberty –
enslavement – as the penalty for a debtor who could not pay
his debts. It was a very ancient law, and its administration
had often been lenient; few plebeian debtors relapsed into
slavery.

But under the patrician consuls, in circumstances of peace,
when the military support of the plebeian 'centuries' was not
so essential, this law was more rigorously administered. And
this rigour closed the ranks of the plebeians, and rich and
poor alike united in discontent and complaint.

It was a revolt, it should be noticed, against the *administration* of justice. But it went so far that the plebeians refused to

perform their military duties and the plebeian city dwellers removed themselves to the Mons Sacer, three miles outside Rome, and set up (or threatened to set up) what was, in effect, a *civitas* of their own. From this position they negotiated with the senate and the patrician consuls.

The agreement reached was characteristically thought of as a 'treaty' between plebs and patricians (afterwards known as the *lex sacrata*).

It provided for the following arrangements, which came into operation gradually in the course of years, and which came to be recognized as constitutionally valid:

(1) First, the plebeians acquired the right to appoint 'magistrates' or 'leaders' of their own, who came to be called *tribuni*.

These tribunes were recognized to have no share in the consular *imperium*, but to have 'powers' of a different sort of their own.

To begin with, the chief of these 'powers' was to give 'help' or 'protection' (*auxilium*) to any plebeian arraigned before a consular judge.

There were, in the first place, two tribunes, but the number was later increased. They were appointed for one year at a time; and the persons of the tribunes were sacrosanct.

(2) Secondly, the plebs acquired the right to meet in an assembly of their own, which came to be called the *concilium plebis*.

This assembly was convened and presided over by the tribunes in the same manner as the consuls convened and presided over the *comitia centuriata*.

The tribunes had the right to put resolutions before the *concilium*; and when such resolutions were voted upon, the manner of voting was neither by 'centuries', nor by *curiae*, but by 'tribes'.

These resolutions, when agreed, were known as *plebiscita* – 'decisions of the plebs'. They were binding only on the plebs and not the whole *populus Romanus*. In short, the plebs were recognized to have the right to make law for themselves.

This was a very remarkable arrangement, for it went a long way towards creating a state within a state.

The only superiorities which the senate and the consular government could claim over the plebeian assembly and the tribunes were:

- that the tribunical 'power' was not recognized as a share in the *imperium*;
- it still required the consuls, the senate and the *comitia centuriata* to make law for the *populus Romanus* as a whole;
- the consuls retained the exclusive authority of military command.

It was not, then, a situation which could endure for long unchanged without the Roman state falling apart. And that this did not happen was due to a series of modifications, taking place over more than a century, which generated a sort of equilibrium between the patricians and the plebeians, the two 'orders' of the *populus Romanus*.

The patrician class became less exclusive by the abrogation of laws which prohibited the intermarriage of patrician and plebeian families.

A new 'nobility', not of blood but of office, emerged in which both patricians and plebeians were sharers.

After a long period of confusion, during which it seems that on occasion a tribune exercised the military *imperium*, it became the custom for one of the two consular magistracies to be reserved for a plebeian holder.

The resolutions of the *concilium plebis* acquired a binding force on the whole *populus Romanus* without requiring the assent of either the senate, the consuls or the *comitia centuriata*. And the *comitia centuriata* was soon left with the single duty of participating in the appointment of the consular magistrates.

Each of these changes was not so much the result of abstract reflection as of accommodation forced upon the patrician senate by contingent circumstances, such as the emergency of war. By early in the third century B.C., then, in a struggle spread over 200 years, it seemed as if the *concilium plebis* had acquired the dominant place in the government of the Roman *civitas*.

9

But long before this another profoundly important change had taken place.

One of the earliest demands of the tribunes on behalf of the plebeians had been for the ancient unwritten law of the Romans to be written down and published. This law was in the custody of the patrician consuls, the senate, and a patrician college of pontiffs, priestly lawyers; and the reason for the demand of the tribunes is clear.

The Romans were governed by a law, the provisions of which were obscure to the plebeians and therefore the administration of which was suspect.

The demand appeared, first, as a demand for the codification and publication of the law relating to the authority of the consuls; but over a period of about ten years it was extended until it became a demand that the whole of the ancient law of the Romans should be revealed.

To satisfy this demand, the senate and the *concilium* agreed to appoint ten patricians for a period of one year to rule the state, to put the law in order and to publish it. (You will remember that a similar demand in ancient Greece was met by the appointment of dictator *nomothetes*, the most famous of which was Solon in Athens.)

The co-called *decemviri* did their work not very expeditiously; its result was the twelve tables of the Roman law, published in 451 B.C.

Henceforth the *populus Romanus* was ruled by a law knowable to all, the keepers of the law (the college of pontiffs) was thrown open to plebeians, and the Roman political experience began to include, with more and more assurance, and activity until then very sparingly engaged in – the activity of 'lawmaking'.

The early centuries of the Roman political experience, then, provided some important topics for reflection:

- How does a collection of tribes become a political society, a *civitas*, and what is involved in this change?
- What is citizenship; and what are its rights and duties?
- What sort of a political community did the *populus Romanus* constitute?
- How may a political community combine executive authority and freedom?
- What is law, and how may it be made?

Editorial Note

LSE 1/1/21, file 3, fos. 168–84. Photocopy of a typescript with autograph corrections.

The Political Experience of the Ancient Romans (2)

1

The political experience of the Romans began as the experience of creating a political community, a *civitas*, a state, out of tribal societies; and of creating the Roman people, the *populus Romanus*, out of a miscellany of different peoples.

With the expulsion of the 'kings' under whom this had been achieved, it became an experience in which the political ascendancy of an hereditary nobility was invaded and gradually modified by the claims of a non-noble class of free land-owners, called *plebeians*.

The result of this struggle for power, which went on for about three and a half centuries, was that, by the beginning of the third century B.C., the city-state of Rome was governed in a very complicated manner.

There were four partners in this republican constitution:

(1) Two ancient assemblies of the *populus Romanus* which had the right to approve or disapprove all legislative proposals, and took part in the election of the executive government.

(2) The ancient patrician senate, which was a deliberative assembly of the heads of noble families.

(3) A new assembly of the plebeian class, the *concilium plebis*, controlled by tribunes, which had the right to propose and approve laws – called *plebiscita* – which applied not only to themselves, but to the whole *populus Romanus*.

(4) Two consular magistrates, elected for one year. These held the *imperium*, the right to rule; and they constituted the executive government. They were elected by the

popular assemblies and by the senate. And they usually belonged to the patrician class.

It was a situation of immense tension, but a temporary *modus vivendi* had been achieved. The ancient prerogatives of an hereditary aristocracy were being invaded by the claim to exercise power of a numerous, wealthy, non-noble class of small landowners and traders. And the plebeian claims were winning.

A great victory had been won in 451 B.C. when the *plebs* successfully demanded the codification and publication of the ancient Roman law, which had hitherto existed as an oral tradition in the care of the senate and in the custody of priestly authorities.

Now, at the beginning of the third century B.C., it looked as if the *concilium plebis* would outshine all other assemblies as an authority for making law, and as if its leaders, the tribunes, would invade the consular magistracies and might capture the executive offices of the Roman state; and thus, give Rome an oligarchical government from which the nobility were excluded.

Nevertheless, this did not happen; and our first question is: why did it not happen?

(1) The short answer to this question is that, just as the *concilium plebis* was in a position to exploit its constitutional victory over the senate, Rome became involved in a war with the other great Mediterranean power, Carthage.

In its first phase, this war lasted sixteen years; but it was nearly eighty years before the destruction of Carthaginian power was achieved. And in the later part of this period of nearly a century, Roman armies, in a major military effort, invaded and conquered Greece, Asia Minor, Egypt, and Spain.

War, in any case, is apt to postpone domestic disputes and ambitions. And a long period of military engagements, in which there were some crippling defeats as well as final victories, is not the most favourable circumstance for an assembly which had hitherto spent its energies on winning new rights for itself to take over the direction of policy and the government of a state.

Indeed, these wars, in which there were not one, but many, Roman armies in the field, in which there were several theaters of war, were beyond the capacity of even the annually appointed consular magistrates to conduct and control.

What was required, in order to provide a continuous policy and an over-all strategy, was a body of persons who could reach decisions after debate and discussion, and which could transmit these decisions, if only in the form of advice, to those charged with executive power.

The *concilium plebis* was completely unequipped to play this part. But this had long been the part played by the senate in Roman politics.

In respect of procedure alone, the *concilium plebis* was at a hopeless disadvantage. It was not an assembly for debate; it could meet only when called together by its tribunes. From being an assembly of protest it had become a legislative assembly; but legislation is one thing and the conduct of policy is another.

The senate, on the other hand, met without having to be called together; it was never a legislative assembly, but an assembly of debate, and its debates terminated in the expression of an 'opinion' or 'advice' to those who held the executive *imperium*: the consuls.

In these circumstances the government of Rome and the conduct of policy fell into the hands of the only constitutional body able to carry it out, namely, the senate. And the emergent power of the plebs remained only emergent.

(2) But there is something more significant to be said about the situation than this.

What we want to know is: (a) How, apart from convenience, could the senate acquire this dominating position so soon after it had suffered a considerable constitutional defeat at the hands of the plebs? And (b) what, in fact, was the composition of the senate in this century of war?

(a) To answer the first of these questions I shall have to open a subject about which there will be a lot more to say later on.

In the Roman way of thinking about politics a firm distinction was made between those who wielded legally authorized 'power' (*potestas*), and those who had 'authority' (*auctoritas*).

Potestas was understood to be specific and definable; it was to hold a particular office and to have the right and the duty to exercise the 'powers' which belonged by law to that office.

Thus, the tribunes had the *potestas* to do what belonged to the office of tribune; and the censor was endowed with the particular *potestas* which belonged to his office.

The consular magistrates were in a slightly freer position; as holders of the *imperium* they exercised a larger and more compelling *potestas* which might on occasion be the *imperium militae* of an army commander in the field; but, even so, it was *potestas* and consequently, in principle, definable. There was, in fact, a law which defined their powers.

On the other hand, *auctoritas* (authority), where it was recognized to be enjoyed, was not limited to any particular sphere of action. Nobody by virtue of having *auctoritas* could command, or make a law; what he could do was to think for himself, to give an opinion or an advice which must be listened to.

Auctoritas meant, not having a narrow sphere of action in which your word was law, but having initiative to think and to deliberate and speak about policy. To have *auctoritas* was precisely not to have *potestas*; and to have *potestas* carried with it no *auctoritas*.

Now, what the patrician senate was recognized to have was, precisely, *auctoritas*. Thus the senate, not only by its procedure, but also by its constitutional character, was less encumbered and less limited than any holder of a *potestas*, even the *potestas* which belonged to the consular *imperium*.

In other words, *potestas* is specific, *auctoritas* is extendable and can grow. And in the circumstances of the time of which I am speaking the *auctoritas senatus* grew tremendously. Before the end of this period of war what had been senatorial 'opinion' and 'advice', given only when asked for by a consul, became senatorial 'decree'.

This is an almost supreme example of duties falling to those who are there and can perform them without any overt or revolutionary change in their character or status.

The declaration of war and peace and the ratification of treaties were matters in which the *populus Romanus* never lost their rights. But it was the senate which settled the terms of peace, which gave audience to foreign ambassadors, which regulated the yearly levies of soldiers, which decreed the annexation of provinces, which controlled supplies, which

considered strategy, which (when a new and more aggres-
sive policy seemed to be called for) dismissed Fabius from
his command and appointed Scipio in his place.

Much of this was done in the form of advice to the consular
magistrates, but it was the senate and not the magistrates
who supplied the initiative.

(b) But what was the composition of a senate which could
wield such 'authority'?

Even before the time of which I am speaking, the senate
had ceased to be a merely hereditary body of patricians. Not
only has a 'nobility' of office appeared beside the old nobility
of blood, but the nobility of blood had become less exclusive
by intermarriage with plebeian families.

In short, the senate had become a body determined to a
significant extent by appointment; the change was not altogether unlike that which has taken place in the House of
Lords during the last fifty years. And a magistrate (called the
censor) had the duty of making appointments to vacancies in
it.

Nor were these vacancies rare; in 216 B.C. in the disaster at
Cannae, more than half the senate was killed on the field of
battle. Moreover, there was by then a well understood order
of preference which the censor was expected to follow in
appointing to the senate.

Thus, the senate, in whose hands was the conduct of policy
at this time, had become more and more a body of ex-magistrates – not merely ex-consuls, but ex-tribunes and ex-hold-
ers of the numerous other magistracies.

So, if it is said that during this period the senate staged a
great 'comeback' from its defeat by the plebs, it must be recognized that it was, in many respects, a new sort of senate
which acquired this dominating position.

2

But wars come to an end; and it is almost a maxim of Roman
political experience that peace and the cessation of danger is
the signal for a renewal of the internal tensions of Roman
politics. There was even a proposal not to destroy Carthage
because war abroad meant the greater chance of peace at
home.

(1) This meant, first, the attempt of the *concilium plebis* to regain the power it had lost during the long supremacy of the senatorial *auctoritas*.

But this, second, great bid for supreme power was also frustrated by circumstances.

The Rome which had come out of this century of war was very different from the Rome which had first defended itself against Carthage. It was the centre and ruler of an immense Mediterranean empire of subject peoples, variously governed.

Outside Italy, this empire was divided into provinces, each with a governor, and each governor was in command of considerable military forces. How were these inevitably powerful governors, the provincial proconsuls, to be controlled? It was a new problem in Roman government.

The *concilium plebis* could hamper and frustrate senatorial control and often did so. But it was utterly incompetent to exercise adequate control itself – and for the same reasons as had made it incompetent to conduct a major war.

The result of this situation was that control over the provincial empire disintegrated; and the disintegration spread to the whole of Roman government.

For half a century Roman politics collapsed into a contest for power, and among these contestants were often successful military commanders from the provinces who returned to Rome with their armies, intent on asserting themselves. It was civil war, not politics.

For a brief period there was some semblance of order under an appointed dictator, named Sulla; but that also collapsed.

(2) Nevertheless, before the Roman republic gave place to a manner of government which, because it was so different, in the end required that a new name should be found for it, there was a final oscillation from one extreme to another.

In 49 B.C., Julius Caesar, the commander of the armies which had just completed the conquest of Gaul, learned that his hopes of appointment to a second period of consulship, and a new command, were likely to be thwarted by his enemies at home. He returned at the head of his veterans and made himself master of Rome by force.

To him the senate was nothing, the *concilium plebis* merely an exasperating survival, and the magistrates fit only to be

his agents. He turned what the Romans had always understood as a temporary expedient – namely, a dictatorship –
into a system of government. He was masterful, and gave
Rome its first taste of genuine autocracy, which lasted five
years.

On the Ides of March 44 B.C. he was assassinated in the
senate-house by patricians who had in their hearts the shadowy ideals of the republic and who hated him as a despot.

Junius Brutus had been the agent by which the Romans rid
themselves centuries earlier of a despotic king, Tarquinius
Superbus; this time it was the hand of Marcus Brutus which
struck for 'liberty': 'liberty' and the restoration of the republic.

But, whatever may have been designed by his assassins,
the death of Caesar did not restore the republic. It was the
signal for renewed civil war, in which revenge for Caesar's
death was added to all the other current political causes.

In this civil war two great figures gradually emerged, commanders of armies: Mark Antony, who made himself master
of the East and took on the habits of a Hellenistic despot; and
Octavian, the great nephew, adoptive son, and designated
heir of Julius Caesar, who held the West as consul and military dictator.

The Roman world was not large enough for these two.
Their armies finally met at Actium, in Greece, in the year 31
B.C. Octavian triumphed, and proceeded at once to re-
conquer the East.

Two years later he entered Rome, greeted as the man who
had restored the sovereignty of Rome over the civilized
world and as the saviour of the republic. The doors of the
temple of Janus were closed for the first time in two hundred
years, signifying that the Roman world was at peace.

3

The authority of Octavian was the prestige of a successful
military commander, and he returned to Rome with the trea-
sures of Egypt, which were lavished upon the *populus*.

His legal position was that of consul – this was the sixth
successive year that he had held the consular *imperium*. The
senate, the *concilium plebis* and the popular assemblies had
survived, though severely battered and demoralized. All the
institutions of the republic were still there.

There were two obvious lessons to be learned from the recent political experience of the Romans.

The first: that merely to 'restore' the republican constitution would be to restore anarchy both in Rome and in the provinces.

The second: that a military dictatorship, like that of Julius Caesar, was intolerable.

Something that was neither the one nor the other had to be generated. And it is a tribute to the political genius of the Romans and to the astuteness of Octavian that in the course of the next forty-four years it was generated.

Moreover, it was generated with remarkable political economy, out of materials which lay ready to hand.

The Romans never indulged in political invention, if they could find among their institutions something suitable to meet the situation.

The new order of government (as it came to be called) which gradually emerged was an immensely subtle rearrangement in which sheer invention played a negligible part. Each phase of the change was unobtrusive because it differed minimally from what had gone before, and nobody could say for certain where the old ended or the new began.

It began, under the renewed consulship of Octavian and Agrippa, with an act of conciliation and oblivion.

Old proscriptions were expunged from the record, ancient enmities were forgotten, arrears of taxation were cancelled, the senate was restored to its ancient dignity, the plebs and the legionaries were rewarded with remarkable indifference to past loyalties, the shrines and temples of the gods were repaired, the irregular enactments of past times were annulled, confidence was restored, and the rate of interest fell from twelve to four percent.

On the first of January 27 B.C., Octavian ceremonially announced his resignation of the extraordinary *potestas* with which he had been endowed less than two years before and (as he said) he 'transferred the *res publica* into the keeping of the senate and the *populus Romanus*.' It was a dramatic move, and the response was equally dramatic.

The senate, with the approval of the popular assembly, forthwith invested Octavian himself, without a partner, for a period of ten years, with the consular *imperium*.

He was given the sole command of all the Roman provinces where there was need of an army (the others remaining within the jurisdiction of the senate); he had sole responsibility for levying troops within the empire, for the declaration of war and peace and for making treaties.

He was to take precedence over all other magistrates, whose nomination was put in his hands.

Thus, firm control was arranged for where it was needed; and the danger of civil war was averted by putting all the legions under the command of one man. No longer could a proconsul from the provinces appear with his army to subjugate Rome.

This was a bold step which might be thought to be in the direction of autocratic government; but it was well within the conventions of Roman republican government.

At the time there were divergent interpretations of what had been done. To some, it appeared as a definitive restoration of republican government; Octavian's position was supreme, but he owed it to the senate and the *populus*; and he held office as a consul. He was, indeed, declared to be the 'champion of the freedom of the *populus Romanus*'.

To others, to the Italian and provincial municipalities, he appeared as 'Caesar', the 'guardian of the Roman *imperium* and the ruler of the world'.

And it was in virtue of this ambiguity that what was to become the new order of government could be launched without opposition or serious misgiving.

The Romans had, in fact, settled for peace and security, and the appearance of republican 'liberty' was saved in the technicality of the manner of Octavian's appointment.

Further, on this same occasion, the name Augustus was conferred upon Octavian, and he was thenceforth known by this title. The name carried with it a vague religious dignity, but what was in men's minds at the time is indicated by the fact that some thought the name Romulus more appropriate than Augustus: he was being connected with a notional refoundation of the Roman state.

4

This, however, was only the beginning of the process in which the new order of government emerged out of the old republic.

Less than four years later, in 23 B.C., Augustus resigned his consular *imperium* and retained only the proconsular *potestas* in virtue of which he governed those provinces of the empire which were under his military command.

The renunciation of the consulship meant the renunciation of authority within the city of Rome itself, of his precedence over other magistrates, his right to convene the popular assembly and to demand advice from the senate. It seemed, in short, to restore a manner of government in which authority at home was separated from authority abroad, which had in the past proved so disastrous.

In their anxiety, the senate and the *populus* pressed upon Augustus various extraordinary powers, including that of dictator for life. All these he refused as unconstitutional. But by a device, which was not here used for the first time in Roman politics, he was offered and accepted 'powers' which, in fact, restored to him everything he had resigned.

The device was that a man might exercise the 'powers' of an office without holding the office itself.

And on this occasion Augustus was invested with the *imperium* of a consul without holding the office of consul (which he had resigned). And when this *imperium* was added to his *imperium* as a proconsul (which he had not resigned) he had powers which no Roman had ever before enjoyed. He had the *imperium militae* of a proconsul, and he was authorized to exercise it *domi*, 'at home', in Rome itself.

To these 'powers' others were added. Without being appointed censor, he was given the 'powers' of a censor; without being appointed *pontifex maximus*, he was given the 'powers' of this office; and without being a tribune, he was given the tribunical *potestas*: and all for life.

Now, all this was constitutionally possible precisely because he did not hold these offices, any one of which would have disqualified him from holding any of the others: a man could not, for example, be a tribune and a consul at the same time.

No office had been terminated, there still remained consuls, tribunes, a censor, and a *pontifex maximus*, but Augustus alone could exercise the *potestas* which belonged to each and all of these offices.

No new powers had been invented, the appearance of 'dictatorship' had been avoided; but an all-powerful ruler had been created by endowing Augustus with all the constitutional 'powers' known to the Roman state.

Without being a 'dictator', in the technical constitutional sense, he was the supreme guardian of the *res publica Romanorum*.

And, as if this were not enough for one man, he was declared *princeps senatus*: 'first senator'.

Now, this might seem an insignificant addition to his position, but in fact it was the most important item of all. He was not the first man in Roman history to be declared *princeps senatus*; but in the case of Augustus what it meant was that besides enjoying the *potestas* which belonged to each of a number of important magistracies, he had also the *auctoritas senatus*. In short, he had everything.

For the first time in Roman history, *potestas* and *auctoritas* were joined in one person. However, as we have seen, although the *potestas* of a magistrate could not increase (it was exactly defined, a matter of law), the *auctoritas* of the senate was something without any exact limits.

In being declared *princeps senatus*, then, Augustus joined *auctoritas* to *potestas* and *imperium* and had acquired absolute supremacy. And from being *princeps senatus* he came to be recognized as *princeps* of the Roman state; and the new order of government acquired the name by which it has ever since been known: the principate.

These, then, were the honours, powers, authority and dignity conferred upon Augustus round about the year 23 B.C. And these were what he enjoyed and exercised for the remaining thirty-six years of his life.

The only significant addition to them came in the year 2 A.D. when he was declared *pater patriae*, 'father of his people'. It was an honorific title (as much religious as political) which, among much else, connected the Roman state with a Roman household and the *princeps* with the *paterfamilias*, and it glanced back to Romulus, the original, founding father of the Roman state.

In virtue of his enjoyment of these powers and authorities, Augustus is commonly thought of as the first Roman emperor, the period of his rule is spoken of as his 'reign', and the principate as the beginning of the imperial government of Rome.

Certainly Augustus was supreme, and his power and authority might properly be thought of as those of an emperor. But he owed every item of his supremacy to the senate and *populus Romanus*; his powers were given him for his sole use and had been expressly renewed and confirmed at intervals during his reign. There was nothing in them which he could bequeath in his will to a successor, as a Hellenistic king could bequeath his kingdom.

Now, the powers and the authority of Augustus must die with him; but, such was the confidence which the new order of government had won, that it seemed clear that there should be somebody able and ready to succeed him.

Nobody doubted, least of all Augustus, that it was the exclusive right of the senate and *populus* to confer such powers; but it was the part of Augustus himself to see that a suitable candidate, versed in the business of government, was available. Whom should he choose? How should he indicate his choice? What steps should be taken to avoid an interregnum and civil war?

In finding a successor, Augustus had bad luck: his first two choices died before they could succeed. In the end Augustus settled for his stepson Tiberius, who had for many years been one of Augustus's colleagues in government and held many of the offices of state.

Tiberius, then, succeeded; and he was invested by the senate and the popular assembly with all the powers and authority they had given to Augustus. Who could not assert that some new system of government had emerged, something comparable to a fresh foundation of the state? And yet who could with confidence assert that the old republican constitution was a thing of the past?

A change had certainly been made; and it was acceptable because nobody new exactly when it had come about, or what had been changed.

5

On the death of Augustus, the political experience of the Roman people had already extended over a period of nearly eight centuries. The major problem that had emerged was that of transforming the government of a city-state into a government appropriate for a vast empire.

A solution to this problem had emerged with Augustus. The Romans had got themselves an emperor – and a characteristically 'Roman' emperor. He was, in character and authority, quite unlike other rulers of empires – oriental despots or Hellenistic kings. He was not a dynast, the Roman empire was far from being his property, his authority was derived neither from conquest *nor* was he surrounded with the myth of divinity.

For some time, indeed for nearly two centuries, the authority of the Roman republican constitution over men's minds was never completely lost. Sometimes it was strong, at others weak; but it can be seen to be gradually dwindling away.

Although the immediate successors of Augustus were a remarkable collection of eccentrics (Tiberius, Caligula, Claudius, Nero) – some of whom were pushed into preeminence by military force and many of whom died by assassination – the path marked out by Augustus was never completely deserted. And it was trodden more exactly by others – like Vespasian, Trajan, Hadrian, and Marcus Aurelius.

Even if no regular and satisfactory method of selecting an emperor was ever devised, the powers he enjoyed were always recognized to be conferred by the senate and *populus*.

The imperial office had, then, been designed to rule an empire and to control the politically dangerous military forces of the empire. The *princeps* was the protector of the Roman state against civil war. This was the principate.

At what point this design began to be seriously modified is difficult to say exactly. In origin it was the firm footprint of Augustus upon circumstance; and each of his successors added their own footprints, not always exactly in the steps of the founder.

But it is commonly understood that the seizure of the imperial power in 192 A.D., 150 years after the death of Augustus, by Septimus Severus, an African general, marks the end of the principate and the beginning of that undisguised autocracy which composes the last three centuries of the political experience of the *populus Romanus* – an experience, not of governing but of being governed.

The rule of these Roman emperors was autocratic, sometimes wise or competent, often negligent and incompetent. They were successful, or not so successful, dynasts. They became surrounded with an aura of divinity, and their power rested upon their command of their armies and upon the faithfulness of their body-guards. The magnificent was mixed with the sordid in their conduct; their word was law.

The last realities of the Roman republican government had long ago disappeared, although the somewhat theatrical relics of patrician dignity remained in Rome.

But it should not be thought that this Roman world was grossly misgoverned under these great autocrats. It enjoyed peace, the *pax Romana*, and (more intermittently) prosperity. The law of Rome gave an orderliness to this world, and Roman citizenship was extended to all who came under their rule. There was more freedom of movement in this empire than there had ever been before in the Roman world.

It was far from being an empire designed by Augustus, but it was far, also, from being a ramshackle empire.

It fell a victim not to the vices and injustices of autocracy but to external forces – a vast and gradually accumulated movement of barbarian peoples over its frontiers, themselves pushed on by others in more distant regions.

It is difficult to imagine any empire with resources adequate to meet and to master this invasion which had been probing the frontiers of the empire from the time of Marcus Aurelius, but the empire of Rome certainly had not got them at its disposal. It was a running engagement which went on, now here and now there, for three centuries.

Peoples known as the Goths and the Vandals, pushed on by the Mongolian Huns, swept over Gaul, into Spain and Africa. And the end, or a sort of end, came in the year 476 A.D. when the city of Rome was captured by the Ostrogoths who established a Gothic kingdom in Italy under Theodoric.

The *civitas Romana*, like the city states of ancient Greece, was, in the end, destroyed by an invasion of foreigners.

There is no way of summing up this political experience of a thousand years.

Later peoples have been fascinated by it because it seemed to contain everything that could possibly happen to a people. No circumstance was absent, and every circumstance met with some kind of response. It is an endless political improvisation, by a conservative people supremely capable of learning from experience.

It left many relics behind. To a significant extent it may be said that the political dwellings European peoples have since lived in have been built out of materials which were left lying about when the political experience of the Romans disintegrated.

But what is more important to us is that this political experience generated a legend of itself in which actions and events acquired poetically universal significance – a legend, unmatched until quite modern times, in which the Romans expressed their beliefs about themselves as a community and about what they were doing in the world. It generated also some notable political sentiments, beliefs, and ideas which gave it a remarkably comprehensive intellectual organization. The philosophical talents of the Romans may have been small; but they certainly did not lack the power to understand their political experience in the idiom of general ideas.

And this is what we must concern ourselves with next.

Editorial Note

LSE 1/1/21, file 3, fos. 185–202. Fos. 185–6 are photocopies of autograph sheets; fos. 187–202 are photocopies of a typescript with autograph corrections.

Thirteen

Roman Political Thought (1)

1

The Romans are always thought of a people memorable for what they did in the world – a race of soldiers, organizers, engineers, colonizers, and rulers. And unquestionably they earned their reputation.

And at the same time they have appeared to be a remarkably 'unintellectual' people, whose thoughts never reached the level of their deeds. It is conceded that there were Roman poets; there were historians and lawyers; but we look in vain for a philosopher – let alone one in the class of the philosophers of Greece.

But, if it is true that they were not much given to intellectual speculative adventures, we should beware of underestimating their powers of thought – especially when it comes to politics.

For, in fact, this empirical-seeming politics of theirs had a remarkably firm and profound intellectual organization.

Any such organization, however deeply it seems embedded in popular sentiment and belief is, of course, the work of writers. But in the case of the Romans, the writers who endowed them with this political self-consciousness were historians, poets, and lawyers, not philosophers.

The manner in which the Romans governed and were governed during the thousand years of their political experience was never turned into a coherent system of abstract ideas. Instead, its intellectual organization was that of a legend in which the events and the fortunes of this remarkable people was endowed with a universal significance by being made to compose a work of art – a drama, or a story, whose moral was always being made explicit in events.

2

I propose to begin with what must be regarded as the central core of this organization of political ideas, namely, the beliefs the Romans had about the sort of community they believed themselves to constitute.

Every people has some beliefs about the kind of community they compose, and usually they are among its more important beliefs.

The Genevan Calvinists of the sixteenth century believed themselves to compose a community engaged in the worship of God; others have used the word 'nation' to denote the sort of community they constitute. Such beliefs are apt to change over the years: recently we seem to have sunk so low as to believe that the community we compose is an 'economy'.

And, of course, one's beliefs about the sort of community one belongs to involve beliefs about the kind of person one is.

In the case of the Romans, it may be said, that over a period of about a thousand years their beliefs about the sort of community they composed did not change very much.

They clustered round the notion of the *populus Romanus*, 'the Roman people', or (as they sometimes said) 'the Roman race'.

We are not, now, concerned with the actual components of this 'people', with where they came from, or with how they emerged upon the scene and what they did. We are concerned with what they came to think about themselves.

The *populus Romanus* was, in fact, the chief, the comprehensive *dramatis persona* of this legend of Roman politics. Everything that happened, happened to the Roman people. Every actor who appeared upon the stage was recognized as a representative of the Roman people. How did they think of themselves?

(1) In this much used expression – *populus Romanus* – there appears, in the first place, the notion of the Romans as composing a single family – both literally and metaphorically.

To think of the Roman people as, literally, a single family entailed some idea of an original progenitor. And the Romans thought of Romulus, not merely as the leader of the mixed collection of Sabines and Latins who settled the seven hills of Rome, and as the founder of a city (*urbs*), and as the creator of the Roman *civitas*, but as the original parent, the 'father', of the Roman people.

Nor was this merely a primitive way of thinking which they grew out of. They took these expressions literally. *Romulus parens*, the Romulus who was the first *pater patriae*, was a figure looked back upon even after centuries of Roman history. In this they are not unique: recall 'father' Abraham.

And later, the supreme figures of Roman politics were thought of, not merely as honorary 'founders' or 'refounders' of the Roman *civitas*, but as honorary progenitors of the *populus Romanus*.

Julius Caesar, for example, was recognized, by those who recognized him to have authority, as *parens* of his people. He was given the title *pater patriae*; his assassins were denoted by the word *parricidia* (murderers of their father); and the Ides of March was 'the day of the parricides'. And when we consider how deeply Caesar was hated, this was going pretty far. Indeed, the Latin expression for a traitor was *parricidium patriae*.

When Octavian was to be honoured with a special *praenomen*, the name Romulus was canvassed, although the name Augustus was chosen.

In short, the Roman manner of expressing profound respect for a man was to attribute to him the character of the progenitor of the Roman race; and the major political crime was identified with the murder of a parent.

But even more significant was the belief that 'the family' was a compelling analogy by which to understand the *communitas* composed by the Roman people. And it is the character of the Roman *familia* which gives point to this analogy.

According to ancient custom, the aristocratic Roman family, which was a household (*domus*) consisting of wife, children, slaves and 'clients' – *clientes* were 'free' dependents, who took the family name and were in the position of 'retainers' who received protection from the family they were associated with and in return gave it their support – was a world ruled by the absolute authority of the *paterfamilias*. At a later stage in Roman history, this absolute authority was limited here and there by law; but, in principle, the 'right' (*jus*) of the *paterfamilias* was absolute except where it was expressly restricted.

He determined the lives and activities of his entire household; the whole family property was in his ownership; he chose husbands for his daughters and wives for his sons; and in early times he enjoyed the *jus vitae necisque*, the right of life and death over his children and slaves.

Now, it is easy to understand what entailments for political thought would follow from taking this 'family' as the model or analogy of the Roman *civitas*. It suggested the notion of governing as an activity which sprang from a 'natural' authority of a 'natural' head: patriarchalism. It suggested a certain sort of relationship between ruler and ruled. And the relationship between the *paterfamilias* and his *clientes* was available to be applied to the relationship between the Roman state and the 'kings' of the Italian tribes which were its first conquests or allies.

Indeed, it may be said that Roman politics was, fundamentally, family politics. Roman political history has often been written in terms of what is called the struggle of the patrician and the plebeian orders, but the real parties in Roman politics were 'family connections', as in eighteenth-century England. A family's 'clients' were its retainers, its political supporters. It is not the so-called politics of family interests; the great Roman families were organizations of opinion about policy, not mere organizations of interests.

In short, to think of the *populus Romanus* as a sort of perpetual family, the patrician elders as its perpetual *patres* gave a specific direction to Roman ideas about government which it never quite lost.[1]

'Government' as a sort of counterpart to the domestic *disciplina* of the Roman family was an idea never far out of sight, though it was also never without qualification.

And this marks the distinction between the Roman and the Greek way of thinking of a political community. All that is most representative of Greek thought expressly rejected the understanding of the *polis* on the analogy of a family or a household.

(2) But besides thinking of themselves as a single family, the *populus Romanus* thought of themselves as a historic *communitas* or 'partnership' which had been composed by a treaty (*foedus*) between tribes and which was held together by a 'treaty' or 'agreement' in which their mutual dependency was recognized.

---

[1] In Oakeshott's hand at this point: 'SPQR', i.e. '*Senatus populusque Romanorum*', the senate and the people of Rome.

If the word *familia* represented the, so to say, poetic unity of the Roman people, the word *foedus* represented the practical operation of this unity. It is almost the notion of a 'contract'.

This notion of their political community being based upon agreement was very ancient: it appeared, for example, in the legend which attributed the foundation of *Alba Longa* to a treaty between the Latin inhabitants of the Alban hills and the immigrant 'Trojans' led by Aeneas. And it might be taken to represent the facts of the case about the founding of the city of Rome.

On the two notable occasions in Roman history (one perhaps legendary, but the other certainly historic), when the *communitas Romanorum* was disrupted by the secession of an important part of it, unity was restored by the renewal of the 'treaty' which was believed to be its foundation.

And, as we shall see, this idea of *foedus* is fundamentally involved in both the Roman religion and the Roman idea of law.

This notion had one supremely important entailment: since the *populus Romanus* was a community founded upon and held together by a 'treaty', therefore the notion of *fides*, of 'keeping faith,' of *bona fides* in the observance of the terms of the treaty, was of unmistakable importance. And so it was: *fides*, 'keeping faith' between partners was a constantly operative idea in the conduct of Roman politics.

And here again there is a divergence from the Greek way of thinking. Aristotle, at least, rejected the idea of a 'treaty' or an 'alliance' as representing the character of the unity of a *polis*. But for many centuries the Roman state revealed itself, and was understood, as an alliance which was not incapable of being disrupted.

The Romans had, what the Athenians never had, namely the notion that they composed a civil association. What united them was *not* engagement in a common enterprise, but respect for the *mos majorem*, ancient customs, and respect for the *law*. And this law was *not* thought of as the organization of an enterprise, but as the terms in which they kept faith with one another. And this is what I mean by a civil association.

So far, then, we may suppose the Romans to think of one another as 'brothers' and as 'partners', rather than (as Aris-

totle said the members of a *polis* should think of themselves)
as 'friends'.

(3) The *populus Romanus* was, then, both a 'family' and a
'partnership'. But further, it was essentially a *sacred* partnership – a *communio sacrorum*, a partnership in the performance
of sacred rites. And this takes the relationship of Roman to
Roman to a deeper level.

Soon I shall have something more to say about the Roman
religion, but for the moment we may observe (a) that the
Roman family was itself understood to be a religious community; it had gods of its own and the head of the family, the
paterfamilias, was the 'priest'. And (b) that the original legal
qualification for belonging to the *populus Romanus* was membership in one of the *curiae* or 'parishes' into which Romulus
is reputed to have organized his followers. And a *curia* was a
local community which had a place of worship and religious
rites and festivals of its own.

In an important sense the *populus Romanus* was a *curia* (a
religious society) composed of *curiae* (religious guilds). Politics never ceased to have an element of religious ritual.

(4) Further, and perhaps not without some contradiction of
what I have already said, the *populus Romanus* was a people
with a 'purpose' in the world, a 'destiny', a *fortuna*; and it was
held together and united in the pursuit of this 'purpose'. In
this respect they were 'comrades'.

How early this notion imposed itself upon the Romans is
difficult to say, but it was already strong in early republican
times. Nor is it easy to say exactly what they thought this
destiny to be.

Early, it was, no doubt, a reflection of their success in
remaining whole and in having overcome the forces which
made for disintegration – a reflection of the feeling of being
blessed by the gods.

Later it certainly became a much more precise idea – the
idea of their destiny to rule the world and impose a civilization and an orderliness upon its barbarisms. But the important thing was that it was thought of as the destiny of the
Roman people. It carried them through every defeat and they
found it confirmed in every victory.

And it was from this belief in the destiny of the Roman
people that the much later idea of the 'eternal' and indestructible city of Rome emerged.

The politics of Rome is the politics of a 'chosen people' who, more fortunate than the ancient Hebrews, were never brought so low as to doubt their 'destiny'. What broke the force of this idea was *not* defeat, but the extension of Roman citizenship by Caracalla to all the subjects of the Roman government. The belief that they were a 'chosen people' was destroyed by dissipating their sense of family solidarity.

(5) Lastly, the fortunes of Roman arms, the extension of Roman power, the achievements of Roman civilization over this period of a thousand years, were always thought of as the fortunes and the achievements of the *populus Romanus*. It was the history, not of Rome, but of the Roman people.

Roman rulers, magistrates, consuls, proconsuls, military commanders, emperors – these were the agents of the destiny of the *populus Romanus*. Roman rule in the world was the *imperium populi Romani*, and the emperor was *custos imperi Romani*.

This, then, was the cluster of related ideas which gathered round the expression *populus Romanus*, and together constituted the terms of Roman political self-consciousness.

3

I want, now, to take up the theme of the *populus Romanus* as a 'religious' community, and say something about the religious beliefs of the Roman people as they enter into their political beliefs.

With the early Romans, as with most emergent political societies, religion and politics, although they may be distinguished, were inseparable activities. Moreover, this was not a feature of Roman history which gradually receded.

In the course of centuries, the relationship between these two activities changed, but they never sprang apart. And yet Roman government was never at any time properly to be described as 'theocratic'; and both Roman religion itself and its relationship to politics were significantly different from anything that appeared in a Greek *polis*.

(1) The Latin word *religio* was understood, by Cicero and others, to be connected with the verb *ligare*, which means to 'tie' or to 'bind'. Thus, it signified the condition of being 'bound' or 'obliged', and the activities which belong to this condition. Hence, religious observances were thought of as the recognition and celebration of a sacred 'bond'.

In earliest times, this 'bond' was the obligation which tied a present generation to its forebears.

Religion centred in the family; it celebrated the sanctities of hearth and home. It was a worship and consultation of ancestors in which the current *paterfamilias* was the officiating priest.

The human disposition it generated and expressed was *pietas* – the veneration, the love and the loyalty of children to parents, alive or long dead.

But when the religious feelings and beliefs of the Romans came to be centred in the larger 'family' of the *populus Romanus* itself, the emotion of *pietas* was directed towards the gods of the new *domus*, the *civitas*, and towards the progenitors and founders of this 'family'.

The custodians of the *sacra*, the priests, of this *communitas Romanorum* were the counterparts of the *paterfamilias* – namely, kings and their partners in ruling.

And in the early history of Rome, King Numa (as his name indicates) was recognized as a preeminent holder of this office of priest-king. After Romulus had founded the city, it is Numa who was reputed to have impressed upon its inhabitants their sense of being a religious community.

Now, the gods of the Romans were local inhabitants, and every human activity had its own providential god.

Unlike the gods of Greece (who were limited in number, who had a home of their own on Mount Olympus and who made only occasional excursions into the human world), the gods of the Romans actually inhabited the temples in which they were worshipped, and perpetually watched over, not only the fortunes of the Roman people, but every activity of every Roman.

It was, then, the preeminent office of the ruler to preserve what the Romans called the *pax deorum* – the 'peace of the gods' – which was the good relations between the *populus Romanus* and its gods.

And these good relations were thought of as a 'treaty' (*foedus*) between gods and men, in which men were bound to reverence, and the gods (in return) to promote good fortune. Thus, *religio* (being bound, by a treaty), *pietas* (reverence), and *fides* (keeping faith) were ideas which belonged together.

(2) Politics, then, the pursuit of policy, was, in the first place, a religious activity. It entailed always, as a preliminary to

action, a process of ascertaining whether what was proposed was in accordance with the will of the gods.

This process was called *auspicium*, divination of the will of the gods by the observation of the flight of birds.

Rex and *augur*, the ruler and the man who had the prerogative of *auspicium*, were joined in a single person, because the chief office of *rex*, one that no other man could perform, was to preserve the *pax deorum* upon which the success of human enterprise depended.

The first *rex* of the Romans was the founder of the Roman *civitas*, Romulus. And all the ceremonies of 'augury' in the subsequent long history of the Roman people were traced back to that never-forgotten legendary occasion when Romulus sought the blessing and approval of the gods for the enterprise of founding the city of Rome, and received it when twelve vultures appeared.

Moreover, this right of *auspicium* was believed to be so overwhelmingly important that there had to be some understood manner in which it was handed on from one *rex* to another in an unbrokered transmission.

Thus it was believed that, between the death of one *rex* and the succession of the next, the custodian of this right was the senate – that body of 'patricians' whom Romulus was reputed to have appointed to be his partners in government, and which (while of course mortal in its members) as a body never died.

And the religious character which was attached to the pursuit of policy was attached also to legislation. The legal arrangements of the Roman state were in the care and custody of the gods.

(3) This identity of religion and politics was never seriously modified during the course of Roman history. But in republican times certain distinctions emerged.

When there was no longer a 'king', the priest-like functions of the former kings were performed by a *rex sacrorum*, a 'king' of the sacred things. And the rights and duties of men in respect of the gods were distinguished from the rights and duties of men in respect of one another: the *jus divinum* was distinguished from the *jus humanum*.[2]

---

[2]   In Oakeshott's hand at this point: 'cp. The distinction between "god palaver" & "man palaver"'.

Nevertheless, some of the earliest politico-religious beliefs of the Romans survived to the time of the emperors. What is called 'caesar worship,' the worship of the emperor as a god (which alone of their civil duties Christians refused to perform), is to be understood as a survival of this sort, and not as a degenerate bowing and scraping to an autocrat.

The ordinary *paterfamilias*, as we have seen, could at death be said to become divine (*divus*) and even a god (*deus*); and the part of him which was believed to survive death (namely, his *genius* or 'spirit') was an object of family worship as *deus parens*.

And the difference between a caesar, an emperor, and an ordinary man was not that a caesar was reputed to be divine and a god and the ordinary man not, but that the *genius* of the ordinary man became a private and family god and the *genius* of a caesar became a public god, a god of the 'family' of the *populus Romanus* and publicly worshipped.

The divinity of a caesar was, therefore, a counterpart of an emperor being recognized as *parens* of his people, *pater patriae* corresponding to the *paterfamilias*.

And when Vespasian said on his deathbed, 'Dear me, I must be turning into a god', he said no more than any dying *paterfamilias* might have said without any tinge of blasphemy. Nevertheless, there was something a little novel when (as happened in the second century A.D.) emperors were worshipped during their lifetime.

It was a novelty learned from the near theocracies of the Hellenistic kings and was more prevalent in the Greek provinces of the empire than in Rome itself. But it can be recognized as a corruption of something that had belonged to Roman religion from earliest times.

(4) *Religio*, then, for the Roman stood for the obligations which 'bound' him to his gods and to his ancestors.

But politically the most significant feature of *religio* was that it stood for a profound, pious, and 'binding' attachment to the great event in which the *populus Romanus* itself emerged, namely the foundation of the city of Rome and the Roman state by Romulus.

All the sanctity which gathered round the hearth and home of the *familia* was transferred to this new 'public' home of the Romans, the city of Rome. And their overwhelmingly religious duty was to preserve what Romulus had founded.

In the Greek world there were innumerable cities and each was a new and independent foundation; in the Roman world there were no new independent foundations, there was only one Rome and the dependent municipalities of the empire.

Indeed, the 'destiny', the 'mission' of the *populus Romanus* was, precisely, to make Rome immortal; and they sought the authority for every enterprise in this original sacred foundation. They dated every event in their history from the year of foundation, *anno urbis conditur*.

Some peoples have looked back to an 'original constitution' and believed it to be their destiny to remain faithful to it. There is something of this feeling in modern America.

But the Romans had no such 'constitution'. What they looked back to, and were 'bound' to, in *pietas* and *fides*, was the event of 'foundation' and the 'founding father', Romulus.

And this, perhaps, is only another facet of the fundamental ancestor worship of Roman religion; turning it, in this case, from an ordinary 'natural' religion, common to many peoples, into an 'historic' religion unique to themselves – a religion which had a specific historical beginning, a sacred moment in time, and was not merely a reflection of the mysteriousness of natural processes.

The Romans, then, may be recognized as a profoundly religious people. Their religion was never elaborated into a theology worth the name. It was a religion of feeling and conduct, a practical faith which kept pace with great social and political changes, and always remained the centre of their self-identity as a people and as a state.

The Roman religion was the energy of Roman politics; and Roman politics was the reflection of Roman religion.

Thus, as might be expected, when, under the rule of autocratic emperors, the vigour ebbed from Roman politics, the religion also lost its vitality.

From the first century B.C., the old Roman religion was on its way out. It was undermined by skepticism; and from this time the Roman empire was invaded by the popular religious cults of the East, the most powerful of which was the religion of Mithras.

Nevertheless, this ancient Roman religion reasserted itself in a remarkable manner in the adoption of Christianity by the rulers of Rome.

And, on any reading of it, this was a tremendous achievement. For Christianity began by being, in Rome, a religion of the lower classes, even the slaves – all those whose share in the religious rites of the Romans was peripheral because a worship of ancestors can make only an indirect appeal to those who have no ancestors and no ancestral homes.

(5) Round about the year 30 A.D., the rulers of Rome began to observe closely the appearance of a new religious sect in the empire, which they had earlier discounted and tolerated, having mistaken it for a Judaic sect.

This sect, whose members called themselves 'Christians', was suspected of treasonable activities and was identified as being politically dangerous.

From the time of the emperor Nero (64 A.D.) there began a long period during which Christians were alternately persecuted and neglected; and during this period the sect grew in numbers and spread itself throughout the empire.

Then, at the end of the second century, Diocletian made a determined attempt to eradicate it. This attempt failed; and it was followed by a policy of toleration, first announced by Constantine (himself a convert) in the so-called edict of Milan in 313 A.D.

In the course of the next fifty years, toleration turned into favour; and then, in 378 A.D. under Theodosius, Christianity was adopted as the official religion of the empire.

The old Roman religion was proscribed, its priests dispossessed, its temples turned into museums, and even the Roman calendar, in which dates had always been calculated from the year of the foundation of Rome and which recorded the festivals of the old Roman religion, was abolished. In its place appeared a calendar based upon Christian festivals, and beginning from *anno domini* – 'the year of the Lord'.

The Roman state, by an imperial edict, had placed itself under the aegis of the god of the Christians.

Of course, relics of the old Roman religion remained for centuries to come; and, indeed, embedded themselves in Christian belief and practice. To this day, in the remotest parts of Calabria, the distinction between Diana and the Virgin Mary is far from certain. But, on any estimate of its effect, this edict constituted a remarkable revolution.

Perhaps it may be regarded as the decisive event which marked the end of the Roman political experience; this, and not the fall of Rome to the Ostrogoths a century later.

Of course, it was not intended to be the end. It was an attempt to give a renewed sanctity to the Roman state in what appeared at the time to be the current idiom of sanctity. It was an alliance with the 'god' who had proved himself to be 'the most powerful god'.

Nor would it have been possible if Christianity had not already acquired features of a profoundly 'Roman' character. Christians by that time were no longer a sect of believers notable for their indifference to what went on in the world, and above all to politics and public affairs.

They constituted a church, organized on a Roman pattern and endowed by law with special 'immunities'. It was a church with a hierarchy of officers, elders, and priests, and a diocesan organization geared into the Roman civil administration.

Moreover, many of the current beliefs about the church reflected Roman ideas. It was a church believed to have been 'founded' in a manner not remotely different from the legendary foundation of Rome itself. And there was an attachment to this 'foundation' at least as strong as the attachment to this 'foundation' of Rome. The authority of its current leaders was based upon the authority of its founder.

There was, further, a profound belief in the authority of the foundation, an authority handed on, from generation to generation, in an unbroken transmission – not at all unlike the handing on of the right of *auspicium* by the undying senate.

But in order to make the Christian church of the third century an adequate religious foundation for the Roman state, one thing remained to be done. This church was rent by divergent doctrines and practices, and it was necessary to impose upon it an orthodoxy of belief and practice. This was achieved in the great church councils of the period, and it was achieved under pressure from the Roman imperial government. The unity of the Christian church was a Roman and a political achievement. Indeed, it was the emperors themselves who summoned the councils of the church. And when they had shed the divine attributes which the old Roman religion had given them, they acquired priestly attributes in the Christian church. If the Christian church could be said to have a 'head' in the fourth century A.D., it was the emperor.

The design of Theodosius was, then, to reunite the empire by allying it with the strongest current idiom of religious belief. But the effect of this policy was something different from the design.

For the Christian church already had an independent organization of its own, and it was impossible at the stroke of a pen to turn its priests into the servants of the state which the priests of the old Roman indigenous religion had been.

In short, the adoption of Christianity as the official religion of the empire introduced a tension between religion and politics which had never before existed. Religion and politics were no longer a single activity. If they did not automatically pull in different directions, at least the possibility that they might do so had appeared.

Bishops were appointed by emperors, and were often the civil governors of Roman municipalities; and the ecclesiastical and municipal organizations were often difficult to distinguish. But the great bishops, like Ambrose of Milan, regarded themselves as the critics, not the servants, of emperors.

If, then, one understands the political experience of the Roman people as the fortunes and achievements of a people who conceived themselves as guided by a religious destiny to rule and civilize the world, then, I think there are *two* important points at which a discordant note is struck.

(1) The extension of Roman citizenship to all subjects of the Roman government. This, so to speak, dissipated, or began to dissipate, the notion of a 'chosen people'.

(2) The adoption of Christianity and the termination of the absolute unity of religion and politics, the last emblem of which had been the worship of the emperors themselves, although the discord struck by this note was profoundly qualified by the *Roman* character which Christian belief and the organization of the Christian church had acquired.

The important change here was not the spread of Christian moral sentiments, somewhat different from those characteristic of Roman civilization, but the appearance of a religion which had an organization at least potentially independent of the civil organization of the state.

Editorial Note

LSE 1/1/21, file 3, fos. 203–17. Fos. 203–12, 214–17 are photocopies of a typescript with autograph corrections; fo. 213 is a photocopy of an autograph sheet.

Fourteen

Roman Political Thought (2)

1

Last week we considered two features of the organizing sentiments, beliefs, and ideas of the Roman political experience:

- What the Romans thought about themselves as a people, and the analogies they used when thinking about the community they believed themselves to compose;
- The religious beliefs which informed and shaped this political experience.

This morning I want to consider the family of related beliefs which, for the Romans, represented their understanding of government, the activity of governing, and the experience of being governed.

2

In this connection the first expression we have to consider is *res publica*. This is not an easy expression to translate. It is of, course, singular, not plural. Literally it means 'the public thing', or 'the public concern'.

It is sometimes translated 'the state'. But this is a little off-centre. The Romans had a word for 'state' – the word *civitas* – which stood for the political community, founded by Romulus, to which all Romans belonged.

Res publica, on the other hand, stood for the 'concern' or the 'affair' in which all Romans believed themselves to be united: the *public* activity of the *populus Romanus*.

Now, the Romans recognized (as most settled communities recognize) a distinction between things which, in some sense or other, may be said to be 'publicly owned' and those which were privately owned. There were the *res publicae* (like roads and harbors), the owner of which was recognized to be the *populus Romanus* (or, as modern Americans would say, 'the people'); it is not a matter of chance that American politics is shot through with expressions that come from Roman politics; the founding fathers had clearly before them the republican constitution of Rome. And there were the *res privatae*, things which were in private ownership.

And further, there were *res communes*, which were things (such as the air, the sea and running water) of which nobody was the owner.

But what distinguishes the expression *res publica* is that it denotes a *political* distinction between 'public' and 'private'. It indicates a notion, not of 'public ownership' contrasted with 'private ownership', but 'public concern' contrasted with 'private concern'.

Res publica was the common, or public, activity or concern of the *populus Romanus*. It was sometimes called, simply, *res Romana*: the Roman concern.

We have noticed, among the Greeks, a distinction between public and private – particularly a distinction between a public place (the *agora*) and a private place (the household). But it was nowhere near as clear and precise as the Roman distinction. 'Public' meant for the Roman very much what it means for us – namely, that which is the concern of, and that which affects all members of, a community indifferently and none in particular.

Now, government was understood, precisely, as the care and custody of *res publica*, the public concern in terms of which all Romans were united. And the 'ruler', whoever he might be, or whatever the name given to his office, was the custodian of the *res publica Romana*.

In these circumstances, it is not difficult to understand how, on different occasions and by different people, this *res publica Romana* might be recognised narrowly as 'the immediate concern' of the Roman people, or widely and more profoundly as the destiny or *fortuna* of the Roman people.

'Public policy' might appear narrowly, in fighting off an enemy or in making a treaty or in a piece of legislation (such as the law which permitted marriage between plebeian and patrician), or in a wider interpretation as pursuing the *fortuna* of the Roman people.

Thus, the Romans recognized a distinction between 'public' and 'private', between 'public law' and 'private law', which the Athenians never quite managed to make.

In virtue of this distinction the Roman *communitas* may be said to have been not only a political community (which Athens certainly was) but also a civil community: that is a community which recognized itself as private individuals or families joined together in the enjoyment of rights and duties in respect of one another. Private persons having not merely 'private', contractual relations with one another, but also 'public' relations with one another.

This is the sort of community we should be at home in; we also live in a civil as well as a political society. We recognise private as well as public law. But Athens was a community of a different sort; one which is much more difficult for us to understand.

Now, we have seen that governing, the care and custody of the *res publica*, for the Romans was understood to be, in the first place, a religious activity: winning and maintaining the favour of the gods for the public enterprise, endeavours, and activities of the *populus Romanus*.

But under this aura of religion and dependence upon the gods, the Romans understood the activity of governing to be a mixture of what may be called 'the exercise of initiative' and the exercise of often great but always exactly and legally defined 'powers'.

A mixture of what they called 'authority', *auctoritas*, and 'legal power', *potestas*, a mixture between 'leading' and 'administration'. And we must understand what they meant by these two words, *auctoritas* and *potestas*.

3: *Auctoritas*

(1) As an abstract noun, the word *auctoritas* stood for the qualities which belonged to an *auctor*. And an *auctor* was a man who originated something – an author, a creator, a founder, or a progenitor.

Consequently, *auctoritas* meant having the quality or characteristic of 'inventiveness' or 'initiative', or of being the source, or cause, or origin of something.

Thus, *auctor* and *auctoritas* were words which could be used in connection with a number of different activities, such as writing a book, designing a building, inventing a machine, or even setting going a course of events.

We are interested in it when it was used in connection with human activities which entail a relationship between a man (said to be an *auctor*) and other men.

(2) The simplest, and probably the most primitive, appearance of this idea of being an *auctor* and having *auctoritas* was in connection with a family.

The 'founder' of a family, its original progenitor (so far as recorded history is concerned), was its *auctor*. (Thus, in one image of the human race, not of course a Roman image, Adam would be recognized as its *auctor*; indeed, Adam is thought of, by Augustine for example, as 'the author of all our misery'. And the Israelites looked back to 'father' Abraham as their preeminent *auctor* or progenitor.)

But, if *auctoritas* is, supremely, the quality of the reputed progenitor of a family, every *paterfamilias* in his own generation must be understood to have a share of this quality of being an *auctor*.

He displays his *auctoritas* in 'carrying on', 'increasing', 'augmenting' what the original progenitor, or *auctor*-in-chief, began or 'founded'. And he derives his *auctoritas* from being the current and temporary successor of the founder.

Both *auctor* and *auctoritas* derive from the verb *augere*, which meant to 'increase', to 'enlarge', to 'augment', or 'to add luster to'. Thus, in a family, *auctoritas* is handed on in an unbroken, legitimate transmission, there being no doubt *who* is, in any generation, its current holder, namely, the *paterfamilias*. He has a 'natural' authority over his family.

(3) Now, we have seen the powerful pull of the analogy of the family upon Roman political thought; and it is a short step from *auctoritas* in the *familia* to *auctoritas* in connection with the *populus Romanus* and *res publica*.

The founding father of Rome was Romulus.[1] In the legend his ancestry was not neglected – the son of a vestal virgin (herself the niece of a chieftain) and Mars. But so far as Rome and the *populus Romanus* were concerned he was the *auctor*, the historic progenitor, and therefore the possessor of a natural *auctoritas*.

Whoever, in the later political history of Rome, was understood to have *auctoritas* was believed to derive it from Romulus and his 'foundation'.

And the activity of every subsequent *auctor* was to 'increase', to 'enlarge', to 'add luster to', to 'augment' this original 'foundation'. 'Authority' in the living always derived from the original *auctor*, the founder of Rome.

Thus, anyone recognized to have *auctoritas* bore a special relationship to the *populus Romanus*, and had a special activity to perform in relation to *res publica*.

---

[1] Oakeshott's marginal note: 'Founder of the "family fortunes"'.

For there to be no contemporary representative of *auctoritas* in the Roman state would have been recognized as a break with the original foundation which would be the equivalent of the destruction of everything that belonged to *res Romana*.

(4) Our questions, then, are: (a) What was understood to be the exact relationship of *auctoritas* to *res publica* and the *populus Romanus*? (b) Who was understood to have *auctoritas*? and, How was it acquired? (c) What was believed to be the proper attitude of the *populus Romanus* towards *auctoritas* and its possessors?

(a) The relationship between an *auctor* and the *populus Romanus* was, fundamentally, a tutorial relationship: to exercise *auctoritas* was to advise, to give guidance, and to educate.

And in relation to *res publica*, what was to be expected from those who were recognized to have *auctoritas* was, *not* command and executive direction, but reflective advice and the sort of initiative in policy-making which could be supplied by men steeped in the *traditio* which joined the present generation to its roots in the original foundation.

Thus *auctoritas* was an activity at once limited in its inspiration and totally unlimited in its range; and, as the Romans thought of it, it supplied something indispensable for the care and custody of *res publica*.

It was a spring of political initiative, not a reservoir of political power; for, to have *auctoritas* was, precisely, *not* to have power (*potestas*); it was to be a teacher, not a commander.

No state could be ruled by *auctoritas*, but a state without *auctoritas* (although it might be orderly and well-arranged) would be only devoid of any sense of direction on account of being cut off from the 'tradition' which flowed from its 'foundation'.

(b) Now, the Roman had no doubt that whoever had *auctoritas* acquired it from some connection, direct or indirect, he had with the original *auctor* of the Roman *civitas*.

This connection must be historical, but the evidence of *auctoritas* might appear in certain observable personal characteristics.

Among these characteristics, some giving more convincing proof than others, were age, birth, force of character, actual achievement, and a recognizable but indefinable 'wisdom' in counsel.

Of these characteristics, 'age' was the simplest and the most significant. But the elderly were considered to have *auctoritas*, not because their opinions might be supposed to be 'mature', but because to be old was to be nearing the time when one becomes an 'ancestor' and might be supposed (having, so to speak, one foot in the grave) to be in direct communication with the founding fathers.

But, however surely a Roman might believe himself able to detect *auctoritas* in the face and bearing of a man, the main evidence that he possessed *auctoritas* was his historical or notional-historical connection with the foundation of Rome.

Now, Romulus had, reputedly, chosen a hundred of the heads of the most distinguished families of early Rome to be his counselors, and this was the reputed origin of the senate.

And the senate, being composed of *patres*, the 'fathers' of the *populus Romanus*, was recognized as the preeminent possessor of *auctoritas*.

This historical connection with the original *auctor* was, of course, weakened by the passage of time and by the changes which took place in the composition of the senate; although a senate composed chiefly of ex-magistrates could still appear as a repository of political wisdom, and thus of initiative.

But the attribution of *auctoritas* to the senate was unmistakably confirmed by its behavior over the centuries of Roman history.

Even at those times, usually times of war, when the senate came near to governing Rome, it *never* pretended to executive power (except, perhaps, in the appointment of army commanders), and it worked always through giving advice and guidance to the consular magistrates.

The right of the senate was the right to be heard and not interrupted when it gave advice; but its advice could be ignored.

And, further, by attributing *auctoritas* to the senate, the Romans acquired the confidence that it was perpetually available to them: the senate never dies, and it is perpetually in session.

During the republic, then, the answer to the question, *Who has auctoritas?* was, unquestionably, the senate.

But, as the republican constitution was gradually modified by Augustus, *auctoritas* was acquired by the *princeps* himself, although it was not lost by the senate. And the notable characteristic of the *princeps* was that, for the first time in

Roman history, senatorial *auctoritas* was joined by magisterial *potestas* in a single office.

But, at least so far as Augustus was concerned, *auctoritas* and *potestas* were never confused. He had *auctoritas* in virtue of being recognised as 'Augustus', as *pater patriae* and as *princeps senatus*, but his *potestas*, his executive power, came from a quite different endowment, which we will consider in a moment.

There was one other set of people in the Roman state who, in later times, were also recognized to have *auctoritas*; namely, the jurisconsults.

These were the learned writers on the law, who had no magisterial office but who (after the desuetude of the office of *pontifex maximus*) were recognized as both custodians and interpreters of the law.

At first they were scholars who were consulted on account of their learning; but later, under Augustus, they were formed into a 'college' of jurisconsults and given official status.

And, appropriately, since what a jurisconsult did was to give an 'opinion' about the law, or an 'interpretation' of it, he was said to have *auctoritas*. He was not a judge, deciding a case, but a man 'learned' in the law.

(c) Lastly, the appropriate attitude towards *auctoritas* was the attitude appropriate towards an *auctor*; namely, *reverentia*, 'respect' and 'deference'.

He was *not* a ruler who commanded obedience, or a legislator who laid down a rule; he was a guide to be consulted and whose opinion should be listened to in all that pertained to *res publica*.

(5) In *auctoritas*, then, the Romans translated what they believed to be an indispensable feature of political activity into the idiom of a general idea: namely, the necessity for reflection about the conduct of public affairs.

But what we have to try to understand is that Roman politics was *not*, what it often is for us, and what it was for the Athenians, an open-ended activity governed by imagined and sought-for desirabilities still to be enjoyed; it was the exploration of the intimations of an original foundation.

Roman politics, understood to be the exploration of the intimations of an original foundation, required an understood and an unbroken connection with that foundation and its *auctor*; and this was supplied, first in the *auctoritas senatus*, and later in the *auctoritas* attributed to the *princeps*.

What, in politics, the Roman asked himself was *not* will this policy or this change in the law have a desirable outcome, *but* is it congruent with the *mos maiores*, the ancient customs of the original foundation to which the *populus Romanus* belongs.

And the bearer of *auctoritas*, the man whose words should be listened to, was recognized to be the custodian of the *mos maiores* of the Roman people and therefore as the guardian of the unchanging standards of conduct which should guide political activity.

Auctoritas was the word the Romans used to denote what they believed to be one of the essential ingredients of government. What it supplied was, *not* merely counsel in connection with *res publica*, but insight into the *fortuna*, the destiny and the traditions of the Roman people, without which no policy could be formulated or successfully pursued.

And, when it is properly understood, *auctoritas* may be recognized as a uniquely Roman idea. It had no proper counterpart in the political ideas of the ancient Greeks.

Authority is defined, *not* in terms of the quality of its acts, but in terms of a procedure of authorization.

4: *Potestas*

Now, to guide, to advise, to admonish, to teach, to provide that connection with the past which endows a people with a sense of their own identity – to do all or any of this, is *not* to 'rule'.

And as the Romans understood it, government, strictly speaking, was *not* the exercise of *auctoritas*, but the exercise of *potestas*.

Potestas we translate as 'power'; but it must be understood that what it stands for is legal or rightful power. It is *not* 'physical power' – the Latin language has another word for that: *potentia* – it is the exercise of legally acquired *potentia*: the *right* to rule.

(1) More exactly, the word *potestas* (in connection with government) stood for the rights and duties which belonged to each of the specified offices of state.

Each office was, in fact, the right and the duty to do certain things; and these rights and duties were legally defined.

On taking up an office the holder would swear an oath to perform the duties of his office exactly and according to law and precedent; and if he were to go beyond this he would be guilty of an illegality for which he might be brought to book at the end of his term. For no office (at least under the republic) was held for more than a specified period of time.

There were many different offices; and during the republic they were greatly multiplied. A position such as that of tribune, which began by being informal, when it was turned into an 'office' was understood as the exercise of a definable *potestas*.

For example, the tribunical *potestas* was, at first, the right to intercede on behalf of a member of the plebeian class if it seemed that he had been unjustly treated by magistrate or senate; and later, it became the right to summon the *concilium plebis*, to put propositions before it, to take a vote and to pass this *plebiscitum* on to the consular magistrate.

Government, then, when it was thought of as the exercise of *potestas*, was an activity distributed between a great number of different offices each with exactly defined 'powers'.

But *all* the rights and duties which pertained to *all* the different current officers of state could be thought of as composing a finite total, and this sum represented the total *potestas* available to be used in government – the total amount of legally authorized power available to the community.

The *potestas* belonging to one office would, of course, be different from that belonging to another: a censor, a consul, and a tribune each had different rights and duties.

But, besides being different, the *potestas* of one office might be recognizably greater or less than that of another: 'dictatorship', for example, was an emergency office to which extraordinary powers belonged; but these extraordinary powers were 'powers' which already belonged to different offices – 'dictatorship' was a composite office; it did not add to the sum total of *potestas*.

And further, the *potestas* of a particular office might vary with different circumstances. For example, the Romans made a very important distinction between the *potestas* to be exercised by an office holder within the city of Rome itself and the *potestas* he could exercise abroad. The military commander of a Roman garrison had far less power over his soldiers than he had over the same soldiers in the field.

This way of thinking enabled the Romans to make an important distinction, which we have already noticed: a distinction between the office itself and the *potestas* which defined it.

In virtue of this distinction they were able to think of a man exercising the *potestas* which belonged to two or more offices while not holding the offices themselves – which in most cases it would be illegal to hold concurrently.

Thus, Augustus was successively endowed with the *potestas* of a consul, of a proconsul, of a tribune, and of a censor, and, in consequence, wielded an amount of *potestas* hitherto unknown for a single man, who had not been appointed a 'dictator', to wield.

Indeed, in theory, the *princeps* was simply a man who not only had the *auctoritas senatus* (though without depriving the senate itself), but also the *potestas* which belonged to all the important offices of state, and to hold it for life. He appeared as supreme guide and ruler of the *populus Romanus*.

Thus, the Romans could recognize the imperial office as constituting no increase in the total *potestas* in the state, but merely as gathering together in one office all the hitherto dispersed *potestas*.

(2) Now, there was one kind of *potestas* distinguished from all others by reason of its magnitude and importance: it was called *imperium*.

This word had a long history, and in the end was used to signify something which simply did not exist when it first joined the political vocabulary of the Romans. Under the republic, *imperium* normally stood for the *potestas* of a military commander; that is, his power over his army. But, since in republican days, one or both of the consular magistrates might (on the outbreak of war) be given command of an army, *imperium* was not infrequently added to the consular *potestas* for the period of a campaign or of a war.

And when he marched out of Rome at the head of his army, and when the *pomerium* (the boundary of the city) was passed, he put on a red toga signifying that from that moment he exercised the *imperium militae*, which, needless to say, was far greater than any consul possessed within the city.

But, at a later stage in Roman history, there were other circumstances, besides those of actual warfare, when *potestas* equal to that of the *imperium militae* was believed to be necessary or appropriate.

The governor of a province, called a proconsul, was endowed the proconsular *imperium* – a *potestas* far greater and more embracing than that which belonged to any consular magistrate in Rome itself.

And it was an extreme step to endow a man with 'dictatorial' *imperium* at home; this was never done except in great emergency and then only for a very limited period of time.

Nevertheless, war, emergency, and the government of conquered peoples made the Romans acquainted with offices to which belonged extraordinary powers. And, I suppose, in a speculative sort of way, the *potestas* which was called *imperium* was thought of as simply a very large proportion of (perhaps, in some cases, the total) *potestas* available to be used in government.

But the most important practical consequence was that there were offices which carried with them so much power (designed to be used only in particular circumstances) that it was more difficult for a man who used them out of place to appear as a monster of oppression. He was, indeed, only using recognizably legal powers – but not quite in the right place.

Julius Caesar returning from Gaul, and setting up a dictatorship in Rome by military force, could be identified as a man, no doubt behaving unconstitutionally, but *not* unrecognisably: he was exercising the proconsular *imperium* (with which he had been endowed) but exercising it in Rome instead of in Gaul.

And when it was thought necessary to endow a man with very great power in Rome itself, the model was there to be followed: he could be given the proconsular *imperium*. Thus, a proconsul was a man who, as governor of a province of Rome, normally had far greater *potestas* than a consul at home. It was when this proconsular *imperium* was added to all the other bits of *potestas* given to Augustus that he became a genuinely supreme ruler, and for life.

Imperium, then, began by signifying that great exercise of extraordinary *potestas* which was entailed in pursuing the destiny of Rome in a military campaign.

(3) But with Augustus the word *imperium* began to be used in a different manner. It no longer meant merely 'rule' or

'government'; it stood for empire: the *imperium Romanum* was the Roman empire as a territorial and administrative whole. It was a 'thing', not an activity. And its counterpart was *imperator*: emperor – who was *custos imperi Romani*: custodian of the empire of the Romans.

And when this change took place, all the sanctity which had before attached itself in the Roman mind to the providential destiny of the Roman people to rule and bring order and civilization to the world, attached itself to the empire itself.

The blessing of the gods was invoked, *not* upon the enterprise and the activity of the Roman people in pursuing their destiny, but upon the empire itself and upon its *imperator* who had rolled up in his single office all the *potestas* available, and held it for life.

(4) But the question we must ask ourselves is: If the Romans thought that the *potestas* (in virtue of which a man might exercise 'rule' at one level or another) was leased out and distributed between the various known offices of the Roman state, *where* did they think it came from?

And, oddly enough for an unspeculative people, the Romans were in no doubt about the proper answer to this question.

The source and donor of all *potestas* was the *populus Romanus* itself. *Potestas* belonged to the 'Roman people', just as *auctoritas* belonged to the Roman senate.

Thus, the Roman people understood themselves to be governed by the *potestas* with which they themselves endowed their rulers. And the bestowal of *imperium* upon a man was the greatest thing the *populus Romanus* could do. Until Augustus, they never did it save for a stated period of time.

Now, this giving of *potestas* always took the form of appointment to an office (or to the prerogatives of an office), the *potestas* of which was already settled by law and custom. And, usually (although not always) the manner of the appointment showed *where* the *potestas* had come from.

During the republic, for example, consular magistrates were elected by the *comitia centuriata*; tribunes were elected by the *concilium plebis*; and either *comitia* or *concilium* had a hand in the appointment of all inferior magistrates.

It is true that the part played in these elections by the popular assemblies was restricted: no name could be proposed from the floor of the house; voting was acceptance or rejection of a name presented to the assembly. And for long periods there were conventions which restricted candidates for certain offices to certain classes in Roman society.

Nor, since *potestas* belonged to the whole *populus Romanus* and not merely to the *plebs*, was the senate left out of this process of appointment of magisterial offices. The formal approval of the senate was necessary for any appointment.

Moreover, the imperial office itself, as it emerged, was not excluded from this procedure in respect of its *potestas*.

Augustus and his immediate successors were properly appointed consuls before they were *princeps*, and they were separately endowed with the *potestas* of various offices in the usual manner.

The only things peculiar about their position were that they often had the *potestas* without the office to which it belonged, and that they were endowed with it for life and not for the usual term of years. It later became the custom to pass a *lex de imperio* on the succession of an emperor which endowed him with comprehensive rights and powers.

In later times there were often irregularities, but they were irregularities which often obliquely demonstrated that *imperium* belonged to the *populus Romanus* – such, for example, as the election of an *imperator* by the acclamation of his army.

(5) *Imperium populi Romani*, 'the rule of the Roman people', then, was *not* an empty expression.

It was the Roman people who ruled themselves and who ruled the Roman world through the agents which it endowed with power. And when *imperium* came to mean, not the activity of ruling, but the empire itself, it was still the empire of the Roman people.

There was, of course, nothing 'democratic' (in either an ancient or a modern sense) in this belief that *potestas* belonged to the people; for the Roman people never imagined that *they* could rule except through their appointed agents.

But, vaguely perhaps, it was felt that while *auctoritas* belonged to the senate, *potestas* and the extreme of *potestas*, *imperium*, belonged to the people. And even some of the most autocratic emperors acquired their power from the *lex regia* passed at the beginning of their reigns.

5

Roman government, then, was understood as a subtle mixture of the exercise of *auctoritas* and the exercise of *potestas*.

Under the republic these were never confused; and even during the period of the Punic wars when the senate took charge of *res publica Romana* and its advice became decision and direction, it never itself assumed executive office; it always worked through the consular magistrates. Indeed it might be said that if there was any theory of the republican constitution it was the separation of *auctoritas* from *potestas*.[2]

But with the rule of emperors, a certain confusion made its appearance. An *imperator* was recognized to have both *potestas* and *auctoritas*; and, having both, they tended not to be so clearly distinguished from one another. And the later jurists tended to ignore the distinction, regarding the will of the *imperator* as supreme, and not worrying to consider very much how he became endowed with this supremacy.

6

Now, there is one other word which is important precisely because the Romans did not normally use it for 'government': the word *dominium*.

Dominium belonged to the vocabulary of the Roman family or household. It referred to a specific *potestas* of the head of a household, namely, his *potestas* as the owner of property and slaves. In respect of his property and slaves, but *not* in respect of his wife, children or *clientes*, the *paterfamilias* was *dominus* ('lord') and exercised *dominium* ('lordship').

But in spite of the fact that Romans found in the government of a family so appropriate an analogy by which to understand the government of the *civitas*, they fought shy of transferring the words *dominus* and *dominium* to their political vocabulary.

Imperium was *not* thought of as *dominium*: the *potestas* of the rulers of the *populus Romanus* was not thought of as springing from ownership: 'subjects' were *not* 'slaves'. Indeed it was from the *populus Romanus* that the rulers derived their *potestas*.

The Romans, however, *were* familiar with other societies whose rulers were the owners of their territory, whose sub-

---

[2] Oakeshott's mariginal note: '*Potestas* = election to office. *Auctoritas* = never election.'

jects (with little exaggeration) might be spoken of as their 'slaves', and whose *potestas* did derive from ownership. And it was in describing the government of *these* societies, and *not* that of their own, that the Romans used the word *dominium*.

In short, the words *dominus* and *dominium* correspond to the Greek words *despotes* and *despoteia*, which, meaning the owner and master of slaves, were rejected by the Greeks in describing even the most autocratic ruler of a *polis*, and were used only to describe the rulers of Persia and Egypt.

Nevertheless, when the Roman emperors acquired autocratic powers, this word *dominus* began to creep into the Roman political vocabulary; but rather as a general indication of the absoluteness of their *potestas* than as a technical word meaning that their subjects were understood to be no better than slaves.

The title *dominus* was offered to Augustus and to Tiberius, but it was refused, by the one out of policy and by the other out of contempt.

But it was accepted by Caligula. Suetonius tells us that Caligula 'did away with any pretense of being merely the chief executive of the *populus Romanus*'.

'Bear in mind,' Caligula is reputed to have said, 'that I can treat anyone exactly as I like'.

This, however, is to be recognized as the boast of a lunatic; at all events it was a desperate departure from the traditions of Roman government. Except that *dominium* might perhaps be recognized as the activity of one who, like an emperor, exercised both *auctoritas* and *potestas*.

The words *auctoritas*, *potestas*, and *imperium* were the words the Romans used to signify the different activities in which the *res publica Romana* was cared for; the different activities which composed the activity of 'governing'.

Dominium, 'rulership' based upon 'ownership', 'lordship', was not, strictly speaking a political word at all; but, although it did come to stand on the edge of the Roman political vocabulary, the distinction between autocracy and despotism was not obscured.

Editorial Note

LSE 1/19. Photocopy of a fifteen-page typescript with autograph corrections, except for the photocopy of the autograph page numbered '7a' in Oakeshott's hand. Another copy is at LSE 1/1/21, file 3, of which fos. 221-7, 229-36 are photocopies of a typescript with autograph corrections; fo. 228 is a photocopy of an autograph sheet.

Fifteen

Roman Political Thought (3)

1

The thoughts of most communities which achieve any high degree of political self-consciousness are usually concerned with such matters as:

- What sort of a political community do we compose?
- What is ruling and being ruled?
- What is the authority of rulers, and how do they acquire it? What are the rights of subjects, and how are they acquired?
- What is law?

And I want to say something this morning about the idea of law among the ancient Romans.

Two things stand out very clearly.

(1) A political experience, or a political culture, is composed of the pro-feelings current in the society, its valuations. And the Romans set a very high value upon something which the Athenians valued very little and scarcely understood, namely, legality.

Legality can never be more than one of a number of values; but the Roman political culture is distinguished in recognizing it to be very valuable. They were most unwilling to sacrifice legality in favour of other values.

(2) The law of the Romans is by far the most comprehensive and elaborate system of law that any people, save in modern times, ever generated for themselves.

And among their contemporaries, the Romans were notable as intrepid law*makers*. They not only valued their law very highly, but they had some very clear ideas about the authority of law and the process of legislation.

Nevertheless, this Roman law, like any other, sprang from very primitive beginnings. But its emergence was, in many ways, very different from that of the law (such as it was) of the cities of ancient Greece.

2

The words we are concerned with are *fas, nefas, jus, lex, edictum*.

Law is concerned with what is right and wrong in human conduct.

(1) The most elementary and primitive conception of right and wrong in human conduct appears in the words *fas* and *nefas*. *Fas* stood for what is permitted and *nefas* for what is forbidden. Now, what was this idea of right and wrong?

In the first place it was a 'tribal' idea. That is, *fas* and *nefas* stood for what is permitted and what is forbidden to the *populus Romanus*.

No doubt it was a redaction from earlier tribal laws; but from the time when the *populus Romanus* emerged, they recognized themselves to be different from other peoples and were proud of that difference.

And when they came into contact with other peoples, the Romans never even expected them to have the same rules of right and wrong conduct as themselves. And so long as they thought in terms of *fas* and *nefas*, they had no law which they could or wished to impose upon anyone else. *Fas* and *nefas* stood for what was permitted and what was forbidden to a Roman.

Secondly, *nas* and *nefas* were religious ideas. The founders of the *civitas* were believed to have made a treaty with the gods in which the protection and favour of the gods was secured in return for certain duties performed; and it was these duties which comprised *fas*.

It was a divine law, representing the will and pleasure of the gods, and it was the product of a covenant between the Roman people and its gods.

A large part of it was a ceremonial law which determined the procedure to be followed on important occasions; and beyond this it was composed of some simple rules of ordinary conduct. The custodians of *fas* were priests. But what distinguished *fas* was its origin in a covenant or a treaty with the gods; and these ideas of covenant and treaty ran through the whole of Roman legal thought; it is this which, more than anything else, distinguished *fas* from the Greek *themis*. The

Greeks had next to no contractual relationship with their Gods.

But, in other respects, it was like most other primitive law in that it identified sin and crime. *Nefas* is socially undesirable conduct because it is displeasing to the gods who, on account of it, might withdraw their blessing.

(2) *Jus*. But, more rapidly than many other peoples, the Romans came to distinguish between religious duties, moral rules, and law strictly speaking. And the word *jus* represents a stage in the emergence of these distinctions.

Jus, in its earliest meaning, meant that which is 'right' and 'fitting', not because it was the will and pleasure of the gods but because it was the custom of the society.

As a late Roman lawyer put it, perhaps a little too definitely: '*fas* is divine law; *jus* is human law'.

At all events, when *jus* came to be the word ordinarily used for conduct proper to a Roman, *two* kinds of *jus* were recognized: *jus divinum*, obligations to the gods, and *jus humanum*, obligations to one's fellows.

And this distinction set the *jus humanum* free to develop, *not*, of course, as a purely secular system of rights and duties, but as a system of rights and duties of which it was thought men and *not* gods were the responsible authors.

Like *fas*, *jus humanum* was thought of as springing from a covenant; but a treaty, *not* between gods and men, but between families and tribal groups.

It was not unlike *thesmos*; except that, whereas *thesmos* was thought of as the product of 'doing' justice to a variety of tribal customs, *jus* was the product of more specific covenants of mutual trust.

The custodians of *fas* were priests, and the *jus divinum* still remained in their care. But the custodians of *jus*, the *jus humanum*, were magistrates.

Later, the word *jus* acquired other meanings. The activity of law-courts was described as *jus reddere* – which may be translated 'to dispense justice'. It was the word used to indicate a whole section of the Roman law: *jus civile* meant the whole body of law which applied to the relations between Roman *cives* (citizens) and *jus gentium* (the 'law of nations') meant the whole body of law which governed the relations between *cives* and those who were not *cives*, that is, foreigners or what in Rome itself were called *peregrini* (temporarily resident foreigners).

As a law governing *gentes* (nations), the *jus gentium* was the inspiration of the later European 'international law'.

(3) *Fas* and *jus* were, then, the words in which the Romans expressed the legal order of the *communio Romanorum*; they were the customary, unwritten law of the Roman people, relating to gods and men.

But at some stage, difficult to determine (because Roman writers were apt to project into the distant past ideas and even words which did not become current until later times), the Romans acquired a third word for law.

It represents an idea of law much more positive and historical than the ideas represented in *fas* and *jus*: the word *lex*.

Various derivations of this word have been suggested, the most likely being that it represented the ideas of something binding and something *read out*, or *spoken*, or *declared*.

But, whatever the truth about that, when *lex* came to be used as the ordinary word for a law, it stood for a law known to have been *made* at a certain time and a written-down law; in short, what we should call a statute.

But, like the earlier Roman words for law, *lex* contained also the idea of an agreement or a covenant. And this idea was kept alive and reinforced by the methods by which *lex* was made.

Law as *lex*, then, distinguished itself from law as *fas* or *jus* because it reflected a process of lawmaking, *legislation*. And what *lex* was believed to be is revealed in the *process* in which it was made.

Reputedly from its first emergence, and certainly from very early times, there was an assembly of the Roman people. The earliest assembly was the *comitia curiata*, but it was the somewhat later *comitia centuriata* which became what may be called the first 'legislative' assembly of the Roman people.

It represented all classes in the Roman community, patricians as well as plebeians. In republican times it was called together by the consular magistrate.

The making of *lex* was a process in which the presiding magistrate made a proposal, followed by the formula: 'Is it your pleasure, and do you hold it to be the divine will that...?'

The proposal was a question, *rogatio*; and if, when the assembly had voted, the proposal was found to be accepted, it became *lex*, requiring only in addition the imprimatur of the senate.

There was no debate; no proposal could be made from the floor of the house; and technically the legislator was the magistrate (*legis-lator*, meaning 'the proposer of law'). All *lex* was recorded under the name of the consular magistrate who proposed it.

Thus, it was (for example) by the *lex Publilia* (471 B.C.) that the lawfulness of an assembly of the plebs was established; by the *lex Hortensia* (467 B.C.) that the *concilium plebis* was recognised as a lawmaking body whose *plebiscite* had the force of *lex*; and by the *lex Canuleia* (445 B.C.) that mixed marriages between patricians and plebeian families became legal. Each of these were the names of the consuls concerned.

Throughout the republic there were in fact two 'legislative' bodies, the *comitia centuriata* controlled by the consuls, and the *concilium plebis* controlled by the tribunes. Both operated with the same procedure of *rogatio* (question) and answer given by a silent vote. But whereas the resolutions of the *comitia* were called *lex*, those of the *concilium* were called *plebiscite* – resolutions of the *plebs*.

Later, after the plebeians had gained entry into the senate itself, *lex* could be made by consular magistrates *senatus consultum*, that is, 'in consultation with the senate'.

The fundamental change in lawmaking came gradually with the imperial constitution. The popular assemblies ceased to be the source of law, and *lex* was made, first, by imperial direction to the senate, and later by imperial proclamation (*edictum* or *decretum*).

In the end the famous principle (which appears in Justinian's *Institutes*) established itself: *quod principi placuit, legis habet vigorum*: 'what pleases the *princeps* has the force of law'.[1]

Lex was the will of the *imperator*: the emperor was *solus conditor legis*, 'the sole source of law.' He had acquired (theoretically by the *lex regia*) the powers and prerogatives not only of magistrates and tribunes, but also of assemblies.

---

[1] Oakeshott's marginal note: 'Even when the emperor pronounced an edict, he did so as representative of the Roman people, who were the sole source of law.'

Now, *lex*, made in these manners, entailed an idea of law which had *two* fundamental features.

(a) *Lex* is a statement that, whatever may have been the approved practice in the past, henceforward this shall be the established rule.

Every *lex* has a date from which it becomes current; and in this it differs from customary law, which has no date.

Consequently, *lex* is a law which should have no retrospective application – it operates only from the date of enactment. And further, since it has been made, it is capable of amendment or even repeal.

The important point about *lex* is that its authority derives, *not* from its reasonableness or convenience, but from the fact that it has been made by the recognized and legitimate law-making process. *Lex* is an artifact, and its counterpart is this specific and narrow idea of 'law'.

You may argue that it is inconvenient, even that it is unjust, but until it has been repealed it requires obedience. This is an idea of law that had very little counterpart among the Greeks.

(b) *Lex* is, in form, a bargain, a covenant or a treaty; and the parties in this covenant are (on the one side) the magistrates, the administrators of law, and (on the other side) the *populus Romanus*.

It has the arbitrariness of a covenant; and its operation depends upon *fides*, the magistrate and the administrator 'keeping faith' with the *populus Romanus*.

This notion of a covenant was reinforced by the fact that, in republican times, *lex* was often a bargain between the patrician order (in whose hands most of the magistracies were) and the plebeian order (whose will was embodied in *lex*).

The famous secession of the plebs from Rome and their settlement on the *mons sacer* was brought to an end by a solemn agreement or covenant in which the patricians promised the reforms demanded by the plebs, and this covenant was called the *lex sacrata*.

And this notion of covenant survived into imperial times, growing more and more a fiction, when the law was thought of as a covenant between *imperator* and *populus*.

(4) In the history of Roman law there was one great event which overshadowed all others.

In early days, the law of the Romans was a customary, unwritten law, the sanctity of which was emphasised by its custodians being priests.

Now, one of the earliest demands of the *concilium plebis*, when it had achieved the status of being a legal assembly, was that this unwritten law should (in the words of Livy) 'cease to be kept secret among the mysteries and sacraments of the immortal gods.' The demand was that the law should be written down and published.

The immediate occasion of this demand was the suspicion that the law of debt was being harshly administered by patrician magistrates.

But the result of the demand was the setting up of a commission of ten patricians, the *decemviri*, whose task was to reduce the law to writing and to publish it.

They took more than a year over the job (and were more than suspected of spinning it out in order to remain in power); but in the end what they produced was laid before the popular assembly by the magistrates (in the usual way) and was made *lex*. Ancient custom was converted into law.

This was the famous twelve tables of the Roman law (*lex XII tabularum*). It was engraved on panels of metal and set up in the forum. And it was for ever cherished as the fundamental, original, sacred law of the Romans.[2]

All *leges* subsequently made were thought of as additions to or amplifications of this fundamental law.

This, also, was thought of as a covenant – a covenant between patricians and plebs, in which it was agreed that law henceforth should be, not secret, but known to all.

(5) The character of Roman law, and the methods of making law recognized by the Romans, then, reveal *two* beliefs of almost equal strength.

(a) The conviction that the *populus Romanus* itself is the source of all law.

This belief is the counterpart of the belief that the *populus Romanus* is the source of all *potestas* – executive power in government. And, together, these beliefs about law and government survived all the vicissitudes of constitutional change.

Even the later emperors, whose word was law, and whose power was used autocratically, were thought of as having

---

[2] Oakeshott's marginal note: 'Cp. Magna Carta.'

acquired their right to make law and their right to rule from the *populus Romanus* itself.

But, it should be recognized, that even under the republican constitution, the function of the popular assembly in lawmaking was never more than the right, without debate, to give or refuse their consent to what was proposed to them.

(b) The belief that, by means of this process of making *lex*, the Roman people were emancipated from the rule of ancient custom.

There are very few societies which have not had some difficulty in divesting themselves of the notion that ancient custom has a prescriptive authority from which there is no escape. There is the feeling that you cannot abolish custom, you can only try to forget it if it becomes too inconvenient.

The Romans, however, *did* manage to emancipate themselves from the rule of ancient custom. In *lex*, a statute, they discovered a means of modifying, and even abolishing, ancient custom.

And they helped themselves to this conclusion, in later days, by coming to think of ancient custom as itself *lex* and therefore capable of being emended in a lawmaking process.

This belief that, by means of a known process of making law, they had command over their own rules of order was an elementary belief in what later came to be called *sovereignty*. A 'sovereign' authority is not merely one that has no contemporary superior, but one which is emancipated from the past.

3

Roman reflection about law was, then, clearly confined to reflection about the processes in which it could be properly made, and to the actual elaboration of a system of laws which embraced all the relationships that made themselves known in the course of their history.

But there was *one* speculative idea, characteristically acquired from the Greeks, which the Romans resorted to in trying to understand the relationship between 'law' and 'justice'.

This was the idea of a law of nature, *lex naturalis*. An idea which had a long subsequent history in European thought.

The experience of injustice is an experience common to all peoples.

One form of injustice is easy to understand – namely, the injustice which springs from a corrupt administration of the law: the injustice which is identified as a denial of what are known to be your legal rights. For here the law itself provides the standard and criterion of justice.

But there is another form of injustice which is less easy to give an intelligent account of – namely, when injustice is attributed to the law itself, to what the law itself commands or allows.

How can the law itself be said to be 'unjust'? What do we mean when we assert the 'injustice' of the law?

This is an important question because assertions of this sort are often made.

There is one simple way out of this puzzle. It is to recognize that an 'unjust' law is simply a law which has not been made in the manner in which it is recognized that all law should be made. In other words, if you cannot fault the way in which the law has been made, it *must* be recognized to be a 'just' law.

And any people which has settled upon a procedure for making law is likely to look first at the way in which a law has been made when considering its 'justice' or 'injustice'.

But this really answers a different question. You may agree that if a law has been made in the proper process, it ought to be obeyed. But to say that a law ought to be obeyed is not necessarily the same thing as to say that it is 'just'.

Thus, a law may be recognized to be legitimate, because it has been made in the proper way, and it may in consequence command my obedience; but it still may be thought to be 'unjust'. How can this be?

This is both a practical and a speculative question with which thoughtful people have always been faced. The Romans recognized it as a sensible question, and they answered it with the aid of an idea which Roman lawyers appropriated from the Stoic philosophy: the idea of a law of nature.

Briefly, it was thought that 'justice' must be the correspondence of a demand or a duty or an act with a law of some sort.

And in order to determine the 'justice' or 'injustice' of *lex*, the man-made law, an appeal must be made to another law, *not* made by men, and therefore *not* to be suspected of being 'unjust' itself.

This other, or higher, law was the *lex naturalis*. And *if* this were thought to be a law embedded in the operation of the universe, or as having been made by a providential god, it could be considered to be itself absolutely and unquestionably 'just', and to afford a criterion by which to *judge* the 'justice' or 'injustice' of *lex*.

This entailed the belief that some forms of human conduct were 'naturally just' and other forms 'naturally unjust'; and *lex* which conflicted with 'natural justice' was, on that account, convicted of being 'unjust'.

This is the nearest the Romans got to a philosophical understanding of law and justice; and they put the idea to a variety of uses.

(1) The law of nature was appealed to in the Roman courts when it appeared that the operation of the law would leave behind it the feeling that, somehow, less than justice had been done. Where *lex* seemed unreasonable in its operation, an appeal could be made to reason itself, embodied in a law of nature.

Or, the law of nature was sometimes appealed to when it seemed to a defending lawyer that the case against his client left nothing else to appeal to.

(2) The law of nature was, rather vaguely, thought of as a source from which just *lex* might be generated.

This was so particularly in those realms of human relationships where the law as it stood seemed unsatisfactory or inadequate or where there was no ancient custom to recognize as its source.

It was under the aegis of the law of nature that the Romans constructed all that part of their law which was concerned with the relations between Roman citizens and foreigners, and was called the *jus gentium*, the 'law of nations', *natio* being the word they used to signify communities – such as the Jews – within the Roman Empire.

In short, even in their most speculative and philosophical moods, the Romans clung to the idea of *legality*.

They could think of *no* other way of criticizing the justice of current legal rules than by measuring them against other and higher legal rules, the rules of the law of nature.

In other words, they recognized no fundamental distinction between the activity of the judge, the activity of the critic of current law, and the activity of a legislator.

The judge decided cases according to the law.

The critic of current law judged its justice by measuring it against a higher law.

The legislator made law which could survive the ordeal of being judged according to this higher law.

It was in virtue of the high value the Romans placed upon legality, and their understanding of what this meant, that the Roman *civitas* became and was what may be called a civil association. That is, a set of private persons joined in the recognition of a law to which they, all alike, owed obedience.

They could at times think of themselves as a people with a destiny to fulfill, and it was only in later times that they began to lose the sense of belonging to a family whose founder was Romulus. But behind all this was the idea that what held them together as a community was their ancient customs and the law which they had made for themselves.

And, just as they shared with the peoples they conquered their technological achievements, so also they shared their law.

They were, besides, a remarkably law-abiding people – at least in the centuries of the republic. For nearly seven centuries, the city of Rome had no police force, and capital punishment was unknown.

(3) More speculatively, the idea of the law of nature was used simply to give a precise meaning to the belief that *lex*, even if legitimate and properly made, could not be considered to be automatically just.

4

I want to end by considering briefly another important word in the Roman political vocabulary: the word *libertas* – 'freedom'.

Libertas was essentially a practical idea. It was *not* connected with anything so speculative as liberation from natural necessity. What was recognized as a bar to being 'free' were certain restrictions (mostly man-made) which were easily observable in the world.

(1) *Liber*, was, of course, originally a deity – the Roman god of the vine, Bacchus, the counterpart of the Greek Dionysus; and *libertas* was, so to speak, being 'uninhibited'.

But for the early Romans 'freedom' was understood as the characteristic of a man's *genius*, which was identified as his immortal part and was also regarded as his procreative spirit.

In the widest possible sense, *libertas* was a condition in which a man's *genius* could fulfil itself and demonstrate its immortality by founding a family or by 'augmenting' a family already founded. Freedom was the characteristic of an *auctor*, of an 'originator'.

This most general sense of *libertas* was exemplified: (a) in the belief that a condition of *servitium* (i.e., being a 'slave') was not 'free', because a slave's genius could never demonstrate its immortality in this manner. He could get children, but never found a family, and he had no ancestors. And (b) in the belief that to become 'adult' and to put on the *toga virilis*, which was a recognition of procreative power, was to attain a certain sort of *libertas*.

Further, freedom was generally connected with the human ability to act, which was also recognised as the work of the human *genius*. History was *res gestae*, 'things done' by human beings which demonstrated their freedom to act, their capacity to be an *auctor*.

(2) But, within this very general context, we are concerned with the political idea of *libertas*, the recognition that Rome began in a 'free act'. And here the fundamental belief of the Romans, the belief to which all other beliefs about freedom were connected, was that the foundation of the city of Rome represented the most momentous 'free act' in their history, the founding of the family of the Romans.

'Freedom' was something that a Roman felt himself to have inherited from the way in which the Roman state came into existence – something, perhaps, a little like the feeling that modern Americans have that freedom is something they have inherited from the way in which the United States came into being.

From almost every point of view, Roman political thought began *ab urbe condita*, from the foundation of the city. And this act of foundation was, for them, the original act of 'freedom'.

To be rooted in this foundation was the first and supreme 'freedom' for the Romans, because (as they understood it) their 'mission' was to explore and elaborate it and spread it through the world.

In short, *auctoritas* indicated the path you must, as a Roman, tread; and *libertas* was to walk in that path.

Thus, while *auctoritas* belonged to the *senatus*, the elders, the *patres*, *libertas* belonged to the *populus Romanus*: *auctoritas senatus*; *libertas populi*. To be free was not to be unguided; it was to follow a *fortuna* which you recognised to be your own.

There was, then, an important sense of *libertas*, in which it was identified with being a citizen of Rome. Roman citizenship was the enjoyment of the Roman inheritance, and that inheritance was the outcome of an act of freedom, an act of the free, 'generative' spirit, the *genius* of Romulus.

Thus, *libertas* was something Roman, and it was something that Romans could, to a limited extent, give to others by drawing them into the world governed by the *imperium populi Romani*.

This is why, when the Romans conquered the cities of Greece, they thought and spoke of that conquest as a 'liberation'. What Rome gave to Athens was *libertas*.

(3) But beyond this, the history of Rome (not unlike our own history) was recognized as the story of a people whose liberty was always being compromised and as often as it was lost it was regained again, usually dramatically.

Junius Brutus, when he organized the expulsion of the last 'king', Tarquinius Superbus, was thought and spoken of as the 'liberator' of Rome; and 'kings' were ever after identified with servitude.

The republic was an era of 'liberty', freedom being identified with the establishment of the consulship.

Julius Caesar, when he entered Rome as a self-appointed dictator in 50 B.C., represented himself as the 'liberator' of the Roman people.

Marcus Brutus, when he assassinated Caesar, was hailed, by many, as a 'liberator'.

Octavian, when, in 43 B.C., he defeated Mark Antony, was a 'liberator', and his rule as Augustus was represented as the restoration of 'freedom'.

On the death of Nero, Suetonius tells us, 'citizens ran through the streets wearing caps of liberty, as though they were freed slaves'; because Nero had come to be recognized as more like a slave-master than a 'ruler'.

Later more than one emperor was assassinated to the cry of 'liberty'.

All this is, perhaps, a little confusing; not unlike the confusion which has overtaken the word 'liberation' in our own time. But there is some logic in it. Behind it was the distinction between *dominium* ('lordship') and *imperium* ('rule').

Dominium was what an owner had over his slaves, and what the Roman was accustomed to think an oriental despot or a Hellenistic king had over his subjects – a despotic 'lordship'.

Imperium, on the other hand, was 'rule' of a different kind. And it was believed that so long as you were subject to *imperium* (even if it was the *imperium* of a temporarily appointed dictator) you were 'free', or at least this was no bar to your being free.

It was because Tarquinius had become a 'despot' that his expulsion established 'freedom'. Lucretia was his property.

It was because the republic was ruled by magistrates who were endowed with their *potestas* by the *populus Romanus* that it was though of as an era of freedom.

It was because Caesar had become a 'despot' that his assassination by Brutus restored 'freedom'.

And it was because the Romans rescued the Greek cities from the 'despotic' rule of the Macedonian kings that they could represent themselves as bringers of 'freedom' to Greece.

And within the Roman empire there were municipalities which were recognised as *civitates liberae*, free municipalities. These lived under their own law, and had financial independence, and their differences with the Roman government were settled by negotiations. The 'unfree' communities were ruled by a Roman 'governor'.

(4) Slaves, then, were 'unfree,' because they lived under the *dominium* of their masters.

Minors were 'unfree' because they lived under the autocratic rule (*potestas dominica*) of their fathers.

To live under a despot or a usurper was to be 'unfree'.

But citizens were 'free Romans', *not* because they enjoyed 'self-government' in any significant sense, nor because they ever themselves exercised *imperium*, but because those who did exercise it were known to have been endowed with it by the *populus Romanus*, and because they knew themselves to be joined in the common recognition of the authority of a law.

The great moments in the history of Roman freedom were recognized to be: the foundation of the city of Rome; the expulsion of the last king; the recognition of the tribunes and the *concilium plebis*; the publication of the twelve tables of the Roman law; the winning of the right of appeal from magistrates to *populus* on certain occasions; and the destruction of usurpers and rulers who had broken 'faith' with their subjects and become 'despots'.

Editorial Note

LSE 1/1/21, file 3, fos. 237–55. Fos. 239–48, 251–4 are photocopies of a typescript with autograph corrections; fos. 237–8, 249–50 are photocopies of autograph sheets.

Sixteen

Medieval Political Experience

1

Today we begin to consider the third of the political experiences we are concerned with. I have called it the political experience of medieval Europe.

The expression signifies a period of time and a geographical area which came to be inhabited by various peoples.

So far as time is concerned I am going to take it to be the period which begins with the unmistakable collapse of the Roman imperial administration, the end of the *pax Romana*. The year 400 A.D. is a reasonable proximate date, though in itself it has no significance.

It is impossible to be any more precise about the end of the period, for this medieval political experience shaded imperceptibly into that of modern Europe – that is to say into the political experience we recognize as our own. But the year 1500 A.D. (which also has no significance in itself) may be taken as the approximate end.

Both these dates are so approximate that each of them might be moved a century either way.

It is, then, a period of something over a thousand years.

It is a little easier to be precise about the geographical area. It may be said to be the political experience of the people who came to inhabit the northern and western parts of the Roman world (*orbis terrarum Romanorum*), namely (from north to south) – Britain, Gaul, Germany west of the Rhine, Spain, and Italy.

When I say that the political experience we are concerned with is that of the peoples who came to inhabit this territory, I mean that it was the political culture acquired by the people who, from the second century A.D., gradually moved into this territory and who mixed with the peoples who already occupied it.

And this political culture distinguished itself from those of ancient Greece and Rome:

- In respect of the dimensions of the territory over which it spread itself
- In respect of the size of the populations concerned
- In respect of the slowness with which it emerged

Now the two important features of this world which these peoples encountered as they moved into it were (1) that it was still significantly Roman, and (2) that it was Christian; and both these features impressed themselves indelibly upon the immigrants and conditioned their political experience.

(1) From its Roman inheritance, medieval Europe acquired a language – the Latin language. This became the language of European law and of medieval political reflection. So far as politics is concerned, the importance of this lies in the fact that it was a vocabulary which already displayed Roman thoughts, and when these peoples, in the course of time, made it a vehicle for their own thoughts, they were unable to exclude (indeed, they did not attempt to exclude) the Roman thoughts which the language carried with it. Nevertheless, these thoughts were transformed in their new context.

With the language, what medieval Europe acquired from Rome was a past-relationship with a Roman civilization in terms of which they came to understand themselves. Even for the immigrant peoples, their acquired past-relationship with Rome became far more important than their relationship with their own past.

(2) Besides this Roman inheritance – or as an indistinguishable part of it – these peoples, coming with religions of their own, were converted to the Christianity which they found in the territories they occupied.

What they encountered, in the first place, was *three* different sorts of Christianity; each with some kind of organization:

- Latin Christianity: the beliefs of an organized church which from about 300 A.D. recognized the bishop of Rome as its head, and called him pope.
- Arian Christianity, which was a version of Christian belief which had been propagated by a man named Arius. It had been condemned by the council of Nicea in

325 A.D., but it continued to flourish in parts of Eastern
Europe.
• Celtic Christianity, a version of Christian belief current
  in the more northern parts of Europe and deeply entan-
  gled with other native religions.

But incomparably the strongest of these organizations was
that of Latin Christianity (*Roman* Christianity). Indeed, the
pope had come to fill the place occupied by the later Roman
emperors as head of the Roman Christian church, and by
about 700 A.D. a uniformity of Latin Christianity had been
established in medieval Europe. But not before 1200 can it be
said that Christianity embraced the whole of the medieval
world we are dealing with.

Thus, the political cultures of medieval peoples may be said
to be the institutions of government, and the thoughts about
them, which emerged gradually from what these immigrant
peoples brought with them, mixed with what they found – a
Christian church, the relics of a Roman civilization, and peoples with laws and customs of their own who had known the
Roman only as an overlord.

2

Our first business is to understand *how* this world of medieval political thought and activity emerged, *who* were the
peoples concerned and *what* they brought with them, and
their fortunes.

The Roman world (*orbis terrarum Romanorum*), at its greatest, stretched from the Cheviot Hills to Egypt, from the Rhine
to the Atlantic, and from Asia Minor to Spain.

From the second century A.D. barbarian peoples were
beginning to seep over its frontiers, particularly from the east
and north-east. And, during the course of two centuries, this
trickle of invaders became an irresistible flood of migrant
peoples.

Where the movement of peoples began, nobody knows;
but it is known that the territory left by those who came over
the borders of the empire was rapidly filled by others moving in from further east. The migrants were displaced
peoples.

During the fourth and fifth centuries these peoples spread
themselves over the greater part of the continental Roman

Empire: Britain, Gaul, Italy, Spain. In 476 A.D. the city of Rome itself was captured.

This movement of peoples was slow enough for the Romans themselves to distinguish between the various peoples, and to give them names: Saxons, Goths, Franks, Burgundians, Alans, Vandals, Avars.

Each of these peoples was a conglomeration of tribes – tribes with their tribal chiefs, their tribal laws, customs, religions, and manners of dealing with their common affairs.

None of them had ever lived under Roman rule; all were alien to Europe.

The circumstances of migration, however, broke up the tribal organization of these peoples. They moved into the Roman empire as 'hordes' composed of non-tribal groups, of various dimensions, which the Romans called *comitatus*.

This is a matter of some importance. Medieval politics, no doubt, began with many reminiscences of tribal organization; but unlike both ancient Greece and Rome, the political communities which in the end emerged in medieval Europe were not unions of tribes. And part of the reason why anything like a recognizable political community was so long in appearing in the post-Roman world was that this world was an immense and almost unqualified chaos of small, local communities. Indeed, apart from what was inherited from Rome, the political experience of medieval Europe was more nearly built up out of nothing than any other political experience we know of.

A *comitatus* was a group or detachment constituted by a 'leader' (*dux*) and his 'followers' (*comites*). It was a small military formation held together, *not* by a tribal tie of common blood, but by a tie of fidelity, displayed in an oath of allegiance to the 'leader'.

The process was one of infiltration; or it became so after the peoples who had for long lived on the frontiers of the empire and who had learned some military skill and organization from the Romans, had actually defeated the Roman defenders.

3

This period of movement and migration was gradually succeeded by settlement. The piece of territory upon which any of these peoples organized in these detachments settled seems to have been determined largely by pressure or absence of pressure from behind. They cast about for a home where they might come to rest. It was a slow process.

The Iberian peninsula, for example, was invaded by the Suevi, the Vandals, the Alans, and the Visigoths, who had crossed Gaul. But the Vandals moved on to north Africa, and the Visigoths first came back over the Pyrenees to settle in southern Gaul and later returned to conquer the whole of Iberia.

Some of the Saxons settled just east of the Rhine, others invaded Britain. The Salian Franks settled in northern Gaul; the Austrasian Franks in southern Gaul and the Rhineland; the Ostrogoths in Italy.

This activity of settlement generated the first, primitive territorial communities of medieval Europe.

Now, wherever these peoples settled there was already an indigenous population, not tribal in character, sometimes living in towns of Roman foundation, and often larger in numbers than the immigrants and having laws, customs, and a religion of their own.

The immigrants mixed with these natives, and the communities which emerged came to be distinguished by the territory they occupied, and neither by a tribal belief in common blood, nor even by a common law.

And it was in these circumstances of settlement and mixture that the first so-called 'kings' of medieval Europe emerged: men of authority who were *neither* tribal chieftains *nor* merely leaders of military formations, but rulers who had managed to impose themselves upon bits of territory. The *dux* (leader of a *comitatus*) became *rex* (king), and a 'king' was a 'lord' – a 'land lord'.

4

In many cases it is, of course, an exaggeration to call these early settlements of European peoples 'communities'; or to attribute to these 'kings' anything so specific as 'government.' Each settlement was a chaos of multiple peoples, laws, customs, and religions.

In any village (to say nothing of larger settlements) there were wandering men who, having been used to carrying their own law with them wherever they went, claimed to be under a different law from their neighbors, and particularly from that of the native who remained.

In short, the situation called for 'politics' – a reconciliation of differences. But there was next to no political experience to draw upon.

These 'kings' were men of violence, who ruled for the most part by force and in virtue of military superiority, possibly with some relics of the authority of tribal chiefs, and always in virtue of the possession of land.

Some of them, in the course of time, carved out considerable 'kingdoms'. Clovis, who styled himself as 'king' of the Salian Franks and took the Roman title of consul, was particularly successful, and managed even to found a short-lived dynasty. And Theodoric in Italy, of course, had the advantage of succeeding to the prestige of a ruler in Rome.

The problem of government was how to impose and maintain the rudiments of law and order in a world in which the *pax Romana* had been destroyed, in which a single, recognized 'law of a territory' had not yet emerged (but in which many different laws were current), and in communities in which there were recognized to be 'noble' families, families of free men, and serfs and slaves. 'Noble' often signifying merely 'conqueror'; 'serf' often signifying 'the conquered'.

Settlement was, in fact, the acquisition of land; the ownership and cultivation of land was the main feature of these communities; government, such as there was, was the exercise of 'lordship': rule in virtue of ownership. All authority was connected with landed property.

The ambition of every ambitious man was for the power that came from the ownership of land. But he could buy power only by giving away part of his land in return for military support. And this is what he did: paid for support by alienating land to men who became his tenants and his subjects.

On the other hand, the need of every man was for a protector more powerful than himself. And to meet this need a practice emerged which perhaps owed something to the old *comitatus*.

Free men who were relatively powerless 'commended' themselves to those who were more powerful. They pledged their loyalty to one more powerful than themselves, thus turning his *potentia* into *potestas*. In this practice a 'lord' – one who owned more land and disposed of more resources – would acquire a retainer, and the retainer would acquire a powerful protector.

A 'king' was often a 'lord', perhaps recognized to have royal blood, but chosen by his fellow 'lords' to organize the defence of a territory or a people, and given the necessary support to perform this service. He was a man to whom others 'commended' themselves for particular purposes; usually *war*.

In short, something like political societies were constructed out of the most elementary materials – the materials of a simple social structure, of authority deriving from 'lordship' and from 'commendation', and a notion of law which went back to primitive tribal times.

Of these communities the smaller were the more durable; 'kingdoms' emerged only to dissolve again.

For, where the possession of land is the only source of power, and where the only way a landowner could acquire 'subjects' was by alienating part of his land to others in return for their support, the process was inherently self-defeating.

These 'kings', for example, created counts and dukes, and the counts and dukes destroyed the power of kings.

Moreover, according to custom, on the death of one of these 'kings' his 'kingdom' would be dispersed among his heirs, and the process of collecting together and consolidating a 'kingdom' would have to begin all over again.

5

Now, these people, the invaders and settlers of this once Roman world, brought with them their religions: religions which, no doubt, had begun in tribal ancestor-worship but which had, in some cases, acquired gods and elaborate theological beliefs.

Coming with these religions, they entered a world in which, for a century or more, the Christian religion had been spreading itself. And they became converts to Christianity. The conversion was, in most cases, the work of missionaries sent out for the purpose from what had already become the centre of the Christian church in the West, namely Rome.

Thus, for a people to be converted to Christianity meant not only throwing out old religious beliefs and acquiring new (which we may suppose was often a very slow process), but also being brought within the orbit of an organized church and of the authority of its head. Indeed, the only authority in early medieval Europe which did *not* derive from the ownership of land was that of the church and the pope.

And since the normal method of 'conversion' was first to convert the 'ruler', the 'king' (who then imposed the new religion upon his people, often by force – in the same manner as the converted Roman emperors had imposed it upon their subjects), these 'kings' acquired an added prestige and the office of king acquired a reflected sanctity.

Christian kings were crowned in an ecclesiastical cere- mony; and among their duties was the duty of defending the Christian church within their realms and, often, of defending Christendom against the attacks of pagan invaders.

Christian beliefs about the duties of kings, in the course of time, penetrated deeply into the political beliefs of medieval peoples; but the immediate political impact of Christianity upon these converted peoples was to add a sanctity to the office of kingship and thus to enhance the authority of rulers whose authority was otherwise often not very great or very durable.

A notable example of this was that of Clovis, who, being elected king of the Salian Franks, established himself in northern Gaul, with his capital in Paris at the end of the fifth century.

He was converted to Christianity, he imposed Christianity upon his subjects, and his alliance with the Christian church gave a religious sanction to his authority – not unlike the reli- gious sanction which the emperor Theodosius had sought from Christianity – which made him the most powerful ruler of his time.

6

Thus, even in these early times, when force was so much more in evidence than recognized and legitimate authority, there emerged an institution and an idea of 'kingship', closely connected with the church of Latin Christianity.

It was compounded of outstanding personality, the resources which came from the ownership of land, the belief in royal blood, the constant need for an organizer of defence, and the sanctity provided by coronation in a Christian eccle- siastical ceremony.

Kingly rule was *not* very far removed from the analogy of family rule; it retained a fundamental element of 'lordship';

but it was on the way to being 'political' rule, and the impact of Christianity pressed it in this direction by adding a new source of authority to it.

7

In this early medieval Europe, incomparably the most successful ruler was Charles, known as Charlemagne, king of the Austrasian Franks.

At the end of the eighth century, he had gathered together by conquest, and held together by a rudimentary system of administration, an empire which stretched from the Ebro (in Spain) to the Elb, and from the North Sea to the Tiber.

It was an empire composed of great counties and duchies, in which counts and dukes ruled as 'lords' in virtue of their ownership of land. But it was a 'political' empire because the authority of Charles himself was not based upon 'lordship' but upon the authority accorded to him by dukes over whom he ruled, and upon an administrative and judicial organization which he superimposed upon the rule of the counts and dukes.

And in the year 800, in recognition of the position in Christendom which he had carved out for himself, he was crowned *imperator* by Pope Leo III in Rome: the first of the medieval 'emperors', who came to represent in their office some shadowy ideal of the political unity of Christendom.

Nevertheless, even with this prestige to support it and the not insignificant administrative system he had built up, Charlemagne's empire did not survive him.

According to Frankish custom, it was divided between his sons, and subsequently suffered further division.

Moreover, even in the ninth century, Europe had not passed out of the era of movement, invasion, settlement and resettlement. Peoples were still on the move, entering, harassing or pressing upon this old Roman world, all of them non-Christian.

A great movement of Muslim peoples from Arabia began in the sixth century. In the course of a hundred years they occupied the whole of north Africa and Spain, and in 722 reached Tours in France. Here they were defeated but they remained in occupation of a large part of Spain until the end of the middle ages.

In the eighth century Europe was invaded by the Norsemen, who first ravaged the northern shores of Europe and later established settlements in England, Ireland, Normandy, Sicily, and the eastern Mediterranean.

In the ninth century the Magyars invaded Europe from the east. They occupied parts of northern Italy and Provence, and withdrew only after their defeat by Otto I of Germany at Lechfeld in 955.

In short, for the better part of eight centuries the territory which had been that of the Roman empire had no rest: nine hundred years of violence and invasions. And not until these had been repelled or accommodated could Europe begin to acquire a durable political shape.

8

From about the ninth century, however, more durable political shapes began to emerge.

The political experience of medieval Europe became:

First, an experience in which, over a large part of Europe, local rulers of various magnitudes, dukes, counts, margraves, bishops (who ruled their tenants and retainers by virtue of their ownership of land) not only became subject to the rule of kings, whom they elected, but themselves gave shape to the laws, institutions, and beliefs characteristic of a medieval monarchy.

Secondly, an experience in which some of the old Roman municipalities of the empire which had retained their independence generated republican governments of their own.

Thirdly, an experience in which, largely under the inspiration of the Christian church, Christendom acquired a semblance of political unity – an experience of empire.

9

There are similarities and differences in the processes in which – to call them by their modern names – France, Germany, England, and Spain, the four great realms of medieval Europe, emerged.

(1) In 987 Hugh Capet, Count of Paris, was elected king of the West Franks by his fellow lords – the dukes of Aquitaine, Burgundy, Normandy, and Brittany, and the counts of Flanders, Vermandois, Champagne, and Toulouse. He regarded himself as the successor of Clovis and Charlemagne, and his

descendants ruled France as kings until the end of the eighteenth century.

But it was nearly four hundred years before the king of the
West Franks could speak of himself properly as king of
France, and before France emerged as a political community.

(2) In 918 Henry, Duke of Saxony, was elected king of the
East Franks by his fellow lords – the Dukes of Swabia,
Bavaria, Franconia, and Lorraine. Their immediate need of a
king was the need of an organizer to defend their lands from
the invading Slavs, Magyars, and Norsemen. But the office of
king was established, and Henry was succeeded over a
period of nearly five hundred years by kings holding this
office.

But Germany, neither in the middle ages nor at any subsequent time, became a 'kingdom': partly because the wealth
and power of the great dukes and margraves enabled them
to retain a large measure of independence, and partly
because the office of emperor, with all its distracting obligations and engagements, became annexed to the office of king
of the East Franks.

Germany remained an agglomeration of semi-independent principalities – duchies, margravates, ecclesiastical
states, and free cities – held together in late medieval times
under an inconsequent imperial constitution.

(3) Britain, first conquered by the Romans, then by the Saxons, a prey to the invasion of Danes and Norsemen, a land of
seven kingdoms, achieved some sort of unity in the tenth
century under Saxon kings – a unity which was tremendously enhanced when the island was finally conquered by
the Normans.

Earlier than any other of the medieval realms, England
became a kingdom whose unity was uncompromised by the
independence of great lords and 'lordships', and over a
period of four and a half centuries it explored a political
experience in which the nobility, the free men, and the king
each participated.

(4) The Iberian peninsula, after the collapse of the Visigothic
kingdom, was overrun by Arab invaders who, early in the
eighth century, penetrated as far as southern France. When
the tide of this invasion receded, the peninsula became a

land, like France, ruled by lords whose authority derived from the ownership of land.

By the thirteenth century it had been composed into four kingdoms – Navarre, Castile, Aragon, and Portugal – and the remaining Arab province of Granada in the south. By the end of the middle ages it had become a single kingdom in which, nevertheless, the pull of provincial independence was strong and has remained so to this day.

(5) Italy, after the collapse of the Ostrogothic kingdom, became and remained a divided territory of small civil and ecclesiastical principalities and free cities.

It suffered perpetual invasion: by the armies of Byzantium, by the Normans who established a short-lived kingdom in the south, by the armies of the king-emperors of Germany, and by the armies of Aragon and France. The Italy of which Machiavelli wrote in the early sixteenth century was, politically, not very different from the Italy of the ninth century: a battlefield of contending 'lords', mostly foreign invaders.

10

Now this, often confused and always changeful, political experience gave medieval people a number of political themes to reflect upon, the most important of which were:

(1) The rights and duties of civil rulers. This theme was reflected upon mostly in connection with monarchy, but it was a theme of considerable complication.

There were monarchies of different sorts; and in each an intelligible relation had to be determined between kings and dukes; and between civil and ecclesiastical authorities; and between the various kingdoms which composed what by the ninth century came to be called Christendom and the church, which in a large manner constituted Christendom.

In general this reflection upon kingship was a prolonged endeavor to understand a ruler who was not a 'lord', a ruler whose authority did *not* spring from ownership: a political head and *not* the owner of an estate with tenants. How could legitimate authority emerge from the rule of force?

(2) The duties and liberties of subjects. This theme is the obverse of the theme of kingship and was a prolonged endeavour to understand a 'subject' who was *not* a 'tenant',

somewhat similar to the endeavour in ancient Greece to understand a citizen who was not a tribesman. And it generated the second great political invention of medieval times. If the first invention was kings who were not mere 'lords', the second was *parliaments*: meetings of men who were 'subjects' and not mere 'tenants'.

(3) The nature and authority of the church. In medieval Europe, religion and politics were related to one another in a manner somewhat different from their relation in ancient Greece and ancient Rome; and this difference conditioned the whole of medieval politics and political reflection.

(4) The nature of law. Here again there was vast complexity. The middle ages inherited a multiplicity of laws and a multiplicity of notions about the authority of law; and it was their fortune to add greatly to that multiplicity. It was a theme of perpetual interest and importance.

(5) The nature of property and 'lordship'. It was in reflecting upon this theme that medieval thinkers may be said to have discovered 'politics'.

(6) The idea of empire. This theme gathered into itself reminiscences of the never-forgotten Roman empire, and was the nucleus round which was grouped the never-neglected ideal of Christian unity in its political aspect.

'Lordship', property, kingship, parliaments, the liberties of subjects, the church, medieval laws, empire: from one point of view these are all recognizable as what are called 'institutions' – that is, patterns of conduct, manners of behaving, improvised in response to situations or in answer to requirements.

And the political experience of medieval Europe is an experience of continuous inventiveness and improvisation; the view that this was a period of European history of even comparative stagnation has nothing whatever to be said in its favour.

These 'institutions' were the product of human choices; and some of them may even be recognized as first designed to serve a particular purpose – although, where this is so, they rapidly outgrew their original design.

A king might be designed to organize the defence of five dukedoms against a common enemy, but he became a unique and durable political character.

The church, which was first the organization of the life and worship of the converts to a new religion, became the mightiest political power Europe has ever known.

A parliament, first devised to provide support for royal authority, might become an indispensable partner in government.

All these, then, from one point of view, are institutions. But from another point of view, they are thoughts and families of thoughts. They are the understanding people had of conduct, the expectations people entertained about behavior, the interpretation they imposed upon events and happenings.

Kingship is what came to be believed about the authority and office of men called 'kings'.

Property is what was believed about the legitimate relations between men and things.

'The church' is what was thought about the relation between the spiritual and the temporal life of human beings.

And it is from this point of view, as thoughts and organizations of thoughts, that I propose to consider them.

11

Lastly, medieval political reflection did not neglect the more general and philosophical themes, themes which had been explored by the ancient Greeks – the nature and necessity of government, the source of authority, the division between the public and the private realm.

And on these matters the reasoning of medieval thinkers was utterly unlike anything we have met in the ancient world. As political philosophers they had a style of their own, of which I shall try to give you some impression.

Editorial Note

LSE 1/1/21, file 4, fos. 257–70. Photocopy of a typescript with autograph corrections.

Seventeen

Medieval Government

1

There are four words commonly used in the middle ages in connection with the authority and the office of a ruler. They are Latin words; they carried with them meanings for the ancient Roman state, but they had new meanings imposed upon them in medieval political thought.

(1) *Potestas*. This was the most general word for the authority of a medieval ruler; it stood for his right to rule.

(2) *Dominium*. This word stood for a special sort of relationship, namely, 'lordship'. 'Lordship' was a relationship which derived from the ownership of land. A 'lord', strictly speaking, had tenants or serfs or even slaves, but *not* 'subjects'. A lord was *not*, as such, a ruler; but as rulers were also, all of them 'lords' – 'lordship' and 'rulership' were connected. A ruler was 'lord' of his own land; for example, John was king of England and lord of Ireland.

(3) *Jurisdictio*. This meant 'to have jurisdiction over'. And it might refer to a territory or to a particular set of people. *Jurisdictio* was the right to do certain things – e.g., to hold a court of law, or to levy a tax. 'Jurisdiction' was always defined and always limited. It was a relationship between a ruler and his 'subjects', not between a lord and his tenants.

(4) *Gubernaculum*. This was originally a maritime word, meaning the activity of a helmsman or a pilot.

It was used by the Romans in a colloquial to stand for 'government'. The ruler is being thought of as the pilot of the ship of state.

In the middle ages it acquired a technical meaning.

It meant all those powers or authorities to decide or to act which belonged to a ruler, but were *not* comprised in his 'jurisdiction'.

A ruler as a judge in a court of law was exercising his *jurisdictio*; a ruler as the initiator of policy, declarer of war and peace, a ruler as a leader, was exercising his *gubernaculum*.

Thus *gubernaculum* was an open-ended activity; *jurisdictio* was precise and limited. And the two words corresponded to, and distinguished between the two different kinds of activity which it falls to any ruler to exercise.

2

Now medieval peoples may be said to have had *two* deeply rooted prejudices, or beliefs, about ruling. They began, no doubt, as feelings, but they came to be written up into principles.

(1) First, they believed that for a man to have authority over others, for him to have a *right* to rule, was something he must have acquired.

No man could be thought of as having a natural right to rule over other men; or, to put it another way, a right to rule could not derive from any natural quality that the ruler, *as a man*, might have – his superior strength; his superior intelligence or virtue.

Now, you will see that this belief excludes any close analogy between the authority of a ruler and the 'natural' authority of a father over his family.

And further, it made it very difficult for medieval peoples to believe in an hereditary right to rule – to believe, that is, that the right to rule could be acquired by inheritance.

Indeed, for medieval peoples, inheritance had to do with the ownership of land and *not* with the right to rule. And the notion of an hereditary right to rule was not really medieval at all; it appeared first in Europe in the sixteenth century when 'kingship' began to be regarded as itself a piece of property.

In medieval times, such things as 'royal families' were certainly recognized, and a man might *succeed* to the office of ruler by inheriting it from his father. But it was *not this* that endowed him with his right to rule.

Or to put it another way, a right to rule belonged to the office of ruler, and although there might be proper and improper ways of coming to occupy this office, it was *not* these which constituted the right to rule.

Where, then, could he get his right to rule from?

As medieval people understood it, he could acquire a right to rule, authority, only be being given it by somebody who had a right to give it.

And the conclusion they reached was that only God could give a man the right to rule over other men. They argued that the *only* self-evidently legitimate ruler in the universe was God, and that, consequently, all human rule must be understood to derive from God.

Omne potestas est a Deo.

Now, as we shall see, they thought that there might be a variety of procedures through which a man may acquire from God the right to rule, but all of them were recognized as bestowing the right to rule only because they were recognized to be *channels* through which God had given authority.

So, in an important sense, all human rulers are deputies of God. They are occupants of offices which have got their authority from God.

(2) The second deeply-rooted belief of medieval peoples was that ruling was the activity of a *monarch*. As a broad generalization it would be true to say that nothing which fell outside monarchy seriously entered into the thoughts about government of medieval peoples.

Monarchy was, in fact, the political inheritance of the middle ages, both from its Roman imperial pedigree and from its Teutonic pedigree. But, although this was the accepted view, medieval ways of thinking required it to be justified and made intelligible. Various general ideas were adduced to support this monarchical experience.

For example, in the monotheism of Christian orthodoxy, God himself was recognized to be a monarch; and all earthly rule (understood to be a 'representation' of this divine rule) must therefore be monarchical also. The sublunary world was the counterpart of the world above the moon; and a human ruler who was not a king would be unintelligible.

But to be a monarch, to 'rule', was always to hold a more or less specified office. And what we are concerned with is the office of kingship, because it was to this office that *potestas* – *jurisdictio* and *gubernaculum* – belonged.

Nevertheless, it cannot be said that the office of 'king' was ever, in the middle ages, a uniform office. There were recognized to be various sorts of king and various modes of kingship. To speak of medieval kingship as if it were a single, settled, and unequivocal institution would be a great mistake.

3

Kingship in the middle ages may be said to have been a complex and manifold institution composed of *two* diverse dispositions and pointing towards two simple and ideal types of monarchy, which rarely, if ever, corresponded exactly to any of the actual monarchies.

These two ideal types of monarchy may be called 'absolute' and 'conditional' monarchical rule. Neither of these words is medieval, and I use them merely to describe the two ideal directions in which medieval belief about monarchy found itself pulled.

(1) 'Absolute' monarchy. Here the ruler was believed to derive his *potestas* directly from God. The authority to rule is a direct gift of God. For example, Coke in Cowdrey's case defines an absolute monarch as one independent of the pope.

The ruler may be elected (indeed, he usually was), but election was understood to be appointment to an office; and the *potestas* belonged to the office. It is 'absolute' if the responsibility it entailed was owed directly to God and to nobody else. This, in medieval parlance, is monarchy *Dei gratia*, by the grace of God.

This does *not* mean that in monarchies which approximated to the 'absolute' type, there were no recognized standards in the conduct of the holder of the kingly office, that there was nothing that he ought not to do.

Such standards certainly existed; but in a monarchy of this sort the king is responsible only to God for their observance. He is, and he remains, king *Dei gratia*, by the 'grace of God'. And grace is neither an indication nor a warrant of good character or good behavior. Grace, in Christian theology, is an unmerited gift of God. Many kings and popes were known to have disreputable characters, but their *authority* to rule was not derived from their 'natural' characters.

(2) 'Conditional' monarchy. Here the kingly *potestas* was, also, believed to derive from God, but *not* directly. The intermediary between the king and God was the king's *subjects*, those over whom he ruled – or *some* of those over whom he ruled.

A king in this position was, of course, recognized to be responsible to God for the performance of his duties, but this was an ultimate responsibility. His immediate responsibility was to his subjects. And in these circumstances his subjects (or some of them) were recognized to have a right to exercise some control over him, and to recall him to his duties if he neglected them, and perhaps *even* to depose him.

Here, again, the middle ages does not provide us with an exact and unmodified example of this type of monarchy; but this was one of the directions of all medieval thought about kingly rule.

These, then, are the two directions in which medieval thought about kingly rule tended to run; and I want to illustrate them by saying something about three different examples of monarchy: the government of the church, the government of France, and the government of England.

4

The medieval Christian church was incomparably the most authoritative and the most sophisticated of all the political institutions of medieval Europe. Nearly all medieval ideas about government were first generated in the church; and the medieval church was the political educator of Christendom. It is from this point of view I want to talk about it.

The word 'church' (*ecclesia*) in the middle ages did *not* stand for the whole body of baptized Christians. The church was *not*, in this sense, a community or society of all those who had common Christian religious beliefs.

It was understood to be a set of men, who, in respect of occupying certain offices, were recognized to have authority to rule over the inhabitants of Christendom in respect of certain, not very exactly defined, activities. Generally speaking, they were activities which were said to concern the soul and salvation as distinct from the body and its earthly welfare.

These men were the holders of a variety of ecclesiastical offices in many different organizations – parochial, diocesan, monastic, and organizations (often under archbishops) annexed to the particular realms of Christendom and composing rudimentary 'national' churches.

But it is possible to speak of *the* church in medieval western Europe because the bishop of Rome very early established his supremacy over the whole of this organization. In

343 A.D. the Council of Sardica authorized appeals to Rome. This supremacy was unmistakably acknowledged in the title of *papa* (pope) which from the fifth to the eleventh century was gradually appropriated uniquely to this bishop. And by about 700 A.D., the papal or Latin church had destroyed the early Celtic church and had suppressed the Arian heresy.

The pope, then, was a 'ruler'; he was the occupant of a recognized office to which was annexed a *potestas*, a right to rule.

The subjects over whom he had this right to rule were of various sorts:

(1) The holders of ecclesiastical offices – bishops, abbots, priests, etc.

(2) In the later middle ages anyone who belonged to the class of persons known as 'clerks' (that is, at its widest, literate persons) was claimed by popes as falling within their rule.

(3) The claim of some of the later popes to exercise their *potestas* over kings and emperors was based upon the view that they, also, were holders of ecclesiastical offices – coronation being an ecclesiastical ceremony. Uncrowned rulers – dukes, counts, margraves etc. – were, as such, outside the papal *potestas*.

(4) *All* persons in respect of some of their activities, for example marriage, family relations, making wills etc. It was, for example, by *church* law that usury was forbidden in the middle ages.

During the middle ages the person appointed to the office of pope was always an already consecrated bishop.

In early centuries, popes were elected by the clergy, the senate and the *populus* of the city of Rome; they were sometimes nominated by kings (Theodoric nominated Felix in 526), and by emperors; but the accepted method of appointment became election by a body of ecclesiastical magnates known as the college of cardinals.

By reason of the rule of sacerdotal celibacy in the Western church, hereditary succession to the office of pope was legally impossible.

But the manner of election had nothing whatever to do with the *potestas* of a pope. That belonged to the office itself;

and the papal 'office' appeared long before that of any of the other kingly offices of Christendom.

A pope, on election, made no promises to his electors or to anyone else. He did not, like other kings, await sanctification in a coronation ceremony. He immediately succeeded to the *potestas* of the office.

This *potestas* was believed to derive directly, without contemporary intermediary, from God himself. The pope was ruler of his subjects *Dei gratia*; and he was responsible only to God.

By what process was it understood that the papal office had acquired this *potestas*?

The *potestas* of the papal office was recognized to be of two sorts: *potestas ordinis* and *potestas jurisdictionis*.

The *potestas ordinis* belonged to a consecrated bishop, and thus the pope enjoyed it already, before his election.

To it belonged the sacramental powers of a priest which he acquired at his ordination or consecration and which were believed to have been handed down in an unbroken succession from bishop to bishop, not unlike the *auctoritas* of the Roman senate.

The *potestas jurisdictionis*, on the other hand, was peculiar to the office of pope. It was the 'right' in virtue of which all ecclesiastics were subject to his rule. This was understood to derive directly from the commission of Christ to St. Peter to found and govern the church, as recorded in the New Testament.

In short, to be elected pope was to succeed to the *potestas* with which it was believed St. Peter had been directly endowed by God. It was the *potestas* of an absolute ruler, responsible to God alone.

As successor to St. Peter, and 'head' of the Christian church in Western Europe, the pope was, then, a ruler exercising an *imperium* over all his subordinates. In the course of time, a great deal of landed property came to be annexed to the office of pope, but his rule was never *dominium*, rule in virtue of the ownership of property. It was *potestas*, political rule, *not* 'lordship'.

This rule was exercised with the assistance of a *curia* of cardinals; and it made itself felt throughout Christendom by means of papal emissaries, known as legates, direct representatives of the pope himself.

The *potestas jurisdictionis* of the pope was the unshared and absolute right: (1) to make decisions about the conduct of ecclesiastical affairs, and (2) to make law for the church, and to judge all ecclesiastical causes according to the canon law, which was, so to speak, the domestic law of the church. It was a *potestas* which went back to that of the Roman emperors, who had been the recognized heads of the Christian church, and who had often been depicted in ecclesiastical robes.

In every realm of Christendom there were ecclesiastical courts, conducted usually by bishops, which had jurisdiction not only over the conduct of ecclesiastics, but over all men in respect of certain matters.

In virtue of this ecclesiastic jurisdiction of the pope throughout Christendom, it was recognized that in every realm of Christendom there were at least two ruling authorities – an ecclesiastical or papal authority, and a civil or kingly authority. And these two jurisdictions were known as the *sacerdotium* and the *regnum*.

But the papal court in Rome was the head of a hierarchy of courts, itself hearing all important cases and settling appeals from lower courts.

Moreover, it was the pope as a judge in his own court who assumed jurisdiction over the disputes of medieval rulers and who sanctioned treaties between kings. It was a papal bull which in 1493 divided the newly discovered but unexplored lands of South America between the kings of Spain and Portugal.

In short, the papal *potestas jurisdictionis* was the rule of a ruler, a legislator, and a judge.

Now, as may be expected, this understanding of the *potestas* of the papal office did not appear suddenly. It emerged gradually and was not fully established until the twelfth century. But it had already been formulated in the eleventh century by one of the most remarkable of medieval popes – Gregory VII, known as Hildebrand.

The so-called *Dictatus Papae Gregorii VII* (1075) set out the principles of the papal *imperium* with absolute clarity.

The pope is declared to be head of the ecclesiastical hierarchy of Christendom; and all *potestas* exercised by any ecclesiastic derives from the *potestas* of the pope.

All are agents of the pope; and his direct agents, papal legates, are declared to take precedence over all others.

The pope has the sole right to appoint, transfer, or depose all holders of ecclesiastical offices.

Every ecclesiastical court in Christendom operates under his authority; the pope himself is the final dispenser of all justice.

He has the sole right to promulgate laws for the church, to create new bishoprics, to ordain clerics. He alone may summon a general council of the church.

Thus, there emerged in the twelfth century the understanding of the papal *potestas* as a *plentitudo ecclesiasticae potestas*; an absolute *imperium*, derived from God alone, responsible only to God; boundless, exceptionless, complete, and imprescriptible – a *potestas perfecta*.

In addition to this 'absolute' *potestas*, or right to rule, the pope claimed (and it was recognized to belong to his office) an *auctoritas*, 'authority'.

Now, we have seen that *auctoritas* for the Roman signified an activity of guardianship rather than 'rule', a right to advise, and to teach, and to admonish. And this is what it also meant in the political vocabulary of the medieval church. It corresponded to the notion of *gubernaculum* – the right to decide policy; to be a helmsman.

The papal *auctoritas* was exercised in respect of two different, but related, matters.

(1) In virtue of his *auctoritas* the pope was recognized to be the guardian, the custodian of Christian doctrine, and its sole authoritative interpreter. This 'authority' he was held to have derived from St. Peter. It might be used to settle, judicially, actual disputes about Christian belief; but it was something much larger and less defined than merely this.

Like the *auctoritas* of the Roman senate, which was the guardianship of the tradition and the *fortuna* of the *populus Romanus*, the papal *auctoritas* was the authority to guard and to 'augment' and to interpret Christian belief according to the tradition founded by St. Peter in response to the commission of Christ and carried on in the great doctrinal general councils of the church in the second and third centuries.

Here, as in so many other respects, the Christian church in the West reflected the beliefs of the ancient Romans: the pope in respect of doctrine was like an emperor who had succeeded to the *auctoritas* of the senate; a general council of the church itself corresponding to the senate.

(2) But the pope was not only recognized to have *auctoritas* over Christian doctrine; he claimed, and he often successfully exercised, *auctoritas* over the kings and emperors of Christendom.

Here, also, *auctoritas* was the right to advise, to teach, to warn, and to admonish rulers. This *auctoritas* went back in an unbroken succession to the *auctoritas* exercised by the great bishops over emperors in Roman days: an ecclesiastic like Ambrose of Milan admonishing an emperor like Theodosius.

The ground of this *auctoritas* was the pope's position as guardian of the Christian church; and it was often used to instruct kings and emperors in their duties as Christian rulers and as protectors of the church.

But in the course of time it went far beyond this, and became the right to instruct and to admonish rulers in all their conduct as rulers.

This is what pope Galasius I in the fifth century believed himself to be establishing when he claimed that, while the kingly and the ecclesiastical *potestas* were separated and were exercised in Christendom by *two* different sorts of rulers, popes and kings; nevertheless, the ecclesiastical *auctoritas* extended to the supervision of the conduct of kings and emperors. Innocent III instructed John to come to an understanding with and make peace with the magnates of England in 1215.

Now, at least from the time of Gregory VII, this papal *auctoritas* over kings began to be interpreted and used as if it were *potestas* – that is to say, a right to rule, to command, and to punish.

For the most part it was used when a monarch ruled in such a way as to neglect or to prejudice the interests of the church in his realm; but in fact the claim went far beyond this. And at least part of the ground of the conversion of this *auctoritas* into *potestas* was the belief that kings, in virtue of being anointed persons, were in some sense ecclesiastics and therefore came under the *potestas jurisdictionis* of the pope.

Nor were the punishments at the disposal of the pope with which to execute the judgments of this *potestas* ineffective. He claimed the right to depose kings and emperors, and to excommunicate them thereby to absolve their subjects of their allegiance.

Gregory VII deposed the Emperor Henry IV; Innocent IV deposed Sancho II of Portugal and appointed a regent in his place; and King John of England was excommunicated and his subjects absolved from their allegiance.

The papal monarchy in the middle ages was, then, a very close approximation to one of the ideal types of medieval monarchy, namely, an 'absolute' monarchy. And, in respect of the pope's *potestas* and *auctoritas* being universal throughout Christendom, he was universally recognized as one of the 'rulers' in every medieval realm. And he was a ruler whose jurisdiction went far beyond narrowly ecclesiastical matters. He was the ruler of all that jurisdiction known as *sacerdotium*.

But, although the papal monarchy is a close approximation to this ideal type of medieval monarchy – 'absolute' monarchy – it did not quite coincide with the type, which remained a merely ideal type.

For the history of the later middle ages is, among other things, the history of the incursion of the beliefs and ideas connected with 'conditional' monarchy even into the papal monarchy itself.

The whole of what is called the conciliar movement in the fifteenth century, all the claims then made on behalf of general councils of the church to share the authority of the pope, and all the ideas you will find, for example, in the writings of Marsilius of Padua about the government of the church – all these are to be understood as the ideas connected with that other ideal type of medieval monarchy ('conditional' monarchy) being applied to the papal monarchy itself.

Nevertheless, medieval Europe never came nearer to a conception of absolute monarchy than it did in the papacy; and when the notion of 'absolute' civil monarchy was later explored, the model in the minds of the explorers was that of the papacy.

When some kings in the sixteenth century claimed a *plentitudo potestas* they were aping a claim made centuries before on behalf of popes.

The church of Latin Christianity was, then, a political institution; and the manner in which it was governed, and the manner in which its rulers exerted their right to rule, represents one of the most important directions of medieval thought about the office of ruler.

And, as a political education and example, the church may be said to have made medieval Europe familiar with two very important ideas.

As we shall see, the authority of the office of a *king* only very gradually emerged out of the authority of 'lordship'. 'Kingship' only gradually became distinguished from 'lordship' – *regale* (kingly rule) from *dominium* (rule in virtue of ownership).

But the *potestas* of the pope was never *dominium*; it never had anything to do with 'ownership' of land. It derived from Christ's commission to St. Peter. Papal authority began by being *'regal'* authority. And thus, the church supplied medieval Europe with an idea of 'rulership' already completely detached from ownership.

Secondly, the papacy supplied medieval Europe with an idea of *absolute* regal authority. And the so-called 'absolute' rulers of Europe in the sixteenth and seventeenth centuries were applying the model of papal rule to a civil state, having themselves in fact acquired some, if not all, the *potestas* of a pope.

5

The second example of monarchical government I want to consider is that of the kings of France.

France, after the collapse of the Carolingian empire, was a land in which the great dukes and counts ruled in their dukedoms and counties. Their rule was 'lordship' – that is, the right to rule based upon the ownership of land. They were *grands seigneurs*.

Each was the immediate owner of an estate, a *demesne*. And beyond this they administered a customary law among their 'vassals,' as these did among those under them. They were jealous of their independence; their titles were hereditary because they were connected with land; and they had a monopoly of military force within their counties or dukedoms, which were often very large.

Among these, in the tenth century, was the count of Paris, whose lands in the Ile de France were, in fact, less extensive than any of the other *grands seigneurs*; he was by no means the greatest 'lord' in France.

There had been kings in France in earlier days, the most notable of whom was Clovis, king of the Salian Franks in the fifth century. A convert to Christianity, Clovis had been crowned in an ecclesiastical ceremony in Paris, and had exercised some vague authority beyond his own lands.

In 987 Hugh Capet, Count of Paris, was elected 'king' of the West Franks by his fellow lords – the dukes of Aquitaine, Burgundy, Normandy, and Brittany, and the counts of Flanders, Vermandois, Champagne, and Toulouse. And a 'king' (though nothing more than a count in his own *demesne*) is something more than a *seigneur*. What more is he? Where does his authority as king come from?

His authority in no sense extended into the lands of his fellow lords and electors. It was solely an authority over *them*, a recognition by them of his value mainly as an organizer of defence against common enemies. He was a 'king' of 'lords', not of France. Hence, whatever the source of his authority, it was certainly not *seigneurial*. Although, of course, his actual power (*potentia*) was derived from the resources which came from being *seigneur* in his own land.

But, he was a ruler, crowned in an ecclesiastical ceremony at least four centuries old even in France; he was the holder of a sanctified office and therefore something very much more than a count of Paris, and his authority was significantly more than merely a 'lord' elected by his fellow 'lords'. He had been elected to an office.

Indeed, tracing his office back to Clovis and to Charlemagne, it was understood that his royal *potestas* had not been given him by his electors, nor did it derive from his royal blood; it was something he had acquired in the anointing ceremony of his coronation. The oil of anointment had, according to repute, been brought by a dove from heaven for Clovis's coronation, and it was preserved from generation to generation, over centuries. He was king *Dei gratia*.

This was the peculiarity of kingship in France. The king in France made no promises at his coronation, he acknowledged no duties to his people – he could scarcely be said to have subjects – but only to God. He was *rex sacerdos*; the bishop's words at the coronation were: 'through this crown you become a sharer in our ministry'.

If his electors, his 'vassals', the great dukes and counts, had given him more authority, there might have emerged a notion of kingship in which the kingly *potestas* was understood to derive from the gift of his 'vassals', the notion of a king accountable to his subjects. But they gave him little and that grudgingly. What power he acquired he took for himself; his authority came from God at his coronation.

Kingship in France, then, began as an approximation to what I have called one of the two ideal extremes of medieval monarchy – 'absolute' monarchy.

This did not mean that French kings had extraordinarily great power; quite the reverse, they had very little. It signified only that their *potestas* was derived, not from their subjects, but directly from God, and was bestowed on them in an ecclesiastical ceremony.

But, having become kings, the counts of Paris began to rule in their own 'country', not only as *seigneurs*, but also as kings. They ruled as *imperatores*, exercising an *imperium*, not derived form 'lordship' but from God. The law of the city of Paris became the king's law, promulgated *de plenitudo potestatis regiae* (out of his absolute kingly right). And the emergence of the French monarchy was a process in which a king, powerful only in his own 'lordship', and coming to rule his own country as a king, and *not* merely as a 'count', gradually extended his authority from this base.

At first, the most he could exact from the great dukes and counts was what they exacted from *their* 'vassals' – namely, 'fealty'; the obligation not to make war on him and to support him in his military enterprises.

And the French monarchy emerged *not* from a king enlisting the cooperation of his mighty 'vassals' and acquiring extended authority from them, but from a king, believed to rule *Dei gratia*, gradually destroying his 'vassals' and extending his *demesne* to take in their land, by conquest, sequestration, marriage, and all the other means by which a medieval monarchy could emerge. It took many centuries. But this was not a process in which he extended his 'lordship', but his 'kingship'.

The result of this was that, in the French monarchy, 'lordship' and kingly *potestas* were joined in a way which they were not joined elsewhere. And if this had not been so, the history of French politics would have been very different from what it has been.

Now, there was one important consequence of these beliefs about the authority of the French king.

Since the king ruled *Dei gratia*, his competitor in authority was not his subjects, but the church. A king ruling *Dei gratia* was a king whose source of authority made him susceptible to papal pressure. And throughout the middle ages the kingly government of France suffered more than that of any other medieval realm from papal supervision and papal interference.

It was, indeed, in an attempt to frustrate the claims of the pope in France that the French monarchy acquired some of the characteristics of that other ideal type of medieval monarchy – 'conditional' monarchy. We shall see later what these were and how deep they went.

6

The third example of kingship I want to notice may be called 'feudal' kingship. It may be thought of as an approximation to that ideal type of kingship I have called 'conditional' kingship.

The word 'feudal' may be taken to stand for an 'order' of an elementary kind which emerged first in northern France and Burgundy and later spread, in various forms, nearly all over Europe, and became a recognized *political* order.

From one point of view it may be seen to be the sort of 'order' which sprang from an extension of the early practice of 'commendation'. The weak, but free, man 'commends' himself to a stranger and thus becomes the 'vassal' of a 'lord'. The 'vassal' owes services to his 'lord'; the 'lord' protects his 'vassal', for example, he holds a court in which disputes between vassals may be settled.

From another point of view, it can be seen to spring from the practice of a large owner of land giving tenancies of parts of his estate to others in return for services. The tenancies may be of various sorts, and the services of various kinds.

Either way, the result is a legal relationship of mutual benefit, based upon the ownership of land, between a 'lord' (*dominus, seigneur*) and his 'vassals'. Both are 'free' men; and there is a compact between them made under oath.

Now, this arrangement may take place at any level of society. But when several great 'lords' 'commend' themselves to one of their number, electing him to perform some office on behalf of all (such as that of an organizer of defence against a common enemy) a 'feudal' *king* may emerge.

Or, when the 'lord' of a very extensive estate parcels out large parts of this estate (in this case called 'fiefs') to lesser 'lords' in return for services, and undertakes to protect his 'vassal' lords, again a 'feudal' king may emerge.

In both cases, the 'lord' who enjoys 'kingship' is legally related to his 'lordly' vassals; they have entered into a mutual compact with him in which each owes to the other a service or services.

The normal services owed by a 'vassal' to his king were *auxilium* (military aid) and *concilium* (advice or counsel), and the duty of not taking up arms against him. The normal protection was a court for settling disputes.

But where a 'feudal' king does emerge, he is something different from merely one 'lord' among others. His authority over his 'vassals' derives from the compact he has with them, and is *not* itself the authority of 'lordship'.

And further, when this king is crowned in an ecclesiastical ceremony he acquires an added authority, quite different from that of either 'lordship' or of compact.

The 'feudal' king's superiority is signified in his duty to protect not merely the 'lordships' of his fiefholders, but the kingdom. And a kingdom is something different from a 'lordship'. And it lies also in his coronation.

The conditional character of feudal kingship is signified in the king's duty to keep the compact he has entered into with his fiefholders to perform the services expected of him, and in their right to hold him to that duty.

A 'feudal' monarchy, then, was an elaborate network of personal legal relationships based upon the holding of land. The king is recognized to be the head of a hierarchy, owing duties to those under him, and being recognized to have the rights necessary for the performance of those duties. These are the rights of kingship.

Now, there was an element of 'feudalism' in most medieval monarchies. Sometimes it was qualified (as in France) by a strong belief in the *Dei gratia* title of a king; sometimes it was strong enough to assert itself as the dominant belief in respect of the king's authority.

This was so in England, in spite of some features in the Anglo-Norman monarchy which gave the king a stronger position and a more independent authority that a simply 'feudal' monarch.

But in England, also, kingship had peculiar difficulty in emerging from 'lordship'.

At the Norman conquest it was established that, notionally, the whole territory of England belonged to William the Conquerer by right of conquest. At the conquest all the ancient seats of 'lordship' were abolished, and William asserted his 'lordship' over the whole land.

This territory was then parceled out as 'fiefs' to 'lords' who thereby became the tenants-in-chief of the king, owing him services. Each tenant-in-chief had sub-tenants of parts of his 'fief'; and the king himself had the rights of 'lordship' over his own *demesne*, upon the resources of which he lived and governed.

But the 'fiefs' of the tenants-in-chief were scattered; there were no enormous estates such as existed on the continent. And the royal *demesne*, also, was not concentrated in one place, but consisted of scattered 'royal' manors.

No tenant-in-chief enjoyed the right of *justicia* (the right to hold an independent court) in his 'fief'. Justice was the concern of the king throughout his realm. And by the Oath of Salisbury a direct relationship was established between the king and, not only his tenants-in-chief, but all his subjects. The Norman kings of England were among the *first* to have 'subjects' who were *not* themselves 'lords'. They are kings of 'England'.

Now, all this was something like a carefully planned 'feudal' monarchy. It gave the king the strongest possible hold over his tenants-in-chief, but it admitted that the king owed duties to his subjects to the performance of which *they* had the right to hold him. And this was recognized in the coronation oath of medieval English kings.

The king in England, then, like the king in France, was certainly believed to be responsible to God for the care of his subjects, and he was certainly believed to rule *Dei gratia*.

But there was something else in the situation which qualified the absoluteness of his authority.

He owed duties to his subjects; he recognized these duties in his coronation oath; and his tenants-in-chief were recognized to have the legal right to hold the king to the performance of these duties – a right which they exercised on several occasions, the most notable of which being the presentation of Magna Charta to King John in 1215.

The authority of the king of England was the authority of the head of a 'feudal' hierarchy of 'lords'. But, if his authority was, thus, 'conditional' or 'constitutional' (in the way in which the authority of the king of France was not, and the authority of the pope certainly was not) it was, nevertheless, very great.

In so far, then, as a 'feudal' element entered into the authority of a medieval king, his 'kingship' approximated to what I have called the ideal type of 'conditional' or 'constitutional' monarchy.

And it was an acute observation of political writers in Russia in the nineteenth century that what stood in the way of converting the 'absolute' rule of the tsars into a 'constitutional' rule was the fact that Russia had never been feudal.

7

These, then, were the main directions of medieval thought about the authority of rulers.

(1) The kingly office (except in the case of the pope) was a notion of ruling which gradually emerged out of 'lordship'.

(2) Since the actual resources of a king were, largely, the resources of his own *demesne*, 'lordship' (the right to rule derived from ownership of land) remained a component of the notion of kingship. The dual personality, or 'two bodies', of a king.

(3) But the *potestas* of a king, his right to rule as a king, was gradually detached from his 'lordship'. And the beliefs which clustered round it pulled in *two* different directions.

- Those beliefs which tended to recognize his authority as *Dei gratia*, and therefore, in respect of his subjects, *absolute*.
- Those beliefs which tended to recognize his authority as that of the head of a feudal hierarchy responsible to his subjects for his rule, and to recognize his subjects as having a legal right to recall him to his duties, and perhaps even (if necessary) to depose him.

Editorial Note

LSE 1/1/21, file 4, fos. 271–94. Fos. 271–5 are photocopies of autograph sheets; fos. 276–94 are photocopies of a typescript with autograph corrections.

Eighteen

The Medieval Theory of Empire

1

The history of medieval political thought is littered with the words *imperium* and *imperator* – 'empire' and 'emperor'. But it is not always clear what these words stand for; and, in different contexts, they have so many different meanings that, at first sight, they seem to stand for nothing specific at all. Nevertheless, they were connected with a direction of medieval political thinking (half practical and half visionary) which is both interesting and very important for understanding medieval politics.

The words themselves were, of course, inherited from ancient Rome; and, although they were often detached from any reminiscence of ancient Rome, there was one connection in which they were used which contained a very clear reminiscence of ancient Rome. How were they used and what did they stand for in the middle ages?

First, we must understand that there were many realms within the political experience of the middle ages which, at one time or another, were called and recognized as 'empires', and were ruled over by 'emperors'.

There was, in the first place, the 'Roman empire' of the East, with its capital in Byzantium. This lasted until 1453 when it fell before the onslaught of the Turks. Throughout the middle ages, after the fall of Rome in 410 A.D. to the Goths, this Byzantine empire was recognized to be the one genuine relic of ancient Rome, dating from Diocletian's division of the empire in the third century.

Then there was a Bulgarian empire, a Serbian empire, a German empire, from the thirteenth century a Russian empire, and the Castilian kings of Spain were rulers over what was known as a Spanish empire. In all of these cases the 'emperor' was a sort of 'king of kings' who exercised a hegemony over various realms and princes and this hegemony was thought of as an 'empire'. They might perhaps be called 'feudal' empires; at any rate they were empires on the ground.

Secondly, the words 'emperor' and 'empire' were used simply to indicate political independence, to indicate that the ruler and the realm were subject to no higher or external authority. This is the meaning of the words in the well-known medieval political maxim: *rex est imperator in regno suo* – 'the king is emperor in his own realm'. And it was reflected also in Henry VIII's claim that 'This realm of England is an empire'. It stood for an assertion of political independence made against the claim of any other ruler to have superior jurisdiction, and (in the case of Henry VIII) made against a claim of the papacy.

Moreover, various kings of medieval Europe took imperial titles (like the title Augustus) – Philip II of France was known as 'Philip Augustus' – intending only to assert their importance in a general way.

But, thirdly, there was a quite different use of these words 'empire' and 'emperor' – a use in which they were neither mere assertions of independence, *nor* indicating a particular piece of the territory of Europe and the supremacy of the ruler of that territory. And it is this use which we have to consider.

2

After the death of the emperor Honorius in 423 A.D. there ceased to be a 'Roman empire' in strict descent from Augustus in the West. From this date the only Roman emperor, in this strict descent, was the emperor in Byzantium.

Nevertheless, from the year 800, for a short period, Charlemagne, the king of the Franks and Lombards, held the title of 'Roman emperor', a title which one of his sons, Louis, also held. Then, from the eleventh century, the expression 'Roman empire' (*imperium Romanum*) came back into currency: from the twelfth century there was something which was called 'the holy empire' (*sacrum imperium*); and from the thirteenth century there was something called 'the holy Roman empire' (*sacrum imperium Romanum*) which was supposed to have lasted until it was destroyed by Napoleon in 1808.

Our questions are: What were medieval people thinking of when they used these expressions: 'Roman empire', 'holy empire', and 'holy Roman empire'? And, what were they thinking of when they used the word *imperator* (emperor), and did *not* mean by it (for example) the ruler of the Bulgars, or a mere assertion of independence on the part of a feudal king?

Perhaps we should be clear, first, that they were *not* thinking about either of two things which we might suppose them to be thinking about.

They were not thinking of a so-called 'revived' ancient Roman empire in the West. They called it (often, but not always) a Roman empire; and I don't believe that they could easily have thought what they did think without having some reminiscence of the empire of ancient Rome in their minds. But they were not thinking of a 'restored' or 're-established', or a 'renewed' Roman empire. They were, in short, thinking of something *new*, something that made sense only in medieval circumstances.

They were not thinking of a piece of the territory of Western Europe ruled over by somebody called an 'emperor'. There were such territorial empires, but the medieval 'Roman' or 'holy Roman' empire was *not* a piece of territory. Consequently, when they spoke of a 'Roman' or a 'holy Roman' emperor, they meant a man who occupied an 'imperial' office, who had duties, functions, and an 'imperial' authority, but whose *imperium* was not a piece of territory; because there was no piece of territory in medieval Europe which could be called the 'Roman' or the 'Holy Roman' empire.

3

Now, to our way of thinking, this appears an odd situation: an emperor without an empire; a 'Roman' emperor, yet *not* believed to be a successor to Augustus. And we may resolve the puzzle by asking: Who were the people who thought and talked in this manner? When did they begin to think and talk in this way? Who were these emperors? How did they acquire their title? What were their duties if they were not, as emperors, the rulers of a piece of territory?

(1) The medieval Roman 'empire', or the holy Roman empire, was, fundamentally, an invention of ecclesiastics;

first of popes and later of ecclesiastical lawyers. And it was a remarkable case of the invention in practice of something that was required by theory but which did not exist until it had been invented. *Expedit esse imperatorem*: 'it is necessary that there should be an emperor'.

What is the necessity? Why must there be an emperor in the sense that if he did not exist he had to be invented? The short answer to this question is that an 'emperor' was required by ecclesiastical theory, and by ecclesiastical circumstances. The situation was as follows:

In the time when the ancient Roman empire in the West was still a reality, and after the adoption of Christianity as its official religion, the emperors were, in a special sense, the secular protectors of the church. Some, like Theodosius in the fourth century, were recognized as performing this function with special zeal. Julian the Apostate, it is true, was notably hostile to the church and its interests, but he was recognized as having failed in one of the duties of a Christian emperor.

On the death of Honorius, however, there were no more Roman emperors in the West, and the leaders of the church (and later the popes) had to seek protectors where they could among the secular rulers of Christendom. In the early centuries they looked to the emperor in Byzantium – and in the fifth century we have seen that pope Galasius I could write to the emperor in Byzantium setting out the ecclesiastical theory (which was merely an abridgment of earlier practice) that pope and emperor were, under God, the joint rulers of Christendom, the pope exercising an ecclesiastical *auctoritas* and the emperor exercising an imperial *potestas* in the interests of the Christian faith – but the emperor was powerless to do what was wanted. After his failure to establish his authority in the West in the sixth century, he was no longer a possible protector.

(2) This is the context of the event which may be taken as the enterprise of the church to make for itself an 'emperor' in the West who should be its sword and its shield, and also its agent in the protection of the Christian faith against its enemies. This event was the coronation of Charles, King of the Franks and Lombards, as 'Emperor of the Romans' by Pope Leo III on Christmas day in the year 800; Charles having been 'elected' (according to the ancient forms) by the people of the city of Rome.

Charles was the mightiest king in Christendom – the obvious choice of a pope looking for a sword and shield for the church in the West. Moreover, there was immediate work to be done on behalf of the church – the protection of Christendom against the invading Arabs. In short, there was a function to be performed and the functionary had been invented to perform it.

What, then, emerged in the year 800 was this strange medieval figure – an emperor without an empire. For Charles was not 'emperor of the Franks'; he was, as emperor, ruler of no territory. But he was the chosen partner of the pope in the custody of Christendom and protector of the interests of the church and the Christian faith. Thus, *imperator* was the title of he who had been chose above all other Christian princes to occupy what might be regarded as an office, in relation to the church, vacant since the death of Honorius.

The office itself might be said to be old – in the sense that ancient Roman emperors, like Theodosius, had been protectors of the interests of the church. But it was really a new office which contained only a dim reminiscence of ancient times. Perhaps, no pope could have thought of creating this office of protector-in-chief of the church if he had not remembered past times when there had been an emperor, a successor to Augustus, to perform this function. But what Leo III did in 800 was to make a secular partner for himself; and this was something new. And what he made was a Roman emperor.

(3) Now, setting aside the practical convenience of having a powerful protector (and the added convenience to the papacy of having an 'emperor' whom the pope had himself chosen and crowned and might therefore be able to control), there lay behind all this what may be called a 'vision', which also had in it some reminiscence of the past. It was a 'vision' which gathered strength and precision during the middle ages, but remarkably enough it was a 'vision' which almost totally neglected the direction which events were in fact taking during the medieval centuries, and did very little to modify that direction.

It was a 'vision' of Christendom as a single realm, guided, directed, and ruled (under God) by a single spiritual ruler in partnership with a single temporal ruler; a dyarchy of pope and emperor. Each of these joint vicars of God having his own duties to perform, but together composing the government and direction of a *respublica Christiana* ('a Christian realm'), or an *imperium Christianum* (a Christian empire), as it later came to be called. Kings and princes, in their own realms, were to be subordinates, almost agents, of popes and emperors.

It is, of course, noticeable that this conception ran counter to the main trend of medieval times which went to the gradual construction of the independent nation states that emerged unmistakably in the sixteenth century. But this does not detract from the supreme importance in medieval politics of this piece of what may be called 'visionary' political thinking. It was the conception of Christendom as a single community. And it was a conception which was capable of drawing sustenance from at least some of the circumstances of the middle ages – the recovery of the ancient Roman law, for example, provoked in some visionaries the notion that here was the common law for the *respublica Christiana*.

4

The subsequent history of this 'vision' and its counterpart in medieval government was full of vicissitudes. The office of 'holy emperor' never, of course, became hereditary during the middle ages. According to the ecclesiastical 'vision' it was an office bestowed by the pope, but in the course of the tenth century it was more or less appropriated, as of right, by the kings of Germany, and thus became connected with the territories of these kings, namely, Germany, Burgundy, and Italy – although, of course, these territories were not the territories of an 'empire'.

But popes found many of these 'emperors' uneasy partners, often unwilling to perform their duties in respect of the church. Gregory VII (in the eleventh century), and his great successors in the papacy, managed for a time to reimpose their control upon the emperors; but by the middle of the fourteenth century this notional 'empire' of Christendom had become a German empire, in which certain of the princes of Germany were the 'electors' to the office of 'emperor'. And it thus remained, more or less, until the nineteenth century. The 'emperor' was still, in these centuries, often crowned by the pope, and he could sometimes be prevailed upon to fight the battles of the church – but less and less frequently.

Indeed, for a long period, it was the king of France, rather than the holy Roman emperor, who answered the call of popes to undertake crusades, to put down heresy and to perform the other functions for which this emperor had been invented. The 'vision', it is fair to say, remained a 'vision'.

5

Now, this vision of an *imperium Christianum*, Christendom as a single whole ruled jointly by a pope and emperor, left some of the most profound political thinkers of the middle ages quite unmoved.

St. Augustine, who could have imagined it in terms of a Roman empire, properly speaking, was indifferent to it. What did it matter under whose rule a Christian lived for the brief life of a mortal man, so long as he was not required to do anything impious? A universal emperor was no better and no worse than a local king or prince as a channel for God's providential grace. Christendom had no need of political as well as ecclesiastical unity.

And St. Thomas Aquinas, in the thirteenth century, was similarly unmoved by it. His realistic attention was turned to a Europe fast separating itself into sovereign states, and he was concerned with the quality of the government of these states and not with any fantasy of an empire of Christendom.

But, before the vision faded, it found some notable protagonists; and of these the most celebrated was Dante, who lived in the second half of the thirteenth century. He was a Florentine poet, and for much of his life a political exile from Florence; and in a book called *De monarchia* ('Concerning Imperial Government') he gave what he believed to be a reasoned explanation of the necessity of the *imperium Christianum*, a 'philosophy' of the *respublica Christiana*.

The most interesting feature of this explanation is that it is carried out entirely in Aristotelian terms. Nobody writing at that time could fail to be profoundly influenced by the Aristotelian understanding of human activity, but Dante performed the *tour de force* of explaining and defending this peculiarly medieval 'vision' of Christendom as a political as well as an ecclesiastical unity in the terms of Aristotelian teleology.

There is, he says, following Aristotle, one universal end in all human conduct, namely, the achievement of that excellence which is potential in human 'nature'.

This end is pursued in all kinds of human associations – in the activity which goes on in a family or household, in that which is characteristic of a village, a city or a kingdom. It is absurd to think that, in each of these different contexts, a different end is being pursued; there is one end being pursued in all, namely, the human *eudaimonia*; and it is absurd to suppose that this single end can ever be pursued by a man out of relation to any other man. Human beings are, naturally, *animalia politica*.

Further, the conditions of the achievement of human excellence are the conditions which it is the proper function of a 'government' to provide – namely, peace, justice, and freedom. Without peace there can be no civilized life; justice is rendering each man his due; and freedom is emancipation from necessity and that opportunity of rational choice which, for Aristotle, characterized a human being.

Now, since there is but one end for man, and since the conditions in which this end can be pursued are also universal, it is better that mankind be under the rule of one than under the rule of many different princes and magistrates; peace will be more sure and justice more certain. In short, the oneness of mankind indicates the appropriateness, if not the necessity, of one ruler and regulator of human conditions, the necessity of a single 'imperial' political association.

This, which I have described in a very simplified form, is the design of the argument which Dante uses to explain and elucidate the centuries old 'vision' of the *imperium Christianum*.

The argument does not stop there. It goes on to demonstrate the appropriateness for Christendom of a Roman emperor, notionally the successor Augustus; and it goes on to show that, while human beings may achieve their 'natural' end (in the Aristotelian sense) only in these circumstances, they also have a 'supernatural' end (final salvation) which is ministered to by the single ecclesiastical authority of Christendom – namely, the church.

Thus, Dante's *De monarchia* is an elucidation of this 'vision' of an *imperium Christianum*, governed jointly by pope and Christian emperor, each with his separate functions to peform in relation to the ends pursued in all human activity.

It is an Aristotelian-Christian theory of government. And one of the remarkable things about it is that it was written at a time when this 'vision' of the *respublica Christiana* has less to correspond to it in medieval politics than ever before. The *De monarchia* was, in a sense, already out of date when it was written. Christendom as a *respublica Christiana* was, perhaps, the greatest of medieval political dreams. But by the end of the thirteenth century Western Europe was fast becoming a collection of emergent independent states, and the political authority of the pope and his emperor was declining.

Editorial Note

LSE 1/1/21, file 4, fos. 295– 302. Photocopy of a typescript with autograph corrections.

Nineteen

Medieval Law

1

We have been considering the disposition of medieval ideas about the right of a ruler to rule – the authority of kings.

I want now to consider an analogous topic: medieval beliefs about *law*, and the authority of law.

Now, what is meant by 'law' is a rule of conduct which demands to be obeyed as a matter of right. It is order induced, *not* by violence, but by authority.

The most fundamental of all distinctions in political thought is the distinction between 'force' or 'violence' and 'authority'; between *potentia*, which is physical, and *potestas* or *auctoritas*, which is mental; between 'might' and 'right'.

Both 'violence' and 'authority' may each produce 'order'; but they produce it in different manners, and the 'order' of 'authority' has a different quality from the order of 'violence'.

'Violence' exacts obedience by making disobedience physically impossible; but 'authority' demands obedience in virtue of a 'right' to be obeyed, and it succeeds in exacting obedience when this 'right' to be obeyed is recognized to be legitimate and is acceded to.

Hobbes understood this better than most political writers. He knew that government must have 'authority'; and that 'to have authority' meant to have been constituted in a manner which was recognized to give it 'authority'. He knew that a government must also have 'power' (*potentia*). And he knew that the two were different from one another.

Thus, a ruler may have both 'authority' and 'power'. But his 'authority' is *not* based upon his 'power'; it is based upon whatever is believed to be his 'right' to rule.

Consequently, when obedience is demanded as a 'right', it is always possible to ask the question: What is the ground of your right to be obeyed? And the answer must be, *not* a demonstration of superior force, but in terms of a *belief* which makes the 'right' acceptable.

We have considered some of the beliefs, current in medieval times, which offered themselves as the grounds of a ruler's right to rule.

And if one seeks for a general movement in medieval thought on this subject, it is a movement away from the belief that the ownership of land ('lordship') gives the 'right' to rule, and towards the belief that a king's right to rule comes either from a divine endowment, or from a feudal compact.

In short, 'authority' rests upon *opinion*; it reflects a belief, found to be acceptable, about how 'authority' may be acquired. To believe that a king's right to rule is based upon a feudal compact is to believe that a feudal compact can endow an office with 'authority'.

Now, what we mean by 'law' is an 'authority' of this sort. It is a rule of conduct which demands to be obeyed as a matter of 'right', and *not* merely because, *if* it is not obeyed, conformity will be exacted by force.

Consequently, all thinking about law is apt to return, again and again, to the question: Whence comes this authority?

All answers to this question will reflect current beliefs about what constitutes authoritativeness. And most answers to this question may be expected to refer to the source from which the law is believed to come, or (*if* the law is recognized to have been *made*) from the *manner* in which it has been made.

What were the medieval answers?

A 'statute' today is recognized to be authoritative *if* it has been properly made by parliament, because we recognize parliament to have the sole 'right' to make a 'statute'.

2

Now, the peoples of medieval Europe were certain of one thing. They may have been doubtful about to whom they owed their loyalty, and their loyalties may often have been divided; but they knew they had *laws*.

In early times, these laws were, for the most part, not written-down laws; they were customs of conduct which were recognized as proper to be obeyed.

Even in the darkest and most chaotic circumstances, when order was apt to be imposed by violence – that is, by men who merely possessed superior force and had no very well-recognized 'right' to be obeyed – the peoples of medieval Europe never lost the sense of being under a 'law'.

Indeed, the difficulty often was, *not* that there was no law, but that the chaos had invaded the law itself. There often seemed to be a distracting conflict of legal duties.

Law, among these people, was, then, *older* than violence; and often enough 'violence' was recognized as breach of law.

These peoples came into Western Europe with their tribal laws; they entered territories whose native inhabitants (with whom they mixed) lived under other laws of their own. The circumstances of movement broke up the tribal communities, and small groups of families might find themselves surrounded by peoples with different laws from themselves.

The circumstances of settlement, in the end, after many centuries, generated more or less homogeneous territorial communities, each with its own law; but local variety of law persisted, and had not disappeared in some places even in the nineteenth century.

Law for medieval peoples was primordial; they might have, as yet, nothing they could recognize as a homeland; they might have almost nothing recognizable as 'government'; but they had law.

And what they recognized as a 'community', in the first place, was a group of people who lived under one law. The differences between communities were differences, *not* between 'governments' but between *laws*.

This applied not merely to communities of one sort, but to communities of all sorts. For example, by the seventh century Western European peoples had become familiar with two great religious communities besides Christians; namely, Jews and Muslims. And they identified these communities as people who had laws of their own – the law of Moses and the law of Muhammad.

Religion was recognized as obedience to a law, and consequently Christians, Jews, and Muslims were three 'legally' distinguishable communities.

Moreover, as the great realms of Christendom emerged, and the legal chaos of the early centuries was modified, these peoples of medieval Europe became familiar with new bodies of law of great variety:

- Ancient, customary law, the folk-law;
- 'Feudal' law;
- Law of the king;
- Local laws, e.g., the forest law of England and the law merchant (the laws of fairs and markets);
- Roman law (rediscovered in the twelfth century in the texts of the great imperial codifiers);
- Canon law (the law of the church);
- *Capitularia* of emperors, and 'statutes' of kings and parliaments;
- Biblical law – the Old Testament and New Testament;
- Speculative laws, like the *lex natura* and the *lex divina*, discovered in classical writers.

And, generally speaking, every law had its own courts in which it was applied to particular cases and administered.

Indeed, it might be said that where there is no court there is no law.

For courts are not merely engaged in administering the law; they are the immediate custodians of the law.

However, I propose to reserve what I have to say about medieval courts of law until I come to deal with medieval parliaments and the ideas which centred round them.

What we have to consider now is medieval beliefs about the authority of law, *not* about the authority of rulers.

The world of medieval European thought was an immensely variegated structure of laws. And this may be taken to reflect the most fundamental of all impulses – the impulse to have rights and duties to know what they are, and to be assured of them. This is escape from the rule of violence.

Anyone who made a claim, whether he were pope, emperor, king, 'vassal', or merchant, always (in the middle ages) tried to show that it was a claim based upon *law*. So important was this that laws were often forged in order to substantiate claims.

What, in these circumstances, did these medieval peoples think about law? Or rather, what was the course and direction of their thought about law? Because these thoughts had to comprehend and adjust themselves to circumstances of immense changefulness.

3

Now, since the first law of which medieval peoples were aware was the unwritten customs of a people, their first attitude towards law was the attitude one has towards a possession: it is there, and it is yours; you may appeal to it. It is steady, whatever else may move. How you came by it is a question which scarcely occurs. Hence, the notion that law is something that has been *made*, the notion of legislation, was far out of sight.

Law was something you inherit; it was old and its authority rested, in the first place, upon its immemorial character. Law belonged to the folk; it was their most cherished possession for it alone stood in the way of the rule of violence; it applied to everyone, the great and the small man alike. It comprised the rules governing the treatment of one man by another.

And if there was added to this the notion that law was *sacred*, then its sacredness, the religious authority attributed to it, derived from its antiquity, and was an indication of its supreme importance.

There was, then, in these circumstances, no distinction between actual law and ideal law – law as it is and law as it might be. The attitude to law was an essentially conservative attitude; change was not merely undesirable, it was something that was not contemplated.

The authority of law cannot derive from its having been made in a certain manner because it is *not* understood ever to have been made. Its authority was believed to spring from its antiquity.

Nevertheless, law understood in this manner could not merely be neglected; it was something to be cherished. It may be lost or it may suffer corruption. It required that *two* activities should be continuously performed in respect of it. And in the course of performing these two activities some new ideas about the authority of law emerged.

First, it must be cared for, guarded, protected, preserved, and administered. And the chief activity of those in authority, of kings and rulers of all sorts, was understood to be the custody of the law.

Their office was the office of the custodian of the law. And this was particularly so of 'kings', whose office in a feudal society was to prevent the local violence of magnates destroying the rights of their subordinates.

Secondly, since the law was ancient custom, imprecise, unwritten and unenacted, it often happened that what it required of you was obscure or uncertain. Therefore, the law had, on occasion, to be *discovered* and restored and made plain. And the method of discovery must be local inquiry – an inquest.

The presumption always was that there is a law, and if circumstances have obscured what the law demands, then the business of authority is to conduct an inquiry of those most likely to *remember*. And this again was the recognized duty of kings.

But inquiries of this sort were often equivocal proceedings.

The presumption was that the only permissible activities in respect of law were guardianship, discovery, and *restoration*. Nobody would admit to the sacrilege of changing the law.

But, in fact, an inquiry to elicit and to settle the law often resulted in the reformation of the law; the law was, in fact, emended in the process of discovery. Nevertheless, it was done in such a manner that what appeared to have been done was to remove a corruption and *not* to have instituted a change.

And it is *only* when law came to be written down that, *if* change *was* made (as was unavoidably the case with changing circumstances), the recognition that a change had been made became unavoidable; and the immensely difficult step was taken from preserving and 'discovering' law to 'making' law.

And understandably, in these circumstances it was easier to admit a new law if it seemed to be merely an addition to law: what, above all, you will not suffer is being deprived of rights you believe yourself to possess.

There were, however, many things which mediated this step.

European peoples were used to their rulers promulgating decrees, although it was always held that these were valid so long as they did not conflict with 'the law'. And the huge task of reducing multifarious local laws to the common law of a realm, undertaken always by royal authority and by royal judges, was an experience which, while it did not shake the belief that the law was the law of the community, did shake the simple view that law was too sacred to be changed.

By the thirteenth century in England, for example, something recognized to be a *lex terrae* (a law of the land) had definitely superseded the ancient *consuetudines* (customs) of the people of England.

But this 'law of the land' was made, in much the same way as *thesmos* emerged from *themis* – by constructing one law out of multifarious local laws; and its authority derived as much from the antiquity of its contents as from the manner in which it had been constructed.

Moreover, when the time came for reconciling a belief in the fixity of law with the notion of legal innovation, it was this belief that the law belonged to the community, and that kings were its custodians, which conditioned the activity of innovation and generated a process by which law could be recognized as having been legitimately made.

The first principle of all medieval legislation was that, while it was initiated by a king, it was valid only if it had the approval of those whose rights and duties are being changed or enlarged, and that it should always appear as the removal of an abuse.

In England, for example, no 'statute' could be made without the approval of those whom it affected. But, even so, it was a long time before 'statute' was recognized as unmistakably superior to the common law. In France, the office of the local *parlements* was to adjust a law promulgated by a king to local circumstance and record its acceptance.

Thus, when, with the greatest reluctance, medieval people admitted the possibility of making new law (nearly always obscuring the process by thinking and speaking of it as 'emendation') they could without great difficulty adjust their thoughts about the authority of law to the new situation.

Law was to be obeyed not merely because it was old and sacrosanct, but because it had been approved and consented to by those whose conduct it rules.

These ideas of approval and consent only very gradually emerged from the parent ideas of 'discovery' and 'declaration'. To discover the law had required an inquiry, an inquest; to make a law required a not wholly dissimilar process, a parliament: 'the great inquest of the realm'.

And yet the change was, in fact, very great – a change from the belief that law is not at the disposal of each succeeding generation, to the belief that, if the innovation follows a recognized procedure, new and valid law can be made; the change from *consuetudines* to *leges*.

Consuetudines draw their authority from antiquity. *Leges* gain authority from the manner in which they have been made.

4

Now, this process in which ancient and unwritten custom and local law was transformed into a *lex terrae*, and the adjustments of thought about the authority of law which it entailed, was profoundly influenced by ideas acquired from outside the communities concerned.

The two great sources of legal ideas which impressed themselves upon this process were the Roman imperial law and the canon law.

(1) Roman law had remained as the customary law of some parts of Europe (particularly in the south of France) where the Roman imperial administration had been strongest. And in Spain, in the fifth century, its Visigothic rulers had made codes which were (and were known to be) alloys of Gothic and Roman laws.

The Roman imperial law, in the texts of Justinian and others, had not been entirely forgotten. But it was not until its virtual rediscovery in the twelfth century that it began to have a notable effect upon the law and the legal ideas of medieval communities.

The texts of the Roman imperial law introduced these peoples to a law far more sophisticated in its terms, its categories and its distinctions, than anything they then possessed. And it came with the still undimmed authority that belonged to anything 'Roman'.

It is, therefore, not at all surprising that it should have been taken in some respects as a model (or at least an aid) in the immensely difficult task of constructing a *lex terrae*, especially in those parts of Europe where this process was still only beginning in the twelfth century.

No lawyer could escape its influence; and even in England where its influence was least notable, it had its effect in detail.

Medieval Europe owed to Roman law two important ideas: (1) It introduced the new and unfamiliar idea of *law-making* – the unmistakable idea of *legislation*. Necessity and Roman law taught medieval rulers and communities to be lawmakers. (2) It introduced a new and unfamiliar idea of the relation of the king to the process of lawmaking.

Law appeared in the Roman texts as the will of an emperor, and as emanating from his limitless *imperium*. The image of a ruler it presents was that of a lawmaker who was himself above the law – not of a king who was the custodian of his people's law.

Oddly enough, however, even in the twelfth century, there were people learned enough in the Roman law to detect a feature of it which pulled in the opposite direction.

How did a Roman emperor acquire this supreme position in respect of the law? Was it not by virtue of the *lex regia* in which the *populus Romanus* had endowed him with this supremacy? Did not the Roman law assume that the law-making *imperium* belonged to the emperor *only* because it had been given him by the *populus Romanus*?

These considerations allowed the Roman imperial autocracy to be interpreted as if it sprang from something like the 'feudal' *pactum*, or treaty, between a king and his subjects which required him to perform his duties as a king and not to infringe the rights of his subjects.

From this point of view, then, the penetration of medieval Europe by Roman legal ideas had an ambiguous result.

It seemed to proclaim an autocrat, but an autocrat who owed his position to popular approval and authority.

It suggested the notion of a 'government' capable of remoulding the law of a community; but it qualified this suggestion by the more familiar notion of rulers owing their authority as lawmakers to their subjects.

The Roman text: *quod principi placuit leges habet vigorem* ('what the king pleases has the force of law'), could be countered by the text: *lex est quod populi jubet* ('law is what the people commands').

The Roman law of property was essentially individualistic – it rested upon the notion of *ownership*. This was fundamentally different from the feudal law of property, which (generally speaking) recognized only *occupation* and the enjoyment of the fruits of occupation in return for services of one sort or another.

And it was the Roman law which, in this respect, mediated the change from the 'feudal' law of property to the modern law of property.

The impact of Roman law was something which all European peoples felt, in one degree or another, from the twelfth century; it was therefore a great unifying force. Thus, later medieval Europe enjoyed two sources of unity – the church (the idea of the community of Christendom) and Roman law.

(2) The other great source of legal ideas for medieval peoples was canon law – the law of the church. Like all other medieval law, this began as a disordered muddle gathered in from a variety of sources; precepts of the Old Testament and the New Testament, decisions of the great councils of the church, decrees of bishops and popes, odd maxims of the Roman civil law surviving from imperial times. It was the *consuetudines*, the folk law, of the church.

But, as with all other medieval law, there came a time when an attempt was made to sort out this muddle and put it in order. And this was done under the influence of the Roman civil law.

One of the earliest canon lawyers to attempt this was Gratian, in the twelfth century. What Gratian produced was not a code of law for the church but a textbook after the style of the old imperial jurisconsults, called the *Decretum*.

But it was the starting point for the lawmaking activities of subsequent popes, for (as we have seen) the popes, at least from the time of Gregory VII, claimed the absolute authority tenants-in-chief make law for the church.

Thus the canon law became an increasing body of ecclesiastical law, generated from the edicts and decretals of the popes. And its authority derived from the uncontested authority of the pope as a legislator, his *potestas jurisdictionis*.

Now, the canon lawyers were not only familiar with the texts of the Roman law, but also with the various speculative ideas which Roman lawyers had used to give authority to positive law. The most important of these ideas was the Stoic idea of *natural law*.

This was the belief that there existed a 'law', common to all mankind, and available to all mankind by their 'natural reason', the law of the *cosmopolis*, the commands of which coincided with absolute justice and therefore could be used as a model for legislators.

This conception had, much earlier, been Christianized; the *lex naturalis* was thought of as a law implanted in human beings by God himself and representing God's will for mankind.

The law of nature was the law of God; it was absolute in its authority, above kings and emperors and even popes.

Here, then, was the notion of an 'ideal' or 'model' law such as had had no place in the earlier conceptions of folk law.

It was a notion which could be used as a criterion for law-making, much more speculatively satisfactory than the older notion that made law must *not* conflict with the ancient customs or that what was Roman was good.

Indeed, in the legal thought of the later middle ages, when the authority of ancient custom was beginning to be lost in the authority of the *lex terrae*, the notion of a 'natural law' as the touchstone of justice took the place of the notion of ancient custom.

Conformity to 'natural law' was something which might be added to the notion of 'approval by those concerned' as the mark of true law; it was something which might even be supposed to govern popular consent.

And medieval European thought began to fill out this idea of a law of nature with all those rights and duties which were believed to be imprescriptible as belonging to men as men.

A late medieval writer, like Marsilius of Padua, is prepared to make a list of the *duties* which the law of nature imposes upon all men.

They are the things which, as he says, are acceptable by almost all men as honourable and worthy of observance.

- That God shall be worshipped.
- That parents should be honoured.
- That children shall be educated by their parents.
- That injuries should be inflicted upon no man.
- That a man should be permitted to enjoy what is his own.

But here there were the seeds of an intellectual conflict: how to bring together the ideas (a) that just law is conformity to natural law, and (b) that just law is what is approved by the community – a conflict which had great practical consequences in the sixteenth century, and which often appeared in later times.

5

In respect of law, then, the communities of medieval Europe found themselves having to assimilate a number of ideas and beliefs which pulled in different directions.

They believed profoundly in the sanctity of law.

They believed that the law was the most valuable possession of a community; their great defence against the reign of violence.

They were reluctant innovators.

They had before them two 'ideal' models: (1) A folk law which embraced rulers and ruled alike, and which could not be emended except with the consent of those concerned; (2) A law, emanating from an authority (a pope, or much more rarely, a king) who enjoyed a lawmaking *imperium* derived from God.

With difficulty they emancipated themselves from the authority of ancient custom. And what took its place was law whose authority derived from its having been made in a certain manner – a manner which could plausibly be thought to represent the consent of those who were obliged to obey.

Editorial Note

LSE 1/1/21, file 4, fos. 303–16. Fos. 303, 308, 315 are photocopies of autograph sheets; fos. 304–7, 309–14, 316 are photocopies of a typescript with autograph corrections.

Twenty

Medieval Parliaments

1

In reviewing the themes of medieval European political thought, I said that it was responsible for two great political inventions.

- The invention of kingship. This was the invention of *political* authority, authority over subjects, distinguished from mere 'lordship' or authority based upon the ownership of land, authority over tenants.
- Parliaments.

And it is about this second invention that I want to say something this morning.

Parliaments appeared in every realm of Christendom during the twelfth and thirteenth centuries.

They cannot, as we shall see, be said to have been designed. They emerged as devices of government out of customs and practices far older than themselves. But long before the end of the middle ages some general ideas about their character and authority had got themselves accepted.

Indeed, parliaments, from the point of view I am going to take, can be recognized as a particular family of ideas about government.

The instruments of government which, in the course of time, came to be known as 'parliaments' or (in other European languages) *parlements, cortes, Diet, Landtage, Reichstage,* etc., were of many different sorts, but they had certain features in common.

They were conferences: this was the original meaning of the word *parliamentum*.

They were conferences called by kings or other rulers, such as dukes or counts. They were called to discuss specific matters or to reach specific decisions.

They were composed of persons who owed allegiance to the king or duke concerned.

They emerged from certain features of a feudally organized society. And of these features two are more important than others, in this connection.

(1) It was the duty of a 'vassal' to provide his 'lord' not only with *auxilium* (aid, chiefly military), but also *concilium* (counsel or advice). And a *parliamentum* emerged when a king called upon his 'vassals' to perform this service of *concilium*.

In a feudally organized society no 'lord' could do without the good will and assistance of his 'vassals'. And the main concerns in respect of which this good will, assistance, and advice were needed were war, the provision of revenue, and the discovery and the settlement of the law. In each of these activities a 'lord', and particularly a feudal king, required to mobilize the loyalty and assistance of his 'vassals'.

A king might have at his disposal a *curia regis*, a council of legal and military professional advisers, but he could not do without the aid and counsel of those without whose support no settled policy could be pursued.

(2) The principle that no law should be emended without the consent and acquiescence of all those affected. From one point of view, parliaments were the medieval answer to the problem of how to reconcile belief in the fixity of law with the need for legal innovation.

These parliaments were all, in the first place, courts of law, in the medieval sense. Those who were called to them were recognized as suitors of a court: it was their feudal duty to attend.

But, being called for one purpose, these conferences of 'vassals' were found eligible to serve other purposes; and in the course of time, both their composition and the business they transacted underwent considerable change.

At what point a 'parliament', properly speaking, emerged is, therefore, impossible to say. But in general it may be said that it emerged out of a conference of 'lords' and 'vassals' designed, not to do something new, but to do better or more expeditiously what was already being done in other ways.

It became an unmistakable 'parliament' when it began to do things which had never been done by anyone before.

Thus, 'parliaments' were the meeting place, or confluence, of a number of different activities current in a feudally organized society which combined to compose a recognizably new instrument of government.

Beyond this general character, the parliaments which appeared during the twelfth and thirteenth centuries in each of the realms of Europe had special characteristics, both in respect of how they emerged and of *what* in the end they became, and of the *beliefs* which attached themselves to them.

2

Let us consider the manner in which they emerged, and find out what this tells us about their character and the ideas they generated. I want to consider three examples.

(1) The simplest and earliest example is that of the *cortes* of Spain.

Spain in the twelfth century consisted of six independent kingdoms – Navarre, Leon, Galicia, Castile, Aragon, and Portugal. And from early in the century it was the custom of the kings of each of these realms each to call meetings, composed of all their tenants-in-chief and of all the bishops of the realm, on certain occasions. An assembly of this sort was called *cortes*, which means 'court'. The king 'held court' with those who, in virtue of the lands they held, owed him immediate allegiance.

The occasions were, at first, comparatively rare and were to deal with specific business.

For example, in 1140 the *cortes* of Portugal was assembled to confirm the doubtful title of Alphonso I to the throne; and in 1160 the *cortes* of Aragon was assembled to swear allegiance to the heir apparent to the throne.

That is to say, these were occasions when it was thought wise to mobilize the allegiance of the chief subjects to a king. The *cortes* was a royal instrument of government; a device of monarchy.

But later it became the custom to summon the *cortes* of these kingdoms at regular intervals (perhaps twice a year, and usually on the occasion of a Christian festival like Easter) to transact business of a more routine nature, such as to get acquiescence to legislation, to consider matters of war and peace, and to get consent to the imposition of taxes.

On these occasions it was found advisable to call, not only the nobles and bishops (who were called individually), but to call, also, representatives of the towns.

Now, the significance of the addition of townsmen to the *cortes* was this.

First, the towns of Spain were ancient Roman municipalities which, even in Roman imperial times had enjoyed self-government and which had retained a large measure of independence until the eleventh century. They had municipal governments.

Secondly, even when they lost their independence, they (like the other towns and cities of medieval Europe) were outside the feudal organization. Feudal tenures, and the obligations and rights which went with them, were never appropriate to town life, in spite of the fact that the terms of feudal laws were often applied to them.

Thus, a *cortes* without representatives of the towns would be an assembly of the king's subjects which left out a significant class of them.

Thirdly, towns were centres of wealth, and if revenue were to be raised other than by the collection of the customary feudal dues, this was the most promising source from which it might come. But because in each town there existed a municipal government, they were in a position to choose and to send official representatives to the *cortes*.

Thus, as a partner with the king in government, the *cortes* of the Spanish kingdoms were recognized to be assemblies of what were called the 'estates' of the realm: the bishops composed the ecclesiastical 'estate', the tenants-in-chief were the 'estate' of the nobility, and the townsmen composed a third 'estate'.

The bishops and the nobles were all called individually and were, thus, not 'representatives' of anyone; the townsmen were present in the *cortes* as representatives, not of their localities, but of their 'estate', i.e., their class, or kind of person.

But the character of all European parliaments was conditioned by the fortunes of the monarchy in which they had place. And as the monarch in each of these kingdoms in Spain increased his power, so the *cortes* turned more and more into an instrument of opposition, of remonstrance and of resistance to the king, criticizing his policy and remonstrating about his extravagance. And consequently they were called with more and more reluctance.

And when, first by the union of the crowns of Castile and Aragon by marriage, and then by the destruction of the inde-

pendence of the other kingdoms by conquest, a single kingdom of Spain emerged, the *cortes* of the defunct kingdoms
became the guardians of that provincial independence
which has remained in Spain to this day.

Thus, within the particular setting of Spain, the *cortes* were
both assistants and critics of royal government: and this is
the dual character of all medieval parliaments.

(2) The emergence of the *cortes* in the kingdoms of Spain was
comparatively simple, and they were the earliest 'parliamentary' institutions to appear in Europe.

Turning to England, the process of emergence and the
result are both infinitely more complicated.

In general, the English 'parliament' may be seen to emerge
from *three* different and not even closely connected circumstances, and was the meeting-place of a variety of different
legal and political beliefs.

(a) By the beginning of the twelfth century, the government of England had come to be carried on by the king, the
set of legal and administrative officials which composed his
'household', and a council of magnates, selected tenants-in-chief, the *curia regis*.

The officials had been divided, according to the nature of
their business, into various 'courts', the most important of
which were the Court of Exchequer, the Court of Chancery,
and the Court of King's Bench.

The work of these courts was administrative and judicial,
but (in the then state of the law) they were constantly faced
with problems to which there was no ready answer. Consequently, they each on occasion turned to the king's council
for help, advice, and sometimes for a definite ruling.

In its first use, the word *parliamentum* stood for the king's
council (*curia regis*) in its capacity as a deliberative body giving advice, and perhaps authoritative rulings, to judges and
administrators.

This is the first strand of the three which were twisted
together to compose the English 'parliament'.

The second strand was this:

(b) The work of the king's courts of justice consisted of *two*
related activities.

First, to determine the law, and secondly, to hear cases
which were, in a large part, complaints from people who had

had duties (payments or services) forced upon them by their feudal superiors which they believed had no legal authority.

That is to say, the chief business of the king's courts was to protect the otherwise unprotected from illegal exactions. And the institution of the justices in eyre, who traveled the country, brought the king's justice in reach of all in the assize courts.

The aggrieved person came before the court and asked for a 'writ', that is, an official pronouncement commanding, in a set legal form, that the illegal exaction should cease forthwith. And the theory was that for every wrong there was an appropriate 'writ'. (Thus, in later times a 'writ' of *habeas corpus* was designed to prevent illegal imprisonment.) For every wrong there is a writ to put it right.

But wrongs may be many and with minute differences between them; and it was, in fact, impossible to devise 'writs' to meet every wrong.

To meet this situation, a new procedure was devised; the aggrieved person could proceed by petition or plea, in which he described informally the precise wrong he had suffered (which might be of such a character as not to correspond to any known writ) and asked for his grievance to be redressed.

These petitions or pleas were heard in the king's courts.

But, since some were particularly complicated (the law often being obscure), and since others might involve whole local communities, it became the custom to present these legal pleas or petitions, not to an ordinary assize court, or even the King's Bench court, but to a court composed of the *curia regis* reinforced by all the available judicial officers – in short to a *high court of parliament*.

This is the origin not only of private acts of parliament, but of a great deal of what was at *first* thought of as the emendation of the law and *later* as legislation.

It embodied the belief that there is no legal tangle that cannot be unraveled; no wrong which cannot be redressed; and that what a judge can't do by issuing a 'writ' a parliament can do in another less formal way, by hearing a plea and responding to a request to put right a wrong.

(c) The third strand is less easily identifiable, but it is in some respects the most important.

It reflected the duty of the king's 'vassals' to give him *concilium*, and the necessity of a feudal king (even one in so strong a position as that of the king of England) of getting the good-will of his 'vassals' by consulting them on important matters of government, and obtaining their approval. It was the right and the duty of a vassal to deliberate with the ruler.

But *this* component of a 'parliament' had two sides to it.

First, it exhibits a parliament as the *curia regis* reinforced by an assembly of the chief 'vassals' of the king, and thus becoming what it was often said to be, the 'common council of the realm'.

And although the people called to this council were all the tenants-in-chief and all the bishops, the social structure of England was sufficiently complex for there to be a lesser nobility who were 'represented' by some of their number: the knights of the shires.

But secondly, the office of a feudal king is the office of an overlord who *must* govern according to the law and not infringe the rights of his subjects. If he departs from the duties of his office, it is the place of his chief 'vassals' to bring him to book, to admonish him and to extract from him a proper recognition of the promises made at his coronation.

And on occasion, during the reigns of King John and Henry III, the barons of England were obliged to take action of this sort.

The most notable of these occasions was that on which the Magna Carta, a reaffirmation of feudal rights, was presented to King John and his agreement to it extracted. The assembly of tenants-in-chief which met on the island of Runnymede to impose the Carta upon John was called a 'parliament'. And Magna Carta itself provided for a periodic meeting of magnates to oversee the activities of the king.

Thus, 'parliament' stood, not only for the *duty* of vassals to give advice and support to kings, but also the *right* of 'vassals' to extract from kings redress, not merely for their particular grievances and wrongs, but for the misgovernment of the realm, if it occurred.

These, then, are the complicated circumstances from which the English parliament emerged. By the reign of Edward I it had become the most notable instrument of government in England.

It came to meet regularly, twice a year. Its business proliferated, because it was found suitable to participate in many of the activities of governing. And its composition changed.

But it never lost its original character as a court of law; and so far as the middle ages are concerned, its main business remained that of a court of law – hearing petitions, dispensing of justice, and expediting matters of administration; activities which imperceptibly passed over into legislation.

But if it is correct to think of parliament in England, even during the middle ages, as a participant in lawmaking, it must be remembered that the principle on which it became a necessary partner in lawmaking was *already* there, long before it emerged – the feudal principle that a man's rights may not be altered without his consent.

What promoted the importance of parliament in this respect was *not* the emergence of a new principle; indeed, when this principle was formulated, often enough it was a sentence from Justinian's *Codex* of Roman law which was quoted: *quod omnes similiter tangit, ab omnibus comprobetur* – 'what touches all should be approved by all'.

The importance of parliament grew out of the fact that the circumstances of the later middle ages called more and more for the emendation of the law, and that parliament offered itself as a ready manner in which the consent of all could be presumed to have been obtained.

If we ask, What made it plausible to recognize the consent of parliament as the consent of the whole realm and in what particular concerns was this consent required?, the answer is to be found in the extension of the composition of parliament which took place in Edward I's reign, and in the king's need for a wider constituency from which to draw financial support.

The earliest English parliaments were composed of bishops and nobles summoned by name. It was preeminently a 'feudal' assembly; and it entailed no element of 'representation'. All the individuals whom it was thought proper and necessary to consult were present. It was the *curia regis* reinforced by the immediate 'vassals' of the king – who, indeed, had a feudal obligation to give *concilium* to the king.

But, gradually, it became the custom, especially when financial matters were to be deliberated upon, to summon representatives of the shires and the towns.

This was done by a writ to the sheriff (the king's personal officer in the counties) commanding him to see that two knights from each of the thirty-five shires should be nominated at the meeting of the shire court, and two burgesses from each of eighty boroughs should be nominated by the town government, and that they should attend an assembly at Westminster on a certain day, having full and sufficient *potestas* to consent, on behalf of their constituents, to what should be decided in parliament.

The execution of this writ was the seed from which the House of Commons grew.

The knights of the shire were 'representatives' of the 'freeholders' of the counties, all of whom had a duty to attend the monthly sessions of the shire court; the burgesses were 'representatives' of the free men of the towns. There was nothing that could be called an 'election', there was no competition to go to Westminster – quite the reverse, it was regarded as a burdensome duty.

In parliament, these representatives were, on occasion, asked to consent to the levying of taxes. This was a recognition of the feudal principle that no man could be required to part with what is his own except with his own consent.

But, in the middle ages, their main activity became the presentation of petitions on behalf of their communities or on behalf of individuals – an activity which recognized parliament as fundamentally a court of justice. And it became a convention that the redress of grievances should precede the vote of taxes.

But, with such an assembly available, it came to be used for any purpose for which it might seem suitable.

Policy and affairs of war and peace (except when they hung upon finance) were not discussed in parliament, which only very slowly became a deliberative assembly.

But in 1302, when it seemed necessary to the king to rebut in the strongest terms the claims of superior authority made by Pope Boniface VIII, the reply to the pope was sent not only with the authority of the king but also with that of parliament.

This was, perhaps, the earliest occasion when the king in parliament 'spoke for England'; it was a notable occasion when the king mobilized the support of his subjects in an affair of policy. And parliament acquired a new dimension.

Now, it will be seen from this that the English parliament, even in its emergence, was an immensely more complicated institution than the *cortes* of Spain.

It did not, in the first place, call upon any new principle. The principle of *consent* was already there in the organization of a feudal society; and the possibility of one man 'representing' others and both speaking and consenting on their behalf presented no puzzles or difficulties. Men 'represented' others long before anyone began to think about 'representation', or to talk about a principle of representation.

The statement of Chief Justice Thorpe in 1365 that 'parliament represents the body of the whole realm' could be accepted without difficulty by those versed in feudal law.

Rex in parliamento – 'the king in parliament' was clearly an authority suitable to 'speak for England'.

But it was, also, recognizably a superior legal entity to that of the king alone.

The king, of course, could dispose of his own rights (as he sometimes did by royal charter), but he could *not* dispose of the rights of others.

To do this he required the consent of those others. And parliament was the means he had of getting that consent.

Before the end of the middle ages, the 'parliament' which met periodically at Westminster had acquired the character of an assembly composed of the nobility and representatives of the towns and shires. And the representatives had the authority to pledge the consent of their localities to what was agreed in parliament.

It was a court of law to which pleas and petitions were presented and which had the authority of a court to redress the wrongs complained of.

It was a legislative assembly without whose consent no man could be deprived of his rights or be given new duties. The principle here is: no man may have his rights and duties changed without his consent given through his representatives.

It was an assembly capable of authorizing the collection of taxes. The principle here is: no man may be deprived of his property without his consent given through his representatives.

It was a deliberative assembly; an assembly capable of giving advice to the ruler in matters of policy, and supporting him in the conduct of policy.

(3) The *parlements* which appeared in France have features which distinguish them from all others.

(a) France in the twelfth century was a kingdom only in the sense that it had a feudal overlord, called king, but who exercised only a very tenuous overlordship over his 'vassals' (the great dukes and counts) and could exact from them only an intermittent allegiance.

Each ruled his own lands, and the king (as count of Paris) ruled his lands, like the others. France was a kind of feudal federation of principalities. This king was the count of Paris, and he was elected by his fellow lords.

Nevertheless, the count of Paris, as king, had kingly duties.

He had a *curia regis* to conduct the affairs of the kingdom. And like other monarchs of the twelfth century it fell to him to provide a 'royal' justice; that is, to provide a court in which complaints about the illegal exactions of his great 'vassals' could be heard.

He was also, by the twelfth century, a legislator, engaged in the task of generating a *lex terrae* for the whole of France.

Like other monarchs in this situation, he found it useful for the conduct of judicial, legislative, and political affairs to reinforce the *curia regis* (which dealt with the affairs of his kingdom as distinct from those of his county of Paris) with magnates (bishops and barons) and lawyers.

But although this reinforced *curia regis* dealt with the affairs of his kingdom, the persons who composed it were all drawn from his own county. This reinforced *curia regis* became known as the *parlement* of Paris.

It was, essentially, a court of law. Its business was the discovery and settlement of law; inquiry into abuses, the redress of feudal wrongs, and the hearing of appeals from the courts of the king's 'vassals'.

From the middle of the thirteenth century it had come to sit four times a year; it had a president who was not the king himself; and so far as the king's own legislative activity was concerned, it had the duty of verifying, of declaring to be valid, and of recording royal edicts. That is, it had the supremely important duty of inquiring into the conformity of royal edicts with the customary law – because customary law was still believed to have prescriptive authority.

But the edicts and ordinances of such a king, although verified and declared valid in the *parlement* of Paris, were not easily to be accepted in the lands of his great 'vassal' dukes and counts.

And, as counterparts to the royal *parlement* of Paris, there appeared local *parlements* in each of the great duchies and counties. By the end of the thirteenth century there were eleven of them.

They, like the *parlement* of Paris, were courts of law and were composed of lawyers and others whose main qualification was a knowledge of the local law – the law of Toulouse, or Anjou, or Brittany, or Burgundy, and so on.

The business of these *parlements* was to examine the royal edicts, to inquire into their conformity with local law, to remonstrate if the conflict were significant, to adjust them to local circumstances, and to register or record them.

Thus, France had twelve *parlements*, of which the *parlement* of Paris was, in most matters, superior, because it was nearest to the king. They were all, strictly speaking, courts of law; their main business was *not* to try cases, but to discover the law and to record it. They were composed of lawyers. They were in no sense 'representative' institutions. And they played no part in authorizing taxation. They belong to the history of the *lex terrae* of France as it emerges from local custom.

(b) Now, altogether separate from these *parlements*, it was the custom, from the eleventh century, for a duke or a count to reinforce his council of administrators by assemblies of his own 'vassals', to discuss questions which were agreed to concern all, questions of politics and taxation.

These assemblies came to be composed, not only of the lay and ecclesiastical 'vassals' of the dukes and the counts, but also of representatives of the towns.

In short, these assemblies were recognized as assemblies of the 'estates' of the duchy or county – the nobles, the ecclesiastics, and the townsmen composing the famous *tiers état* ('third estate').

Now, the existence of these provincial assemblies of the estates provided the opportunity for the emergence of an assembly of the same sort for the whole kingdom.

And at a crisis in the affairs of the kingdom, in 1302, the king, Philip IV, called in Paris the first meeting of the 'estates' of the realm, as assembly which came to be known as the *états genereaux*: 'the states-general'.

The occasion was that of the publication of Pope Boniface VIII's bull, *unam sanctam*, in which he claimed an authority over the affairs of the realms of Christendom which, if it had been admitted, would have turned the kings of Christendom into mere lieutenants of the pope.

It was an occasion when, as we have seen, even the king of England thought it wise to mobilize all the loyalty of his subjects and to reply to the papal claim, not only on his own authority, but also on the authority of parliament. In France the same procedure was followed in replying to the pope.

This states-general, or meeting of the estates of the realm, was composed of the nobility and the bishops of the realm and 'representatives' of the towns. The great 'vassals' of the king, the dukes and the counts, themselves appeared. But, unlike the English parliament, the states-general was in the nature of a 'congress of ambassadors', an assembly representing the great, still semi-independent, provinces of France.

But its meetings were rare; it never acquired any settled procedure; it was in no sense a court of law and had nothing to do with the authorization of legislation. It never became a normal instrument of government, but its value was recognized as a possible means for the king to get consent to taxes.

Thus, in France, law and legislation became the business of the king and the *parlements* and particularly the *parlement* of Paris; politics and finance became the business of the estates – a separation of functions which had momentous consequences.

It cannot be said that there was any design in this; it must be understood as the product of the peculiar circumstances of France. But the result was that a strong 'parliamentary' partner with the king in the government of France never appeared in the middle ages.

Indeed, although 'parliaments' of various sorts appeared everywhere in medieval Europe, none except the English parliament managed to establish itself as a permanent partner with the king in government.

And the reason for this is perhaps that it was a single, all-purpose assembly; and that it was not an assembly of the estates of the realm.

4

Now, a parliament is an institution which may be seen to reflect certain general beliefs. But I think it is true to say that parliaments were the means by which certain old ideas about government were enlarged and more firmly impressed upon medieval peoples, rather than that they represented or generated any entirely new beliefs.

The chief beliefs concerned may, perhaps, be stated as follows:

(1) That every man has rights and among these rights is the right to be protected by law against the infringement of his rights. Parliaments (above all in England) were devices by which wrongs (wrongs suffered by individuals and by whole local communities) could be redressed more expeditiously, and less at the mercy of the formalities of a 'writ', than before.

The 'writ' which required the sheriff to see that representatives of the shires and towns came to Westminster was a 'writ' which opened the door wider to procedure by plea and petition instead of 'writ', and closed the gap between 'discovering' and administering the law and making new law. For making new law was recognized first as the redress of wrongs.

(2) That every man has a vested and legitimate interest in the present condition of his rights, which should not be changed without his consent. Here what parliaments provided was an enlargement; they provided a manner in which this consent could be given or presumed to be given.

The legitimate interest in the preservation of one's current rights led, in some places in Europe, to an extraordinary 'parliamentary' deadlock.

The *liberum veto* in the Polish diet, whereby unanimity was required for any decision – every man having the right to refuse to consent, and without the consent of each and all nothing could be done – was, no doubt, an eccentricity. But it was an eccentricity based upon the universally held assumption that rights may not be altered except with the consent of each holder of those rights.

What the English parliament generated was the recognition of the necessity of reaching decisions in which many men were participators; the necessity of compromise; and in doing so they went beyond the immediate range of feudal ideas. Other parliaments never achieved this, and consequently did not survive.

(3) That what was a man's 'own' may not be taken away from him or curtailed without his consent.

It was this principle of private property which lies behind the settled view in the middle ages that to pay a tax was to surrender what belonged to you and therefore requires your consent.

The theory of medieval taxation is that (where it goes beyond the dues and services which belong to the tenure of land) the king may not impose a tax unless he has reached an understanding with every man who will be required to pay. And parliaments were a device for reaching this understanding and getting the required consent.

(4) That there are some persons who have a right to oppose misgovernment, not by rebellion, but by calling the attention of a ruler to his errors and by notifying him that he will not get the necessary support if he rules in neglect of the rights of his subjects.

(5) But, on the other side, we may notice that medieval parliaments neither rested upon, nor generated, the belief that their participation in government concerned the formulation and conduct of policy.

They did not discuss policy, and their influence upon it was remote and indirect: it was confined to the authorization or the refusal of that part of the resources necessary to conduct policy which was in their control.

(6) Lastly, the practice of calling parliament entailed, in the end, the practice of 'representation'. But I think it would be hard to find anything that could be called an 'idea' or theory of representation in the middle ages, though some thought was given to the problem of how, and in what sense, one man could be said to 'represent' another.

5

Now, this review of the beliefs which were associated with medieval parliaments and their place in the activity of governing and the experience of being governed leads us back to medieval kingship: medieval government.

It enables us to understand a feature of the office of king which, so far, I have only referred to; a feature which may be supposed to correspond with the necessities of government itself.

A medieval ruler was recognized to have *two* tasks:

(1)   He was the custodian of the rights of his subjects; the judge who could redress the wrongs they suffered, who could take the initiative in emending the law, and who preserved the peace of the community. And here a feudal king often found himself redressing the wrongs which the ordinary man might suffer at the hands of his feudal superiors; his task was often to hold the balance between the nobility of his realm and the ordinary free man.

(2)   He was custodian of the interests of his realm, with the task of defending these interests against external enemies. He was the man who initiated and conducted policy.

These two tasks were recognized to require different sorts of *potestas* for their performance. And the names these different sorts of *potestas* were given were, respectively, *jurisdictio* and *gubernaculum*: the authority of a judge or custodian of the law, and the authority of a guide, a 'helmsman' or a 'pilot'.

And, in medieval England at least, this distinction came to be embodied in the distinction between 'the crown' and 'the king.' *Jurisdictio* belonged to 'the crown'; *gubernaculum* belonged to 'the king' personally.

His rights of *jurisdictio* were all those rights which the king required in order to perform his duties as custodian of the law. These were the 'rights of the crown'. And in England, by the time of Edward I, 'the king in parliament' (*rex in parliamento*) was identified as 'the crown'.

It was these rights which the royal judges exercised on behalf of the king. It was in respect of having these rights that a king could be thought of as 'the fountain of justice.'

That is to say, a *parliamentum* was the recognized partner of a king in the exercise of his *potestas jurisdictionis*.

His rights of *gubernaculum* were different.

In respect of these he was not bound by law; their virtue was precisely that they enabled him to move in a region where there is no law – in the conduct of foreign policy, for example.

It was in virtue of his *gubernaculum* that a king negotiates with other kings, and can act as a guardian, in a more general sense, of his realm. *Gubernaculum* belonged to him, personally, as king.

Sometimes, but rarely, his *gubernaculum* conflicts with his *jurisdictio*. In the pursuit of policy he imposes upon his subjects liabilities or duties which go beyond what the law allows, especially in time of war and in defence of the realm.

But if this is so, he must be prepared to show good reason for it; he must be prepared to show that he is acting *ex justa causa*, and to demonstrate the *necessity* of the unwonted demands he is making on his subjects.

This, no doubt, is a subtle distinction. But two things are obvious:

(1) That a ruler denied the rights of *gubernaculum* would be ill able to deal with the emergencies of politics and ill equipped to guard the interests of the realm.

(2) That a rule in which *jurisdictio* was constantly being invaded by *gubernaculum*, a rule in which a king constantly governed on the edges of the law, appealing always to his personal, gubernatorial, 'prerogative' rights, would constitute a serious breach of the notion of medieval kingship.

A profound student of medieval politics (Gierke) has said that the modern state emerges from the medieval realm when the famous Ciceronian tag, *salus populi suprema lex*, becomes the dominant principle of government.

That is, when ruling is recognized not as *jurisdictio* supplemented by *gubernaculum*, but as *gubernaculum* inspired by an ad hoc judgment about what the *utilitas publica* requires. Or, in other words, when rulers regard their own realms and their own subjects as the objects of 'policy'.

Editorial Note

LSE 1/1/21, file 4, fos. 317–34. Fos. 317, 327–8 are photocopies of autograph sheets; fos. 318–26, 329–34 are photocopies of a typescript with autograph corrections.

Twenty-one

Medieval Political Philosophy (1): Augustine

1

Our study of the political thought of medieval times has been concerned with the practical understanding which medieval people had of the institutions of government with which they were familiar: lords, kings, popes, parliaments; laws and courts of law. And with the practical answers they found for such questions as:

- Who is my ruler and whence comes his authority to rule?
- Where do my loyalties lie? What are my duties? What are my rights?
- What sort of a society do I belong to?

At a slightly higher level of generality, there is a vast medieval literature of political reflection and criticism, still concerned to explore the workings of political institutions, but doing so on a more extended scale.

There are treatises on the duties of rulers, like the *Policraticus* of John of Salisbury (1150).

There are the defenders of civil and imperial prerogatives against the claims of the church – like Dante and Marsilius of Padua.

There are writers like Sir John Fortescue, in the fifteenth century, whose book called *The Governance of England* is the first genuine interpretation of the British constitution.

And there are innumerable controversial political writers.

All this I propose to leave on one side, because I want to end what I have to say about medieval politics by saying something about medieval political thought at a more philosophical level.

Generally speaking, philosophers are concerned, *not* with answering practical questions, like: Where do my loyalties lie? but with the presuppositions of practical questions – like, What does it mean to say that one has an 'obligation'?

And, in respect of politics, all the details of philosophical reflection may be seen as contributing to answering the question:

What is the place of civil society and the activities which keep it going on the map of the universe?

You will remember that when the thinkers of the ancient world asked themselves this question – Plato or Aristotle, for example – they put it in the form:

What is there in 'human nature' which indicates that *polis*-life is necessary for the good human life?

In other words, they recognized *polis*-life as a particular kind of human life, and they tried to relate it to what they understood human beings to be.

And, further, they set out their conclusions in an abstract argument designed to display their relationship.

And this is a way of thinking and speaking which we easily understood because, whatever adjustments we may have made in it, it is our own way of thinking and speaking.

Now, a medieval thinker, considering this question, may almost be defined as a man who assumes that a form of human life, like being in a civil society, is to be accounted for, *not* by relating it to human 'nature', but by relating it to divine 'nature'.

In other words, the question he asks himself is not: What is there in the nature of human beings which accounts for civil society? but: What is the place of civil society in the universe which God has designed?

In short, the characteristic assumption of the medieval thinker is the image of the universe which by the fourth century A.D. had been generated out of three centuries of reflection and meditation and which has come to be identified as 'Christian'.

And further, *instead* of stating his conclusions in an abstract argument, he was much more likely to put them in the form of a dramatic story.

It is true that in considering these matters, writers from the thirteenth century onwards returned to the idiom of abstract argument, but throughout the middle ages the relationship of God to the world, and of man to man, never ceased to be dramatic.

Now, in order to illustrate this medieval way of thinking about civil society and its place in the intellectual map of the universe, I propose to say something about St. Augustine's writings on this subject.

2

Christian thought about politics and government began slowly and in an unmistakably practical mood. In early times, Christians composed small communities of families whose manner of life and whose relation to the world around them sprang from one over-mastering conviction – the conviction that soon (at least in the life-time of the young or middle-aged) Christ would reappear, and an immense and long-promised transformation of the world would take place; a 'new age' would dawn in which a redeemed human race would be released from all suffering, wrong, evil, and misery. Peace would reign instead of war; freedom instead of subjection; and God himself would rule in a 'heavenly city', instead of the corruption and injustice of the current rule of men.

In these circumstances, Christians were, and could afford to be, as indifferent to everything that comprised politics and government as a school-boy on the last day of term can afford to suffer with indifference the rules of his school and the enormities and injuries of his masters. The order of life of these Christian communities was faith (in the promise of the Lord), hope for the 'new age' and charity towards one another. This was enough; and it was, indeed, a foretaste of the rule of God himself. It is not going to last very much longer.

But the second coming of Christ did not take place. And in the letters of St. Paul we can see a man trying to adjust the beliefs of himself and his fellow Christians to this disappointment. Christians, it was clear, would have to live in the world-as-it-is longer than they had expected. Consequently, they would have to come to terms with the world-as-it-is; and, if possible, their immediate expectation of an historical event would have to be replaced by a faith in a 'salvation' of a slightly different kind. The genius of St. Paul accomplished this adjustment of attitude and belief for Christian people. Government, he wrote, to the Christian community in Rome (that is, the current Roman government), was something to be grateful for; at least, it maintained peace and order and was tolerant of the beliefs of its subjects. Christians should perform their civic duties, and honour the rulers of Rome. The whole disposition of this early Christian teaching was in the direction of what (much later) came to be called passive obedience. No Christian should aspire to political power; but neither should he fail to render unto Caesar the things that are Caesar's.

In the days of persecution there was, naturally enough, a revulsion from this view – a revulsion which sometimes expressed itself in the extreme view that all civil government was evil and belonged to the devil, and that the emperor was anti-Christ – that strange figure who Christians believed would appear before the second coming of Christ. And this left its permanent mark on Christian thought, though later it was recognized as a heresy.

But when Christianity was first tolerated and then adopted by the Roman government, and when the church had acquired an organization and a government of its own, there was room for new thoughts about government and politics, because there was room for new thoughts about the current condition of the world.

Indeed, there appeared a doctrine that the current course of historical happenings and the current strivings of human beings (so far from being merely filling in time before the redemption of mankind) should be understood as themselves the events and the strivings in which that redemption was being achieved. In its simplest form this was the doctrine of Pelagius; in a more complicated form, in which human history was understood as human beings gradually acquiring the ultimate truth about the universe, it was the belief of a set of Christian heretics known as the Gnostics.

But the orthodox Christian belief remained that God, in his good time, would redeem mankind, and that meanwhile the Christian was a pilgrim passing through a world which would come to an end.

And yet...and yet...Christians might legitimately ask: What, then, is politics and government? What is the explanation of the current organization of the world? Has it no place in the design of God?

It was to this theme that St. Augustine, early in the fifth century A.D., addressed himself. And in answering it he produced the first great 'Christian' political philosophy; that is to say, an explanation of political activity, of government and civil order, conceived in the Christian idiom.

And to show the seriousness of his philosophical purpose he undertook, at the same time, to give, also, a philosophical explanation of the Christian church. The church, as every Christian recognized, had been founded by St. Peter at the direct command of Christ; and, for most, this was explanation enough. But not for a philosopher. Augustine, in effect, undertook to show why Christ had given this injunction to St. Peter – to show the place of the church in the total designs of God.

3

Now, Augustine was a voluminous writer, but his thoughts on politics are mostly contained in a work which has an unmistakably 'political' title – a work called *De civitate Dei*: 'Concerning the City of God'. Somehow, he is going to show us that the 'cities' of this world, the political organizations of mankind, and particularly that of the Roman empire, are to be explained by relating them to a 'city' of which God is the ruler, a 'heavenly' city.

What reminiscences there are here of Plato and of the *cosmopolis* of the Stoics, who shall say? But whatever Augustine took from the ancient pagan world, he transformed, translated into a Christian idiom. And the dramatic representation of the story of mankind which started in the garden of Eden and would end in heaven, this drama which four centuries of Christian thought had created out of Hebrew, Greek, and Roman materials, became in Augustine's hands an integrated philosophical theory.

Like most of Augustine's writings, the *De civitate Dei* is a work of controversy. It was designed to prove two fundamental propositions:

That the fall of the city of Rome (the eternal city, as the Romans had thought) to the invading Goths in 410 A.D. was not an event of any great significance. Pagan and Christian alike believed this to be the end of the world; Augustine denied it. The ground of this denial was the belief that no event in human history is of any decisive significance, except the death of Christ. The world is 'marking time'; nothing that happens either brings nearer, or puts farther away, the final salvation of mankind, or contributes anything to it. In short, the first of Augustine's propositions was anti-Pelagian.

The second proposition was that the fall of Rome was not brought about (as some suggested) by the Roman adoption of Christianity. And here Augustine's argument was that whatever the merely secular calamity involved in the fall of Rome, it was due to the undestroyed relics of the ancient Roman religion and not to the adoption of Christianity as the official religion of the empire.

But in the course of arguing these two propositions, Augustine elaborated what may be called a political philosophy – an explanation of both the civil and the ecclesiastical *potestas*.

It is a long and intricate argument, and instead of trying to follow it step by step I propose to describe it to you and then comment on some of its features.

4

(1) The world as God created it was an orderly universe. It was rationally constructed; its part fitted together and were congruent to one another. Or, to put it another way, God's created universe had a law according to which its parts worked and moved in relation to one another.

Everything in it had a specific place or 'function'; and in its place, everything was 'good'. This is what the word 'good' signifies for Augustine.

The divinely created world, is, then, what Augustine called an *ordo universi* (a 'universal order'), or an *ordo rerum* (an 'order of things'); complete, coherent, and expressing the rational design of God.

(2) The vast variety of things which composed this universe fell into two broad categories:

- Those things which were incapable of getting out of their allotted place, those which could not fail to obey the law of God and thus fulfil their proper function;
- Those which were capable of disobedience and could wander from their proper place and thus fail to fulfil their proper function. In particular, angels and human beings belong to this category.

And if one were to ask Augustine why God should have created a universe in which some of its components were capable of getting out of place, his answer was that, as everyone knows, it is boring for a ruler to have subjects none of whom are capable of disobedience, and that there is a special satisfaction to be got from being obeyed by those whose obedience is not necessary.

(3) God's attitude to this created universe is two-fold:

(a) He naturally desired that its order should be observed and preserved – that each component part should remain in its proper place, fulfil its appointed function, and thus exhibit its own specific excellence. This is recognized by Augustine as an attitude of strict 'justice'; a desire that the *ordo universi* should not be disrupted.

In respect of many things in the universe it was, of course, impossible for this desire of its creator to be disappointed. Most of its components could not wander from their proper places: for example, the planets could not diverge from their orbits, and fire could not fail to generate heat.

But in respect of some of its components, particularly angels and men, God's desire for the order of the universe to be maintained might be disappointed; for these were created capable of disobedience.

Now, if disobedience were to occur, the errant part of the universe must, of course, expect to feel the weight of God's displeasure. God's attitude of strict justice would come into play, and the errancy would be punished.

(b) But disruption, disobedience brings into play, not only God's attitude of strict justice, but also the second of God's attitudes towards the universe of his creation; namely, what Augustine calls 'love' or 'forgiveness'.

In short, as Augustine understood it, God has an 'affection' for what he has created which is not destroyed by disobedience to his law.

For Augustine this is a logical conclusion. His argument is that, if God's nature had contained nothing but a desire for absolute and unvarying order, he would never have created a universe in which disorder was possible. But having created a world in which some of its components are capable of disorderly conduct, his nature must be supposed to contain an appropriate response to disorder – and this appropriate response is not mere repression, but what Augustine calls 'love' or 'forgiveness'.

The two-fold attitude of God to his creation is, then

- Strict justice: the condemnation and punishment of disorder.

- Love: the forgiveness of errancy and disorder.

(4) Now, human sin is, precisely, a man wandering from his proper place in the *ordo universi*. It is a disruption of the order by a component capable of disorder, being disorderly. It is disobedience of the law of the universe.

But what is meant when it is said that a component has got out of its proper place? Two things:

(a) That the errant component is trying to occupy another place, not its own proper place. For in this universe there are no vacant spaces into which any of its parts may slip if they move from their appointed places. Of course, the attempt to occupy another place cannot succeed; no part of the universe could ever succeed in performing a function other than its own. But in trying to do so it must fail to perform its own proper function. If a pawn on the chessboard tries to be a king it will fail, but in trying it will cease to be a good pawn.

(b) That to endeavour to occupy a place in the order of the universe other than your own proper place is to prefer yourself to the order of the universe. It is to imagine another order with yourself at its centre. Every act of disorder is the destruction of one order in favour of another. Every pawn that tries to be a king is *not* merely breaking the law; it is proposing a new set of *laws* in which pawns move as kings.

(5) This, then, is the general nature of evil, and the particular nature of sin: it is a component of the universe preferring itself to the order in which it belongs.

Now (Augustine continues) we know that there was one 'original sin' in human history. It was committed by Adam, the first man; and has been inherited by the human race as an indelible stain or corruption of human nature. It disrupted the *ordo universi*; and this disruption goes on reverberating down the long corridor of all subsequent human history. But this 'original' sin was not only a primordial act of self-preference on the part of Adam; it is also the emblem of all subsequent human sin. All sin is of the same fundamental character as the first sin.

Disappointingly enough, this original sin has nothing to do with sex. Augustine identifies it, not as concupiscence, but as pride. And it is not difficult to understand why.

Pride is, precisely, thinking of yourself as, and behaving as if, you were other than in fact you are. It is trying to occupy a place in the *ordo universi* other than that which properly belongs to you. Pride, then, for Augustine, is self-preference, and is the universal character of all sin.

And since it is not only preferring yourself to the *ordo universi*, but is also attempting to replace that order with another of which you are the centre, pride (and therefore all sin) is the attempt of a part of the created universe to become the creator. Pride is a man attempting to become God. A king which tried to move only as a pawn might be thought to be a very humble sort of king; but not so. His pride lies in thinking that he can improve the laws of the game.

The fall of man, then, was not caused by pride; it *was* pride. And it was preceded by the 'fall of the angels'; 'the angels fell by pride'.

(5) Now, the self-preference of sinful man has a two-fold consequence:

(a)   It results in the estrangement of man from God. Man, disrupting God's *ordo*, and setting himself up as the creator and centre of another imagined order, denies God and separates himself from God. The emblem of this consequence is the expulsion of Adam and Eve from the garden of Eden: the sinful pride of Adam cut him off from God.

(b)   It results in each man preferring himself, his own happiness, to that of every other man. This is simply another aspect of the disruption of the *ordo* inherent in sin: the strife and contention in which men are estranged from their fellow men. The emblem of this is the story of Cain and Abel, the story of the first murder.

(6) This 'original' sin, then, has taken place. Adam imagined himself to be God and disrupted God's universe, and human nature acquired an indelible stain, a corruption of will, so that, not merely the actions, but the desires and intentions of mankind diverge from God's design.

This, an offence against God's sense of order, a perpetual disposition of disobedience and self-preference, lays the human race under the punishment of God. Punishment is the visitation of sin with its due; and the wages of sin is death.

But secondly, it brings into operation God's 'love' and 'for-giveness'. And in 'love', and 'forgiveness', God:

(a) Pursues the human race in order to rescue it from the consequences of sin; namely alienation from himself and alienation from one another. For this purpose (that is, to miti-gate these consequences of sin) God gave mankind a specific, positive rule of life, and he gave them institutions of govern-ment. Moses was the first law-giver; Nimrod was the first king.

These, however, were temporary measures, designed, not to abolish sin and restore mankind, but merely to mitigate some of the immediate consequences of sin.

(b) Has promised, in the end, to redeem the human race from sin and to restore human nature to its original inno-cence. This ultimate redemption has been prefigured in human history by many partial redemptions: Noah was saved from the flood, Lot from Sodom, Isaac from sacrifice, the Israelites from Egypt. But now, this redemption is not merely a promise; it has specifically been set on foot. For God has sent his son into the world to reconcile mankind to him-self and to one another. And the faith of a Christian is the belief that he shall inherit the kingdom of heaven.

But neither this ultimate redemption, nor the temporary measures by which God has mitigated the immediate conse-quences of sin, can in any sense be said to be merited or deserved by mankind. They are examples of God's grace, his gracious love and forgiveness.

(8) We live, then, (says Augustine) in an interim period of human history: awaiting with renewed expectation final sal-vation; and meanwhile enjoying God's gracious mitigations of some of the consequences of our alienation from himself and from one another.

Thus, the present condition of the world exhibits two fun-damental characteristics:

It is temporary. It is to be succeeded by a new condition in which the disrupted *ordo universi* is finally restored. And nothing that now happens or may happen can hasten or retard this final event. In relation to this final salvation there is, for Augustine, only one event that has a causative or con-tributory character; namely, the crucifixion of Christ. All other events, before and after, are merely insignificant clouds which pass across the sky.

It is a mixed condition. It contains order and disorder, good and evil, divine punishment and divine love.

Now, this mixed condition of the current world and of current human character appears in the lives of human beings as a divided loyalty. We are citizens of two 'cities'; we owe allegiance to two different rulers.

(a) As he was created, man's allegiance was to the *ordo universi* of God. He was a citizen of a *civitas Dei*, a 'city of God', a city whose order was unbroken, unmixed good. And this, in spite of human sin, remains the true allegiance of mankind.

(b) But, in respect of being sinners and having corrupt natures, human beings are citizens, also, of a *civitas diaboli*, a city of the devil, a city of the proud, a city of those who love themselves more than they love God. This second city Augustine also calls the *civitas terrena*, the 'city of earth', *not* meaning that it is one of the cities of the world, but in order to contrast it with the *civitas coelestis*, the 'city of heaven' or the 'city of God'.

'Two loves', says Augustine, 'have created two cities': the love of God, the *civitas coelestis*; the love of oneself, the *civitas terrena*.

Now, the *civitas Dei* and the *civitas terrena* are not, of course, actual cities, situated in this world. They are 'ideal' cities which represent two 'ideal' allegiances – one towards absolute good and the other towards absolute evil. They represent 'ideal', 'unmixed' extremes of disposition and conduct, which (because they are unmixed) do not belong to the present world. The two cities, says Augustine, 'lie confused in the world'. There is something of the city of God and something of the city of the devil in every human soul; but neither has existed unqualified by the other since the fall of man.

(9) We are concerned, not with what Augustine thinks about final salvation (except insofar as the expectation of it makes us 'pilgrims', foreigners – 'here we have no abiding city but we seek one to come'), but with what he thinks about our present condition.

This is a world in which God's grace operates to mitigate the immediate consequences of sin. And to this end God has ordained the two distinguishable authorities in current human life: the church and civil government; sacerdotal and regal authority.

Both the church and civil society belong to the present, temporary condition of the world; both exhibit the mixed character of the present world; both mitigate the consequences of sin; neither causes or contributes to ultimate salvation.

The two consequences of sin are: the alienation of mankind from God, and the alienation of man from man.

The church was designed by God, and its foundation was commissioned by Christ, in order to give relief from the first consequences of sin: alienation from God. It is a *corpus permixtum*, a mixed body of human beings, containing saints and sinners, some worse and more corrupt than others; but all suffering from the original 'stain'. It is a *civitas*, a city of believers, to which the Christian owes a duty. Its significant *potestas* is the *potestas ordinis*, the *potestas* of administering the sacraments. These sacraments – baptism, marriage, the mass, and so on – are the positive means of keeping alive in a corrupt world that love of God and preference for the *ordo universi* which is man's first allegiance. They are the gifts of God's grace; a kind of compensation for having been expelled from the garden of Eden. The church is not itself, of course, the *civitas Dei*; and to be a Christian believer, and a good church-goer, does not ensure 'salvation'.

The order of a civil society, on the other hand, is designed by God's grace to give relief from the second consequence of sin: the alienation of man from man from which springs contention, strife, murder, war, and so on.

The civil order, for Augustine, represents the human race being prevented by God's grace from that complete self-destruction which would be the result of sin if sin were allowed to have its full consequences. Thus, it is itself a consequence of sin; and it is a gift of God's grace to an undeserving human race to relieve it of a particular consequence of sin. Civil society is not the *civitas terrena*; it, like the church, is a *civitas permixtum*, an order in which good and evil lie confused together.

But, like all other 'cities' (except the *civitas diaboli*) a civil order exhibits, in some degree, the two fundamental characteristics of 'order' – namely, *justitia* and *pax*, 'justice' and 'peace'.

Justitia is order generated, not by violence, but by law and authority. It is giving each man his due where what is 'due' (however circumstantial it may be) is *not* arbitrary and shifting, but firm and known. *Remota justitia quid regna nisi magna latrocinia*, writes St. Augustine: 'without justice, what are kingdoms other than great gangs of robbers'.

Pax is that cessation of strife which comes with an authority which, as the custodian of the law, forbids resort to violence and itself provides remedies for wrongs.

Of course, the *justitia* of a civil order is very imperfect; and the *pax* it provides is fragile and uncertain. They are only the pale reflections of the *justitia* which belongs to the *ordo universi*, and the *pax coelestis* of the *civitas Dei*. But however pale the reflection, the *justitia* of a civil order distinguishes it from a band of brigands; and its *pax*, however imperfect, is an unmistakable mitigation of that war of all against all which would otherwise spring from the unhindered self-preference of each man. And, that even these pale reflections of *justitia* and *pax* exist in the world, is something that the human race owes to the love and the forgiveness of a providential God.

6

Now, if this is the place which Augustine finds for civil society on the map of the universe, there is no doubt about what he considers to be the most significant features of a civil *civitas*. They are: the arrangement of duties and rights characteristic of a legal order under the *potestas* of a legitimate ruler; military force in the custody of this ruler; the right of private property; and the subordination of one man to another in a social order, including the institution of slavery.

It is these particular institutions which Augustine sees standing between sinful man and the complete chaos of unrelieved self-preference which would otherwise be the result of sin. Each makes a contribution to the prevention of the strife between man and man which would otherwise lead to the destruction of the race by mutual murder.

The particular civil order Augustine had in mind was, of course, that of the Roman empire. And consequently his political theory is in the nature of a sanctification of the Roman imperial government. It is the *pax Romana* seen *sub specie aeternitatis*. Not that he thought of Roman government as indisputably just – that is not the point. The point is that all order has some semblance of justice; and any order (that is, anything which rescues mankind from the rule of violence) is valuable – even if it were the order of a pagan government. But imperial Rome had the virtue, for Augustine, of having adopted Christianity as its official religion; and he could recognize Theodosius as a ruler blessed by God's grace.

Nevertheless, Augustine did not think that civil society had been instituted by God immediately after the expulsion of Adam and Eve from Eden. Nobody, not even God, could then know just how much disorder sin would generate in the world. Augustine thought that civil society had been instituted by God as a kind of last resort of mercy when it appeared that mankind were bent upon self-destruction. Nimrod was the first king; and since Nimrod's day Augustine thought that there had been only two dominant 'kingdoms' or civil orders in the world, the one succeeding the other, and each of which in its own time had performed the same service for mankind: the kingdom of the Hebrews, and the Roman state.

7

The civil order, then, is a device of God's grace designed to prevent men, who had surrendered to pride, from destroying themselves in contention and strife. But Augustine recognized it as a slightly equivocal device. A civil order in which each man has his rights and duties and is assured by law of the enjoyment of what is his own, may certainly be recognized as a defence against the disorder of the unhindered and continuous pursuit by every man of his own disordered desires.

But such an order requires a custodian, a king or an emperor; a ruler, *not* (as others are) subject to the restraints of the civil order, but, under God, creating and maintaining those restraints. But such a man will be undefended against the sin, the self-preference, against which he protects others. Kings, in order to be kings, must (it seems) be 'proud'; and unless God himself were to rule there is no easy way out of this dilemma.

As Augustine understands it, kings (that is, custodians of a civil order) can peform their office only with the aid of a kind of vicarious sinfulness. Their 'pride' saves others from the dismal consequences of universal pride. The vice of an emperor makes possible the order of a civil state. And, in a subtle sense, the *populus Romanus* when it endowed the emperor with the *imperium* unloaded upon him their opportunity to sin, just as Christ takes all the sins of mankind upon himself.

8

Now, what comment can be made on this political philosophy of St. Augustine?

(1) First, we may perhaps understand it more fully by contrasting it with what we found in ancient Greek thought.

In both Plato and Aristotle, *polis*-life, a civil order, was understood to spring from human nature itself and to be a necessary condition of a good human life. A just *polis* was recognized as a great and difficult achievement; but an achievement made possible by certain uniquely human capacities (their powers of speech and their aptitude for action and reasoning); and made necessary on account of the uniquely human *eudaimonia* which these capacities entailed. *Polis*-life was explained as a reflection of the rationality and virtue of which human beings are naturally capable. The mystery of its historical emergence was removed by understanding it as already embedded in human nature.

St. Augustine's explanation, on the other hand, introduces to us a remarkably different set of considerations. Government is said to be *propter peccatum*, 'on account of sin'. And a civil order is recognized as an unmerited gift of the grace of a providential God, and to be designed to mitigate a particular consequence of the current sinful disposition of human beings.

And if we ask ourselves, Why could not Augustine look (like so many of the ancients) for the explanation of civil order in human nature itself and pin his faith to the precept 'follow nature'? The answer is that, unfortunately, the 'nature' (which would have been a reliable guide) has been lost. For, in Augustine's way of thinking, the word 'nature' signified that original, free, innocent condition of mankind as it was created by God. But, during the whole of the post-lapsarian history of mankind, this nature had been corrupt and vitiated by sin. This true, original human nature would, indeed, be restored in God's good time; but meanwhile it is lost. What exists now is utterly corrupt nature; incapable, itself, of generating any kind of order.

In short, if it is order which has to be explained, nothing in current 'nature' (so far as Augustine was concerned) could possibly explain it. If order exists among men it must have been given to them by God's grace.

And further, for Plato human excellence was a certain condition of the human soul, and for Aristotle the human *eudaimonia* was a certain manner of living in the world, and for both *polis*-life could be recognized as a necessary condition of this excellence. But for Augustine the current world might afford opportunites for a better or for a worse life, and a civil order might be recognized as a defence against the worse; but all this had nothing whatever to do with that restored union with God hereafter in the *civitas coelestis* which, in Christian thought, had taken the place of the Greek notion of human excellence. And on this account, also, his reading of the world differed from theirs.

(2) Secondly, we may notice that Augustine's manner of thinking is a preeminently Roman manner of thinking. And were it not for Augustine it would have to be admitted that the Romans produced no great philosopher. Augustine, of course, is a Roman with a difference; he is a Christian. But Christian thought had acquired many of the characteristic features of Roman thought.

For the Roman, Rome had been founded by Romulus with divine approval; this 'foundation' was the authority for all the subsequent activities of the Roman people; the Roman calendar took the year of 'foundation' as 'Year 1'; and the *imperium* exercised by an emperor was the *imperium* of Romulus. The Roman people were a people who had a destiny to fulfil in the world, a destiny which was imposed upon them by Romulus and their gods. Rome itself was an 'eternal city'.

Similarly, the Christian church had been founded by St. Peter at the command of Christ; this 'foundation' was the authority for all the subsequent activities of the sacerdotal authority in Christendom; the Christian calendar took the year of the birth of the 'founder' of Christianity as 'Year 1' (although, of course, Christ was something much more than the 'founder' of the Christian church). But the 'eternal city' was no longer a city of this world; it was the *civitas Dei* to which the allegiance of all men was due and which would, in God's good time, be the single and undisputed centre of allegiance.

Meanwhile, the history of mankind is seen as the history of God's providential grace wrestling with man's corrupt and vitiated nature in a contest which has only a temporary and contingent significance. For salvation and union with God is not the victory of God in *this* contest; it lies in the cessation of this contest in an act of final redemption.

Thus, Augustine's explanation of the civil order is an explanation in the idiom of the Christian thought of his time, an idiom so deeply marked by the Roman conception of the *civitas* that it may be recognized as a characteristically Roman political philosophy.

Editorial Note

LSE 1/1/21, file 4, fos. 347–64. Fos. 347–9, 351 are photocopies of autograph sheets; fos. 350, 352–64 are photocopies of a typescript with autograph corrections. The lecture on 'Medieval Political Philosophy' (fos. 335–46) is omitted because it is a shorter version of the two lectures on Augustine and Aquinas published here.

Twenty-two

Medieval Political Philosophy (2): Aquinas

1

The second example of medieval philosophical reflection on political activity and government I want to consider is that which is to be found in the writings of St. Thomas Aquinas, whose life covered the central fifty years of the thirteenth century. Aquinas was a philosopher and a theologian who turned his attention to the problems of political philosophy. He wrote a fragment called *De regimine principum* ('On Kingly Government'): and the rest of what he had to say about government and politics appears incidentally in his *Summa theologica* and in his commentaries on Aristotle's *Ethics* and *Politics*.

What I have called 'political philosophy' – that is, an attempt to *explain* political activity and the experience of governing and being governed by elucidating its place on the map of human activity in general – is a comparatively rare appearance. It may be provoked when some strikingly new political experience emerges; that is, when what has to be explained seems to be different from what others may be thought to have already satisfactorily explained. But a genuinely fresh turn will be given to this explanatory enterprise only when there emerges some new understanding of what has to be said in order to explain.

For example, Plato's philosophical explanation of *polis*-life sprang from his 'doctrine of ideas', which was his understanding of what had to be said in order to explain anything; and Augustine's explanation of the civil order was one which he (and others of his time) believed to be entailed in the Christian view of the universe.

Now, by the thirteenth century the political experience of Western Europe had acquired some features which distinguished it from the political experience Augustine had before him; there was, however, nothing in it which defied explanation in Augustinian terms. But the turn of events in the intellectual history of the early thirteenth century produced a situation which (to anyone alive to what was afoot) went a long way towards depriving the Augustinian manner of explanation of its power to give intellectual satisfaction.

It was not, of course, that people had ceased to believe in that view of the universe which Augustine (calling upon four centuries of Christian thought) had elaborated. The creation of the world out of nothing, and of the human race, by an omnipotent God; the sin of Adam; the ensuing corruption of human nature; the love and forgiveness of God; the promise of redemption, and the interim operation of God's grace rescuing the fallen world from chaos – all this was as intelligible and as acceptable to Christian people as it had ever been. But, in the second decade of the thirteenth century something had been added to it; something which (because it was impossible to ignore it) had to be reconciled with this Christian understanding of the world. Nevertheless, it was something very difficult to reconcile. This was the ethical and political writings of Aristotle, newly recovered after having been lost to Western Europe for the better part of ten centuries.

The importance of these writings of Aristotle in the thirteenth century was twofold:

They gave an understanding of human activity, of human personality, and of the excellence characteristic of human beings, radically different from the view of these things contained in the accepted Augustinian or (more generally) Christian way of thinking. They contained nothing about the creation of the world, nothing about divine providence, nothing about the church and nothing about the salvation of mankind. And further, they were not writings which merely omitted these important considerations; they composed a coherent explanation of things into which (it appeared) these things could not be fitted. In short, these writings presented the thirteenth century with a manner of explaining things to which it was unaccustomed; and it is not surprising that these writings first met with hostility.

Nevertheless, the explanation of things they contained could not be merely ignored by thirteenth century thinkers.

Aristotle, on account of many of his other writings which had long been known to Christian thinkers, had already, by the thirteenth century, achieved a position of undeniable philosophical authority. The current 'Christian' view of the physical universe was already thoroughly Aristotelian; much of what the middle ages knew of astronomy and biology was owed directly or indirectly to Aristotle; and he was the acknowledged father of the logic characteristic of the 'scholastic' manner of argument. He already sat, brooding over Christendom, with Cicero and Donatus, carved in stone on the West front of the cathedral of Chartres – a logician, an orator, and a grammarian. He was, in short, an honorary 'father' of the Christian church.

The question, then, which confronted the generation of Aquinas was: What was to be done with an Aristotle who (in the newly recovered *Ethics* and *Politics*) was now found to have an explanation of human character, human activity, human virtue which seemed to conflict radically with the accepted Christian view? All that was certain was that he could neither be ignored, nor simply declared a heretic, nor easily accepted.

The impact of these ethical and political writings of Aristotle was slow. They came to the thirteenth century first by way of Latin translations from Arabic translations; and from Toledo (that great centre of medieval intellectual activity) they gradually seeped into the consciousness of Western Europe. It was the generation of Aquinas which had to discover how to come to terms with them.

And, briefly, the undertaking Aquinas set himself (among much else) was to compose an explanation of the civil order in which the writings of Augustine and the writings of Aristotle were reconciled to one another. This is what is meant when Aquinas is described as the first Christian Aristotelian; and this is why he could hardly escape the task of reconciling the two. It was an enterprise which required great subtlety, great sincerity, and great liberality of mind.

2

Our first business is to see clearly the difference between the Augustinian understanding of human nature and human activity and the Aristotelian understanding of it.

(1) For Augustine, current human activity is determined by two things: (a) the original sin of Adam, inherited by all mankind as a vitiation of human nature; (b) God's gracious activity in the world, mitigating some of the immediate consequences of this sin, and exemplified in particular by the institutions of the church and the civil order.

Government and the civil order are recognized as *propter peccatum*, 'on account of sin'. They are necessary for the survival of the human race; but they are possible only because they are the providential gifts of a loving and forgiving God. They do not, they could not, spring from current, vitiated human nature – although it was admitted that there remained some relics of man's uncorrupt nature. They are supernatural gifts to mankind. They belong to current human history, not to 'nature'. The true, original, uncorrupt 'nature' of man did not require them; the present 'corrupt' nature of men could not generate them.

In these circumstances the activity of rulers is understood to be fundamentally 'penal' – that is, the suppression of the propensity of their subjects to sin and strife. The authority of rulers is *a Deo*, 'from God': they are God's vicars. The order imposed by rulers is an order which has some semblance of 'justice' – that is, it differs from the order which might be opposed by mere violence. And the product of civil rule is a condition which bears some resemblance to 'peace'.

And further, government, and the civil order it generates (for there can be no civil order without government), is of no permanent significance. The good behaviour it exacts from its subjects merely enables them to get through this interim period of human history, after the fall of man and before the promised redemption of man. The rise and fall of kingdoms, better and worse behaviour, more and less just rulers – all these are relatively insignificant contingencies. The hopes and longings of mankind are fixed, not upon the achievement of anything upon earth, but upon their final salvation and reunion with God in the *civitas Dei*. And this salvation is neither merited by human beings, nor is it the product of historical events; it is an undeserved gift of divine grace.

(2) Now, when we turn from Augustine to Aristotle (and when Aquinas turned from Augustine to Aristotle) a totally different understanding of the situation appears.

Human beings, like everything else in the world have an inherent 'nature' which is at once the cause of their activity and the end at which that activity is aimed. The specific and unique character of human beings is that they pursue the peculiar excellence which is potential in their 'nature' by making choices for themselves. These choices are rational choices if they promote the achievement of the peculiar excellence of human nature. Rational conduct, then, the conduct proper to human beings, may be described as voluntary activity designed to realize the excellence potential in human 'nature'.

This rational conduct may be hindered by irrational impulses inseparable from voluntary conduct, but there is no inborn propensity to be guided by irrational impulse – quite the reverse – and certainly nothing has happened to the human race (like an 'original sin') to increase this propensity.

Further, human beings are capable of speech, and this makes possible a co-operative enterprise for the achievement of human excellence. This co-operative enterprise is a political activity: *polis*-life is at once 'natural' to human beings and an achievement of human beings in which potential human excellence becomes actual.

Consequently, human conduct is not understood as requiring to be directed by an angry or an affectionate God. *Polis*-life is the product of rational human choice, and is therefore natural to human beings; it is certainly not a device to mitigate the consequences of a corrupt human nature.

In this understanding of things there is no place or need for the Augustinian divine grace; it would simply be redundant. Nor is current human life an interim (made tolerable by divine providence) between an original corruption and a final redemption: it is all there is. The hopes and expectations of human beings are fixed upon the realization of the potentialities of their rational 'natures'. There is no heavenly city; there is no place or need for the gracious gift of 'salvation'; there are only better and worse manners of living.

It is true that the good citizen may be distinguished from the good man; but that is only because ultimate human excellence (though it is impossible without *polis*-life) lies in an activity which is not a civic activity; namely, in 'contemplation' or a life of reflective reason.

In short, it would seem that no two readings of human nature, of human activity, and of human virtue, could be more different from one another. And as an emblem of the differences we may take the respective explanations which Augustine and Aristotle give of slavery.

Slavery is unintelligible to Augustine unless it is understood as a divine institution; something authorized by God. And when it is understood in this manner it may be recognized as both a punishment for sin and as a remedy for the disorder brought into the world by sin. It is part of that contingent subordination of man to man authorized by God as a mitigation of the chaos generated by sin. Thus, it is 'historic', not 'natural'; it is something expressly instituted by God.

For Aristotle slavery is intelligible only if it is a condition of living which corresponds to 'nature'. It is explicable only if it can be seen to be in some manner 'natural'.

Now, it is obvious that it will take a very clever man to reconcile these two readings of human beings and human activity. But Aquinas was a very clever man; and without going into all the intricate detail of his argument, I want to show you how he induced an agreement between what may be called the Augustinian and the Aristotelian inheritance of his generation, and to consider some of the consequences of this agreement.

3

In the generation of Aquinas (roughly the middle of the thirteenth century), and subsequently among medieval philosophers, there were many who found in the writings of Aristotle much that attracted them and much that they could make use of; but it is safe to say that no other medieval thinker studied Aristotle so deeply as Aquinas; and there was none who accepted, as Aquinas did, the central Aristotelian conception of a natural world, operating according to its own internal laws, a self-contained, self-moved universe requiring nothing outside itself to make it work or to make its operation intelligible.

Aquinas's two categories of (1) movement which is *secundum natura* ('natural', or 'according to nature') and (2) movement which is *contra natura* ('against nature'), are Aristotle's two categories of 'natural movement' (in which the thing that moves is moved by its own inherent potentiality), and 'accidental movement' in which the natural movement of one thing may be frustrated by the natural movement of another.

And having accepted this Aristotelian conception in respect of the world in general, Aquinas accepted it also in respect of human conduct.

Human behaviour is *not* determined by something outside human nature, and it is *not* directed to the achievement of an end imposed upon it by some external authority; it is the potentialities of human nature seeking to realize themselves.

And further, for Aquinas (as for Aristotle), the unique and specific character of human behaviour is that it is *voluntary*; that is, it is a response to choice. It is rational behaviour when the choices which generated it are directed towards the realization of the potentialities of human nature. Human excellence is achieved by human beings knowing what belongs to their 'natures' and achieving it by means of specific choices or decisions.

Now, in this Aristotelian understanding of the world and of human activity there is no place for an external authority (a god, for example) to impose laws of movement or rules of conduct; the excellence of things does not lie in their conformity to an externally imposed standard, but in their achievement of what is already potential in themselves.

Aristotle had imagined that it was logically necessary to suppose a 'first mover' who originally set this natural system going. And at this point Aquinas departs from Aristotle by thinking (according to the Christian idiom) that this 'first mover' or 'God' was not merely an original impulse, but was the designer and 'creator' of the natural world. God is *auctor naturae, or conditor naturae*; and therefore the internal movement, the order and system, which characterizes the natural world, exemplifies divine reason. But this does nothing whatever to qualify or modify the Aristotelian belief in the self-moved, self-operating natural world of things.

Human activity, then, is movement, in response to rational choices, in which the human *eudaimonia,* or the excellence characteristic of human beings, is achieved. And the divergence between this view of things and the conventional Augustinian view may be illustrated as follows.

From early in the Christian era it had become the convention to think of human excellence as the exercise of what were known as the seven cardinal virtues (to which there corresponded the seven deadly sins, signifying human

viciousness). These virtues were justice, temperance, forti-
tude, prudence, faith, hope, and charity.

In the Christian way of thinking, the first four of these
(which had been derived from the morality, chiefly Stoic, of
the ancient world, and were known as the 'moral' virtues)
had no value in themselves. These 'moral' virtues were 'indifferent', they had no significant 'effect' unless they were
inspired by the last three (faith, hope, and charity), which
were known as the 'theological' virtues. Thus, merely
'moral' conduct had no autonomous standing; and human
excellence was understood as a condition of the human soul
which required the intervention of divine grace; it was something which human nature unendowed by divine grace
could not achieve.

Now, Aquinas, following Aristotle, asserted that the
'moral' virtues (those which sprang from rational human
nature) were *not* valueless in themselves, and that they composed an autonomous condition of 'natural' human excellence. If they were informed by the 'theological' virtues they
were supremely valuable and represented the fundamental
character of a good human life.

The first great modification, then, of the Augustinian
understanding of human activity which Aquinas introduced
was a modified view of the relation of grace to nature.

For Augustine, the original, innocent, perfect, 'nature' of
man had become absolutely corrupted by sin; it no longer
existed. What existed was a completely corrupt human
nature, protected against itself, and in the end destined to be
redeemed, by the external intervention of God's providential
grace. Grace was understood to be a supernatural substitute
for a lost human 'nature'.

Against this view, under the guidance of Aristotle's conception of 'nature', Aquinas proposed the principle *gratia
non tollit naturam, sed perficit* ('grace perfects or fulfils nature
and does not oppose it'). And together with this he rejected
the doctrine that the original sin had wholly corrupted
human nature, and put in its place the doctrine that the original sin had wounded human nature but had left it capable of
making rational choices and therefore of achieving the
human excellence signified in the 'moral' virtues, without
the need of the intervention of divine grace. *Id quod est
naturale totaliter perdi non potest.* ('What is natural cannot be
wholly corrupt.')

Nevertheless, Aquinas was not a Pelagian. He did not hold that the salvation of mankind was possible without the intervention of divine grace, or that a good human life as exemplified in the 'moral' virtues would get a man to heaven. He merely held that a good human life could be achieved from the resources of current human nature, and that it was something valuable in itself.

4

Now, the general understanding of human activity and life in the current world which emerges from these assimilations of the Augustinian to the Aristotelian doctrines is something like this:

There is what Aquinas called a *duplex ordo in rebus*, a 'twofold order in the world'.

(1) There is the order of 'nature'; and within 'nature', 'human nature'. This is, as Aristotle had held it to be, a self-contained, self-moved order in which each thing is seeking the excellence which belongs to its own nature. The 'natural' order was created by God and its arrangements exhibit the rationality of God's character. Within this order, then, human activity is the activity of rational beings seeking the excellence which is potential in their rational natures.

It is true that, so far as human beings are concerned, this order of nature is not wholly uncorrupt. Men (as Aristotle knew) are often disposed to refuse rational choices in favour of choices which lead away from the achievement of their political excellence. And (as Aristotle did not know) this corruption is an inheritance from the original sin of Adam. But human nature is not so corrupt that 'natural' excellence is impossible of achievement. And the achievement of this natural excellence is a worthwhile achievement whatever else may also be desirable.

(2) There is the order of divine grace, or the order of *supra natura*. This, from one point of view, penetrates the 'natural' order, not compromising it, but holding in check its propensity to corruption. The natural excellence which is signified in the 'moral' virtues, is made less uncertain of achievement by the addition of the 'theological' virtues of faith, hope, and charity, which are unsought, unmerited gifts of divine grace, and belong to the supernatural order.

But, from another point of view, the order of grace is that which concerns, not a virtuous life on earth, but something quite different – namely, the final salvation and redemption of mankind. For human beings are (what Aristotle had never guessed them to be) immortal souls. Their destiny is not merely to achieve the 'natural' excellence of which they are capable but is to enjoy, also, by the providential grace of God, a life of union with him in the *civitas Dei* which is to come.

Thus, in this *duplex ordo*, Augustine (with some of his extreme beliefs modified), was assimilated to the grand and compelling Aristotelian conception of 'nature' and human nature.

5

Now, as Aquinas understood it, political activity (the experience of governing and being governed in a civil order) belongs unmistakably to the 'natural' order. Human beings are 'by nature' *animalia socialia et politica* – creatures whose natural excellence requires that they should live together in a civil order. Therefore, a civil order is not to be understood as an 'artificial', or 'supernatural' condition of human life, a gift of divine grace to mitigate the consequences of the original sin; indeed, a civil order is not to be understood as *propter peccatum* at all.

It was never 'founded' (as Augustine believed) at a certain point in human history by divine authority. It is (as Aristotle thought) 'natural' to human beings. And since it is a condition necessary to the achievement of the excellence potential in human nature, it must be understood as an achievement of human rational choices designed to supply human natural needs.

Thus, as Aquinas understands it, a civil order is potential in human nature; and what it supplies is that peace and orderliness which is necessary to the *civilitas* (civilized life) in which alone 'natural' human excellence can be achieved. It is (as Aristotle thought) more than a mere *congregatio hominum* (a coming together and association of human beings); it is a *corpus politicum et morale* ('a moral and political order'), supplying the whole circumstantial context necessary for the achievement of *bene vivere* (a good human life on earth).

It follows from this that the civil order may be understood as a *communitas perfecta*, a complete and self-sufficient community of human beings (as Aristotle had understood the *polis* to be); it has the authority of 'nature' and it needs no other additional authority, such as that of a church or of divine grace.

6

Now, when the civil order, the *civitas*, is thus placed firmly within the natural order, the activity which concerned it – political activity and the activity of governing – appears as a *practical* human activity. And *scientia politica* appears, not as a speculative or theoretical science, but as a *scientia operativa*, a practical science, or what Aquinas identified as an 'art'.

Government is not concerned with educating its subjects, or with making them good men or even better men, but with the preservation of public order and decency in public conduct; it is concerned with *utilitas hominum*. Political activity does not prepare human beings for their ultimate salvation; it has to do only with the infinitely variable contingencies of earthly human life.

It is concerned with the local, the temporary, and the convenient, not with the universal, the eternal, and the necessary; it is concerned with the 'natural' *eudaimonia* of human beings, not with their final happiness; it is concerned with crime, not sin; with the public conduct and the ostensible relations between human beings, not with their 'merits'. It may even have to do with a community in which there are wide differences of religious and moral beliefs, and its object is to make possible *civilitas*, a civilized life, even in these circumstances. Strictly speaking, for Aquinas, a pagan civil order might be as good as a Christian civil order.

Civilitas, of course, won't get a man to heaven, and Aquinas is not a Pelagian who thinks it will; but living on earth is as necessary to men as getting to heaven, and politics is concerned with living on earth and the essentially mutable conditions of earthly life.

Now, in following Aristotle, Aquinas has, nevertheless, modified the Aristotelian position. The civil order of Aquinas is not quite the *polis* of Aristotle.

Aristotle had understood the *polis* as a morally and materially self-sufficient community of human beings, an autonomous human society. And the context of this understanding of the *polis* was, among other things, that union of moral and religious belief characteristic of a Greek city. There was no room for the moral or religious eccentric.

But when Aquinas thought of the civil order as a *communitas perfecta*, an autonomous and self-sufficient human society, he meant something less than Aristotle meant. Aristotle was concerned with a moral unity; Aquinas was concerned with an autonomous legal unit. For Aristotle *polis*-life was not merely a life in which *conduct* conformed to known legal standards, it was a life in which *belief* was also a public and legal concern. For Aquinas the civil order has no such comprehensive character. And Aquinas can take a more limited view of the office of civil government, confining it much more narrowly to the care of public order and *civilitas*, because there is some *other* authority in whose care are matters of belief and education; namely, the church.

In short, the autonomy of political authority, for Aristotle, derived from its being a total activity; but for Aquinas, it meant freedom from ecclesiastical control or supervision. And we shall see, in a moment, what he thought was the peculiar office and authority of the church.

But what about the authority of the ruler in a civil order? What has Aquinas to say in elucidation of this vexed medieval question?

Nothing, I think, very new; but enough to make clear his opinion on the current controversies.

Every civil order, as Aquinas understood it, needs a good and just head; even Aristotle could not convert him from the universal monarchical presupposition of medieval political thought.

The authority of a ruler is certainly not derived from ecclesiastical authority; the *potestas* of a king is in no sense subordinate to that of a pope. His authority must be understood to come ultimately from God, because all *potestas*, in the last resort, is *a Deo*. But his office is the care of his subjects, the protection of their rights and the custody of their laws, and therefore his authority must be taken to depend more upon his just performance of the duties of his office than upon anything else.

To rule in despite of the laws and customs of the country (to become a 'tyrant') is for a king to lay himself open to the just rebuke of his subjects and even to their resistance to his rule, so long as that resistance does not take the form of mere rebellion.

In short, Aquinas's understanding of the civil order led him to favour what was called in the thirteenth century a *regimen politicum*, in which the ruler is *under* the law, and to frown upon a *regimen regale* in which the ruler, ruling *Dei gratia*, has obligations to God alone. A ruler, of course, has a responsibility to God; but he fulfils it by ruling his subjects justly.

7

This philosophy of the civil order, of political activity, and of government (with which is mixed some mere opinions about desirable political institutions) is accompanied in the writings of Aquinas by a philosophy of the church, the ecclesiastical order. And here, although he finds little in Aristotle to guide him, he nevertheless finds something.

Unlike the civil order, the church belongs not to the order of 'nature' but to the order of grace. It is not a *corpus naturalis*, but a *corpus mysticum*.

It was 'founded' by divine command; whereas, the civil order is 'natural' and was never in this sense 'founded'. The office of the church is to supply, not the 'natural' needs of mankind, but the supernatural needs of Christians. It is concerned, not with the human *eudaimonia*, but with ultimate salvation. Its *auctoritas* is derived directly from God; it is an organization with a government and a law of its own; and, as such, it is ruled by a ruler who has *potestas*. But this *potestas*, that of a pope, has no direct concern with the civil order; it is certainly not superior to the regal *potestas*.

In short, for Aquinas, there could be no relevant conflict between *sacerdotium* and *regnum*; each has its own sphere of activity, each with its own office to perform. And the ecclesiastical *auctoritas* can be said to be superior to the civil *potestas* only in the sense that it is concerned with a matter of superior importance; namely, eternal salvation through the grace of God.

But, in this matter there was one hint in Aristotle which Aquinas made use of; namely, Aristotle's distinction between the good citizen and the good man. Aristotle had said (*Politics*, III. iv. 4) that the good citizen was not to be identified with the good man, meaning that the excellence inherent in human nature went beyond the excellence indicated in civic virtues. Aquinas takes up this Aristotelian distinction. He understands the good citizen to be the man who has realized the excellence potential in the 'natural' *animale sociale et politicum*; and he understands the good man to be the man who, not only faithful to the 'moral' virtues, but inspired also by the 'theological' virtues of faith, hope, and charity, and assisted by the sacraments of the divinely 'founded' church, belongs not only to the order of nature but also to the order of grace.

8

Now, this philosophy of political activity and the civil order is partnered in the writings of Aquinas by a philosophy of law. In this respect Aquinas owes less to Aristotle (although his somewhat meagre thoughts on law are taken into the account) and more to Christian speculation which from early times had played round themes drawn from the Old Testament, Roman law, and the Stoic philosophy. And the powerful intellect of Aquinas imposed coherence upon these speculations.

The starting point of these speculations had been a conception of God, not as a capricious oriental potentate, the victim of random and omnipotent impulses, but as a mind capable of coherent design; and a conception of the created universe, not as a fortuitous concourse of unintelligible things and events (representing divine impulses), but as an 'order', the product of deliberate, rational design. And this, also, is the starting point of Aquinas.

He begins with a *lex aeterna*, an 'eternal law', which is, in fact, the coherent organization of the mind of God and which is consequently reflected in the character of the universe of his creation.

(1) The immediate reflection of the *lex aeterna* (that is, the mind and design of God) in the created universe is the *lex naturalis*, the law of nature; that is, the manner in which the things of the created world move and behave.

But since the world contains two kinds of beings, those endowed with intelligence, and those not so endowed, the law of nature operates in two diverse manners:

In the 'unintelligent' order of beings (in the animal and vegetable creation, for example) the law of nature appears as the law of their 'natures' which directs them to the achievement of their own inherent excellences, which they obey blindly, and are incapable of disobeying.

For the 'intelligent' order of beings (for example, angels and men), the law of nature is no less a law which directs their conduct to the achievement of their potential excellence, but it appears as a pattern of life perceived by reason to be necessary for the achievement of excellence, and followed, not blindly, but by conscious, rational choice and decision. And since this is the manner of obedience to natural law characteristic of human beings, they are recognized to be capable of diverging from the precepts of the law of nature. And such divergence is sin.

The law of nature, then, delineates the rational choices which must be made and pursued if human beings are to achieve the excellence of the 'nature' with which they have been endowed by God. It is the 'measure' or standard of the conduct of the good man. It contains, however, two kinds of precepts – primary precepts and secondary precepts.

The primary precepts of the law of nature are those which are simple, direct, necessary, and require little or no adjustment to circumstances: precepts such as that one ought to keep one's promises and ought to tell the truth. Divergence from these precepts is recognized as positively destructive of the excellence of which human beings are capable.

The secondary precepts are those which are not so universally necessary, which often require interpretation and in the interpretation of which some allowance for circumstances must often be made. For example, the principle that a man should be allowed to enjoy what is his own, and the institution of monogamy.

(2) Now, while this law of nature may be relied upon to provide the large outline of the pattern of a good human life, it lacks detail, it often leaves human beings without specific guidance, and it concerns only what may be said to be common and necessary to all men, whatever their circumstances. It therefore requires supplementation.

Moreover, both God and human beings (as rational creatures) are capable of making law of another and more specific kind. This other kind of law, which supplements the law of nature, Aquinas calls *lex positivus*, positive law.

Now, the word *positivus* signified two things:

(a)   It meant that which is made or imposed, as distinct from
      that which is inherent. Thus, a positive law was a rule of
      conduct could not simply be *deduced* from human or
      divine nature, as the law of nature could be deduced;
      and which existed only if it had been expressly made on
      a certain occasion.

(b)   That which is not necessary, but is accidental, or contin-
      gent, or temporary, or circumstantial; that which is con-
      cerned with what is mutable.

Thus, *lex positivus* is a law which does not entail a choice
between good and evil, between right and wrong; it is a law
which is specially made to meet a particular circumstance; it
is a law which is 'arbitrary' in the sense that it cannot be
shown to be necessary to the achievement of human excellence; and it is a law which does not pretend to be of universal application. Aristotle called this law *ideos nomos* (local
and temporary law) as distinct from *kronos nomos*, universally and permanently applicable law.

As Aquinas understood the situation, there were three
kinds of *lex positivus* current in his world: the *lex divina*, the
lex canonica, and the *lex civilis* – the positive law of God, the
canon law, and the law of a civil order.

We need not concern ourselves greatly with the first two of
these. The *lex divina* comprised the 'positive' precepts which
God, on specific historical occasions, had added to the law of
nature. They are to be found in the Old and New Testaments
(the ten commandments belong to the 'positive' law of God);
and, in general, the *lex divina* is the 'gracious' or providential
gift to mankind, as distinct from the *lex naturalis* which is
inherent in nature.

The *lex canonica* comprised the positive rules of conduct,
devised by popes and councils of the church, for the government of ecclesiastical persons on all occasions and of lay persons on some occasions. It is 'human' law (though made
under divine authority), and it is concerned with accidentals.

But what Aquinas has to say about the *lex civilis* is a brief
summary of his philosophy of the civil order. He was writing
at a time when the rulers of the civil order of Christendom
were beginning to engage in the activity of making law, and
consequently he was able to expound his understanding of
the activity of governing by explaining the characteristics of
civil law and of the activity in which it is made.

(3) The positive law of a civil order has four main characteristics.

(a) It must be 'reasonable'. This meant that it should not
conflict with any of the 'necessary' conditions of a good
human life, and that it should not offend against the reasonable expectations of those for whom it was made.

This characteristic of 'reasonableness' indicates, for Aquinas, the relation between the *lex civilis* and the *lex naturalis*.
The law of nature stands superior to all other law, and no
other law can repeal any of its precepts. Even the positive
law of God (the *lex divina*) perfects, but does not repeal, the
law of nature.

On some rare occasions the law of a civil order may seem
to put (so to speak) a precept of the law of nature on the statute book of a civil realm – for example, this might be the
interpretation of a civil law against murder, an act certainly
forbidden by the law of nature. But normally the relation of
civil to natural law is not the positive relationship of a copy
to a model, or of a conclusion to a premiss, or of the application of a principle to the principle itself, but the negative relationship of a rule which lays down what seems to be
convenient in the circumstances to a principle which gives
no specific guidance but must not be rejected. It is, perhaps,
the relationship of a tactical move to a strategic plan: the one
cannot be deduced from the other, but elaborates and
extends it.

(b) It must be directed to the *utile communitati*, the common good of the society. This means that a civil law should
serve the public interest; and that if it gives rights or duties to
a particular class or section of the community (as it may well
do), it must be in the public interest that these should enjoy
these rights or have these duties.

(c) It must be made by a legitimate ruler. This is very
important. A civil law cannot claim the character of being a
rule *necessary* for the good human life, but only the virtue of
being convenient in the local and temporary circumstances.
Therefore, its authority (the reason why it should be obeyed)
must lie, in the first place, merely in the fact of its having
been made by one who has authority to make such a law. The
test of legitimacy is, of course, current opinion. If it is
believed that a parliament should be the partner in legislation with a king, then *rex in parliamento* is the legitimate
authority.

(d) It must have been promulgated in such a manner that it is commonly known to those who are obliged to obey it. This characteristic follows directly from it being *lex positivus*. It may be presumed that any adult, rational man knows the precepts of the law of nature because they are precepts inherent in the nature of man and ascertainable by human reason. But without specific information, no man can know a positive law. The *lex divina* is binding because God has published it in the Scriptures; and the *lex civilis* can only be binding when it has been expressly published.

(4) If these are the characteristics of the law of a civil order, what conclusions did Aquinas draw from them about the activity in which they are made and cared for?

It is a practical, not a theoretical activity; it does not consist of establishing true propositions but of making practical rules for current human conduct in a particular community which has a history and circumstances peculiar to itself. *Scientia politica* (one of the chief parts of which is to make positive law) is a practical art which calls into play, not the explanatory 'theoretical' reason, but *prudentia politica*, 'political judgment'. It is responding to current circumstances by making rules which promote the *utile communitati* in the most convenient manner.

On most occasions the political activity of lawmaking will be a response to a specific contingent emergence, and will consist of devising the most feasible arrangement, all things considered. On many occasions, it will be the choice, not of an unqualified good, but of a lesser evil. But it can never be the activity of making deductions from general abstract premises; that is, the activity of making deductions from the *lex naturalis*.

The activity in *prudentia politica* will be, for example, devising a writ to be able to remedy a wrong which has circumstantially made its appearance; or providing other methods of redress when writs prove themselves to be too narrow or too cumbersome procedure; or (like Edward I in the statute *Quia emptores*) a way of circumventing a specific disutility which has emerged from feudal tenures.

Moreover, this *prudentia politica* teaches a ruling authority that not all sin can be conveniently be made punishable as crime; that what cannot be abolished except at too great a cost must be tolerated; that the expectations of subjects (even if they are not manifestly just expectations) must not be peremptorily overridden; that the *lex civilis* is not an instrument of 'salvation' but only of *civilitas* and *bene vivere*; and that to correct an evil in a manner which may destroy the *fides* (mutual trust) and the *amicitia utilis* (bonds of affection) which hold a society together, is political suicide.

But governing a *corpus politicum et morale* is not merely an activity requiring knowledge (knowledge of the particular, historic circumstances), and judgment and moderation. It is also an 'autonomous' activity.

The civil order is a *communitas perfecta*, a self-sufficient society with its own positive law appropriate to its own circumstances. And consequently a ruler must resist an external authority, like a church, if it seems anxious to impose laws upon his realm which, although they may have the pretended authority of natural law, are nevertheless foreign to the manners and customs of his community. Rulers finding themselves in this situation may have to say, as the king and barons of England said in 1234 at the Council of Merton: *Nolumus legis Angliae mutare* ('We are unwilling to change the laws of England'), when the pope pressed upon them a change in the law in regard to legitimacy. For to rule is to have the custody of the laws of a civil realm, to protect them as well as to emend them appropriately.

In short, Aquinas made a conception of political activity and the activity of governing spring from a consideration of the character of the law of a civil order. This, he says, is the character of politics and government, because politics and government are activities concerned with the positive law of a civil order, and this is the character of *lex positivus*.

(5) Aquinas, who was nothing if not systematic, filled out his survey of the different kinds of law current in the universe by noticing (among some other laws of less importance) the *jus gentium*, or the law of nations.

The relations between the civil rulers of Christendom were claimed by the great popes (particularly by Innocent III) to be within papal jurisdiction. Treaties between monarchs were sworn-to in church; the safe-conduct of ambassadors and the emissaries of kings was in the custody of ecclesiastical authorities; the rules of war were sanctioned by papal authority.

But with Aquinas, these and matters like them were understood to come, not under canon law, but under a law called *jus gentium*. This was an ancient expression from the Roman law which stood for the law operative between persons of different *nationes* within the Roman state. But Aquinas used it to denote a law operative between realms and the rulers of realms. As he understood it, it was a particular mixture of *lex naturalis* and *lex positivus*, having the universality of the law of nature and also the characteristic contingency of positive law, in respect of having to take account of local and variable circumstances.

9

This, then, is a description of the achievement of Aquinas in political philosophy; that is, in the enterprise of *explaining* political activity and the activity of governing. It is a subtle union of Christian theology and the Aristotelian philosophy of 'nature', in which these two components were brought together, and made to modify one another and generate an explanation, not only remarkably new in the thirteenth century, but one that has had a profound influence upon all subsequent explanatory enterprises in this field.

Editorial Note

LSE 1/1/21, file 4, fos. 365–84. Photocopy of a typescript. Fo. 366, headed 'Aquinas', is a diagram in Oakeshott's hand of the divisions of the *lex aeterna*.

Twenty-three

The Character of a Modern European State

1

I propose to spend this term considering the last of the political experiences we set out to study: that of modern Europe.

2

During the last four and a half centuries, a certain kind of political association, a certain manner of engaging in political activity, a certain political vocabulary, and a certain style of governing and being governed, has emerged in Europe.

It is appropriately called 'a modern European state'. And it is the scene and the occasion of all modern European political thought.

This kind of political association (the kind to which we ourselves belong) began to appear in Europe in the late fifteenth century. New 'states' of this sort have gone on emerging even in our own day. The model has been extensively copied outside Europe.

For this reason, I do not think it fanciful to consider European politics in these modern centuries as composing a specific political experience, different from, but comparable to the political experience which constituted the *polis* of ancient Greece, for example.

And, just as the political experience of the ancient Greek *polis* has a certain singleness of character, in spite of the fact that the world of the Greek *polis* was composed of many cities in some respects unlike one another, so the political experience of the modern European state may be discerned to have a certain singleness of character, in spite of the fact that modern Europe is composed of many states in some respects unlike one another.

I want this morning to try to describe to you what I will call the 'character' of a modern European state: the common 'character' shared by the political associations of modern Europe.

3

Now, there are two very general ways of understanding this character which I believe to be mistaken and which I want, first, to get out of the way.

(1) Some interpreters of the modern European state have suggested that it is so similar to an ancient Greek *polis* that it is illuminating to lump ancient and modern together, and to speak of an antique-modern political experience, contrasting it with that of medieval Europe.

This, I believe to be a very great mistake.

The condition of the emergence of modern European states and the materials out of which they have been composed were utterly unlike those of any Greek *polis*. Modern European politics is, I think, quite incomprehensible unless it is seen emerging from that of the middle ages. The pedigree of all modern European states is unquestionably medieval.

(2) It is sometimes suggested that the modern European state has a discernible character because it is the work of a designer, or (more plausibly) of a number of designers, all working to a common specification.

The excuse for this view lies in the fact that the states of modern Europe did not all emerge at the same time, and that what had been achieved in one was sometimes imitated in another.

But, it is a lame excuse. And, as I understand it, the modern European state was never designed by anybody. The political dwelling we inhabit never had an architect.

A modern European state is, of course, the product of human choices and activities; it did not descend from heaven. But it is to be understood as the net result of all the temporary and contingent enterprises ('failures' as well as 'successes') of these centuries of European politics.

The path and direction of modern European political activity is neither more nor less than the footprints of those who engaged in politics.

Some footprints have been firmly placed and remain individually distinguishable; others are blurred and obscured, the trampling of many feet which have gone this way and that.

But they are all the marks of men necessarily ignorant of any ultimate destiny, who took their direction from their immediate circumstances, and whose purposes and choices were often modified or frustrated by those of others.

Nevertheless, the political experience of modern Europe is not to be understood as a sequence of aimless choices.

As I understand it, the course of this political experience has been more like the fortunes and adventures of a man whose character (like the characters of us all) has come to be composed of a limited variety of dispositions, and whose activities consist of responding to the circumstances he encounters according to those dispositions.

Some of these dispositions are, of course, stronger than others; and they by no means pull in a single direction.

The modern European state, then, is to be understood as the kind of political association which has emerged during the last four and a half centuries from the conditions of medieval politics.

And the different idioms of it, which constitute the different states of modern Europe, represent, for the most part, a single set of political dispositions working upon marginally different medieval experiences.

4

The political experience of modern Europe begins with an important addition to the European political vocabulary: the word 'state', *l'état, stato* etc. It is a word for a new political experience.

This word derived from the Latin word *status*; and like *status* it was not originally a political word. It meant a 'condition' of any sort, but particularly a 'social' condition.

When the Romans used the word politically they showed they were doing so by qualifying it by another word: thus, *status civitatus* meant 'the political condition or state of the Roman community'.

Politically, in English, the word 'state' is a contraction of an older word – 'estate'. In French no such contraction took place: *l'état* continued to be used for both 'estate' and 'state'.

The word 'estate' in medieval times had various meanings; but for our purpose two are more important than any others.

- 'Estate' = a man's property, and particularly the land he held or owned; e.g. his 'manorial estate'.
- 'Estate' = a man's condition or situation in the world. Thus, the expression 'man's estate' or 'the human condition' (as Montaigne called it). Or, more narrowly, a man's condition or 'place' or 'status' in his society.

Thus, each of the more notable 'degrees' in a medieval society was recognized as an 'estate', and to constitute a specific 'status' in society.

There was a 'kingly estate' – the 'status' of being a king. There were 'noble' and 'knightly' estates. There was a 'clerkly' or ecclesiastical 'estate'. And (according to the French way of speaking) there was a *tiers état*, the 'condition' or 'status' of a free town-dweller, outside the feudal organization.

Now, when the political word 'state' emerged from this word 'estate' in the sixteenth century, it carried with it both these meanings, and added a third.

(1)   'State' = a piece of territory, on the analogy of a 'landed estate'. For example, the expression 'the manor of England' was used in the sixteenth century to signify the whole territory of England understood as a single landed 'estate'.

(2)   'State' = the ruler and the apparatus of rule. This derived partly from the notion that the 'kingly estate', or the condition of being a ruler, was the estate par excellence; and partly from an identification of the land with its ruler. In Shakespeare, for example, the word 'France' may mean both 'the King of France', and the 'land of France'.

(3)   State = an association of human beings in respect of political activity and in respect of those matters with which political activity is understood to be concerned – instruments of government, policies, and laws. It is the formal word for a *political* association; and it is distinguished, on that account, from less formal, non-political words, such as 'country'.

Thus, the political experience of modern Europe is the experience of generating, living in, ruling, and understanding a new sort of political association.

And when it is said (with some exaggeration) that there was no such thing as a 'state' in medieval Europe, what is meant is that the particular sort of political association characteristic of modern times had no exact counterpart in the middle ages.

5

Now, the main features of this sort of political association which came to be called a state are:

(1) A specific territory. What in modern Europe and elsewhere in the world is recognized as a 'state' is, in the first place, a well-defined piece of territory.

Normally, this territory is continuous. But there are exceptions: e.g. Alaska is detached from the USA; East and West Pakistan are discontinuous.

The territory is defined by frontiers which have come to be drawn exactly on accurate maps. Where this boundary includes the sea, a defined area of 'territorial waters' is included in the territory of the state. And, more recently, the so-called 'airspace' above the territory, similarly defined, is also included. Everything to do with the territory of a modern state is as precise as it can be made.

Moreover, in modern Europe there is no piece of territory which is not part of some state.

(2) The second feature of a modern state concerns the character of the inhabitants of its territory.

Generally speaking, in modern Europe, every man belongs to a state, and no man can belong to more than one state. And, for the most part, those who belong to a state live in its territory.

Thus, a modern European state allows no recognition to nomadic habits, and it could not have emerged until the peoples of Europe had lost those migratory urges which prevailed throughout a large part of medieval times. Hence, once one of the difficulties which this model of a political association has had in establishing itself outside Europe – e.g. in Africa and in the Arab world, where nomads still exist.

(3) But the human components of a modern European state have something to distinguish them besides normal residence within a certain area of territory.

They enjoy in common what may be called a certain sentiment of solidarity.

Now, the sentiment of solidarity in virtue of which the members of a modern European state compose a specific collectivity of human beings is much easier to detect than to define. And, as we shall see, one of the great enterprises of modern European political thought has been concerned with attempts to understand and to interpret it: an enterprise which may remind us of Aristotle's effort to discern the nature of a *polis* and to distinguish it from other human collectivities.

We must consider, later, what has been thought about the sentiment of solidarity enjoyed by the members of a modern European state, but three things may be said about it:

First, it is based neither upon a belief in common blood, nor upon a common language, nor upon common religious beliefs, although any of these may be present and may contribute to it. It is less definite and less powerful than the sentiment of solidarity characteristic of a tribe and it does not entail the same degree of homogeneity in those who share it.

Secondly, it is a unique kind of sentiment of solidarity; it is one of the characteristics which most distinguish these political associations from all others; and, being a product of circumstance, each modern European state has achieved it in an idiom of its own.

Thirdly, just as the early history of all modern European states was greatly concerned with the consolidation of their territories, so it was also greatly concerned with the promotion of this sentiment of solidarity among its members.

Nevertheless, it is characteristic of modern European states that this solidarity has always remained limited. Just as Europe is (and in modern times has always struggled to remain) a manifold of independent states, so each of these states has, characteristically, an internal variety which qualifies its solidarity.

This internal variety, absent from the Greek *polis* and from the Roman *civitas*, is one of the inheritances of modern from medieval Europe, and it is the heart of modern politics.

6

A modern European state is, then, distinguished by having exactly defined and carefully maintained frontiers to its territory, and by being composed of inhabitants who have acquired, or are on their way to acquiring, a variously interpreted sentiment of solidarity.

Its third important characteristic is that it has a government exclusively its own.

This ruling authority may take different forms. And, for the most part, modern European thought has identified and understood these forms of government in the old Aristotelian terms. This is unfortunate, because these terms are misleading. But where they have been seen to be particularly misleading some new terms have been invented.

But, underneath this variety of forms, the governments of modern European states have their most important characteristics in common.

The modern European state, and any state elsewhere which has been modelled upon it:

Is ruled by a single, centralized authority.

No part of its territory, and no person, is exempt from this single ruling authority.

All who participate in the activity of governing are either principals, or agents whose powers derive from these principals.

There is a single hierarchy of courts of law which permits no independent jurisdictions.

One of the main reasons why a modern European state is said to have no exact counterpart in medieval Europe is the absence from medieval realms of this single, centralized ruling authority.

7

The activity of governing in a modern state is recognized to be a twofold activity:

- Making law, administering it, and applying the law to particular cases in a judicial procedure;
- The pursuit of policy.

Neither of these activities is peculiar to modern European states. They correspond fairly closely to the medieval terms: *jurisidictio* and *gubernaculum*. But in the modern European state they have changed both their characters and their relations to one another.

(1) Law. Nothing distinguishes a modern European state from a medieval political community (or, indeed, from any other historic polity) more than the freedom and confidence with which its government makes new law; the formality and exactness of the process in which law is made; and the very precise distinction between what is law and what is not law.

Nevertheless, as these modern European states emerged out of medieval communities (even if, in some cases, the emergence was rapid and revolutionary), they were each conscious of already having a law. No modern state began *de novo* in respect of its law.

The ruler, or government, of each of these states was recognized to be the custodian of the law and the dispenser of justice. This is what the middle ages called the *jurisdictio* of a ruler: what a government does under the law.

In most modern European states a distinction was recognized between law not known to have been made in any legislative process (like the common law of England), and law known to have sprung from a legislative act: statute. Though the distinction was often vague.

But the unique characteristic of a modern European state is to recognize the supremacy of the legislative act and to regard all other law as authoritative simply in virtue of its not having been changed or repealed by a legislative act.

Further, in a medieval realm no very firm distinction was made between processes of ascertaining what the law is, making a law, and applying it to a particular case.

All this was done in a 'court of law', and legislatures were courts of law. The process was a judicial process.

But when (in a modern state) lawmaking became an every-day affair, and came to be distinguished from a merely judicial process, a considerable change had taken place: to make law had become the exercise, not of *jurisdictio*, but of *gubernaculum*.

For legislation, when it ceased to be recognized as a judicial activity, became assimilated to the pursuit of policy: *gubernaculum*.

Thus, the modern European state appears as an association in which the medieval distinction between *jurisdictio* and *gubernaculum* had become compromised. And that distinction having become compromised in respect of legislation, the door had been opened for *gubernaculum*, the pursuit of policy, to invade more specifically judicial processes – the determination of cases in a court of law.

Law courts which decide cases on grounds not of law but of policy are not eccentric to the character of a modern European state; they are one of the potentialities of its character. They were common in the sixteenth century, and they have become common again in the twentieth. And to accommodate them the expression 'the rule of law' has received appropriate reinterpretation.

(2) The pursuit of policy. The most direct form in which *gubernaculum*, the pursuit of policy, appears in the government of a modern European state is, of course, in connection with the conduct of a foreign policy.

The authority of a modern government in this activity is often determined by constitutional law and custom: the conditions in which treaties become binding, the formalities of a declaration of war and the conclusion of peace, etc., though these have become less, rather than more, significant in the history of modern European politics as the distinction between war and peace has become more indefinite.

But the conduct of policy is not, itself, the making or the administration of any law. It is pursued by means of negotiations, agreements, suggestions, bargains, indirect pressures, conditional undertakings, threats, promises, advances and withdrawals, etc., all designed to achieve some immediate purpose. And in this conduct of policy a modern European government is considered to be free from any legal obligation to its subjects save, in some cases, the constitutional obligation to reveal what it has done and to justify it in argument.

The government of a modern European state, then, is recognized to be the sole authoritative custodian of the interests of the state in relation to other states – as it was in medieval times. And its authority in this respect is the necessarily unlimited authority of *gubernaculum*.

But, as I have said, it is characteristic of a modern European state that the pursuit of policy is not confined to the conduct of a foreign policy. Their governments also pursue policy in relation to their own subjects: sometimes this entails making law, often it does not.

This, like most else, is not entirely new. In any medieval realm the ruler's *gubernaculum* was liable to invade his *jurisdictio*, though he was expected to justify such an invasion when it took place.

What is new, and characteristic of a modern state, is that this invasion is taken as a matter of course. A government is recognized to be, not only the custodian of its subjects' law, but of the *salus populi*.

In other words, the activity of *jurisdictio*, in a modern state, has become hopelessly compromised by the activity of *gubernaculum*. A modern state is a 'policy' state; and this, in its extreme, is a 'police' state. For what constitutes a 'police' state is not the 'knock on the door' (that is a minor detail), but the pursuit of policy by a government in relation to its own subjects.

8

Now, these characteristics of modern European governments may be summed up by saying that in a modern state

- Governing is recognized to be a sovereign activity
- Governments are exceedingly powerful.

These features refer, respectively to (a) *potestas*, the legal authority of governments; and (b) *potentia*, the actual, physical power a modern government disposes.

(1) The word 'sovereignty' was admitted into the vocabulary of modern European politics to describe two main features of a modern European state.

We speak of a modern European state as a 'sovereign' state, and we mean that it is an association whose government is not legally obliged to any other, or higher, authority unless it expressly accepts such an obligation.

Thus, a medieval king whose acts as a ruler were subject to the legal veto of a pope or an emperor, was not a sovereign ruler.

Sovereignty, here, means independence of all other authority. In the sixteenth century, a 'sovereign' state, in this sense, was called a 'free' state.

But, secondly, the word 'sovereign' is used to signify a legal quality or characteristic of a government in relation to its own subjects and the law of which it is the custodian.

Governing in a modern state is a recognized to be a 'sovereign' activity, not because the ruler can do anything he likes, but because its legally authorized government is supreme over all other authorities, and it is recognized to be the sole source of law.

It is the second of these qualities which is, perhaps, the more important and the more characteristic of modern European states.

It denotes that, in its legislative activities, it is legally independent of any other authority and proof against prescription. In other words, in a modern state, there is no law so ancient or so 'entrenched' that it lies outside the authority of the government to amend or to abolish it; and in every modern European state there is a known and recognized procedure by which this can be done.

This, then, is the sovereign *potestas*, the legal authority, of a modern government. By its nature it is 'absolute'. In this a modern government differs from the government of a medieval kingdom; and we shall have to consider how and why it acquired this quality.

(2) The second notable characteristic of modern European governments is their *potentia*, the actual power they dispose of. This is of a magnitude unknown in earlier times to any government; but, by its nature, it can never be 'absolute'.

A government may be said to be 'powerful', not in respect of its 'sovereignty' (which is a legal authority it may not be able to exercise effectively), but in respect of its ability:

To formulate its designs clearly, to make them known in utterances which readily reach and are understood by all those whom they involve, either agents or subjects;

To enlist continuous support or to compel continuous acquiescence;

To act quickly, economically, and with the certainty of achieving what is desired and of being as little hindered as may be by the intrusion of undesired consequences.

These are the attributes of *potentia*. And a government may be said to lack *potentia* if it makes laws which it is unable to enforce, or embarks upon policies which it cannot carry to the desired conclusion.

Now, the *potentia* of modern European governments derives chiefly from having acquired a large share (though rarely a monopoly) of the ability to control men and things which distinguishes modern European civilization from that of earlier times.

By what means have European governments since the sixteenth century been able to exercise the minute control over their subjects that they are increasingly able to do?

It is because they have at their disposal an apparatus of inquiries, records, registers, files, dossiers, indexes, passports, identity cards, licenses, etc.

It is because their paid agents can move and communicate quickly.

It is because they enjoy settled and guarded frontiers which none may pass without scrutiny and perhaps permission.

It is because they have:

Methods and instruments of administration by means of which policy may be rapidly and effectively carried out, and agents who can be directed from one centre.

Extensive and organized civil and police services.

Military forces easily mobilized and supplied with uniform and powerful equipment.

A ready supply of paper and ink and the reports and records (of births, deaths, marriages, incomes, occupations, the resources of the territory etc.) which spring up wherever paper, ink, curiosity, or ambition are joined.

Efficient techniques for collecting revenue.

Control over the issue of money; banking and monetary techniques which enable governments to live on credit with a permanent debt in which the future productivity of their subjects is mortgaged. Debtors are always more powerful than creditors.

Accurate maps and precise means of measuring time.

Literate subjects upon whom the duty of reading notices and filling in forms may be imposed with confidence.

A settled common language and almost unhindered ability to disseminate utterances of all sorts, whether of command, persuasion, encouragement, or prohibition.

Effective means of identifying their subjects individually by means of names, signatures, photographs etc.

The telegraph (which in the last century enabled Abdul Hamid to massacre his Armenian subjects with incomparable efficiency), the telephone, broadcasting, the Holerith machine, and the computer.

I need not continue the list. These are the sources of a modern government's *potentia*. They have been acquired slowly over the last four and a half centuries; but now, even the least powerful government enjoys a mastery quite unknown to the most powerful in earlier times.

As Lenin remarked, a system of ration cards gives a government greater power over its subjects than was ever possessed by a prophet who could convincingly threaten his followers with hellfire. The prospect of starvation is more persuasive than the prospect of damnation.

These, then, are the characteristics of a modern European state. It is a well-defined territory, inhabited by a people who have acquired, or are on their way to acquiring, a certain sentiment of solidarity, ruled by a government endowed with sovereign authority and very great power. And in all these respects it constitutes a large modification of the medieval political community from which, in most cases, it sprang.

9

There is one further feature to be noticed. It belongs to the character of a modern European state to be one of a number of similar states, with which it is in continuous diplomatic relations. And it is recognized to be the first duty of its government to maintain the integrity of its state in these circumstances.

In the conduct of a foreign policy a government claims and exercises rights over its subjects' persons and property which are absolute.

The manifold in which the modern state emerged was European. The conduct of policy was recognized to be an activity in relation to other *European* states.

In the early centuries of modern history the only external threat to this European manifold of states was the Ottoman empire, and by the mid-seventeenth century that had ceased to be significant.

In these circumstances there emerged a pattern of activity the immediate design of which was to maintain a so-called 'balance of power' within the manifold.

The principles of the policy of each state were:

- To ensure, by agreements and alliances, that a working preponderance of power lay with itself.
- To ensure that no one state acquired so great a preponderance of power as to constitute an imbalance dangerous to the rest.

Against such an overwhelming power, all other European states have habitually united: successively against Spain, France, Germany, and Russia.

If one may speak of a 'European policy', it was to preserve the multiplicity of states which constituted Europe.

The conduct of this foreign policy has involved this manifold of modern European states in almost continuous war.

In the political experience of modern Europe there have been short periods of relative stability, the longest of which was in the late nineteenth century. But the normal condition of most states has been one of preparing for war or engagement in war, defensive or offensive.

This pattern of European politics, in later times, extended itself, without serious modification, to the rest of the world, just as the model of a modern European state imposed itself on political communities outside Europe.

10

Now, this characterization of the modern European state might be greatly extended; there are many features which I have not mentioned. But its chief defect is its abstractedness.

Not until we have seen how these features actually emerged shall we understand the political experience which modern European political thought explored and reflected upon.

Editorial Note

LSE 1/1/21, file 5, fos. 386–99. Photocopy of a typescript.

Twenty-four

The Generation of a Modern State

1

Last week we recognized a modern European state as:

- An association of legally 'free' human beings, among whom a certain sentiment of solidarity had emerged;
- Occupying a territory with defined and settled frontiers;
- Organized by a single system of law exclusively its own, and a single hierarchy of courts, which allowed no independent jurisdictions;
- Ruled by its own exclusive, centralized, sovereign government, which disposes of very great executive power;
- A member of a manifold of states which has come to be recognized as 'Europe', and having territorial possessions (sometimes called 'colonies') outside Europe;
- Normally preparing for war, fighting a war, or recovering from a war, designed to maintain a balance of power in this system of European states.

Now, this 'character' of a modern state is all too neat and abstract.

First, it is nothing more than an 'ideal' model of a modern state; a model to which the states of modern Europe merely approximate. It may help us to identify the more important features of modern European politics, but it can hardly do more.

Secondly, it is abstract. Solidarity, stability, sovereignty, war – these are concrete conditions of things which have been generated in particular circumstances. Each of them is a modification of some feature or other of a medieval realm. And they cannot properly be understood unless we see them coming into being.

The real political experience of modern Europe is not an experience in which the states of modern Europe came to approximate themselves to this model; it is an experience in which these states, each in its own peculiar idiom, and each in its individual circumstances, came to acquire characteristics from which, by a process of abstraction, we are able to extract something like this ideal model.

A modern European state may be thought of as a political dwelling which has been constructed largely out of second-hand materials.

It is like a house which has been built, without the aid of an architect, by many hands, over many years, in response to many different circumstances, out of materials got from the ruins of a medieval castle and a medieval abbey.

Some of the stones have been recut and reshaped; others have been left very much as they were pulled out of the ruins. All have been fitted together differently and put to new uses: what was a battlement has become a doorstep, and what was the top of an altar has become a hearthstone.

And a certain amount of freshly quarried material has been used when the ruins could provide nothing to correspond with current wants.

The political thought of modern Europe is to be regarded as the intellectual organization and understanding of this oddly constructed political dwelling.

It is what has been felt and thought and said by those who helped to construct it and by those who have tried to find their way about it. And we cannot understand this political thought unless we descend from the ideal model to the actual conditions which generated it.

2

A modern European state is, in the first place, a unified landed 'estate' whose territorial boundaries are precise and jealously guarded.

This is in the greatest contrast to the political map of medieval Europe, where frontiers were often vague and always imperfectly controlled.

The change represents movements in two opposite directions, which have gone on, without serious intermission, in modern times; and which still continue: (1) A movement of consolidation in which the provincial and local independencies of medieval realms have been destroyed. (2) A movement of disintegration in which new states have emerged from the breakup of medieval empires.

The processes concerned have been diverse.

European states have been territorially constituted by conquest, by rebellion, by legislative acts, by treaties, by the marriage of rulers, by the hereditary succession of rulers to territories hitherto diverse, and by the transformation of feudal suzerainty into definitive sovereignty.

Almost everywhere these processes have left behind traces of local and provincial independencies.

There is no mystery about how these territories were consolidated; in most cases it was in an arbitrary manner; there is nothing, strictly speaking, rational about it. Territorially, none of the current European states is more than four and a half centuries old; most are of a far more recent creation.

The United Kingdom of Great Britain emerged territorially with the termination of the semi-independencies of Wales and the palatinate of Durham; the accession of James VI of Scotland to the throne of England (to be followed, a century later, by the Act of Union of England and Scotland); the conquest of Ireland, and the loss of Calais.

Ireland was the first of the British 'imperial' possessions; for a short while it became part of the state of Great Britain; later, it became, in part, a separate state, by treaty.

The territories of the British colonial empire which began to be acquired four hundred and fifty years ago have been depleted or transformed over a period of two hundred years.

Spain emerged territorially in a process of conquest and the marriage of the rulers of Castile and Aragon in the fifteenth century. But a profound and unappeased sentiment of independence has remained in Catalonia and Navarre.

Portugal, after a brief period of incorporation, became an independent state in 1640. And both Spain and Portugal acquired colonies outside Europe which were part of their territories, and later lost them.

France was slowly consolidated in processes of conquest and reversion under monarchs who graduated from the status of feudal overlords to sovereign rulers.

Brittany, Calais, and other territories were added by treaty.

The lands adjacent to the Rhine remained, for a long time, ambiguous: Alsace and Lorraine, after nearly two centuries of incorporation in France, were lost to Germany in 1871 and recovered in 1918. And even as late as the nineteenth century, Provence remained somewhat imperfectly a part of the territory of the state of France.

The territories of the French empire, like those of the British, have been depleted or transformed, becoming, in many cases, independent states or parts of independent states, over a period of about two hundred years.

During the sixteenth century the Hapsburg lands in Germany disintegrated into a great number (over three hundred) independent states of various territorial dimensions. Parts of these dominions were reconsolidated into the modern German empire, partly by Prussian conquest and partly by treaty. And this German empire has, in living memory, suffered division, also by conquest.

The sixteenth century Austrian empire lost territory to the Turks in the seventeenth century. Belgium achieved its independence by treaty in the nineteenth century. In the twentieth century this empire dissolved into three independent states – Austria, Hungary, and Czechoslovakia.

The Balkan penninsula, which began in modern times as part of the territories of the Ottoman empire, became in the nineteenth and twentieth centuries, first six, and later five, independent states.

The first genuinely new state to appear in modern Europe was the United Netherlands, composed of a number of territories which emancipated themselves from their Spanish-Hapsburg rulers by rebellion in the sixteenth century.

Switzerland was composed out of a miscellany of independent territories, and survived a civil war.

Italy became a state in the nineteenth century, collected out of a number of independent territories, some formerly belonging to Spain. The Tyrol remained a long time a disputed territory.

The four Scandinavian states, after many vicissitudes, achieved their present form in the nineteenth century.

The territories of the medieval kingdom of Poland have, in modern times, twice lost and regained their independence, on different occasions being partitioned between Austria, Prussia, and Russia, and incorporated in the Russian empire.

The territory of the Russian state was gradually consolidated and extended, mostly by conquest, during a period of about four centuries.

It remains the last of the old-style European empires. It has swallowed, disgorged, and swallowed again territories with long histories of independence in the north, on the Baltic Sea, and in the south.

In the large movements in which the boundaries of these states have been settled for the time being, smaller territories (mostly of medieval origin) have survived by chance: the Grand-Duchy of Luxembourg, the Principalities of Monaco and Andorra, and the Republic of San Marino.

The movement continues, precisely in the same manner as it began in the fifteenth century. If you want to know how, territorially, the states of modern Europe emerged you may observe the process in Ireland forty years ago, in Eastern Germany, and in Cyprus.

Thus, for most of modern European history, the considerations which have determined the territorial boundaries of states have been notably arbitrary; the conformation of medieval settlements, the estates of dynastic rulers (often enlarged by marriage or contracted by rebellion), the alleged requirements of defence, or merely the lines on which contingent hostilities have temporarily come to rest – this being the preeminent character of most of the latest changes.

But, in recent times a notable addition has been made to these considerations, namely, boundaries of states drawn in such a manner as to correspond with what are alleged to be 'national communities'. To some people this has seemed to introduce a much needed 'rational' principle into a supremely arbitrary and contingent political world.

I shall have more to say about this later. But for the moment it may be observed that the territorial boundaries of no modern European state have ever corresponded to anything that may reasonably be called a 'national community'.

3

Turning from territories to people, it may be noticed that one of the conditions which distinguish modern Europe is the relative settlement of peoples. After centuries of wandering to and fro, the migrations of European peoples subsided. And this is one of the conditions of the emergence of modern European states.

And the supremacy of territorial considerations appears in the fact that, in modern Europe, it has been usual for its inhabitants to go with their territory; when a piece of territory changed hands, its inhabitants went with it. This is not universally true: whole communities have left their lands to stay with their folk, and sometimes have been forced to do so.

But a modern European state, composed as it is of bits of territory, acquired at different times, has normally had a diverse population, some components of it often with memories of different allegiances or even of independence. Every modern European state began, in respect of its population, with diversity.

And the task of its rulers has been, not only to consolidate the territory, but also to consolidate its diverse population – to generate in it a sentiment of solidarity which was notably lacking.

The most important diversities which stood in the way of this sentiment of solidarity have been those of local communities of various dimensions, often very ancient, and distinguished by various characteristics: race, religion, language, and social status. The only diversity notably absent at the dawn of modern European history was tribal diversity.

But here we are introduced to the first of the numerous ambivalences of modern European politics. In modern European states, in this matter, two opposed dispositions have been at work: the disposition to generate solidarity by *destroying* diversity, and the disposition to generate solidarity by *containing* diversity.

Let us consider these two dispositions separately. They run through the whole of modern politics.

(1) The distribution to generate solidarity by destroying diversity has been pursued in processes of exclusion and suppression.

(a) In the early years of modern European history, diversities of 'race' and religion were the commonest candidates for exclusion.

The notion of a 'racially' homogeneous state goes back to the sixteenth century. It appeared in Spain where a policy of imposing uniformity led to the exclusion of Arabs and Jews. In later times, an alleged 'racially' homogeneous state was projected in National Socialist Germany, the so-called 'Aryan' race.

And, as a counterpart to this notion, there has appeared the idea of a 'racial' state which should include within its territories all people alleged to belong to a certain race, e.g. pan-Slavism and pan-Teutonism in the nineteenth century.

The other chief candidates for exclusion have been religious minorities and aristocracies.

Muslims and Jews were exiled from Spain and Portugal in the sixteenth century. Catholics were excluded from Protestant states, Protestants from Catholic states. And this has sometimes entailed considerable movements of population. The North American continent was significantly populated by religious dissidents from Europe, both Catholic and Protestant. And in France, Calvinists, at first tolerated, were later excluded, and removed themselves in considerable numbers to England and Brandenburg.

The aristocrat exiled because he conflicted with the desired solidarity of a state is a familiar figure in modern European history, from the fifteenth to the twentieth century.

(b) Where exclusion was difficult or impolitic, the disposition to suppress often came into play in order to generate the desired solidarity.

Local territorial communities have been destroyed or suppressed in almost every state in modern Europe; guilds and ghettoes have been dissolved, gypsies have been harassed and suppressed, associations with affiliations outside the territory of the state have been proscribed.

The disposition to generate solidarity by imposing a single legal status upon all has led to the suppression of aristocracies.

Catholics have been suppressed in Protestant states, Protestants in Catholic states, Jews and Muslims in Christian states.

Linguistic diversities, recognized as perhaps the greatest hindrances to a sentiment of solidarity, have been suppressed, with varying success, in most European states; though some states have had to settle for at least two official languages.

In France and Germany, a process of attrition generated late in the nineteenth century single official languages. Belgium, and more recently Ireland, have settled for two official languages. In Great Britain, Welsh was first excluded as a recognized language and later readmitted.

In short, it has belonged to the character of a modern European state to seek to generate a sentiment of solidarity among its members by the exclusion or suppression of indigenous diversities. And it is in this manner that the so-called 'nations' of modern Europe have been created.

(2) But a disposition opposed to uniformity has also been at work, and unavoidably so.

Every European state began with diversities; and these diversities have promoted a belief that politics is an activity in which diversities are accommodated to one another, and that the necessary sentiment of solidarity may be achieved without their suppression.

This style of politics has always been difficult, but in spite of constant rejection it has managed to survive. And after the first great drive for uniformity in modern European states, which in some cases generated a durable sentiment of solidarity, many have felt themselves stable enough to endure diversities of religion, moral opinion, language, local communities, and even conspiracies to subvert public order.

Some governments, indeed, have felt themselves strong enough, and their subjects sufficiently united, to give legal recognition to conscientious objections of individuals to the performance of some of their legal duties – like military service.

It may be noted that, in the eighteenth and nineteenth centuries, federal constitutions were recognized by some as a device for accommodating and containing diversities in a single state. But the fact remains that every modern European state is, and always has been, 'plural' in respect of its population. Each, in some respect or other, is a barely stable balance of diversities.

A modern European state, then, is to be recognized as an association of human beings which, both territorially and in respect of its people, has been created by a government out of the diverse materials of the European continent.

And in this process two major dispositions may be seen at work, both responses to circumstances, neither by any means getting the better of the other throughout modern European history: a disposition to impose uniformity and homogeneity, and a disposition merely to contain diversity.

4

We now turn to the governments of these states.

In our abstract formulation, the government of a modern European state appeared as a single, centralized, ruling authority, operating by means of its own appointed agents, sovereign, independent of all external authority, proof against prescription, and exceedingly powerful.

Its main activities appeared as lawmaking, the administration of the law, and the pursuit of policy both in respect of its own subjects and in respect of neighboring European states.

What is the historical quality of these abstract characteristics? And how were they acquired?

The nucleus of the government of every modern European state, as it emerged, was a monarch: a king, a prince, a margrave, a grand duke, a prince-bishop. And even those states which had republican constitutions fell into the hands of a single ruler.

The authority of medieval monarchs was limited. They had partners in the activity of ruling whom they had not chosen, aristocracies and parliaments. They were in very incomplete command over their realms, often being considered as no more than the first among many authorities. They were harassed by the claims of the great international authority of the pope, which was displayed in their realms in the independence of ecclesiastical authorities and courts.

The characteristic independence, singleness, and centralization of the government of a modern European state emerged in a process in which monarchs extinguished their unchosen partners and appropriated the authority (and often the property) of those whom they extinguished, and divested themselves of all obligations to hitherto superior authorities.

And when, as happened at a later stage, monarchs were, in some states, succeeded by governments of other kinds, these newly constituted governments inherited the undisputed authority which these monarchs had created for themselves or had come to enjoy by the efforts of their servants.

In short, the *jurisdictio* of rulers was swamped by their authority of *gubernaculum*; they became more the makers and executors of policy than judges in a court of law.

The partners, competitors, or superiors in authority to be extinguished were parliaments, a politically significant nobility, imperial rulers, and the church.

(1) Everywhere in Europe, except in England, the medieval parliamentary institutions were extinguished, extinguished themselves, or made subservient to the ruler. In any case, these new-style rulers were policy-makers, and policy-making had never been a function of a medieval parliament.

(2) The nobilities were deprived of their political significance by circumstances and by means of various devices.

In England, the great noble houses were decimated in civil
war.

Spain was denuded of its aristocracy who led the armies in
the New World.

In France, after a long period during which the government was in the control of factions of the nobility, these
nobles were deprived of political position and authority and
converted into powerless 'courtiers', often bribed into submission by exemptions from taxation.

But, everywhere, what was lost by a nobility did not disappear; it was acquired by the ruler.

In place of the nobility, the new rulers governed with the
aid of a professional class of administrators, who were their
creatures and their agents. It was these who composed the
king's council, the central organ of government which was
established everywhere in Europe, by indigenous growth or
by imitation.

In the sixteenth century, England was ruled by a monarch and a council of about thirty commoners whom he
appointed.

In the seventeenth century, France was ruled by a king and
a council of eleven commoners.

Spain had a similar pattern of government. And this model
emerged in Denmark, Sweden, Brandenburg, Prussia, and
most of the Italian states.

The tasks of the council, under the monarch, were to consider policy, to legislate or to prepare legislation, and to exercise administrative, fiscal, and judicial control over the
whole realm.

(3) The authority of the emperor was repudiated everywhere.

(4) But by far the most important source of the increased
authority of the rulers of modern Europe came from their
acquisition of the authority (and often of the property) of the
church.

Rulers who, in the sixteenth century, elected for Protestantism at once extinguished the independent authority of
the church in their states.

The Protestant reformation, both in its Lutheran and its
Calvinist idiom, began as a genuinely religious movement to

get rid of ecclesiastical abuses and later to reform Christian doctrine.

But no state in Europe ever became Protestant except by the decision, and usually by the command, of its ruler. The motive of this decision was always political – to acquire independence and the power that came with independence. Usually, Protestantism was established only in those states whose rulers were unable to acquire control of the church in any other way.

By electing for Protestantism, the competing authorities which were extinguished were: everywhere, the papacy, the independent ecclesiastical courts and the bishops; in Germany, the emperor; in Holland, the Spanish government; in Sweden, the nobility.

But a Protestant ruler in the sixteenth century did not merely get rid of superiors or partners in government; he acquired an authority which thitherto no Christian ruler had ever enjoyed.

First, he acquired the property of the church – lands, buildings, benefices, and valuable rights of many different kinds. In the sixteenth century the property-map of Europe was transformed, and the very institution of private or corporate property (the firmest of all medieval institutions) was shaken.

The new Protestant territorial states were areas of spoliation and confiscation. And the loot gained by Protestant princes was the capital with which they went into business as modern rulers.

Secondly, he acquired the authority to choose his subjects' religious confession, and to impose upon them the single religious confession of his own choice. Thus, the Protestant prince constituted himself the supreme ecclesiastical as well as political authority in his state.

Thirdly, he acquired for himself the tutelary authority of the church, the authority to guide, to educate, to lead, to engender the habits of a good life, and he turned this tutelary authority into a political *potestas*.

Here is the beginning of that authority by which modern governments not only rule, but also lead, and manage, the lives of their subjects; and the beginning of subjects who have been transformed from adults into parishioners.

And when in later times these political rulers became indifferent to the religious beliefs of their subjects, and embraced policies of 'religious tolerance', they did not resign, but rather increased, their authority as educators and moral leaders.

Nor was this situation peculiar to Protestant states. The rulers of states which remained Catholic in the sixteenth century acquired a no less complete control over the church in their states, but acquired it by other means.

In Spain, royal control over the church had always been great, and in the sixteenth century it was extended. The inquisition was a royal instrument for enforcing religious uniformity and political solidarity. Appointments to ecclesiastical offices, and the operation of the ecclesiastical courts, were in the hands of the ruler; and papal legates had for long enough set foot in Spain only by royal permission.

In France and in Bavaria, a similar control over church property was acquired by their rulers by means of concordats (treaties) with the papacy.

In Austria, the emperor became master of the church in his dominions. He conducted a dissolution of monasteries and an appropriation of church property scarcely less extensive than that which took place in Protestant states.

In Bohemia, the lands and property of the church and of monastic corporations had been extensively confiscated and secularized as far back as the fifteenth century.

Thus, by taking over from the church its courts, its jurisdictions, its independent authority, and often its property, the rulers of both Catholic and Protestant states acquired that concentration of authority in the hands of a single, centralized, government characteristic of a modern state. In this respect there is only a marginal difference between the Emperor Rudolph, Queen Elizabeth, and Gustavus Adolphus.

This important contribution to the immense policy-making authority exercised by modern governments is not less real merely because it appears under another heading in our current political accounts. The rulers of modern states, whether they are kings or ministers, or party secretaries, are (in the Catholic idiom) thinly disguised prince-bishops, (in the Protestant idiom) thinly disguised 'godly princes'.

Thus, the authority of the new rulers of modern states, whoever they were, was composed of what they inherited from their medieval counterparts and what they acquired from the authorities they destroyed or suppressed. It was clear to all that whether the uniform and enforced religious confession of a state was Catholic or Protestant, it was what it was by permission or command of its ruler.

5

The governments of modern states are distinguished not only for their authority in policy making, their *potestas*, but also for the actual power they dispose of: their *potentia*.

Last week I suggested some of the technological inventions and devices which have contributed to this power. I want, now, to notice what I think has been the single greatest contribution to this power.

In sketching the character of the modern European state I said that it was, normally, a state preparing for war, waging war, or recovering from war. And this has been so since its emergence.

The objects of those wars have been various; but if we consider their effect upon the relation of a government to its subjects, there is reason to think that modern governments owe their extraordinary power more to war than to any other single circumstance.

(1) War is expensive; and European wars (and the prospect of war) have become progressively more expensive during the last four centuries.

In the earlier years of modern history wars were fought on savings and out of current resources; and this is why European governments were so concerned to conserve their stock of bullion. Later, they have invariably been fought on credit, the anticipation of the productivity of the inhabitants of a state.

But, either way, war has always required that a government should take command over extraordinary revenue. It has not only been the occasion for the imposition of extraordinary taxation, but also of taking extraordinary command over the resources of a state and the productivity of its subjects. Most of the opposition to modern governments has come in respect of their demands in respect of war. War, in modern Europe, has generated and extended the devices of opposition.

(2) War has always been the occasion for rapid technological advances. That is to say, human command over men and

things has been generated by the requirements of warfare more than by anything else.

(3) Each of the great European wars of modern times, and many of the lesser ones, have taught the governments concerned how to mobilize the resources of their territories and their subjects; and the lessons learned in wars have never been forgotten.

War has accustomed the subjects of modern governments to the experience of having their wealth, their property, their occupations, and their activities managed by those in authority. It has reinforced all those other circumstances from which the single, independent, centralized powerful governments of modern states have sprung. It has been a generator of 'equality' more important than any other – the equality of the besieged. And it has left an indelible mark upon our political vocabulary.

6

There is one other feature of the governments of modern European states, the generation and actual quality of which we must consider.

These governments are recognized to be 'sovereign' in respect of lawmaking. What, in fact, is described by this word 'sovereignty'?

'Sovereignty' is the quality recognized in a government (1) when it is recognized to be the sole authority in the state to make law; (2) when its authority to make law is believed to be unfettered by any superior authority; (3) and when there is believed to be no law current in the society which this government may not repeal or amend.

Now, these beliefs, and this recognition, are inseparable from the character of a modern European state. And the question we have to ask ourselves is, How did the governments of modern Europe acquire this 'sovereignty'? For there is nothing that marks them off so firmly from their medieval predecessors. The supremacy of statute, which is what 'sovereignty' is, was not something easily learned; it was a novelty.

Oddly enough, it may be said that the governments of modern states acquired this quality of 'sovereignty' in response to the felt needs of their subjects.

This is odd because 'the law' is, usually, regarded as a private man's most cherished protection against the exactions of a powerful government. To hand over to a government the unlimited authority to make and to repeal law would seem to be a dangerous adventure. Why has this adventurous course been pursued by every state in modern Europe?

The short answer to this question is: Because a modern European state is, and has been since the sixteenth century, significantly composed of people who have found the activities which they wished to pursue to be restricted and hindered, rather than promoted, by the current legal organization.

What these people looked for from their rulers was release. If land were not released from its old tenures, how could it be freely bought and sold? If trusts 'in perpetuity' were really unalterable, how could capital be invested to the best advantage? If the world of getting and spending were hedged about by antiquated laws, how could productivity be increased? If the old frustrating rights and duties remained sacrosanct, if the law could not be readily changed, how could modern happiness be pursued?

The predominant consciousness was that the old rights and duties were frustrating. And to feel the need for new rights and duties was to know the need of a government recognized to have the authority to abolish old rights and inaugurate the new. 'Sovereignty' in government was the counterpart of 'freedom' in the subject – freedom from a frustrating past.

This, then, was the context in which modern European states acquired governments with 'sovereign' lawmaking authority. Nevertheless, the situation was not quite so simple as that. It had two other features to qualify it.

First, although this may have been the predominant mood, there remained many who were more interested in having their current rights protected than in acquiring new rights.

These often included the highest and the lowest in the state: the nobility and the peasant. There was, and there has always remained, in all modern states, both the disposition to want and to recognize a 'sovereign' lawmaking authority as an emblem of emancipation from the past, and the disposition to be nervous of 'sovereign' governments.

Secondly, as soon as it began to emerge, a 'sovereign' law-making authority was recognized to be dangerous to all subjects alike, if useful to some.

There were many who would have liked to put at least some rights, the most important, out of the reach of its authority to change and to innovate. It was this which gives meaning to the perpetual talk in modern times about 'natural', 'imprescriptible', or 'inextinguishable' rights.

But, to put some rights out of the reach of a government recognized to be 'sovereign' is impossible. The power (*potentia*) of a government is always limited; there are things it cannot do because it has not the means to do them or does not know how to do them. But 'sovereign' *potestas* cannot be limited. It is either sovereign or it is not.

Moreover, it was clear that it was not merely peripheral rights which it was desired to make malleable, but the most fundamental rights of person and property. Thus, any disposition to limit the lawmaking authority of governments was unlikely to protect the more important rights, which were precisely those which many wished to be changed.

Consequently, attention was turned from the dead-end question, How can a 'sovereign' lawmaking authority be limited? to the much more relevant question: How can a government be constituted so that it may safely be trusted with 'sovereign' lawmaking authority?

It was to this question that much of the political thought of modern times has been addressed.

7

The modern European state, then, constituted a new political experience – the experience of living in a 'state'. And this experience was not any the less new because its components were, for the most part, old. 'State-life' in modern Europe, like *polis*-life in ancient Greece, was an unfamiliar experience to those upon whom it supervened.

The political thought of modern times is the activity in which the possibilities of this new political experience were explored and in which attempts were made to understand it and answer the questions which it raised.

Editorial Note

LSE 1/1/21, file 5, fos. 400–14. Photocopy of a typescript.

Twenty-five

Modern European Political Thought

1

We have considered the main features of a modern European state; and I have said something about how these features were acquired and their historical quality.

- Territories gradually amalgamated in a variety of, mostly arbitrary, manners;
- Populations of great diversity gradually acquiring a sentiment of solidarity;
- Governments acquiring unique authority by gathering together at one centre authorities thitherto dispersed; and acquiring unique and tremendous power from the experience of almost continuous war, and from sharing in the vastly increased command over men and things characteristic of modern Europe.

Now, modern European political thought may be understood as the play of the modern European intellect around this experience of living in a 'state'.

It is comprised of the beliefs, sentiments, analogies, myths, ideas, doctrines, interpretations, and explanations which have emerged in the enjoyment of this experience and in terms of which it has been made intelligible.

These beliefs and doctrines should not, therefore, be thought as the foundation, or the cause, or the origin, of this political experience. They are the experience itself translated into the idiom of general ideas.

For example, we should not imagine somebody – like Henry VIII, Richelieu, or Bismarck – saying to himself: 'What we need is a government with sovereign authority: how can we construct it?'

The idea of 'sovereignty' emerged as a description of a quality of the sort of government which chance, circumstance, contingent events, and the pursuit of policies gradually generated.

It was a concept which helped to make intelligible a government recognized to have the authority to destroy feudal tenures, to abolish ecclesiastical courts, to amend the common law and, on occasion, to take command over the property of its subjects.

And what writers like Hobbes, or Locke, or Rousseau, or Bentham were doing was not inventing a concept, but seeking a more profound understanding of the experience of living under a government which was recognized to have the sort of authority it was recognized to have, and seeking more adequate reasons for such a government.

2

We begin, then, with a political experience.

And the first thing to notice about the political experience of modern Europe is its richness and variety; this far exceeds anything we have met in earlier political experiences.

The inheritance of modern politics from the middle ages was, in any case, one of great diversity, offering a variety of paths to be explored. But everything that has happened in the last five centuries has extended the horizons of political activity and beckoned it in new directions.

The geographical exploration of the world, the variety offered in the manifold of European states, the exploitation of the resources of the world by means of the inventions and devices of modern technology – in short, all the changefulness and enterprise of modern Europe has been reflected in its politics.

Further, all the more important human sentiments and desires which politics takes account of and reflects have been in a condition of rapid and incessant change: feelings about the relationship of one human being to another, beliefs about what constitutes happiness, about right and wrong in conduct, and beliefs about good and bad conditions of things.

Of course, there have been limits. The modern European state and the sort of government which went with it, was perceived to have certain important characteristics; and it is these which have composed and limited the world of the modern political imagination.

But they were diverse characteristics, they unfolded themselves gradually, and they were as much possibilities and potentialities as settled characteristics.

Consequently, there has been room for choice, opportunity for reinterpretation, occasion to think of them differently combined or invested in different enterprises.

Governments both 'sovereign' and 'powerful' were, so to speak, the capital with which modern European politics went into business; and a substantial part of modern political thought has been concerned with how and in what enterprises this capital shall be invested.

And even the least tied-down of all pieces of political reflection – a modern utopia – is an imaginary reinvestment of what the political experience of modern Europe had to offer.

3

But political reflection is not only the exploration and understanding of a particular political experience; it is reflection which takes place within a context of general beliefs about the world in general.

An interpretation of a political institution, if it is to be convincing, must appeal to beliefs about the world which currently appear to be reasonable. An enterprise to be pursued must fall within the current imaginative picture of the world.

And, in modern times, these general beliefs and imaginations about the world have been as changeful and as diverse as the political experience itself.

Beliefs which were common enough in the sixteenth century to be appealed to in political discourse, had often ceased to be so even a century later. And what appeared to be a 'reasonable' explanation in the nineteenth century now often appears to us as little better than a superstition.

A world which could be satisfied with understanding the authority of a ruler as derived from his 'divine right' is not very far distant from us in time, but it is utterly remote in feeling and understanding.

In short, that transformation of our understanding of the world which we connect with modern science, anthropology, psychology, etc., has constituted a transformation of the

intellectual apparatus used in interpreting and making intelligible our political experience

In some cases one whole idiom of political reflection has
superseded another. For example: until well on in the eighteenth century the accepted idiom of political reflection was
theological, and even biblical: the beliefs appealed to were
those which composed the Christian cosmology; but it is
comparatively rare to find this idiom in use during the last
hundred and fifty years.

Other changes have proved to be merely temporary fash-
ions of thought. The notion of 'laws of social development',
the notion of 'social evolution', the explanation of political
experience in terms of mechanics, are among the notions
which have gone the way of all fashionable concepts.

Thus, modern Europe, in connection with politics, has provided both material for thought (a political experience) and
manners of reflection which are unmatched for their changefulness and diversity.

The literature of modern political reflection is so immense
and so varied that I cannot attempt more than a description
of the main lines upon which it has run.

4

This vast literature contains writings of many different
kinds.

Statements of policy; diagnoses of political situations; precepts of political conduct; approvals, criticisms, disapprov-
als, and interpretations of political institutions; preferences
for this or that feature of a modern European state; writings
in which some hitherto unexplored potentiality of modern
government is opened up; speculations; utopian imaginings;
and historical and philosophical explanations.

In order to understand this literature, it is very important
to learn to distinguish between the designs and enterprises
of different writers, different pieces of writing, different
arguments.

The assumption, commonly made, that all writing about
politics is really of the same kind and is all part of one great
inquiry, is a ruinous assumption.

A large part of this literature of political reflection is concerned with expressions of opinion, and the recommendation, or criticism, or justification of beliefs about the

situations, enterprises, policies, and institutions which have been thrown up in the course of this political experience.

And perhaps the most interesting part of it is concerned with what may be called the more durable features of life in a modern European state.

It is with this large cross-section of modern European political thought that I shall be chiefly concerned: on the whole, less attention to the philosophers and more attention to the sentiments, beliefs, analogies, opinions, myths which appear in the practical political discourse of modern Europe.

5

Now, these beliefs, opinions, ideas, etc., are of a kind that cannot be proved to be true or false; and the arguments in which they appear are not, as a rule, designed to prove anything to be true or false.

They are designed to be convincing in a pragmatic manner. They are to be understood as the recommendation and the intellectual organization of practical attitudes. And they are much more like suggested rules for conduct than explanations.

These arguments are designed to persuade people what should be their attitude towards situations and institutions in modern European politics; and consequently, their reasoning appeals to whatever is generally believed about the world, about human beings, and about the course of human history by those to whom they are addressed.

They rarely embark upon new intellectual adventures; they use whatever has managed to get itself accepted and believed, and bring it to bear upon politics.

Let me give you two examples.

John Locke in his *Two Treatises of Government* was not, in any profound sense, trying to explain anything, he was saying (among other things) something like this:

> Look; it appears that, in order to get ourselves out of an intolerable situation, we may have to get rid of this government; we may have to have something like a revolution.
>
> I know you are nervous of revolutions. They conflict with loyalties you are accustomed to believe in, and they are apt to be indiscriminately destructive. But take courage.
>
> Here is a set of beliefs about human societies and the activity of ruling them, none of which is new and all of which you and I are substantially agreed about, which suggest that get-

ting rid of a government does not conflict with your real loyalties and will not have the effect of throwing the whole social
order into the melting pot. Let me remind you of these beliefs.

There are, I suggest, bonds which hold a society together
quite independent of any government, and rights and duties
which you enjoy, not as citizens, but as human beings. And if
you once understand that this is so, you will be able to take
quite a different attitude towards government from that
which others (like Sir Robert Filmer) have taught you to take.
And it will be a much more confident attitude to the prospect
of its overthrow.

In short, Locke's aim was to encourage, to give intellectual
confidence, rather than to explain.

And, characteristically for his time, his argument was in a
theological idiom. He was writing for a public who expected
to be convinced by an argument in a theological idiom.
Human beings, for example, are identified in this argument,
as children of a providential God; and their important relations with one another, their rights and duties, derive from
their relations with God.

In short, what Locke purports to be doing is settling a matter of conscience on behalf of his contemporaries.

Rousseau in the *Contrat social*, in at least one of his many
moods, seems to me to be saying something like this:

The laws under which we live and the political decisions
taken on our behalf by our rulers seem to be very hit-and-miss
affairs.

They represent somebody's opinion about how we should
behave and about what should be done. But these opinions
are unmistakably arbitrary and interested, and they are as
much likely to be wrong as right.

This is disconcerting. It gives us no confidence in the justice
of our laws or in the correctness of our policies. And, moreover, it makes us feel like slaves under the arbitrary authority
of somebody else. And whether the ruler is a king or a parliament makes very little difference in this respect.

But, if you listen to me, I can show you a method of making
laws and decisions which is completely emancipated from
this arbitrariness and liability to error and injustice.

Take confidence. Freedom, justice, and government, which
you and I have so long thought to be unrelated or even
opposed to one another may in fact be united.

And, characteristically for his time and his audience, Rousseau's argument is not in a theological idiom.

6

Now it is the kind, or level, of political thinking that I am going to concern myself with chiefly; though it will by no means all come from writers as systematic and thoughtful as Locke and Rousseau.

In considering it, I propose to range up and down the political literature of modern times seeking what has been thought and said on what I think are the four main topics with which modern European thought has concerned itself.

These four topics are:

- The nature of a modern European state;
- The constitution and the authority of governments;
- The activities of governments;
- The nature of political deliberation and argument.

Let me say something, by way of introduction, about each of these topics.

7

The modern European state was a new sort of political association, and we can hardly exaggerate its unfamiliarity to those whom its character and potentialities unfolded themselves.

Often, quite directly and without beating about the bush, and more often implicitly, from the sixteenth century to our own day, the question has been asked: What sort of association is this state?

For example, in the sixteenth century there was a whole literature, full of controversy and contention, devoted to trying to answer the question: What is France?

Thus, we have to get ourselves into the mood in which we can understand people to whom the question: What is France? was both difficult and important to find an answer to.

Now, this reflection on the character of a modern state was not designed merely to distinguish the features of this new sort of political association. It had a supremely practical aim.

People wanted to know what to believe about this modern state; what to expect from it; how to behave appropriately in it. They wanted to know what it was and what it entailed to be a member of such a state. They wanted to be given some convincing analogy for it, so that they knew where they stood in relation to it.

The situation was not, perhaps, so mysterious as we have seen it to have been in ancient Greece. There, *polis*-life emerged out of a quite different sort of life – tribal life. And 'citizenship', being a member of a *polis*, was an absolutely new experience.

But the conditions out of which the modern European state emerged were not those of tribal life – except perhaps in Scotland. What it emerged from was the non-tribal conditions of a medieval realm.

But, if the modern state was not, and could not be understood as, a union of tribes – it was, nevertheless, a union of some sort, and of a new and unfamiliar kind. And it is not at all surprising that people should have searched their experience for ideas by means of which to understand what it was.

Moreover, it is fair to say that these questions: What is this state? What should be my attitude towards it? were not only asked in the dawn of the political experience of modern Europe; they have been reflected upon throughout the whole of modern history.

It is as if we had never quite got used to living in a modern European state; never quite understood it, or resigned ourselves to it. It is still capable of puzzling us; and arguments to justify it are still sought.

As we might expect, much of the reflection on this topic has consisted in seeking the most appropriate analogy in terms of which a modern state might be understood for practical purposes.

The question being asked is often the question: What is a state *like*? For it was believed that if only we knew what it was *like*, we should know more about how to behave in it and what to expect from it.

And the range of analogies which have suggested themselves has been enormous – a family, an organism, a nation, an economy, a joint stock company, a public services corporation, etc., etc. Each of them, perhaps, provides some degree of enlightenment, and each recognizes some feature of a modern state.

It was only the philosophers who looked for something more than an analogy – a definition.

8

The second great topic of modern European political reflection has been concerned with the constitution and authority of the government of a modern state.

This is a more conventional topic; it has its counterpart in every political experience. The questions: Whence comes the authority of a ruler? and, Who should occupy the office of the ruler? are perennial questions.

But they are not academic questions. A political society which has not found some acceptable beliefs about the authority and constitution of its government is a political society with only a very tenuous stability. It is in some degree at the mercy of rival claimants to authority, each of whose claims chime in with some current belief about authority and therefore are recognized to have some validity.

In its simplest form, this is the question: To whom do I owe my allegiance and why? or, What is loyalty in a modern state?

There are some states, even in contemporary Europe, which have been only moderately successful in generating acceptable beliefs on this matter, and which are, consequently, in some degree unsteady and unsettled.

The political history of France in the nineteenth century is, from one point of view, a prolonged search for acceptable common beliefs about what constitutes an authoritative government.

But, by reason of the very diversity of the populations of modern European states this question of the grounds of 'loyalty' has been uniquely important in modern European political thought.

Many of the states of modern Europe have emerged in a process of 'revolution'. And the first thing that had to be done was to generate some acceptable beliefs about the authority of their governments.

This has not been easy; and as a sign of its difficulty, it has often not been achieved without civil war. In modern times, setting on one side the normal violence from which most modern states have sprung, and setting aside wars of so-called 'liberation', a civil war (as part of the process in which governments recognized to have authority have

appeared) has taken place in England, France, the Netherlands, Switzerland, the USA, Ireland, and elsewhere.

In trying to answer the first of these questions – What and
whence is the authority of a government? – we are seeking to
establish and to understand the distinction between might
and right, between violence and authority – the distinction in
which a political society, properly speaking, is constituted.
All states have emerged in violence: how, then, could their
governments acquire 'right'?

In trying to answer the second question: Who should rule?
or, What is the proper constitution of a government? we are
trying to establish an intelligible connection between our
understanding of the office and authority of ruler and the
character of one appropriate to occupy that office and exercise that authority.

9

The third topic of modern European political reflection is
concerned with the activities of governments. The question,
here, is: What are the proper occupations of governments?
What should they *do*? What *is* 'ruling'?

This topic, unlike the earlier two, is almost unique to modern European political reflection. It has no significant counterpart in any other political experience.

Briefly, what a government does, what it is disposed to do,
and what it is expected to do, depends upon two things:

- What it is believed to have the authority to do.
- What in fact it has the power (*potentia*) to do.

Generally speaking, in more distant political experiences,
rulers have had more authority than they have had power.

A medieval king had only a very limited authority. There
were, for example, long periods in the emergence of kingship
in France, when the duty of his subordinates (the great dukes
and counts) did not extend much beyond the duty of not
making war upon him. And this exiguous duty defined the
limit of his authority.

But such a king was lucky if he had power (*potentia*)
enough to enforce even this duty upon his subjects.

In short, a medieval king had, so to speak, no surplus
power to go beyond the limits of his authority, and often he
lacked the power to exert what was recognized to be his
authority.

His authority being settled by convention, and his power being certainly no greater than what was required to maintain his recognized rights, nobody was ever seriously faced with the questions: What are the proper occupations of a ruler? Is he exceeding his authority in what he is doing?

But as the governments of modern Europe began to amass the immense resources of power which they now have at their disposal, the question: What are the proper activities of government? became a supremely relevant question.

In modern times political reflection has been faced with the relatively new situation of rulers who may have much more power than they have authority, and rulers disposed to live up to the extent of their power and even to confuse their power with their authority.

Indeed, it is the enjoyment of these huge resources of power by modern governments which has turned political reflection on to a reconsideration of the benefits of 'sovereign' authority.

In other words, 'sovereign' was a recognized quality in the government of a modern state before that government came to possess the great power which all government now have. But when that power had been acquired, 'sovereign authority' began to look more dangerous than it had earlier seemed to be.

10

The last of the topics of modern European political reflection I shall try to deal with is concerned with the nature of political deliberation and argument.

It is a very old topic. It was reflected upon in ancient Greece. But in modern times it has become, perhaps, the most important of all centres of political reflection.

The questions it embraces are questions such as:

- What are we doing when we deliberate about a political situation or come to a conclusion about what response is to be made?
- What is a political ideology?
- What is sort of talk is political talk?
- What is the logical design of political reasoning and argument?

These are questions which have been continuously considered and reconsidered in modern times. All the great political thinkers from the sixteenth century have had something to say about them.

Indeed, in the dawn of the modern European state there appeared a writer who gave the discussion of these questions a profoundly new direction; namely, Machiavelli.

11

Now, I need hardly say that these four topics of political reflection cannot be separated from one another. They often overlap, and we must be ready to recognize this overlap.

But they can be distinguished from one another, and I propose to start on the first of them next week.

Editorial Note

LSE 1/1/21, file 5, fos. 415–26. Photocopy of a typescript.

Twenty-six

Interpretations of the Modern European State (1)

1

We begin today to consider the first of the main topics of modern European political thought; namely, the answers which have been given to the question, What is a 'state'?

That a state was a collection of people occupying a defined territory was obvious enough – or it became obvious fairly early in modern European history.

But this observation left unanswered a number of important questions:

- What sort of a collectivity of human beings is a 'state'?
- What is the bond between the human components of a 'state'?
- How are the human components of a 'state' related to one another?
- What is the nature of the solidarity characteristic of a 'state'?

Now, when it is understood that living in a modern European 'state' was a new and puzzling experience in the sixteenth century, it will be seen that these are important practical questions.

They are the same sort of questions as Aristotle explored on behalf of the tribesmen of ancient Greece when they were entering upon the new and puzzling experience of *polis*-life.

And what we are concerned with is the sort of practical beliefs which have appeared in modern European political thought on this important topic.

2

The simplest and often the most illuminating way of answering questions like this is to seek an analogy for a modern state among the various collectivities of human beings you are already familiar with.

In other words, the question asked is, What is a modern European state *like*? Is it like any of the communities or associations I am already familiar with and think I understand?

This, you will remember, is what Aristotle did at the beginning of the *Politics*. He asked himself: Is a *polis* like a tribe or a household? And in the end he found himself obliged to reject these analogies as unilluminating – although he did find some similarity between the relation of citizen to citizen and the relation of husband to wife.

Consider it this way:

- You know what it means to be a member of a family, a guild, a fraternity, a church, or a religious sect;
- You are familiar with the bonds of personal loyalty and mutual protection which constitute a feudal relationship;
- You know what it is to live in a village or a town, and you are aware of the bonds which constitute a neighborhood.
- You have, perhaps, acquired the experience of being a member of an assembly, a crowd, an army, or a court of law (as a juror).

In all these cases you know enough about these collectivities to know what to expect from other members of them, and how to behave yourself.

Do any of them offer any useful analogy in trying to understand this new and puzzling experience of life in a 'state'? And if not, where else might we look among what we *do* know in order to illuminate what is puzzling?

Now, an analogy, if it is convincing enough, will often provide the sort of understanding which is practically satisfying. But every practical question is potentially a theoretical question, and a mere analogy will not provide the intellectual understanding which is sought by a philosopher.

Consequently we must expect to find this topic explored at different intellectual levels in modern European political thought. And where analogies are often found acceptable for practical purposes, philosophers like Hobbes or Hume or Hegel will be found to be pressing on to definitive understandings of the nature of a 'state'.

In short, modern European thought on this topic appears at different levels of sophistication.

One further point:

In trying to answer this question, modern European thought has been apt to hover between two somewhat different sorts of questions; between the question: (1) What, in fact, is the bond which unites the members of a 'state'? and (2) What ought to be the bond which unites the members of a 'state'?

But if there is some confusion here, it is an understandable and excusable confusion.

Living in a modern 'state' has always been an unfinished experience.

And what was often being sought was some beliefs which would give practical guidance about the relationship between the members of a 'state' – beliefs which could hardly avoid being a mixture of alleged fact and aspiration.

3

Now, there is one answer to this question about the bond which unites the members of a 'state' which I want to notice here, but to put on one side and return to later.

It is the answer that the collectivity of a modern state lies in the allegiance which each of its members owes to its ruler or government. The answer that the bond which unites the members of a 'state' to one another is solely the loyalty each owes to his ruler.

This answer clearly had some plausibility for members of a European 'state' in the sixteenth century. These early modern 'states' were often arbitrary collections of diverse peoples, brought together by conquest, treaty, or the marriage of rulers. And it was clear that such solidarity as they possessed was, to a large extent, owed to their rulers.

Beyond question, one of the most important differences between a Frenchman and an Englishman in the sixteenth century was the allegiance each owed to his different ruler. And, in some cases, this difference seemed to be definitive.

It is true that Englishmen in the seventeenth century could think of themselves as composing a single community in virtue of being under a common law which was not the product of any ruler's legislative act. But Great Britain could not be thought of as a community of this sort: Scots and English law were different and have remained so. And the best Frenchmen could do was to think of themselves as all alike subjects of Louis XV – they had no common law.

But while this view of the collectivity of a modern 'state' had a good deal to recommend it, even those who seemed most inclined to take it rarely found it a satisfactory account of the situation.

Machiavelli, for example, is very apt to take the view that a 'state' is a collection of people who own allegiance to a ruler. But even he believed that even the most authoritative, the most powerful, and the most energetic ruler would be incapable of imposing a unity upon his subjects if they were not already a community of some sort. The bond of common allegiance could not be the only bond.

Moreover, in the often revolutionary conditions of early modern Europe this was a dangerous belief. It implied that the dissolution of allegiance signified in the ejection of a ruler entailed the dissolution of the 'state' itself. This, you will remember, was a belief that Locke thought to be so dangerous and destructive that he urged his audience to reject it.

But, in any case, this view of the collectivity of a 'state' is so closely connected with beliefs about the authority and the office of a ruler in a modern 'state' that it is better considered, later on, in that connection.

The question which now concerns us is: What, if anything, besides the common allegiance of its members to their ruler, constitutes the collectivity of a 'state'?

4

Now, at the risk of imposing too rigid a classification upon modern European beliefs on this topic, I am going to suggest that most answers to this question fall into one or another of three different classes – though some beliefs seem to overlap these classes.

In general, it has been believed that the collectivity of a modern European 'state', and the bond which ties its members, is either:

- natural: a 'state' is a 'natural community'; or
- artificial: a 'state' is an artificial association; or
- neither natural nor artificial, strictly speaking, but something that partakes of both: a 'historic' bond.

Each of these general views has appeared in a variety of different versions. And I propose to begin with some of the more important versions of the belief that a 'state' is a natural collectivity of human beings.

5

The simplest and most extreme version of this view is the belief that a 'state' is an 'organic' unity, and that its government is merely something superimposed upon a natural or 'organic' whole.

Now, the idea of an 'organism', when used to interpret the nature of a 'state', is, in appearance, a highly sophisticated idea, the sort of thing only a philosopher would think of, and also, in some respects, an obviously inappropriate idea.

Strictly speaking, if a human society were a generated 'organism' it would require no government. It would live and move as a vital unit, its vitality being continuously distributed in all its parts.

And an interpretation of the collectivity of a 'state' which, thus, recognized no place for a 'ruler' or 'government' could not even begin to be plausible.

We must, then, understand what is being suggested in this view is not that a 'state' is an 'organism' and has an 'organic' unity, but that it is something like an 'organism'.

The purport of this interpretation is not so much the strict concept of an 'organism' as the idea of a natural whole of functionally related parts. And understood in this manner, the idea clearly has some practical implications by way of suggestion about how the members of a 'state' are related to one another, and how they ought to behave in relation to one another.

(1) The most naive and direct version of this interpretation of the collectivity of a 'state' *likens* it to that of a human body.

Thus, Rousseau says: 'The body politic may be considered as an organized, living body, like a man. . . The life of both a man and a state is the self common to the whole, the reciprocal sensibility and internal correspondence of all the parts'.

And Hobbes is another writer who used this analogy to indicate his understanding of the nature of a 'state'.

Now, this way of thinking was not, of course, the invention of modern writers. It goes back to Plato; it was a favourite analogy with medieval writers, used to interpret the character of a medieval community; and it was used by St. Paul to interpret the character of an early Christian community.

But the human body never quite offered the analogy which was being sought – the analogy of an 'organism'.

For the image of a human being is not, strictly, that of an organism whose vitality is continuously distributed in all its parts. It is (as it was for Plato), rather, the image of a whole which acquired and maintained its unity by virtue of the operation of one of its parts – the brain or the mind.

And when the Christian church, in medieval times, was spoken of as being composed of a head (the pope) and 'members' or 'limbs', its unity was not thought of as a, strictly speaking, 'organic' unity, but a unity derived from the control exercised by its single 'head' or ruler.

(2) But, if the analogy of a 'human body' is rather farfetched, the natural world offered other analogies to be pursued in trying to understand the collectivity of a 'state'.

Ants and bees (the so-called 'social' insects) have always offered tempting analogies to political thinkers, and not less so in modern times than in others: a 'state' is like a colony of ants or a swarm of bees.

But these could not be regarded as anything but very rough analogies. Although their intention is clear – namely, to recommend a belief that a 'state' should be regarded as a society of functionally related components in which each component (quite apart from what a government might impose) is an individual contributor to a common condition of life.

The analogies remained favourite images in modern times for the collectivity of a modern 'state', although Hobbes (in the seventeenth century), following Aristotle, may be said to have conclusively demonstrated their inappropriateness.

(3) A less farfetched analogy in which a 'state' was interpreted as a 'natural' whole likened it to a family or a household.

The image of a family, here, was not, of course, the family as we know it; it was the so-called 'patriarchal' family which still existed in Europe in the sixteenth and seventeenth centuries.

What a 'state' was being likened to was, in fact, a household which contained not only a husband, wife and children, but more distant blood relations, family servants, and retainers as well.

The best known political writers who interpreted the collectivity of a 'state' in this manner were Jean Bodin and Robert Filmer.

For these writers, and for many others, the family was the emblem of all 'natural' human relationships; and a 'state' was understood as a 'family' composed of 'families', a 'household' composed of 'households'. And government was something added to this 'natural' bond.

Here, again, this interpretation was not original to modern European thinkers. Fundamentally it was a 'tribal' analogy which, you will remember, Aristotle rejected in respect of a *polis* because it seemed to him to miss the characteristic unity of a *polis*. Nevertheless, it is not surprising that modern thinkers should have been attracted by this analogy – even though its practical implications might be somewhat obscure.

The 'family' is, after all, the most obvious analogy for a human society; and the background of this analogy in modern times was biblical and no doubt contained some reminiscence of the ancient Roman notion of the *populus Romanus* as composing a single family, whose progenitor was Romulus, both father and first ruler.

(4) But, in modern times, incomparably the most important version of this understanding of the collectivity of a 'state' as a 'natural' collectivity is that in which a 'state' was identified as a 'nation', and which found the word 'nationality' appropriate to describe the bond which tied the members of a 'state' to one another.

It is true that the word 'nation' when it was used to describe the collectivity of the members of a 'state' did not always carry with it the idea that this was a 'natural' collectivity. But this is the idea which the notion of 'nationality' clung to as it emerged in the eighteenth century. And it always stood for a notion of a 'unity' upon which government was superimposed.

Now, what was meant when it was claimed that the most illuminating analogy to use in describing the collectivity of a modern 'state' was that of a 'nation'? Because, we must understand that this *was* an analogy; the word 'nation' already had a meaning, and what was being claimed was that a 'state' should be understood to be *like* a 'nation'.

The Latin word *natio* was originally understood for a group of human beings, larger than a family but smaller than a 'people' (*populus*), which was distinguished from other groups in respect of certain common and exclusive characteristics.

The most common of these characteristics were a language of their own, perhaps the presumption of common blood, and an exclusive religion. Such groups were a familiar feature of the Roman empire: the Jews, for example, were recognized by the Romans as a *natio*.

Further, the word 'nation' was used in the middle ages (and even down to the eighteenth century) to refer to groups of various sorts who were distinguished, more or less firmly, from those who surrounded them by characteristics at least some of which were regarded as 'natural'.

This, then, was the analogy being used when it was claimed that a 'state' should be understood as a 'nation' – and when this claim was made, the word 'people' was often used as an alternative to the word 'nation'.

For the framers of the French *Declaration des droits de l'homme et du citoyen* (1789) the expression *la nation Française* meant the same thing as *le peuple Français*.

Now, when the word 'nation' began its career in the political vocabulary of modern Europe it was used in connection with two different but related claims: (1) The claim that over and above the unity with which a ruler or government might endow a 'state', it had another, 'natural' unity – that of being a 'nation'; (2) The claim that there were 'natural' communities in Europe, to be called 'nations', which were not themselves 'states' and did not have government exclusively of their own, but that, in virtue of their being 'nations' they ought to be 'states'.

Generally speaking, these two claims appeared respectively in French and in German political thought in the eighteenth century.

(1) In France, the word *nation* came to stand for the collectivity of the inhabitants of the territory of France ruled by the king of France.

Thus, it was asserted that, apart from the unity imposed by their common allegiance to a ruler, Frenchmen composed a 'natural' community of a vaguer sort (based mainly upon a common language) – a unity denoted by the expression *la nation Française* or *le peuple Français*.

The step taken by the framers of the Declaration of the Rights of Man was the assertion that the 'nation' was the sole source of political *potestas*.

And, from one important point of view, the political history of France after the revolution is the story of the efforts of whole classes of Frenchmen, who felt themselves excluded from the French 'nation', to get themselves included within it.

(2) In Germany the word *nation* denoted a 'natural' collectivity of human beings – roughly, those who spoke the German language or any of its dialects.

But in Germany (unlike in France) this 'nation' was not a 'state'; indeed, it was fragmented into about three hundred separate 'states'. And it was claimed that this fragmentation was 'unnatural' because a 'nation', properly speaking, was to be understood as the 'natural' unity of a 'state'.

(3) There was, however, a third circumstance in which the idea of 'nationality' was used in modern Europe.

It was claimed that there were 'natural' communities, to be recognized as 'nations', which were subjected to the rule of other nations. The Poles were a 'nation', but they were ruled by the Czar of Russia; the Hungarians and the Czechs were 'nations', but they were ruled by a Turkish sultan.

And it was this circumstance which generated the genuine doctrine of 'nationalism' in modern Europe – the doctrine, not merely that the fundamental unity of a 'state' is the tie of 'nationality', but that every 'national' community should be a 'political' community with a government exclusively its own.

Here, then, was a massive interpretation of the collectivity of a modern European 'state', in which the bonds which joined the members of a state were understood to be 'natural' bonds and not merely a common allegiance to a ruler, and in which these 'natural' bonds of common 'nationality' were understood to constitute a valid claim to 'statehood' or political independence.

And, of course, this understanding of the nature of a 'state' has since spread itself from Europe to other parts of the world.

There are, perhaps, three observations which may usefully be made about it.

(a) There is something in the circumstances of many modern 'states' to correspond to it; but these circumstances suggest that what is called a 'nation' is not so much a 'natural' collectivity of human beings as a 'historical' collectivity, and that it is often rather the result of a common political allegiance than the occasion of it.

(b) A 'nation' as a collectivity of human beings who speak a single, common language (and in Europe this was the predominant characteristic taken to distinguish a 'nation') was remote from any eighteenth-century European state, and is pretty remote from most contemporary European states.

And the notion that a 'language' community is in any significant sense a 'natural' community does not have very much to be said in its favour.

Its 'language' may be one of the most important characteristics of a society, but it is a 'historic', not a 'natural', characteristic.

(c) Nothing even remotely corresponding to what were in Europe identified, and often approved, as 'national states' exists anywhere else in the world. The notion that nationality is the bond which unites the members of a state, or which should unite it, when exported from Europe, has been the mother of political illusion.

6

Now, before we leave this interpretation of a 'state' as a 'natural' collectivity of human beings, it is worth noticing the idiom of this idea which appears in the writings of Montesquieu, a French writer of the early eighteenth century and perhaps the most profound political thinker of his time.

Montesquieu was concerned with the character of the modern European state; this theme was the centre of his thought.

He has much to say about the constitutions of the governments of modern European 'states'. But he believed that every 'state', whatever sort of government it might have, had what he called an *esprit général*. This expression may, perhaps, be translated: 'general mental character'.

This 'general mental character' comprised the manners, the customs, the beliefs about the world, the moral dispositions, and even the religious convictions of a 'people'.

Thus, he would consider that Englishmen would have a different *esprit général* from Frenchmen or Spaniards.

Now, the important thing about this *esprit général* is that it does not spring from the activities of a government, and it is certainly not something imposed upon a people by its government.

Indeed, it is something which a government has to accept as a condition of being able to rule. A legislator can never successfully oppose it, because it is something stronger and more 'natural' than any code of civil law.

In short, this *esprit général* is the 'natural' tie which constitutes the collectivity of the 'state'.

Nevertheless, Montesquieu did not imagine this *esprit général* to be self-generated, or even to be a solely 'historical' acquisition.

It is the principal 'cause' of a community of human beings; but it is, itself, 'caused' by the 'natural' conditions in which a set of human beings live: their physical environment and particularly the climate of their locality.

Thus, it may be thought of as the 'natural' basis of a 'state', which conditions, or even determines, all the other characteristics of a state – its laws, its constitution, and its instruments of government.

7

Now, there are two important things to be observed in this whole enterprise of seeking the collectivity of a 'state', and the bond which unites the members of a state, in a *natural* tie.

First, it is preeminently understandable.

A modern European 'state' was manifestly a contingent collection of human beings – a matter of chance and circumstances. In some 'states' there were communities which could look back upon long common histories, and in which the familiarity of living together was apt to silence all questions about how they had come to do so. But no modern European 'state' was, itself, a community of this sort.

In these circumstances, the search for some bond of union deeper than mere allegiance to a ruler is easy to understand. The search for a 'natural' unity for a 'state', something to correspond with the lost 'natural' (blood) unity of a 'tribe' or a 'people', is not difficult to account for.

Or, from the other direction, to live in a modern 'state', upon which its government was daily imposing a more exclusive solidarity by the destruction of diversities, could hardly fail to provoke a desire to find some 'natural' or 'rational' base for this solidarity.

The warmth and 'naturalness' of local communities was being lost; and who would not desire that the community by which they were being replaced should be not less warm, 'natural' and familiar?

Indeed the very durability of a modern 'state' seemed to depend upon there being some 'natural' bond between its members.

Secondly, the extreme difficulty of interpreting the solidarity of a modern 'state' as a 'natural' solidarity is to be noticed.

Apart from the 'family', there seems to be no 'natural' bond which may be understood to join human beings into separate, exclusive communities such as modern European 'states'.

The notion of a 'natural' bond between human beings would seem much more likely to generate the idea that, in some manner, the human race itself composes a 'natural' community than the idea that a modern European 'state' composes a natural society.

When Locke looked for a 'natural' bond between human beings he found it in the tie which unites all human beings together as children of one God, or members of one race. And this was a bond which had in some sense to be dissolved if there were to be such a thing as a 'state'.

And when, in the nineteenth century, Mazzini preached a doctrine of 'nationalism' – a doctrine that each 'state' had, or should have, the 'natural' unity or solidarity of a 'nation', he ended up by preaching a doctrine of natural, 'human' solidarity which conflicted with his 'nationalism'.

In short, however understandable it is that a 'natural' basis for the collectivity of a modern European state should have been sought, it is equally clear that the enterprise was likely to be frustrated.

A modern European 'state' was so empirical a construction, was so manifestly a contingent collection of human beings, that to seek a 'natural' unity in it would seem to deny its most notable feature.

Editorial Note

LSE 1/1/21, file 5, fos. 427 – 39. Photocopy of a typescript.

Twenty-seven

Interpretations of the Modern European State (2)

1

Last week we considered some of the directions taken by modern European political thought in the enterprise of understanding a modern European 'state' as a 'natural' collectivity of human beings.

It was, we saw, a somewhat forlorn enterprise, but one which could hardly be avoided. The durability, even the moral validity, of a 'state' seemed to many people to depend upon its success.

The interpretation I want now to consider is that in which a modern 'state' is understood, not as a 'natural' community (its members joined to one another by 'natural' bonds), but as an 'artificial' association of human beings, its members joined together by 'artificial' bonds.

2

This understanding of a 'state' as an 'artificial' association of human beings may be seen to reflect: first, an intellectual disposition; and secondly, something in the actual political experience of modern Europe.

(1) The intellectual disposition it reflected was the assumption that everything in the world is either 'natural' or 'artificial'; that what was not 'natural' must be 'artificial'.

This belief, inherited from the ancient world, may be said to have been commonly held in Western Europe down to the eighteenth century. On one side, there was the 'natural' world, understood in Christian thought as the work of God; on the other side, there were the works of men, the world of 'artifice'.

And, in these circumstances, it is only to be expected that the difficulties encountered in trying to interpret a 'state' as a 'natural' collectivity of human beings would suggest (what was believed to be the only possible alternative) that it should be understood as an 'artificial' collectivity.

But a 'state' understood as a work of human art suggests the question: Who is the artist?

In the circumstances, the most obvious answer to this question was: 'The ruler is the artist'.

This was the answer given, for example, by Machiavelli. And it is the answer implicit in the common way of talking which recognizes, for example, Bismarck as the 'maker of modern Germany', or Cavour as the 'maker of modern Italy'.

But this answer not only recognizes a 'state' as an artificial collectivity of human beings, but also as a collectivity whose bond of union lies in the allegiance of its members to their ruler. And on this account, this answer may be said to have become progressively less acceptable.

What was being sought was a tie between the subjects of a ruler which, however artificial, was not merely a tie of common allegiance to a ruler.

The alternative answer to the question: Who is the artist? was 'the members of the "state" themselves'. It is they who 'make' the 'state' by agreement with one another.

Thus, a 'state' is recognized as a collection of human beings united, by agreement or choice, in pursuit of a common purpose or enterprise. The purpose or enterprise may perhaps be recognized to have some foundation in 'human nature'; but a 'state' is a specific and limited set of people who have chosen to be associated with one another in its pursuit.

This interpretation of what a 'state' is, was, of course, greatly elaborated by philosophical thinkers. But there was, ready to hand, in current experience, an analogy which might be appealed to. A 'state' is something like a joint stock company, distinguished only in respect of the purpose being pursued by its members.

And there was, also, ready to hand, a word to denote a 'state' understood in this manner – the word 'association'. Indeed, this interpretation of a 'state' can be seen as emerging in European thought when a 'state' begins to be spoken of as an 'association' of human beings, rather than as a 'society' or a 'community'. And this way of speaking was emerging in the seventeenth century.

This, then, is the intellectual disposition reflected in the idea of a 'state' as a work of art.

(2) The actual political experience which this understanding of a 'state' reflected was, no doubt, in the first place, the simple observation of the manner in which many modern European 'states' had in fact emerged upon the scene.

They emerged in violence, in the imposition of territorial boundaries which cut across 'natural' communities, which severed 'natural' ties, and which destroyed ancient allegiances. They emerged in treaties of union or dissolution; in the marriages of rulers which joined communities which might have next to nothing in common; and in 'revolutions' which broke old ties and created new.

In short, almost everything about the emergence of a modern 'state' suggested that what had emerged was *not* a 'natural' community. And if it were not a 'natural' community, then (according to the current intellectual assumption) it must be recognized as an 'artificial' association.

Whatever solidarity a modern 'state' might possess was, almost manifestly, the work of man. But this interpretation of a 'state' reflected, alas, a somewhat deeper experience than a recognition of events of association of this sort.

It reflected a sentiment, a belief, about the 'nature' of human beings, and it was designed to recommend the importance of this belief.

The deeper assumption of this interpretation of a 'state' was the belief that each individual human being was a 'natural' unity and had no 'natural' ties with any other human being.

Such individuals were, of course, assumed to be capable of composing themselves into associations; but such associations must be understood to be works of human artifice. And they may be expected to appear if they serve some utility recognizable by a 'natural' human individual.

They may be perceived to be necessary to civilized life; but they have been made, they are liable to dissolution, and they are not 'natural'.

In short, a 'state' must be considered to be an 'artificial' association because what is 'natural' is a human individual, sovereign over himself.

Those who took this view did not necessarily believe that if you went back far enough into the history of any 'state' you would come upon a specific act of association, like the formation of a joint stock company.

What they did believe was that a 'state' must be understood as if it were the product of an act of association, because any other way of understanding it seemed to deny the belief that what was 'natural' to a human being was precisely what made him distinct from every other human being.

Now, this is one of those changes in human sentiment and belief which I have spoken of as characteristic of modern Europe, and it can be made intelligible by considering it in its context.

First, its context was the dissolution of those communal ties, easily mistaken for 'natural' ties, which composed the structure of life in a medieval community. A modern 'state' was itself, from one point of view, an emblem of this dissolution; it generated the unattached individual.

The ties of 'feudal' relationships were being converted into a cash nexus; tenancies of land were coming to be in terms of contracts for money rents.

The corporate and guild organization of industry was giving place to individual enterprise and partnerships springing from individual choice. The relationships which were beginning to count were derived not from *status* but from voluntary acts of agreement.

Family patrimonies were being broken up; estates, freed from entail, were being broken up. And movement was tending to make family ties of shorter duration.

In short, the separate, individual man, with no apparent 'natural' ties, was appearing on the scene. The boy who left home at an early age to seek his fortune among strangers became associated with others only in partnership which he made for himself.

Secondly, this sentiment for individuality was reflected in current religious belief, particularly in Lutherism.

The Lutheran was persuaded that he, under God, was responsible for his own salvation. And this salvation was to be achieved, not by obeying rules common to all men, nor by performing virtuous social actions, but by that which, above all, distinguishes one man from another, namely, his personal 'faith'.

In pursuit of this salvation, no priestly intermediary could help. Each man was alone with God. Moreover, a protestant 'church' was not something into which a man was born; it was an association of believers each of whom had made an individual choice to belong. This is what a religious 'sect' signified, as distinct from what the sixteenth century recognized as 'the church'.

In short, there was very much afoot in early modern Europe to promote the sentiment of individuality and together with it the belief that a 'state' was an 'artificial' association of independent individuals, and to provide appropriate analogies for such a 'state': e.g. a 'joint stock' company, or a religious 'sect'.

3

Here, then, is an interpretation of the nature of a 'state' and of the character of the ties which join its members. It is an 'artificial' association, the bonds of which are the agreements to associate entered into by its members.

Now, an 'association', recognized as a product of human 'artifice', is designed to achieve some end. And one association will be distinguished from another in respect of the end or purpose being pursued.

Thus, each of the versions in which this understanding of a 'state' has appeared in modern European thought is to be recognized as the attribution of a particular purpose to what all understand as an 'artificial' association of human beings.

The purpose itself may, of course, be understood to be in some manner inherent in 'human nature'; but a 'state' is understood to be a specific and 'artificial' association of human beings joined in the pursuit of this purpose.

Let us now consider some of the versions in which this idea of a 'state' has appeared.

4

In early modern European history, perhaps, the most notable version of this idea was religious; and it is best illustrated from the political thought of Calvinism.

A 'state' in the thought of John Calvin and his followers was an association of human beings united in the pursuit of a single end, namely, the glorification of God in their manner of living.

The members of a Calvinist 'state', such as Geneva, were understood to have chosen the particular manner in which they would pursue this end; they were 'converts'; and what united them was not any 'natural' bond, but the tie of what they had chosen to pursue in common.

This understanding of a 'state', then, implied a religious unity and a religious uniformity. And potentially within it was the notion that all Calvinists should compose a single 'state' – an association of all those who had made the same choice.

A somewhat more sophisticated form of this religious version appears in the writings of John Locke.

The human race, as Locke understood it, composes a single 'natural' society, the bonds of which are the common allegiance of its members to the God who had created them and who had prescribed a 'law' which they should obey – the so-called law of nature or law of God.

But a 'state' was an 'artificial' association of certain members of the human race who had agreed to place themselves under a civil law and a civil jurisdiction, the purpose of which was to administer the law of God or nature among themselves.

5

This religious version of the character of a 'state' as an 'artificial' association had, as its counterpart, which may be called a secular *moral* version.

European political thought from the eighteenth century contains many examples of this view of a 'state'.

Here, again, the pursuit of the virtuous life, the life proper to human beings, was understood as the 'natural' end in which all mankind is joined in pursuing.

But a 'state' is a specific association of human beings who have agreed among themselves to pursue the life of virtue in a manner peculiar to themselves. They have expressed their own particular notion of the life of virtue in laws and arrangements peculiar to themselves, and they are joined to one another in pursuing it in this manner.

The moral perfection which, in this understanding of a 'state', is recognized to be that which unites its members, of course, received a variety of semi-philosophical expressions:

In Rousseau and in other eighteenth-century writers, moral perfection was understood (in the Aristotelian manner) as the subordination of passion to reason.

In the nineteenth century, in such writers as Mill and Green, a 'state' appears as an association of human beings in pursuit of 'moral progress'.

And, earlier, Hobbes had understood a 'state' as an 'artificial' association of human beings united in an agreed pursuit of 'peace' among themselves.

6

But among those who have been disposed to understand a 'state' as an 'artificial' association of human beings, the version of this belief which in European thought may be said to have come to supersede all others in importance, is that in which the common purpose in respect of which the members of a 'state' are united is understood to be the exploitation of the natural resources of the world.

A 'state', in this understanding of it, is an 'economy', or (in a cruder formulation of the same idea) it is a 'factory'.

This idea of a 'state' is one now so commonly held that it is worth reminding ourselves that it goes back to the sixteenth century, where it was connected with the notion of a 'state' as a landed 'estate': a territory whose inhabitants are joined in the agreed enterprise of exploiting its resources.

The earliest unequivocal expression of this idea I know of appears in the writings of Francis Bacon. And there it emerges as a moral, or even a religious, doctrine, for which authority is found in Scripture.

God (Bacon and other writers tell us), as recorded in the Book of Genesis, informed Adam that the whole earth and the vegetable and mineral creation was at the absolute disposal of the human race.

And Adam was further informed that the proper occupation of mankind was the enjoyment of these resources. This is what the human race exists for: the glorification of God in the enjoyment of his gifts.

And the sin of Adam, and the fall of man, modified the situation in only one respect – namely, that this enjoyment entails 'work'. The whole duty of man is the glorification of God in the 'work' of exploiting the natural resources of the world.

Thus, a 'state', as Bacon understood it, is a specific association of human beings united in the organized enterprise of exploiting the resources of their territory – united (as we should say) in the common enterprise of 'production'.

After Bacon (and often with express reference to his writings) this idea of a 'state' was elaborated by St. Simon, by Fichte, and by a whole host of writers in the nineteenth and twentieth centuries.

It has now shed some of its original religious and moral connections. And sometimes the crude emphasis on 'production' has been modified by the distributive notion of 'welfare'; and an analogy for the 'state' has been found in a 'public service corporation' in which all members of a 'state' are equal partners.

What is now often called a 'welfare state' is a modern European 'state' understood as a specific association of human beings, united in the common purpose of generating and enjoying such material prosperity as the material and human resources of its territory permit.

7

Now, it is obvious that each of these versions of the belief that a 'state' is an 'artificial' association of human beings joined in their pursuit of a common and agreed purpose will have as its counterpart some beliefs about the role to be played by its government in relation to the pursuit of this purpose.

Calvin, Locke, Bacon, Rousseau, Bentham, Mill, Green, etc.: each has his beliefs about this. And this is a matter which we will have to consider later when we come to beliefs about the authority, constitution, and activities of governments.

But, for the moment, what I have tried to put before you is one whole idiom of thought in modern Europe about the character of a 'state' and of the bonds which unite its members, other than bonds of allegiance to a government which may, also, be understood to unite them.

8

There are, then, two notable interpretations of the collectivity of a 'state' in modern European thought.

In the first, a 'state' appears as a 'natural' society with a 'natural' solidarity.

In the second, a 'state' appears as an 'artificial' association, the product of agreement, the bonds which unite its members being a specifically chosen purpose and the specific arrangements agreed upon for its pursuit.

But there is a third interpretation of the collectivity of a 'state', more difficult to describe, but not less important. It represents a breakout from the intellectual disposition which assumes that everything in the world must be either 'natural' or 'artificial'.

It represents the belief that there is a third kind of thing, neither 'natural' nor 'artificial', but 'historical'; and the belief that a 'state' is properly understood as a 'historical association'.

To recognize something as 'historical' is to recognize it as belonging to some other order of things than the 'natural' order.

Nothing that is 'natural' can be conceived to be other than it is; the world of 'nature' is the world of 'necessity'. But the world of 'history' is the world of things which are contingent, and might have been other than they are.

Similarly, to recognize something as 'historical' is to recognize it as belonging to some other order of things than the 'artificial' order.

Every genuine artifact is designed and made to serve some specific and premeditated purpose. But the essence of something recognized to be 'historical' is that, though it is the product of human choices (and therefore not 'natural'), it is not designed and made to serve any specific and premeditated purpose.

Here, then, is a plausible category of things: neither 'natural' nor 'artificial'; neither 'necessary' nor 'designed.' What we call them does not very much matter; but in the eighteenth century they were beginning to be recognized as 'historical'.

Now, the belief we are to consider is the belief that the collectivity of a 'state', the bond which unites the members of a 'state', is neither a 'natural' bond (like common blood) nor 'artificial' (like an expressly chosen common purpose, as in a joint stock company), but that it is forged by time and circumstance and is 'historical'.

In short, a 'state' is to be understood as a collection of human beings who have no 'natural' ties, who are not united by common blood, who cannot be supposed to have entered into an express agreement to associate with one another for the achievement of a specific purpose, but whom chance has brought together, and who have acquired a sentiment of solidarity from having enjoyed, over the years, a common and continuous 'historical' experience.

Who can tell what 'historical' events, experiences and processes, all of which might have been other than they were, go to make a 'state' and bind its members to one another?

Sometimes it is a war; sometimes the continued rule of a government. But always it is the memory of shared experiences.

A common language, a literature, common laws, folk-tales and legends, songs – all these take their place in the total of contingent circumstances. None by itself is enough to constitute the collectivity of a 'state', but all are apt to be contributory. And all are plausibly independent of any allegiance to a ruler.

Moreover, none of these things is properly to be understood as either 'natural' or 'artificial'.

A language is not 'natural' to a 'people'. Yet nobody invented it to unite a collection of human beings; it was not designed for that purpose. It is the product of 'history'; it is a component in the undesigned and circumstantial ties which constitute the collectivity of a 'state'.

Indeed, it may be said that if there is one analogy more than another which is appealed to in this interpretation of a 'state', it is the analogy of a 'language'.

Moreover, the collectivity of a 'state' understood in this manner suggests that it is always a matter of degree; it is never absolute as it would be if it were either 'natural' or genuinely 'artificial'.

A 'state', like a language, is as stable as it has managed to become. The ties which unite its members, all of them the products of time and circumstance, are as strong as they have managed to become.

9

Now, this interpretation of the collectivity of a 'state' is as 'practical' as either of the other two. It, also, is designed to recommend how the members of a 'state' should think of their relations to one another and how they should behave towards one another.

It suggests that we should get rid of the illusion of 'natural' ties and recognize the contingency and circumstantial character of a 'state'. And it suggests that a 'state' should be thought of as something more substantial than a joint stock company whose members have chosen to associate with one another for the achievement of some specific and designed purpose.

It is neither an agreed purpose nor a 'natural' affiliation which unites the members of a 'state', but a common 'historical' experience.

What unites them is something less substantial than a 'natural' bond, and something less fragile and changeable than a chosen purpose. It is the experience of living together which they have enjoyed over the years; it is all that they have done or refrained from doing, all that they have suffered, believed and felt.

And this, it has been contended, corresponds much more closely to what a European 'state' in fact is than either of the other two interpretations.

10

Now, as might be expected, this interpretation of a 'state' emerged in European thought only with great difficulty. It was not easy to throw off the categories and analogies of 'nature' and 'artifice' and the presumption that everything must be understood in terms of one or the other of these categories.

The writers who first explored this interpretation of the collectivity of a 'state' in the eighteenth century were a set of English and Scottish writers, of whom perhaps the most distinguished were Adam Ferguson, Hume, Burke, and Coleridge, an Italian writer named Vico, and several German writers – Herder, Savigny, and Hegel, for example.

But its emergence is, perhaps, best seen in the writings of Burke, whose hesitations illustrate the difficulty it had in emerging.

In one mood, Burke is all for 'art'. The idea of a 'state' as an artificial association seems to him acceptable.

'The idea of a "people" is the idea of a corporation. It is wholly artificial.' A 'people,' he says, is the product of a 'common agreement'. A 'state' is a 'partnership'.

Nevertheless, Burke is persuaded that a 'state' was never literally 'made' in any specific act of agreement, in a compact

or a contract between hitherto tieless and independent individuals. And therefore he modifies the theory of 'artifice'
and speaks of a 'state' as 'a compact of all the ages'.

A 'people' is, clearly, a 'partnership' of a very odd kind.
Nobody ever drew up, and no persons ever signed, its arti-
cles of agreement.

But still, a 'state' seems to Burke to be very much more like
an artificial association, the product of choices, than it is like
a 'natural' phenomenon.

On the other hand, a 'state' seems to him to lack many of
the characteristics of a 'partnership', with its focus upon the
achievement of a premeditated and designed purpose, and
the ease of dissolution whether or not that purpose has been
achieved.

For its members, it is almost as difficult to escape from as a
'natural' community would be. It is something, like a family,
into which we have been born; and it represents ties which it
would be a great exaggeration to say that they were chosen
ties. They are ties which are acquiesced in and acknowledged, rather than made or contracted.

How, then, is thought to escape from this dilemma: 'art' or
'nature', 'choice' or 'necessity'?

What is it (Burke appears to be asking) which is both 'natural' and 'artificial', and which is neither to the exclusion of
the other? For that, it seems to him, is what a 'state' is.

The answer towards which Burke was feeling his way is an
answer in terms of 'history'. For a product of human history
is, like a work of art, the product of human choices; but it is
not the product of an express design. And, also, it is like 'nature' in having the durability and the unavoidable character
we associate with 'nature'.

What analogy offers itself?

Perhaps the analogy of a 'language', or even of a 'landscape'.

A 'landscape', as it opens before our eyes, is (in Europe at
least) a blend of 'nature' and 'art', a blend of the 'necessary'
and the 'chosen', of the 'given' and the 'made', in which the
'given' and the 'made' are indistinguishable. It is the product
of history.

Moreover, like a 'state', a 'landscape' is both stable and
malleable. It is something that provokes neither an attitude
of mere acceptance (because we know we can impose our

designs upon it), nor an attitude of mere rejection (because it cannot be avoided), but an attitude of conditional acceptance.

A 'state' understood in terms of this analogy is neither a god to be worshiped nor a formless chaos to be merely endured. It is something for which we are conditionally responsible. And it suggests that the relations between its members are neither the relations of 'natural' and 'necessary' ties, nor the relations of partners in pursuit of the achievement of specific and chosen utilities, but the relations of those who share a common experience.

8

So far we have been considering the least tangible of the themes of modern European political thought: that which is concerned with the character of a 'state' and the ties which bind its members to one another.

It can't be said that European thought on this matter has reached any single and unmistakable conclusion. How could it?

The idea that a 'state' should be understood as a 'natural' community is represented in contemporary thought most clearly in the notion of 'nationality' as the principle of the collectivity of a 'state'. For whatever reinterpretation in terms of 'history' the idea of 'nationality' has received, it still derives its power from its quasi-natural character.

The idea of a 'state' as an artificial association of human beings united in pursuit of a chosen purpose is most clearly represented in contemporary thought in the notion of a 'state' as an 'economy'. But alongside these two notions there lies the notion of a 'state' as a 'historic' society, the principle of whose collectivity is the long enjoyment of a common experience of living together.

And since each of these interpretations is, in fact, a recommendation about how the members of a state should behave towards one another, it is not surprising that our political behavior, our conduct as members of a modern 'state', is often ambiguous.

At all events, these seem to be the points between which, in this particular matter, the political imagination of modern Europe has ranged.

Editorial Note

LSE 1/1/21, file 5, fos. 440–52. Photocopy of a typescript.

The Authority of Governments and the Obligations of Subjects (1)

1

We have considered some of the beliefs thrown up in modern European thought about the nature of a 'state' as a collectivity of human beings and about the ties which bind the members of a 'state' to one another. This is the first of the great themes of modern European political thought.

I want, the morning, to begin on the second of the great themes; namely, that which is concerned with the bonds which tie a member of a modern European 'state' to his ruler or government.

The relationship here is between ruler and subject, between government and the governed.

The question may be formulated from either of two points of view – that of the ruler, or that of the subject. But, either way, it is the same question.

We may ask: What is the character and the ground of the allegiance a subject owes to his government? Or, we may ask: What is the character and ground of the authority of a government over its subjects? But, at bottom, we are asking the same question.

In considering the answers which have been given to this question in modern times we are seeking the sentiments and beliefs which have gathered themselves round this relationship between rulers and subjects.

And, as with other topics, we must expect reflection on this topic to take place at a variety of levels of thought; from the unmistakably practical level to the philosophical level.

At the bottom of this scale of thought the question appears in the simple form: To whom do I owe my loyalty, and why?

This is an intensely practical question. To be without an answer to it has often been, in modern Europe, the prelude to civil war. Indeed, all civil wars are to be recognized as conflicts between competing claimants to authority, or as confessions that we are uncertain about our loyalties.

But what this practical question demands in answer is often nothing more than a means of identifying authority and some plausible reason for regarding it as authoritative.

And when we turn to the philosophers (like, for example, Hobbes, or Green) the question is the same, but the answer is given at a much higher level of generality. The answer becomes a genuine 'theory' of political obligation.

I shall hope to say something about what has been thought in modern times at various different levels of reflection, but most of it will be concerned with a middling level where what is demanded is something more than a merely plausible analogy and something less than a fully articulated philosophical 'theory'.

2

Now, it would not be unreasonable to expect to find, among those beliefs about the ties between subjects and governments, some which seem to correspond to the beliefs we have already considered about the ties between the members themselves of a 'state'.

And at certain points there is a correspondence of this sort.

For example, just as it has been thought that the tie between the members of a 'state' is a contractual tie (the belief that a 'state' is a 'partnership' or 'association'), so it has been believed that the tie between ruler and subject is a contractual tie.

Further, if a 'state' is thought of on the analogy of a 'family', it would seem appropriate to think of the allegiance of subject to ruler on the analogy of child to parent.

But, in general, it may be said that no understanding of the ties which bind the members of a 'state' to one another necessarily carries with it any particular understanding of the ties which bind a subject to his ruler.

We are, then, embarked on a genuinely different theme from the theme of the nature of a 'state.' The two themes coincide only in the belief (held by very few in modern times) that nothing binds the members of a 'state' to one another save their common obligations to their ruler.

And I want to say something, first, about the question we are now to consider.

3

The first, and most important, thing to notice is that our question concerns the *right* of a ruler to rule, and the *duty* of a subject to obey.

The question being asked is *not*: Why, in fact, do I submit to those who rule me' or, Why do I, on occasion, feel disinclined to submit?

It is the question: Why *ought* I to submit? or, What would absolve me from my *duty* to submit? or, By what *authority* does a ruler rule?

This is a peculiar sort of question; its logic is the logic of *right*, not the logic of *fact*.

Thus, there are a number of things which might, quite correctly, be said about governments and their relation to their subjects, but which are not relevant to this question of *right*.

The authority of a government is nothing to do with the power (*potentia*) it disposes of.

The power of a government is its ability to compel obedience to its commands; and, if it is a modern government, this power is certain to be very great and may be overwhelming.

But the power of a government to compel submission is not the same thing as its right to be obeyed. And the absence of power to compel submission is not to be identified with the absence of a right to be obeyed.

In other words, force may get obedience, but it cannot establish a right to be obeyed.

The right of a government to rule cannot be made to rest upon the fact that it does things which I find agreeable, or does things which I approve of and think it ought to do.

Nor, conversely, may the right of a government to rule be denied on the grounds that it has failed to do certain things which I would like it to do, or things which I think it ought to do.

In short, no government may be said to have authority in virtue of what it does, or not to have authority because of what it has not done.

Let me put it like this:

A ruler who has power and exercises it to compel submission, but who has no right to be obeyed, is called (in the vocabulary of European politics) a tyrant. He is a 'usurper' – a man who may have power but has no right.

But a 'usurper' cannot acquire a right to rule merely by pleasing his subjects – that is, in virtue of what he may do. By this means he may acquire the compliance of his subjects and the reputation of being a not disagreeable ruler. But, whatever he does, he must always remain, by definition, a ruler who has no right to rule.

The authority of a statute (that is, the duty of a judge to enforce it and my duty to comply with it) does not derive from what the statute commands or forbids; it does not have more authority if I approve of what it commands and less if I disapprove.

Its authority derives from something quite different; namely, from the manner in which it was made – from the fact that it is a statute properly so-called.

Or again, a man who has a right cannot be deprived of it merely by denying him what he has a right to.

If, as a pedestrian, I have a right to cross the road, the motorist who runs me down does not deprive me of my right, he merely deprives me of my life. And the fact that he has not deprived me of my right is demonstrated when my widow recovers damages from him.

In short, the right, or the authority, of a government to rule is a question, not about its power or about its activities, but about its constitution.

If you ask the question: By what right does this government rule? the answer *must* be, not in terms of what it does, has done, or may be expected to do, but only in terms of the manner in which it is understood to be constituted.

Now, it is important to understand that this does not mean that *any* question we ask about the constitution of a government is a question about its authority.

We may, and often do, consider the constitutions of governments from many different points of view. And by the constitution of a government I mean, not necessarily a written document, but the manner in which it has been constituted, composed, got together, appointed, established, or has succeeded to the office.

We may, for example, consider a constitution from the point of view of its efficiency, its costliness, or its aptitude for doing the sort of thing we approve of.

But if we do consider the constitution of a government from any of these points of view, we are *not* considering it from the point of view of the right of the government to rule.

In short, if we are inquiring into the authority of a government we are always inquiring into its constitution; but if we are inquiring into the constitution of a government we are not necessarily inquiring into its authority – we may be inquiring merely into its efficiency.

And it may be noticed that, in modern times, attempts to change the manner in which a government is constituted have usually sprung from a belief that the constitution to be changed conflicted with current beliefs about authority.

The American revolution sprang from the belief that the government in Westminster had no authority over the colonists, not from any objection to what the government in Westminster was doing. What was asserted was, not that tea should not be taxed, but that 'taxation without representation' was not legitimate, or rightful.

Kant believed that a republican government (that is, a government constituted in a certain manner) was the only government 'upon which *rightful* legislation' could be based.

Bentham believed in some sort of representative constitution for a government because he believed that only a government constituted in this manner had a *right* to rule.

Even so banal a question as that of the reform of the House of Lords goes back in the end to a consideration of the extent to which its present constitution conflicts with our current beliefs about the right to be a participant in ruling.

The limitations imposed upon it by the Parliament Act were limitations on its right to participate in legislation; and they were defended by arguments designed to show that, in virtue of its present constitution, its right to participate in legislation ought to be limited.

Now, the point I have been emphasizing is that the question of the authority of a government, or of its right to rule, is a unique kind of question, not to be confused with any other. And, in particular, it is not to be confused with other sorts of questions which may be asked about the way in which a government is constituted, or with questions about what a government actually does or commands to be done.

This is worth emphasizing because, as it happens, one of the most important families of political beliefs in modern times has almost systematically obscured it: I mean what is called 'liberalism', in its general or European sense.

Among much else, the 'liberal' was a man who was disposed to judge governments almost entirely from the point of view of what they did, or what they failed to do, or of the manner in which they did whatever they did.

He believed that what mattered was whether or not a government was a 'good' government; and that any government was to be counted 'good' which promoted what he understood to be the 'common good' of the society.

Thus, he thought of governments in terms of whether or not they were 'oppressive', or competent, or indolent, or overactive, etc. And, so far, his position was secure: these are things which may properly be thought about.

But, unfortunately, when the 'liberal' came to the question of the authority of government, its right to rule, he thought he had already answered it by what he had said about a 'good' government. And this was a mistake in logic.

In short, in the doctrines of 'liberalism', the terms 'oppressor' and 'usurper' were apt to be confused with one another. But they are really quite different characters. An 'oppressor' is a man who may have a right to rule, but rules badly; a 'usurper' or tyrant is a man who has no right to rule however well he may happen to rule.

4

The question of the authority of a government to rule and of the duty of a subject to obey is, then, a unique kind of question; and it is an important question in any circumstances.

In connection with a modern European 'state' it is a more than usually important question.

A modern European 'state' was often a new creation. The frontiers of its territories were new, its component members were people who had had other loyalties and who had never before belonged together, and often its ruler was new.

In these circumstances the question: To whom do I owe my loyalty and why? became a question which could not be brushed aside as of marginal practical importance.

Modern European governments are, in general, very powerful. Consequently, to have a means of distinguishing between power and authority, between force and right, is much more important than it would be if we had to do with governments which have very little power. With very powerful governments we feel we need, above all, to know their authority to rule.

Modern European governments came to claim what was called 'sovereign' authority. And to have some acceptable beliefs about authority is much more important when you are faced with a claim of this sort than when you are faced with a much smaller claim.

Whatever was believed about the ties which bound one member of a 'state' to another, it was obvious that the solidarity of a 'state' depended to a very large extent on its government, and thus on what was believed about the *authority* of its government. For this belief alone, of all the beliefs one may have about a government, is a cohesive belief.

Approval of what a government does, of its policies, is a divisive force in a 'state', because nothing that any government does can ever meet with universal approval. If there is to be cohesion, it must come from common beliefs about its authority to rule.

5

We are, then, concerned with the beliefs and sentiments which have been entertained and found acceptable in modern times about the right, or the authority, of a ruler to rule, and the duty of a subject to obey or to comply.

What are they?

On the threshold of modern times we are met with a belief, inherited from the middle ages, but transformed by modern thought: the belief that all authority exercised by man over man comes from God. *Omne potestas est a Deo.*

The ground of this belief was the view that a man in authority is a man who has the right to be obeyed; and that since all rights come from God, and all duties are owed to God, the right of a man to be obeyed by other men must come from God.

There is no doubt that, in early times, this belief was not intended to magnify human authority; rather the reverse.

It expressed the profoundly held belief that for a man to have authority over other men was so 'unnatural' a thing that it could not be imagined to be rightful unless it had been ordained or permitted by God.

Even the authority of a father over his children (which the Romans thought of as a 'natural' authority) was turned, in Christian thought, into an authority derived from God.

In respect of the authority of a civil ruler over his subjects, this belief (that his right to rule came from God) was never more than one component of the family of beliefs which medieval people were apt to hold on this topic. But it was a very important component.

It is the belief referred to whenever a king was held to rule *Dei gratia*, 'by divine appointment'.

But the belief which emerged in the sixteenth and seventeenth centuries, and which remained the most effective belief about political authority until the nineteenth century, was an elaboration of this medieval belief.

It appeared in various versions. Sometimes it was related to things, but it was a doctrine about the authority of governments which was applied to a great many different sorts (indeed, all sorts) of ruling authority.

Its central idea is that a government which has a right to rule must be one which can be shown (or can be believed) to have derived its authority from God. Or, conversely, the idea that the duty of subjects to obey their rulers derives from the divine commission to rule held by rulers.

This belief has appeared in modern times in two somewhat different forms.

6

Since modern European 'states' began almost everywhere with monarchical governments, the first version of this belief we should consider is that in which it was applied to kings.

It came to be called the doctrine of the divine hereditary right of kings to rule.

Now, this belief no doubt contained many reminiscences of primitive notions about the sanctity of monarchs which remained effective even in modern times: kings were the 'Lord's anointed'.

But it was very far from being a mere superstition. It was a serious attempt to understand political authority in a manner appropriate to a modern 'state'.

How could a king, an ordinary man like other men, be understood to have a right to rule?

The answer that he derives it from God and that he has a divine hereditary right to rule was designed to replace, or to outflank, two other current answers, both of which seemed to be destructive of the order of a modern 'state'.

(1) The first of the answers to which this belief was opposed was that a king's authority to rule his subjects was derived from the pope's authority to rule all Christendom – an authority which, itself, was believed to come from God.

This was a view of civil authority which had been emerging in the fifteenth century. But it was clearly opposed to that 'sovereign' independence which was the mark of a modern European 'state'.

Thus, to claim divine authority for a king was a way of claiming autonomy for a 'state'.

(2) The second answer to which a belief in the divine hereditary authority of kings was opposed was the belief that a king's authority was derived from his subjects, who (of course) were held to derive *their* authority from God.

This doctrine was rejected because it seemed to be no answer at all to the question: Whence comes the authority of a king? and also because it seemed to be destructive of the internal order of a 'state'.

It might be a good answer to the question: Where does a king get his power from? But it was no answer at all to the question: Where does a king get his authority from?

What could it mean to say that the subjects of a king have a right to rule which, individually or collectively, they could hand over to a king?

It could mean one of two things, both of which seemed absurd.

First, it could mean that every man had a God-given right to rule all his fellows, a right which he could hand over to a king. This was obviously absurd.

Secondly, it could mean that each man had a God-given right to rule himself, which he could hand over to a king.

This was not so obviously absurd, and it was a belief which was later elaborated (by Hobbes, for example) into an alternative doctrine of civil authority. But, for the adherents of the doctrine of divine right, it had insuperable difficulties.

There seemed to be no imaginable process by which each man could permanently divest himself of his right to rule himself. And if he did not permanently divest himself of this right, his duty to obey his ruler would remain always a matter of his own choice – that is, no *duty* at all, but a mere inclination.

Thus, those who rejected both these views, as self-contradictory or as destructive of the order of a modern 'state,' were left (in the case of monarchy) with the belief that a king's right to rule must have been acquired directly from God.

And their main task was to find reasons to support this belief.

The belief in the divine hereditary right of kings to rule their subjects emerged towards the end of the sixteenth century. It is a doctrine, whatever its medieval reminiscences, intimately connected with modern European 'states'.

It emerged first in France, where the doctrine of kingship *Dei gratia* had always been strong.

It was commonly held in England in the seventeenth century among the 'royalists', and later among the Jacobites. And it remained an exceedingly influential view in Europe until the late nineteenth century.

It was the common belief among the 'legitimists' in France and in Spain; and it was understood to be the ground of the authority of the emperor or Austria and the Czar of Russia even into the twentieth century.

It was a genuinely 'popular' belief – that is, a belief which, for ordinary people, seemed to answer an important practical question: Who has authority over me, and why?

But, of course, it was greatly elaborated by writers, and was turned by them into a quasi-philosophical doctrine.

In the sixteenth century it was elaborated by William Barclay in *De regno et regale potestate* (1600) as an argument against the supreme authority of the pope.

In the seventeenth century it was taken up by James I in *The Trew Law of Free Monarchies*, as an argument against popular consent as the ground of a king's right to rule.

It is the doctrine to be found in Bodin (*The Six Books of the Republic*), Filmer (*Patriarcha*, 1681), and in Bossuet (*Politique tirée des propres paroles de l'ecriture sainte*). And each of these writers supplies marginally different reasons for holding this belief.

The doctrine, of course, was a severe one, entailing the belief that to disobey a legitimate king was equivalent to disobeying God.

But it never entailed the view that a king was a 'despot'. Indeed, it was an argument against 'despotism'. A 'despot' is a ruler who derives his authority to rule from his ownership of the territory he rules and of all who live on that territory. His authority is 'seigneurial', that of 'lordship'. A king by divine right has quite a different sort of relationship with his subjects.

The main feature of this doctrine of divine right which carried it beyond anything to be found in medieval belief was the hereditary feature. This was understood to be an emblem of the immunity of a king's authority from any dependence upon popular consent or papal approval.

But this hereditary feature was a matter of convenience rather than principle. To succeed to the office of king by lawful descent from a previously legitimate monarch was a device which served several important uses.

It was a way of avoiding a disputed succession. And it left less room for serious doubt about where a subject's loyalty lay. It was a means by which to identify a legitimate ruler, rather than part of the definition of a legitimate ruler.

But this belief in the divine hereditary right of a king to rule was, of course, convincing only with a certain view of the world. Within this view, which actually prevailed in Europe (though not without competitors) until quite recent times, it was a reasoned and reasonable belief. It really did, so far as logic is concerned, provide an answer for the question: Whence comes the authority of a king?

7

But the belief in the divine hereditary right of a king to rule was by no means the only version in modern times of the belief that civil authority derives from God and that the duty of a subject to obey his ruler is a duty to God.

The two other important versions of this belief are to be found in the writings of John Calvin, and in the doctrines of some of the English Puritans of the seventeenth century.

(1) We have seen that, for Calvin and for Protestants who thought like him, a 'state' was an association of human beings engaged in what was held to be the proper occupation of all human beings; namely, glorifying God. This was the common purpose which united them.

But in every such 'state' there was a ruler of some sort. Calvin called him 'the magistrate'. This ruler is distinguished by having the right to be obeyed by his subjects.

And, as Calvin understood it, this 'magistrate' was a 'minister of God', deriving his authority to rule directly from God.

Of course, in such a 'state' there were also ecclesiastical officers, 'elders', who were also 'ministers of God'. And they, somewhat like the Roman senate, might be said to have the *auctoritas* to guide and to advise in all matters concerning the correct conduct of a Christian man.

But these ecclesiastical officers did not have *potestas*, the right to rule and to be obeyed. This belonged solely to the civil 'magistrate', and he got it straight from God.

There were, however, some difficulties in this view of civil authority.

In the case of a king believed to rule by divine right, there was a ready means of identifying who had been endowed by God with this right; namely, hereditary succession to the office of king.

But this means of identification was lacking for the Calvinist. And it might appear that any man had authority to rule who was so strongly convinced of his mission to represent God that he set himself up as a ruler. This was not at all what Calvin intended. And to correct this misconception of the office of ruler, an elaborate doctrine was evolved.

It ran as follows:

The world was understood to be composed of two orders of being: the order of nature and the order of grace. And the order of grace was understood to be superior to the order of nature.

Grace, therefore, had an absolute right to rule over nature, because it is by means of the rule of grace that the order of nature may be drilled into glorifying God – which is the purpose of all government.

Now, all men, in respect of their corruption, their sinfulness and their propensity to sin, belong to the order of nature. But the two orders are represented in the world by two, quite separate, classes of men: (a) The class of those who are, and must remain, merely 'natural' men, because they are untouched by grace. These are the 'ungodly', or the 'reprobate'. (b) The class of those whom grace has emancipated from bondage to the order of nature. These are the 'elect', or the 'chosen'; and they have been chosen by God.

It follows from this that the 'elect' have an absolute right (given them by God) to rule over the 'reprobate'.

And the mark of those who have this right to rule is neither a legitimate claim to office by hereditary succession, nor is it the behavior of the ruler (what he *does*). It is simply the distinction of belonging to the 'elect' of God.

The right to rule comes from divine 'election'. And this may be called the doctrine of the divine right of the 'elect' by grace to rule.

This doctrine might be applied, and was applied, to a variety of different kinds of government – even to monarchical government.

The so-called 'godly prince' of the sixteenth century was not necessarily a man of saintly life, nor did his authority to rule derive from his virtuous conduct. It derived from the fact that he was held to have been appointed by God.

Thus, in this view of things, all civil authority derived from God.

And those who held the divine commission to rule were not a vague and indistinct class of person, like the 'good', or the 'virtuous', or the 'wise'. They were an absolutely separate class of person: those who belonged to the order of grace.

They were, in short, a spiritual aristocracy, not of birth or blood, but of divine 'election'.

The main defect of this view of civil authority was that it did not provide any easy and unmistakable way of identifying those who had the right to rule.

(2) This doctrine about civil authority spread far and wide from Geneva. It established itself among certain Puritan sects in England in the seventeenth century, where it was called the rule of the saints.

It appeared in connection with the so-called 'parliamentary' government which succeeded to kingly rule after the execution of Charles I. It was one doctrine of the divine right to rule succeeding to another.

But its true character emerged when those who held it revealed that they thought it indecent that rulers should be elected by the votes of the 'reprobate'. Such an 'election' concealed their true character.

They wished to convert Parliament into an assembly of saints. They believed that those who had the right to rule were the 'elect' of God, and had been 'elected' by God, and not by other men.

Indeed, they preferred to see in military victory (which they took to represent divine approval) a sign of their 'election', rather than in the votes of the 'reprobate'.

8

Now, this belief, that the authority of governments derives, in one way or another, from a divine commission to rule, is a genuine belief about the *authority* of governments.

It understands the authority of a government to derive from its 'constitution', and not from anything the government does or commands, or from the physical force it may have at its disposal.

It is an answer to the question: Who is my rightful ruler, and by what right does he rule? which agrees with the idiom of the question.

Its convincingness, of course, depended upon a view of the world which, for the most part, has now disappeared from Western Europe. But, so far as the modern 'states' of Europe are concerned, it has been the most long-lived and successful of all modern beliefs about the authority of governments.

Indeed, it is a belief which has shown itself capable of being translated into idioms which may still be found acceptable to some in the contemporary world.

For example, the belief in the right of the 'proletariat', at least temporarily, to rule may be recognized as an offshoot of the belief that only a divine commission can give a right to rule.

Here, it is true that 'history' has taken the place of God as the 'elector' or authorizer of the ruler. But the belief, in principle, remains the same. And the 'proletariat' has the advantage of the Calvinist 'saints' in being a trifle more easy to identify. And the temporariness of the rule of the 'proletariat' corresponds to the temporariness of the rule of the saints in Puritan theory.

Editorial Note

LSE 1/1/21, file 5, fos. 453–68. Photocopy of a typescript.

The Authority of Governments and the Obligations of Subjects (2)

1

Last week we began to consider the answers which modern European thought had returned to the questions: By what right does a ruler, or a government, rule? And, what is the ground of the duty of a subject to obey, or to submit to rule?

I said something about the general nature of these questions, and I pointed out that, logically, they could not be answered *either* by referring to the power (the physical force) at the disposal of a government, *or* by referring to what a government does, or commands, and our approval or disapproval of what it does.

These questions can be answered only by referring to the constitution or the composition, or the character of a government.

A government has authority only in virtue of the manner in which it is constituted. It has authority if it is constituted in a manner which coincides to current beliefs about how an authoritative government must be constituted.

There is, however, something more to be said about beliefs of this sort.

They are not beliefs which can be proved to be either true or false.

They are pragmatic beliefs, which provide an acceptable answer to the practical questions: Who is my ruler? By what right does he rule? and, Why should I obey?

Whether or not a particular belief does provide an acceptable answer to these questions will depend upon whether it fits in with current beliefs about human beings, and about the world in general.

And one of the reasons why beliefs about the authority of governments have been so variegated and changeable in modern times is because of the changeableness of current beliefs about the world.

Indeed, it is not difficult to find occasions in modern times when there was very great uncertainty about what one could believe in regard to the authority of rulers.

And on such occasions anyone wishing to argue that such and such a ruler had, or had not, authority was obliged to appeal to a variety of beliefs, hoping that his audience would find among them something persuasive and acceptable.

For example, when the House of Commons met in January 1689 to consider the flight of James II, the overwhelming majority believed him to be no longer king of England. They believed he had lost his right to rule.

Their task was to explain this belief to themselves and to the people of England. And they could do so only by appealing to current beliefs about the authority of kings.

But, these current beliefs were so various that the document they produced had to offer a variety of reasons for believing that James II was no longer king.

This is what it said: James II, having endeavored to subvert the constitution of the kingdom by breaking the original contract between king and people, and by the advice of Jesuits and other wicked persons, having violated the fundamental law, and having withdrawn himself from the kingdom, had abdicated the government, and that the throne was now vacant.

Now, here was something for almost everybody. If you didn't believe in an original contract between king and people, then you might be persuaded that James II had lost his authority because he had fled the kingdom, or because he had broken fundamental laws.

What, naturally enough, does *not* appear in this list of reasons is any reference to a divine hereditary right to rule – and it does not appear because, if this were believed to be the basis of his authority, it would be difficult to imagine how he could ever lose his authority, except by dying.

Kings by divine hereditary right can lose their authority only by being disposed of: thus, the execution of Charles I, Louis XVI, and the last Czar of Russia.

But, even then, they may have legitimate successors.

2

Last week we considered the belief that a ruler's or a government's right to rule came from a divine commission to rule.

This is an important belief in modern times; it provided the kind of answer required by the question, By what right does a ruler rule? Its fault is that it could not sustain itself among people who were ceasing to believe all the others things about the world which went with it.

It was not refuted, it could not be refuted; it was left high and dry on a receding tide of belief.

Today, I want to consider some other beliefs on this topic current in modern times.

3

First, let us consider a whole set of beliefs which attributed authority, the *right* to rule, to a government in virtue of its possessing what is represented as some 'natural' quality.

In ancient times, it was frequently believed that the natural quality which gave a man the right to rule was the quality of being old.

I doubt whether this has ever been seriously believed in Europe in modern times, although (as we shall see later) it has been believed that the 'age', or the 'long-standing', of a 'constitution' was, at least, an important *sign* of its authority.

But there are other 'natural' qualities, besides age, which have been held to endow a ruler with authority.

In modern times the most important of them have been: blood, virtue, wisdom, and knowledge.

All these are beliefs about the authority of rulers which have satisfied the demands of ordinary people. And each of them has been written up into a 'doctrine' of some sort, in modern times.

(1) The belief that 'royal', or 'aristocratic', or even 'commoner' blood gives authority to rule has not been absent in modern times. It has even been believed that certain 'races' (defined in terms of 'blood') have a right to rule.

But, except in the case of 'royalty', beliefs in authority derived from 'blood' are apt to be unsatisfactorily vague or even meaningless.

First, what blood flows in a man's arteries is a very speculative question, especially in modern Europe. To say the least, this is a very uncertain way of identifying those who have a right to rule.

And secondly, when this belief is extended to a large class of persons, or to a 'race', it is clearly an answer to some other question than the question: Who has authority to rule and why?

No large class of person, let alone a whole 'race' has ever, or could ever, exercise *rule*. This might be a belief about whose interests a ruler should serve, but it couldn't be a belief about who should rule.

If there were a 'master race', defined by blood, we should still need to know by what right it is ruled by those who in fact rule it.

In the case of 'royalty', however, the belief that those of 'royal blood' have the right to rule has been a not unimportant belief in modern times – especially in France, where the royal house traced its descent, and its right to rule, from Hugh Capet.

This belief is affiliated to the belief in the divine hereditary right to rule; but, of course, long before modern times 'royal blood' had become a matter of convention, especially in Russia.

Napoleon wished he had 'royal blood', thinking that, if he had it, his authority would be enhanced. And this, indeed, was correct; 'royal blood' was certainly something which his subjects believed to give authority.

(2) It has been believed that virtue and wisdom are the qualities in virtue of which a ruler has the right to rule.

Now, that our rulers should be 'good' and 'wise' is a universal hope. But this hope does not reflect the belief we are considering here.

What we have to consider is the belief, in modern times, that 'virtue' and 'wisdom' are, not merely valuable qualities in rulers, but are the source of their right to rule.

And here, 'virtue' and 'wisdom' are understood to be 'natural' qualities, and not (for example) gifts of God's grace.

The inspiration of this belief in modern times has often been Platonic.

Plato joined 'virtue' and 'wisdom' in such a manner as to make them the inseparable qualifications of rightful rule. It was *because* he was a philosopher that the ruler had authority: if he were not a philosopher he would be, not only an incompetent ruler, but a 'usurper'.

But, often, in modern times this belief has owed nothing to Plato. It has reflected much less well-thought-out beliefs about 'virtue' and 'wisdom'.

In the eighteenth century the qualities of 'virtue' and 'wisdom' which were believed to give the authority to rule were called 'enlightenment'. And this belief was one of the components of what was understood as 'enlightened government'.

The authority of kings (like Frederick the Great of Prussia), imperial rulers (like Catherine of Russia and Joseph II of Austria) was, in the opinion of most of their subjects, based upon an indefeasible, divine, hereditary right to rule.

But they, and the ministers they appointed, liked to appear up-to-date, and often preferred to base their claim to the obedience of their subjects upon what they called their 'enlightenment'.

The 'wise' and the 'enlightened' have a right to rule the 'foolish' and the 'unenlightened': so ran the doctrine.

This belief rears its head whenever it is suggested that the right to rule rests upon superior 'enlightenment', upon the claim that the ruler 'knows best'.

And there have been participants in ruling who have preferred to base their right to rule upon their alleged 'enlightenment' rather than (for example) on their having been elected to their offices.

This belief in the authority of 'virtue' and 'wisdom' is, of course, the stepbrother of the belief that the 'elect of God' have a right to rule; the difference is only that, here, 'enlightenment' is regarded as a 'natural' quality and not an endowment of God's grace.

And it may be noted here that there have been several notable modern political thinkers who have believed that there are more 'enlightened' and less 'enlightened' members of a political society, but who have expressly denied that 'enlightenment' gives a right to rule.

This was the view of both Coleridge and J. S. Mill, and I think also of Bentham. They expressly rejected 'enlightenment' as giving authority to rule.

(3) The belief that the authority to rule derives from 'knowledge', in the sense of 'information', belongs to a somewhat different category of beliefs.

For while 'knowledge' of this sort is not usually thought of as a 'divine endowment', neither is it usually thought of as a 'natural' endowment. It is something acquired.

No doubt, this belief, in modern times, is a reminiscence of very ancient beliefs in which 'rulership' and the possession of 'information' (often of an esoteric kind) were joined.

Tribal rulers were often distinguished from their subjects by what they 'knew'. Often it was a knowledge of ritual, of how things are done, and of the right words to speak. And they were thought to derive their authority from the exclusive possession of this 'knowledge', which was handed on from ruler to ruler.

This belief, in modern times, certainly goes back to a Christian heresy of the third century: the heresy of Gnosticism.

The Gnostics were a Christian sect who believed that there was a body of information about the world, mysterious and difficult to acquire, which gave, not merely 'power', but also authority to those who possessed it.

And this belief in the authority of *gnosis* has never been far under the surface of modern European beliefs of this sort. It is, for example, only just under the surface of some of the beliefs of Karl Marx.

But, in modern times, the 'knowledge' which has been believed to give a right to rule has not, usually, been 'esoteric' (that is, secret) knowledge; it has been what is called 'scientific' knowledge.

And the belief that the possession of 'scientific' knowledge gives the right to rule has had considerable vogue in modern times.

It appears in the writings of Francis Bacon, in the sixteenth century. It has been written up into elaborate doctrines. It forms a not insignificant component of the beliefs of such writers as Comte and Marx.

And, in recent times, our political vocabulary has been enriched by the word 'meritocracy' – meaning the right of those who have 'merit' (usually thought of as an intellectual quality) to rule.

Now, what those who have held, or who have promoted, beliefs of these sorts about the authority of rulers are saying is that the relationship of ruler to subject is to be understood as like the relationship of:

- the old to the young

- the parent to the child
- the virtuous to the vicious
- the wise to the foolish
- the enlightened to the unenlightened
- the informed to the ignorant.

We are all aware of the kind of relationship which properly subsists between people of these various sorts. And what is being said here is that a relationship of this sort should be understood to subsist between rulers and ruled, and that the possession of these qualities is the source of a ruler's authority to rule.

The weakness of this way of understanding political authority is that it is always on the verge of being irrelevant.

'Virtue', 'wisdom', 'enlightenment', 'knowledge', appear in how a ruler behaves, in what he *does*. But, we have seen, the question: By what right does a ruler rule? can be properly answered only in terms of the character or the 'constitution' of a ruler or government.

If my obligation to obey depended upon the 'virtue' or the 'enlightenment' of my rulers, it would not be a duty, but merely a matter of opinion.

And a subject could claim to be absolved from his duty to obey on the ground that, in his opinion, the ruler was 'foolish', or 'misinformed', or 'unenlightened'.

(4) This would seem to be the place to notice the beliefs which, in modern times, have centred round the view that the right to rule belongs to what is called an 'elite'.

This has never been a view with any great popular appeal. It is the child of the so-called 'intellectual'. But it has had a considerable impact upon the political experience of modern Europe, particularly in recent times.

Some who have held it have spoken of such an 'elite' as a 'ruling class', and this has led to an important confusion.

An 'elite' is not a 'class', in the 'social' sense. And a 'social' class (such as a 'nobility'), when it has been thought to have the right to rule, has never been thought of, and has never thought of itself, as an 'elite'.

Plato's 'guardians' are an 'elite' in the proper sense. The Japanese samurai and the Russian boyars were not 'elites', they were 'nobilities' who claimed no superiority but of 'blood'.

Perhaps the best know writer to understand the authority to rule as belonging to an 'elite', properly speaking, is Vilfredo Pareto, an Italian who died in 1923.

There have, of course, been a great many others. And talk about 'elites' occupies a large place in current nonsense.

Pareto believed that ordinary men were incapable of rational behavior. Their conduct is determined by what he called 'residual beliefs', which are little better than primitive superstitions.

Consequently, they have no reliable knowledge about their needs or where their 'welfare' lies. They are ignorant of themselves and of the world in which they live.

They have to be 'ruled'.

There are, however, some who have emancipated themselves from this condition. And in virtue of this emancipation they are both powerful and have a right to rule.

Their 'rule' consists of getting obedience by playing upon the superstitious beliefs of their ignorant subjects.

But, although this belief in an 'elite' appears to answer the question: Who has the right to rule?, in fact it is no answer at all. And, it is fair to say that what Pareto himself believed about his 'elite' was only that they were a set of men who, in virtue of their superior knowledge, were actually powerful. They composed what is now often called a 'power elite'. But, as we have seen, power cannot give right.

In short, what Pareto has to say may be a plausible belief about the nature of 'good', or 'efficient', government – the rule of an 'elite' equipped to control irrational subjects. But it tells us noting whatever about the right to rule, or about the obligation to obey.

Plato believed that the 'rational' man, the 'philosopher', had a right to rule the 'irrational' man, because he believed that 'reason' had a right to rule 'unreason'.

But for Pareto, and most of the so-called 'elitists', the sole significant thing about an 'elite' is that it is powerful in virtue of its acquired mental characteristics.

4

So far, we have considered two different beliefs about the authority of governments: (1) the belief that the authority to rule is a divine endowment; (2) the belief that the authority to rule is a 'natural' endowment.

But modern European thought has other beliefs to show.

And I want to consider next the belief that the authority to rule is an endowment which the ruler gets from his subjects.

This is clearly a belief about the constitution of a ruler, and so it may be a belief about his authority.

This belief, as it appears in connection with the government of a modern European 'state,' has, like other beliefs on this topic, reminiscences of earlier beliefs.

We noticed the common belief of the ancient Romans that the *potestas* of a ruler, his right to rule, was the endowment of the *populus Romanus* itself.

A consul, or even an emperor, was held to have a right to rule because he had been given it by his subjects. And there were ceremonies, elections, and acclamations which were thought of as occasions when this endowing of a ruler with authority took place.

Similarly, there is an important strain in medieval thought which attributes the ruler's right to rule to a gift from his subjects.

This belief, no doubt, was, in part, a reflection of the manner in which the office of king emerged in the middle ages. A king was the creation of his peers; and his authority to rule them was something they had endowed him with.

It is fair to say that, in medieval Europe, this belief never stood alone. It was usually combined (however inconsistently) with other beliefs, such as the belief that a king's authority was *Dei gratia*. But it was one of the contributing beliefs to the modern view that the authority of a government was a gift from its subjects.

Calling upon reminiscences of these earlier beliefs, what emerged in early modern European history was the belief that the authority of a ruler was derived from the consent of his subjects; or (to put it another way) the belief that the relationship between ruler and subject was a relationship of compact, or contract, between the two.

The circumstances in which this belief emerged are interesting. It was often a belief promoted by religious dissidents (Catholic or Protestant) who were anxious to absolve themselves from the duty of allegiance to a ruler intent upon imposing upon all his subjects a religious confession which they abhorred.

In its modern form, the belief that the authority of a ruler was an endowment of his subjects was, indeed, the invention of Jesuit writers, designed to undermine the authority of Protestant princes.

It became, however, a popular, operative belief; and it seemed to many the best answer available to the question: Whence comes the right of a ruler to rule?

After it had, first, been used in connection with the authority of a king to rule, it was, perhaps, more plausibly, used to elucidate the authority of other sorts of government.

And the idea developed hand in hand with the development of methods of constituting governing authorities which could, on this principle, be believed to be authoritative.

From it emerged what may be said to be the two principles of modern 'democratic' government: for the word 'democracy', in one of its meanings, signifies a belief about the way in which a government which can be recognized to have the right to rule is constituted.

These two principles are: (a) that only a government constituted in a certain manner, a manner which may be plausibly taken to suggest the consent of its subjects, has the right to rule; (b) that there is a known and a recognized manner of constituting a government which has the right to rule; and this manner includes specific and periodic occasions when a government is, in fact, endowed by its subjects with a right to rule, in processes spoken of as 'election' or 'appointment'.

Now, the power of this belief, that the authority of rulers derives from the consent of their subjects, its ability to give a convincing and acceptable answer to the questions: Who is my ruler? and, Where did he get the right to rule?, depends very much upon its vagueness.

We must exclude, of course, the notion that what requires the consent of its subjects is the individual actions of a government: this was never part of the belief.

But when we have excluded this, the notions of authority derived from 'consent', or from 'approval', or from an 'agreement', or a 'compact', are the most difficult of all notions to work with.

All known meanings of giving 'consent', all known means of becoming a 'representative', have a very large element of arbitrariness in their composition: arbitrary occasions, arbitrary constituencies, arbitrary methods of voting, and so on.

And, unless a distinction is made between 'individual choice' and the 'consent' necessary to give a government authority, the belief will certainly collapse.

No modern government has ever been the 'choice' of all its subjects; no modern government has ever had the approval of all its subjects. And yet all modern governments have claimed authority over all their subjects. How can their authority be said to derive from 'consent'?

It is not, then, surprising that so vague and difficult a belief as this should have provoked immense efforts on the part of political writers to elucidate it and to make it intelligible as a belief about the authority of a government to rule.

You will find in Hobbes's *Leviathan* a profound and philosophical attempt to understand the authority of government as springing from the consent of its subjects.

But the examples of writing in this idiom I want to notice are those provided by Locke and Rousseau.

5

Locke understood a 'state' to be a collection of human beings, united by a common obligation to obey the law of nature, which had composed themselves, by agreement, into an 'artificial' association, under a civil government.

This civil government has authority to make laws, and conduct the affairs of the 'state'. Where does it get this authority from?

Locke's answer is that it is endowed with this authority by its subjects, by their express or by their tacit consent.

But what is more important is Locke's view of what the authority of a government is. It is the authority of a 'trustee'.

Ruling is a 'trust'; and the relationship of a ruler to his subjects is *like* that of a 'trustee' to the beneficial owner of an estate.

Now, this was a notion of considerable subtlety. It was designed to get over some of the obvious difficulties inherent in the naive understanding of the authority of a ruler based upon a 'contract' or 'compact' entered into by ruler and subjects.

The difference between a 'contract' and a 'trust' is that, in a 'contract' both parties have interests to secure, both are beneficiaries, whereas, in a 'trust', the 'trustee' is not a beneficiary; he is merely an agent with no independent interest of his own.

A 'trustee' has the duty of administering an estate according to the conditions of the 'trust'; if he fails in this duty, he may be dismissed. But while he remains the 'trustee' he, and no one else, has the right to administer the 'trust'.

The authority of a government, according to Locke's way of thinking, was the authority of a 'trustee', and it gets it by a revokable appointment.

Locke, then, was concerned to recommend a way of thinking about the authority of a government which displays this government as deriving its authority from its subjects.

His chief concern was to interpret the authority of a ruler in such a way that it could be understood as revokable by his subjects, in certain circumstances.

For Locke, then, it was enough to persuade his audience that the authority of a government was such that it could be revoked by its subjects – which, of course, would be impossible if its authority were either a divine or a 'natural' endowment.

But Rousseau wished to go further. He wants to persuade his audience that the decisions and actions of a government are rightful and worthy to be obeyed only if they embody the will (and not merely the 'consent') of its subjects.

For Rousseau, an acceptable government must satisfy three conditions:

- It must have authority; it must have a right to be obeyed and not merely the power to enforce compliance.
- It must be constituted in such a way that its right to rule is known to be derived from its subjects.
- It must operate in such a way that what it does may be understood to be the will of its subjects.

The satisfaction of these conditions, Rousseau finds in what he called the 'general will'. A government which represents the 'general will' alone has the right to rule.

The positive content of this idea of the authority of governments is exceedingly complicated, and it would be grossly misleading to try to abridge it.

But its general character may be seen in what Rousseau rejects.

- The 'natural' will of a man has no authority over another man. No man's 'natural' will has a right to be obeyed.
- No mere collection of 'natural' wills has authority. And this is true whether the collection of 'natural wills' represents a minority, a majority, or even the total of a society.

- Therefore, the only will that has a right to be obeyed is an 'artificial' will.

This 'artificial' will, the 'general will', is a will which each man recognizes as his own will, and in which all conflicts between 'natural' wills have been overcome.

It must be confessed that the generation of this 'general will', as Rousseau describes it, is something of a miracle.

But it should be noticed that at least Rousseau keeps to the rules which govern argument about the authority of rulers.

He knows that the questions: Who is my rightful ruler? and, Why ought I to obey him? *must* be answered in terms of the constitution of the ruling authority.

And his so-called 'theory' of the 'general will' is a description of the way in which a government with the right to rule may be constituted.

6

We have considered a variety of beliefs, current in modern times, about the authority of governments.

- Divine commission, connected with hereditary succession to authority or divine election.
- Natural endowment; blood, virtue, wisdom, knowledge, merit, etc.
- The consent of the governed, variously understood and connected with beliefs about 'election' and 'representation' as the manner in which a rightful government may be constituted.

But these beliefs do not quite exhaust what has been thought and said on this topic in modern times.

There are two other important beliefs which I must say something about next week.

Editorial Note

LSE 1/1/21, file 5, fos. 469–83. Photocopy of a typescript.

The Authority of Governments and the Obligations of Subjects (3)

1

I want this morning to explore some of the other directions which modern European thought about the authority of governments has taken.

(1) Every government has power (*potentia*): a certain degree of ability to get its demands complied with.

This power may be very great. For practical purposes it may be said to be 'overwhelming' if it is always enough to overcome whatever resistance it meets. But it can never, properly, be said to be 'absolute' because it is always finite.

When we speak of 'absolute' governments we are not referring to their power but to something else. Indeed, in modern Europe rulers who have been called 'absolute' have often been notable for their comparatively small resources of power.

The power of a government is like the weight of an object: it is simply a function of the resistance it is capable of overcoming. It does not depend upon the recognition or acknowledgment of those upon whom it is exerted.

This common feature of governments has provoked inquiries of various sorts, which have resulted in 'understandings', or 'theories', about how governments of different kinds acquire and exercise their power. The word 'bureaucracy', for example, is a word which signifies a particular manner of organizing the exertion of power.

Indeed, this is so notable a feature of governments, especially of modern governments, that it has sometimes been considered to be, not only their most interesting feature, but the only feature to be taken account of.

Thus, 'states', under their governments, have been recognized simply as 'power systems'; and politics itself has been thought of as nothing more than the 'science of power'.

(2) This, however, is a mistake. For, in addition to their character as 'systems of power', 'states' are 'systems of authority'. And, in addition to inquiring into the *potentia* at the disposal of a government, we may also inquire into its 'authority' to govern.

And this is a different inquiry, because the 'authority' of a ruler to rule is not a function of the *potentia* he has at his disposal; it is a matter of his *right* to rule, his right to use whatever *potentia* he may have.

How, then, may we distinguish unmistakably between a ruler's power and a ruler's right?

A ruler's power, we have seen, does not depend upon the recognition or the acknowledgment of his subjects. But a ruler's right to rule, his 'authority', depends entirely upon the recognition or the acknowledgment of his subjects.

'Authority', or 'right', is something 'attributed' to a ruler; it is something believed about him. And if he is not believed to have 'authority', then he quite certainly has not got it.

An inquiry into the power of a ruler is an inquiry into his ability to compel obedience to his commands; it is an inquiry into what *causes* him to be able to overcome resistance: e.g. 'he has the maxim gun and we have not'.

But an inquiry into the right of a ruler to rule is an attempt to find convincing *reasons* why 'authority' is attributed to him. Or, alternatively, it is an attempt to find convincing *reasons* for believing that we have an obligation, or a duty, to obey.

Power does not have 'reasons'; right does not have a 'cause'.

'Authority', unlike power, is, then, a matter of opinion or belief; and consequently it makes sense to ask: What *reasons* can be given for holding the belief that, for example, Charles I has a right to rule?

(3) Nevertheless, although 'power' and 'authority' are quite different from one another, there is some sort of relation between the two.

It is a one-way relation, which reflects and emphasizes the difference.

No amount of 'power', however great, can give 'authority'; and no defect of 'power' can constitute a defect of 'authority'. But to be acknowledged to have 'authority' may, and probably will, itself generate some 'power'.

For, to acknowledge a man to have 'authority' is to believe that he *ought* to be obeyed. And subjects who believe that they *ought* to obey are subjects already disposed to obey, although they may not always do so. This decrease in resistance is an increase in the power of whoever is believed to have authority.

The actual power, its effectiveness, of a police force is increased wherever there is a widespread belief that its control is legitimate and ought to be complied with.

But this is by-the-way; and it does nothing to approximate 'power' to 'authority'. It is merely the observation that a belief in 'authority' is likely to be one of the *causes* of power.

2

Inquiries into 'authority' usually begin by being inquiries into the 'authority' for an act or a command. On a particular occasion what I may want to know is: on what 'authority' has the command been given or the act done.

Such inquiries usually reveal a hierarchy of authorities each 'authorized' by a higher authority. For much of the way they take the form of 'legal' inquiries, and refer to successive legal authorizations: e.g. an action is authorized by a bylaw, which is authorized by a statute, which is authorized by a parliament.

But there will come a point when we are obliged to break out of this legal frame of inquiry, because what is sought is a reason for believing that a government has the right to rule. This is the realm of *political* thought, properly so called.

Now, this reason for a belief in the 'authority' of a government must always be given in terms of the constitution of the government about which the inquiry is being made.

A government can never have the right to rule in virtue of its power, or of the agreeableness of what it does, but only in virtue of the manner in which it is constituted, composed or got together.

And a government will be acknowledged to have the right to rule, 'authority' will be attributed to it, if the manner in which it has been composed or got together accords with beliefs about what constitutes 'authority'.

Thus, each of the words in our political vocabulary which signify a form of government stands for (1) a government constituted in a certain manner; each of them may, and usually does, (2) indicate some belief about its authority; and each, in addition, usually signifies (3) an approval or acknowledgment of this authority.

The expression 'democratic government', for example, signifies a government got together in a certain process – shall we say, a process of election.

It signifies, also, a government whose 'authority' to rule is believed to stem from its having been got together in this way.

And further, this expression very often signifies recognition that this belief in what constitutes an 'authoritative' government is approved and is acceptable.

Thus to say: 'This government is not a democratic government', usually means both that this government has not been got together in a process of election, and that, because of this defect, it cannot be recognized to have the right to rule.

And if I were asked to go further and give reasons for my belief that 'authority' is properly attributable only to a government got together in a process of election, I might say something like this:

> In my opinion, the only good reason for attributing to a government a right to rule is because it has the 'consent' of its subjects, and I recognize the process of election as one in which this 'consent' is given.

In the end, then, 'authority' is something attributed to a government in virtue of the manner in which it is got together or composed, and the attribution rests on some general belief about what constitutes a right to rule.

So far, we have seen that modern European political reflection has thrown up two substantial beliefs about what constitutes a right to rule: (1) a divine commission; (2) the 'consent' of its subjects.

And each of these general beliefs has been elaborated by political philosophers whose business it is to find the best reasons they can for holding the beliefs that they do.

3

But, besides the words and expressions which signify forms of government, and usually indicate also some belief about their 'authority', our political vocabulary has other words designed to signify *pseudo* forms of government and to indicate that, because they are *pseudo*, they are devoid of any right to rule. They are *merely* 'power systems' with no 'authority'.

For example, the words 'tyranny' and 'usurpation'.

A 'tyrant', or a 'usurper', is a man who occupies the office of ruler but who, because of the manner in which he has come to that office, has no right to rule.

His lack of a right to rule may be because the way in which he has come to office conflicts with all known beliefs about ways in which a ruler may acquire 'authority', or it may be because he has come to office in a way which would, perhaps, at one time have been recognized as legitimate but is no longer so.

Thus, the Romans, after they had thrown out the Etruscan kings, branded them as 'tyrants'; Milton called Charles I a 'tyrant'; and the American colonists (or some of them) spoke of the government at Westminster as a 'tyranny' in relation to themselves.

4

But the political vocabulary of modern Europe has another word, used in connection with the authority of governments, which is quite unlike any other: the word 'despotism'.

At first sight, it looks to be like the word 'tyranny' – a word signifying a government which has no right to rule because the manner in which it has established itself conflicts with all the current beliefs about 'authority'.

But, in fact, it means something different. In the political vocabulary of modern Europe, a 'despot' is not a man devoid of 'authority'; he is a man who has a sort of 'authority' inappropriate for the ruler of a modern European 'state'.

Now, the peculiar 'authority' of a 'despot' was, as it happens, the sort of 'authority' out of which the kinds of 'authority' believed to be appropriate to the ruler of a modern state emerged. And it is the sort of 'authority' back into which the 'authority' of the ruler of a modern state has shown some tendency to relapse. Hence, the expression 'despotic authority' has a special, and somewhat ambiguous, place in our political language.

The word 'despot' is, of course, derived from the Greek word *despotes*. For Aristotle and his contemporaries, *despotes* meant a man whose 'authority' to rule was based upon his ownership of what he ruled – territory and subjects alike. And it was thought by the Greeks to be a sort of government characteristic of parts of Asia, but one that conflicted with the idea of a *polis*.

In other words, if one had been asked to give a reason for believing that the king of Persia had a right to rule his subjects, it would be: because he owns them and the land on which they live.

And, in giving advice to Alexander, Aristotle recommends him to behave like a *hegemon* (that is, a 'leader' of free men) to the conquered Greeks, but to behave like a *despotes* to the conquered barbarians, because this was their notion of political authority.

The corresponding Latin words were *dominus* and *dominium*; they stood for the right to rule based upon ownership of what is ruled.

Now, in early medieval times, the most significant relation which emerged from the chaos was that between a man and the land which he owned and the people who lived on that land and cultivated it.

These people were of various sorts. Some servile and others occupying land on different sorts of tenancies. But they were all *his* people, the suitors at his court. They owed him services and he owed them protection.

In short, he had 'authority' over them, not merely power, and his 'authority' was recognized to derive from his ownership. This 'authority' was called *dominium*; 'lordship' in English, and *seigneurie* in French.

It was from this situation, a situation in which the accepted belief about 'authority' was that it derived from ownership, that a new kind of 'authority' gradually emerged – 'kingly authority', the 'authority' of a feudal 'king'.

Now, every 'king' was, in the first place, a 'lord' in his own 'estate'. And since *dominium* was the normal way of thinking about 'authority', it is not surprising that 'kingly' authority was often thought of as if it were the 'authority' of 'lordship'.

Indeed, to establish his 'authority' as a 'lord' was often the most effective way for a king to establish his 'authority' as a 'king'. At the Norman conquest of England, William claimed 'lordship' – that is, the 'authority' of ownership – over the whole land.

Nevertheless, the 'authority' of a 'king' was not, and sometimes quite clearly was not, that of 'lordship'. The kings of France were not, and could not pretend to be, 'lords' of France; they were 'lords' in their own *demesne*, but not in relation to their subjects outside this *demesne*.

A medieval king, then, came to be recognized to have two different kinds of 'authority' over two different kinds of subjects. The 'authority' of 'lordship' over his own *demesne* and his tenants, and the 'authority' of a 'king' over his kingdom and his subjects.

This difference appeared unmistakably in what we should call public finance.

In early times, the resources with which kings financed their activities as 'kings' came from the proceeds of their 'lordship' – from the revenue of their own 'estates'.

But when this became insufficient, it was supplemented by revenue raised from those over whom the king did not exercise 'lordship'. And this revenue required the consent of those required to pay, for they were 'free' men and not tenants on his estate.

The difference is like the difference between raising revenue by putting up the rents of your tenants, and raising revenue by instituting a poll tax to be paid by all subjects.

Now, it was these circumstances which generated new beliefs about the 'authority' of rulers. The 'authority' of kings, as such, was *not* the authority of 'lordship'. What was it? What reasons could be given for believing that a 'king' had a right to rule those over whom he did not exercise 'lordship'?

As we have seen, the first incipient medieval beliefs about the 'authority' of kings were in terms of authority derived from God and of authority derived from the 'consent' of their subjects. And these beliefs were inherited and transferred in modern European political thought.

They were beliefs about the 'authority' of rulers obviously appropriate to a modern European 'state', because they recognized the ruled as 'free' men – that is, as men not bound to their rulers by tenancies of land and services arising out of those tenancies.

Modern Europe, then, inherited the great achievement of medieval political thought – the idea of political 'authority' distinguished from the 'authority' of 'lordship'.

But it inherited also a sort of ruler who became the progenitor of modern governments. He was a ruler who, though he had become a 'king', had not quite ceased to be a 'lord'. He was a ruler in whose person the notion of the 'authority' of 'lordship' had not yet been laid to rest. And he was a ruler not incapable of regarding his kingdom as his *demesne*, and of being regarded as having the 'authority' of 'lordship'.

In the main, the great effort of modern European political thought has been directed to suppressing the relics of 'lordship' in beliefs about the 'authority' of modern governments.

In the seventeenth century, political writers observed, in Muscovy and Turkey, governments whose 'authority' seemed to be that of 'lordship'. And they found appropriate expressions to denote this sort of government.

Hobbes called it 'despotical government', 'lordly monarchy' and 'paternal dominion'; Bodin called it *l'empire seigneurial*; Filmer called it 'masterly government'.

And they did not doubt that the 'authority' of a government of a modern European 'state' was not to be understood in these terms.

Nevertheless, the belief in the 'authority' of government as that of 'lordship' did not perish. It survives, largely unrecognized, wherever a 'state' is thought of as an 'estate' (land and its inhabitants) and a government is thought of as the manager of this 'estate'.

Wherever a government acquires an extensive ownership of the land and resources over which it rules, and an extensive command over the activities of its subjects, it has been impossible to detach the 'authority' attributed to it from being connected with these 'lordly' rather than 'kingly' characteristics.

When Mme. De Staël said, in the eighteenth century: 'Despotism is new, liberty is old', she referred to these two kinds of 'authority', 'lordly' and 'kingly' authority. And what she meant was that there had been a recrudescence of a belief in 'lordly' authority after Europe had seemed to have embraced the sort of 'authority' which recognized its subjects as 'free' men – namely 'kingly' authority.

And, on the whole, she was right. In modern times 'despotism', the right to rule based upon ownership, has been the creature of popular revolutions.

5

There is, then, a deceptive simplicity in the view that modern European political thought, having, in its early days, settled for an understanding of political 'authority' in terms of some sort of divine commission, has come to understand it in terms of the 'consent' of its subjects.

First, the notion of 'authority' as divine commission is not without its contemporary counterparts. And secondly, neither of these substantial and well-thought-out theories of political 'authority' has been able to overwhelm the belief in 'authority' understood in terms of 'lordship'.

6

Now, for the rest of my time I want to explore a little another aspect of this question about the 'authority' of governments, their right to rule.

It is an aspect which brings us into contact with a strand in modern political thought which we have not yet noticed.

As it first occurs, the question of 'authority' is a practical question: 'Who has "authority" over me? To whom do I owe loyalty? And why?'

This question may be not unsatisfactorily answered in terms like these:

> *He* (perhaps pointing to a man) has the right to rule because he has succeeded to the office of ruler in the approved manner.

This, so to speak, is a model answer. It may be filled in for any office and any approved manner of succeeding to it.

If it is Henry VIII, the office is that of 'King of England' and he succeeded to it (shall we say) by 'hereditary right'.

If it is President Kennedy, the office is that of president of the United States, and he succeeded to it in the approved process of election.

This is all right as far as it goes. And it may be carried a little further by looking more closely at the approved process by which a man acquires authority to rule and recognizing it as an emblem of some deeper beliefs.

462   *Lectures in the History of Political Thought*

The ceremony by which a man becomes king may, for example, include rituals like anointing with holy oil, which may be taken to be emblematic of a belief that his 'authority' owes something to what may be called 'divine appointment'.

The ceremony by which a man becomes president may include a process of election, which may be taken to be emblematic of a belief that his 'authority' owes something to what may be called the 'consent' of those he is to rule.

But, even so, many questions remain unanswered, questions which must be answered if we are to pretend to an understanding of this 'right to rule'.

(1) First, it is to be noticed that 'authority' belongs to the office and to the occupant of the office only as an occupant.

All that has been said, so far, refers to how a man may come to enjoy the 'authority' of the office he succeeds to. Nothing that has been said so far even begins to account for the attribution of 'authority' to the office itself.

(2) Secondly, let us suppose that the ruler has *not* succeeded to the office in the approved manner: does this mean that he is without 'authority'? If so, half the rulers in medieval and modern times have been without 'authority'.

William I became king of England by conquest. This was not the approved manner of succeeding to the office, yet he and his successors were acknowledged to have a 'right' to rule. How could he have acquired it?

One way of understanding the situation appeared when men in later times began to speak of 'the right of conquest'. But this is not very satisfactory. It merely gets over the difficulty by a questionable *ad hoc* addition to the rightful ways of coming to occupy an office endowed with 'authority'. If this is permissible, anything is permissible.

I have chosen William I because in the seventeenth century he was, by some, identified as a 'tyrant' – a man who had no right to rule. And this brought into question the 'authority' of all his successors.

But, of course, modern European history is filled with parallel cases. By what right did Maria Theresa rule that part of the ancient kingdom of Poland which fell to her by conquest? What was the 'authority' of the British government in Ireland?

In short, how can 'authority' be acquired when all you have got is 'power'?

(3) Thirdly, 'authority' belongs to an office and to a man or men only as occupants of the office. But suppose there is no office.

William the Silent was the first *staatholder* of the United Netherlands; Washington was the first president of the United States. The office had first to be created and endowed with 'authority'. How can this be done?

By the decree of a constituent assembly? But where does the assembly get its 'authority'? By 'election'? But why should I believe that election gives 'authority'? And so on.

In short, the serious intellectual difficulties begin when we have left behind the simple proposition that a man is a rightful ruler if he succeeds to the office of ruler in an approved manner. What we have to go on to inquire is how the office itself can acquire 'authority'.

7

This question was tackled in modern European thought in three different manners.

(1) It was thought to be a question of origins – of how the office of ruler began. And the inquiry was conducted within each of the two current general understandings of political 'authority' – divine commission and the 'consent' of subjects.

If the 'authority' enjoyed by the office of king were to be interpreted as a divine endowment, then there must have been some occasion, long ago, when this endowment was actually made. Let us seek it where it may be found, in ancient records.

This sort of question had been raised in the fifteenth century with regard to the 'authority' of the papal office.

Divine endowment was claimed for the 'authority' of this office; and the occasion of this endowment was asserted to be Christ's utterance to St. Peter, recorded in Scripture.

But just how vulnerable this whole method of argument was, was demonstrated by Marsilius of Padua when he questioned this interpretation of the record. A large part of the *Defensor pacis* is concerned with the alleged origins of the 'authority' claimed for the papal office. And he reached the conclusion that this office had not got the 'authority' claimed for it because what had been relied upon was a misreading of Scripture.

The writer most notable for the attempt to determine how and when the office of king had been endowed by God with its 'authority' was Sir Robert Filmer, in the seventeenth century.

The argument of *Patriarcha* was ambitious, because it concerned 'kingship' in general. Its general conclusion was that the kingly office had been endowed with 'authority' in a conversation between God and Adam, as recorded in Scripture.

This was ingenious; but whatever might be thought of the argument in general, it manifestly failed to connect this original endowment of the kingly office with the office of any particular king. It could, unfortunately, provide no specific information about the kingly office in England, for example.

If, on the other hand, the 'authority' of the office of ruler (whatever form this office might take) were to be interpreted as an endowment by the ruled, then, there must have been some occasion, long ago, when human beings set up an office of ruler and endowed it with 'authority'.

A 'contract', an 'agreement', a 'covenant' of some sort must have been made signifying the 'consent' of the human race to be ruled.

Where were these title deeds of government? Perhaps those who thought in this manner were not quite clear about what they were looking for in this search for this 'original contract'. But sillier things have been looked for – although the inquiry cannot be said to have been very promising.

Montesquieu reported that this 'original contract' had been found in the wood where the barbarians who had overwhelmed the Roman empire had lived. But this was an over-optimistic report. This 'contract' was to be found neither there nor anywhere else.

This belief that the question of the 'authority' to rule might be settled in a quasi-historical inquiry is easy to make fun of. But it was a serious belief, and it generated a large and notable effort of research into the origins of political society.

Indeed, this is the beginning of what we now call social anthropology. And it suggested another and more profitable line of inquiry which we will notice in a moment.

But perhaps its most important outcome was that (as Hobbes remarked) the origins of all governments are disreputable, no argument about the 'authority' of rulers can be got from them, and the less said about them the better.

All governments began in violence; and their acquired 'authority' is not to be accounted for by referring to their origins.

(2) Secondly, the problem of how the office of ruler can have acquired 'authority' was regarded as a philosophical problem.

Much of the writing which belongs to this philosophical inquiry (at least, in the seventeenth century) made use of such ideas as 'divine authorization', 'contract', 'consent' and so on; but these were not thought of as events which took place in the past: they were given the status of necessary assumptions.

Hobbes never imagined the process in which he described the endowment of a ruler with 'authority' as a historical event; it was a necessary process.

The arguments of the philosophers revolved round the necessary character of 'authority' and the nature of those who were under 'authority', namely, 'free' men.

They employed much of the brilliant philosophical talent of the seventeenth century; and the writers who emerge as the masters in the inquiry were Hobbes and Spinoza. Locke hardly competed; but Rousseau was concerned with the same problem: What was the nature of the 'authority' which could rule 'free' men without depriving them of their freedom?

(3) But there was a third approach to the problem, less sophisticated than that of the philosophers, but also less fanciful and doctrinaire than the approach of those who sought evidence for the 'authority' of governments in the origins of governments.

The writers who contributed most to this third line of inquiry were Montesquieu, Burke, and Hume. And behind Burke and Hume there was the very considerable development of anthropological study which had its home in eighteenth-century Edinburgh.

The starting point of this line of inquiry was the admission that we know nothing specific about the origins of government, but that it is safe to assume that government begins in the exercise of *potentia*, power, force, violence.

Nevertheless, to rule is to enjoy 'authority'. Every ruler claims the right to rule; and 'authority' is attributed to it by its subjects.

Indeed, if we were to recognize governments merely as seats of 'power', we would have to recognize ourselves in relation to governments merely as slaves.

But how can 'authority' emerge from what begins as no more than 'power'? In the account of it offered by these other writers, this emergence of 'authority' from power is a historical process, but it is not a historical event. The account runs something like this:

Many of the demands of the powerful are, no doubt, conceded by the less powerful because they are impossible to resist. And some of these demands may be supposed to be conceded because compliance carries with it some valuable *quid pro quo* or reward which makes it worthwhile to comply.

Neither of these situations, however, turn the demands of the powerful into 'rightful' demands or their power into 'authority'. But it may be imagined that, in the course of time, some of the demands of the powerful will acquire the force of custom. That is to say, they will be yielded to not under an express threat of harm, nor because to yield brings with it a valuable recompense, but because it has become 'the done thing'.

This 'done thing' is still merely indicative and not imperative. But, imperceptibly, the 'done thing' becomes recognized as a customary duty; and to recognize a duty is to have acknowledged an 'authority'.

Thus, 'authorization' (the recognition of 'authority') is not a historical event (as Filmer, for example, supposed it to be), nor is it a necessary hypothetical act (as Hobbes and the philosophers understood it); it is a process in which 'power' is 'moralized'.

In this process there may be dramatic moments, as when William the Conqueror extracted an oath of allegiance from those whom he had conquered. But the notion of a 'contract' entered into is far too definite to represent what is going on. And even the notion of 'consent' is too specific.

It is much more like submission becoming acquiescence, and the absence of objection broadening down into customary recognition and the acknowledgment of demand 'rightfully' made.

Just as it is said that, in ancient China, each village readily understood the language spoken in its neighboring villages, but that two villages a hundred miles apart spoke languages quite incomprehensible to one another, so the gap between 'power' and 'authority' is bridged in a series of minimal steps no one of which may be said to be itself the bridge.

In short, the 'authority' of rulers is like the 'rights' of squatters. They begin in acts of power, they grow out of acquiescence and the absence of objection, and they are acquired, by prescription, when what was once a demand receives recognition as a 'rightful' claim.

Burke's formulation of this understanding of the 'authority' which belongs to the office of ruler is hesitating and is hedged with reservations.

> Our constitution, [he says] is a prescriptive constitution; it is a constitution whose sole authority is that it has existed time out of mind.

This seems confident enough. The analogy of 'squatters' rights' is unconcealed. It is offered as a revision of the belief that the 'authority' of rulers is the product of an express 'agreement' or 'contract' signifying the 'consent' of subjects. And it is offered as a rational alternative to 'authority' understood as an express divine endowment.

But Burke is not quite ready for so 'positive' a doctrine of 'authority'. He asks himself the question: But, how *can* prescription create right? And his answer is that prescription itself does not create right: it is merely the means by which God bestows right.

What seemed to be a doctrine of prescriptive 'authority' turns out to be a reformulated doctrine of divine endowment. But it is a radical reformulation, and it is supported by an argument.

Prescription is the product of the lapse of time. But to say that the right to rule rests upon the continuous and recognized exercise of power is to say nothing, unless this continuous exercise of power is taken to signify divine approval.

As Burke understood it, this is precisely what it did signify; and he explained it thus:

The lapse of time, the course of human history, is composed of human choices and human actions – some right, some wrong. But the course of human history is not merely this chance mixture of right and wrong choices.

It is a course of events which is being continuously corrected by God's providential grace. And this divine correction of human errors guarantees that what survives in the long run has the approval of God. What gets itself established and endures does so under God's 'authority'.

Thus, the 'authority' which belongs to the office of ruler, the authority of a constitution, is not understood to spring from a single set act of divine endowment; nor is it understood to spring from anything so specific as a 'contract' in which the ruled endow the ruler with authority by giving 'consent' to being ruled. It springs from prescription recognized as the sign of divine approval.

Hume's version of this doctrine is much more 'positivistic'. For him there is nothing more to be said than that the 'authority' of the office of ruler is the counterpart of the subjects' belief that it has authority.

Men acknowledge their duty to obey, and in this acknowledgment the ruler acquires 'authority'. It is unthinkable that he could acquire it in any other way.

But, this acknowledgment of a duty to obey is not an event; it is nothing so specific as a 'compact'. It is a disposition which is expressed in acts of obedience, rather than admissions of duty; and it requires the lapse of time.

Each 'state', no doubt, will have its own acquired beliefs about the process in which a man must succeed to the office of government if he is to be regarded as succeeding to its 'authority'. And these beliefs may be expressed in specific choices.

But the 'authority' of the office itself cannot be accounted for in this way. Like the rights of squatters, it is prescriptive and is acquired (as it were) by default, by compliance which breeds a belief in 'right'.

8

Here I must end what I have to say about modern European reflection on the 'authority' of governments.

It may seem strange to leave it in the eighteenth century; but nothing very much that is new has been said in recent times. This is not because there is nothing new that could be said, but largely because more recent thought has concerned itself with other things.

One of the chief of its concerns has been with questions about, not the 'authority' of governments, but the activities of governments. And this is what I propose to go on to next week.

Editorial Note

LSE 1/1/21, file 5, fos. 484–500. Photocopy of a typescript.

Thirty-one

The Office of Government (1)

1

So far we have considered some of the beliefs, sentiments, ideas, analogies which have gathered themselves round two important questions thrown up in the political experience of modern Europe.

- What sort of collectivity of human beings is a modern 'state'?
- Whence comes the 'authority' of a government to rule, and the duty of a subject to submit to being ruled?

Both these questions were of great practical importance to the members of a modern 'state'; both provoked elaborate historical and philosophical inquiries; and both generated highly sophisticated systems of ideas.

But, while modern European political reflection has, over the centuries, come to reject some answers which these questions have received, it cannot be said to have arrived at any universally accepted answer. What exists here, as elsewhere, is a set of dispositions to think in certain manners, rather than a set of conclusions.

2

I want, this morning, to begin to consider the sentiments, beliefs, opinions, and ideas which have gathered themselves around another important question:

What is the activity of ruling? What is the proper office, or business, of the government of a modern 'state'?

Here, as elsewhere in political thought, a question about what purports to be fact is run together with a question about what is desirable or to be approved. But this, I think, is unavoidable, if a little confusing.

In their simplest form beliefs about the proper business of governing appear in the analogies which have been suggested for the activity of ruling. In modern times, there have been a vast variety of these analogies. Here are a few.

It has been thought that the proper business of the government of a modern 'state' is:

- To *manage* the activities of its subjects, like the manager of an estate or a factory.
- To *provide*, as a housekeeper provides for her household.
- To engage in an activity called *social engineering*.
- To *organize* the activities of its subjects so that they conform to a 'vision' of society.
- To *lead*, like the leader of an expedition exploring unknown territory.
- To *command*, like a general commanding an army.
- To *conduct*, like the conductor of an orchestra.
- To *navigate*, like the pilot of a ship bound for a known destination.
- To *distribute*, like a quartermaster distributes rations.
- To *educate*, like a schoolmaster educates his pupils.
- To *umpire* the disputes of its subjects, like an arbitrator or a referee.
- To *keep order*, like an usher or a steward at a public meeting.
- To *guard* its subjects' interest, like a night watchman guards the property of his employer.
- To *keep up the momentum* of its subjects' activities, like the flywheel of an engine.
- To *mete out justice* to its subjects, like a judge.
- To *'govern'* the activities of its subjects, like the governor of an engine.
- To *redeem* its subjects from their frustrations and to provide them with an earthly equivalent of salvation.
- To give a *united purpose* to its subjects' activities.

Now, each of these analogies of 'government' expresses a belief about the business or the activity of governing, not about the authority of government. They are answers to the question: What should government be doing? not to the question: Whence comes the authority to rule?

And there is nothing in any of them which necessarily allies it with any particular view of the authority of governments.

Some of these analogies *suggest* an answer to the question: What sort of a collectivity of human beings is a 'state'?

E.g. it is like a 'hungry family'; or a 'schoolroom full of children'; or an 'army'; or a 'factory'; or a set of people playing a game.

But these suggestions are oblique. The centre of attention, here, is the question: What should a *government* be doing? What is governing?

At first sight, it seems a miscellaneous collection of beliefs, each expressing a 'bright idea' about the business of government.

But on closer inspection I think you will find that all the analogies which have been used in modern times to illuminate the business of governing tend in one or another of two opposite directions of thought.

They tend to attribute to the activity of governing *either*: (a) the business of organizing its subjects in the pursuit of a single, premeditated end or purpose; or (b) the business of providing the conditions in which its subjects may pursue their own chosen and various ends while still remaining a single association.

In short, all these analogies of government represent one or the other of two opposed dispositions of thought about the activity of governing.

The first of these tendencies or dispositions of thought I shall call the understanding of governing as a *telocratic* activity: that is, an activity designed to impose a single end or purpose upon its subjects and their activities.

The second of these tendencies or dispositions of thought I shall call the understanding of governing as a *nomocratic* activity: that is, an activity which provides rules for the conduct of its subjects, but rules which do not themselves impose any single and premeditated end or purpose upon that conduct.

3

By *telocracy* I mean the proper business of governing understood as the organization of the energies and activities of its subjects, and of the resources of its territory, for the achievement of a single, premeditated end.

Now, this disposition of belief is a view of the proper business of governing, and not a belief about the authority of a government.

It may be held, and it has been held in modern times, in conjunction with any of the current beliefs about the authority of governments: 'divine commission'; the 'consent' of their subjects; authority which springs from prescription.

But I think it is a belief about the business of government which is closely affiliated with the belief that a 'state' is something like 'natural' community of human beings.

That is, the business of government is here being understood as the guardian or organizer of the solidarity of a community, a solidarity which is itself understood to spring from the pursuit of a single end or purpose.

Nevertheless, this understanding of the business of government does not necessarily entail the constriction of the activities of its subjects within any very narrow limits.

What it means is that activities will be permitted only in relation to the chosen end and only in so far as they contribute to this end; and that they will all be interpreted in relation to that end. And what is being believed is that it is the business of government to see that this happens.

Thus, in a *telocracy*, 'education' will be recognized as the training of the members of a 'state' to participate in the pursuit of the chosen end. 'Art' will be understood as an adjunct of 'policy'. All particular subordinate associations are judged in terms of their contributions to the overall end of the association.

In other words, in this view of things, nothing but the chosen end or purpose is regarded as being valuable in itself.

Further, *telocracy* does not necessarily mean the absence of law. It means only that what may roughly be called 'the rule of law' is recognized to have no independent virtue, but to be valuable only in relation to the pursuit of the chosen end.

Now, within this general disposition towards the activity of governing there is clearly room for a certain limited variety of belief about the business of governments.

And, in the main, *telocratic* beliefs about government will differ from one another in respect of the end specified as the proper end to be pursued.

But this does not mean that the end to be pursued is necessarily chosen and imposed upon its subjects by the government itself.

This may be so, and those who in modern times have taken up with the idea of *telocracy* have often believed it to be necessary. But it is always possible that, within this view of the business of governing, the end to be pursued is merely elicited from its subjects by their government.

But the end having been either elicited or imposed, it belongs to this view of the business of governing to understand government as the focussing of all the activities of its subjects and the resources of its territory upon that single end.

This end, then, however it is specified, will be regarded as the 'social purpose', or the 'common good', of the 'state' itself.

And a 'state' will, appropriately, be understood as a collectivity of human beings united in the pursuit of a common end under the direction of its government.

Lastly, this end will always be understood as a substantive condition of life.

By this I mean a condition of *things*, like actually having a job, or a house of certain specifications, or a specified share of the productive activities going on in the 'state', or a turn in the management of affairs, as distinct from there merely being no legal impediment to the enjoyment of any of these things.

Telocracy, then, is the belief that it is the business of government to generate or to impose an 'end' recognized as a substantive condition of things. An 'end' which members do not choose to enjoy or eschew, it will be a necessary condition of the existence of them all.

4

Now, it is important to understand that this general belief about the business of government is not an arbitrary and unaccountable disposition of thought in modern times. Indeed, the circumstances in which modern European 'states' emerged were such that it would have been very remarkable if a disposition of thought of this kind had not appeared.

Further, this belief is not the product of very recent times. Those of our contemporaries who hold it most firmly are apt to suggest that it is the rational response to our current circumstances. This is a mistake: in fact it is one of the dispositions of belief about government which emerged in the sixteenth century, and it has never been absent from the political experience of modern Europe.

Consider the circumstances of a modern European 'state' which would tend to generate this belief about government.

(1) Every modern 'state' was born in diversity. The first task of rulers was to generate solidarity, a task which, itself, pushed the activity of governing in a *telocratic* direction.

(2) Civil rulers of modern 'states' inherited the *potestas* of medieval kings and they acquired, in a large measure, the *auctoritas* of the medieval church.

They incorporated in themselves the whole of the 'authority', and what might be called the 'conscience', of the associations over which they ruled.

(3) A genuine belief in *telocracy* depends upon large resources of power (*potentia*). Without such resources it is a dream rather than a significant belief; with them, *telocracy* becomes an intellectual and practical possibility.

The accumulation of these resources of power is one of the main features of modern European government; and the only reason why *telocratic* government seems more rational now than it did in early modern times is because power has made it more possible.

(4) War has always been the occasion for government to turn in the direction of *telocracy*: in war a 'state' is organized (within the existing technical competence) for the pursuit of a single end to which all activities are subordinated.

And war has been the normal condition of modern European 'states'. What 'states' learned in war, moreover, tended not to be forgotten in the infrequent intervals between belligerency.

(5) Colonies were, in the sixteenth and seventeenth centuries, regarded as 'estates' to be 'managed'. Their government was usually *telocratic*; ruling them was the organization of their resources for the benefit of the parent 'state'. Settlers were never unqualified subjects; they were agents or tenants holding commissions, concessions, licenses.

Most modern European 'states' acquired colonies, and their experience of 'colonial' government was reflected in a *telocratic* tendency at home.

Indeed, there is much to be said for the view that the art of *telocracy* in modern times was learned in colonial rule, and that, in Europe, it may be recognized as governing a European 'state' as if it were a colony.

(6) This belief about the business of government is likely to appear when, in a 'state', a single 'problem' obtrudes itself so overwhelmingly that its solution may be taken to be an end (like 'victory' in war) to which all other purposes may properly be subordinated.

And a problem of this sort, inviting *telocracy*, has, in fact, been characteristic of modern European politics since the sixteenth century.

Various expressions have been used to denote it. At its simplest it has been thought of as 'the problem of the poor'. But, in a wider context, it has presented itself as the problem of 'underdevelopment' or of 'underemployment'.

This, of course, appears as a political problem only where there is a tendency to understand a 'state' as an 'economy'.

There is, then, much in the political experience of modern Europe to promote a belief in *telocratic* government. And I want now to illustrate the fortunes of this belief in modern European political thought by considering some of the versions in which it has appeared.

5

The belief that the proper business of government is to manage the resources of its territory and the activities of its subjects in such a manner that they serve a single, specified end or purpose emerged first in a religious idiom.

In this idiom the condition of human circumstance to which all activities without exception should be subordinated, the end or purpose to be imposed by government, was denoted by the word 'righteousness'.

The Geneva of Calvin and Beza, the Zurich of Zwingli, and England in the central years of the seventeenth century were places and occasions when this version of *telocratic* belief came to the surface.

This belief, as it emerged, however, was not the belief that the business of government was to turn each and every subject into a 'righteous' man. *That*, on the view that 'righteousness' is a matter of divine election, would have been an impossible purpose to pursue.

What was believed to be the business of government was the creation and maintenance of what was called a 'righteous community' – that is, a substantive condition of things identified as 'righteous conduct' among its subjects.

The office of government was understood on the analogy of a military commander whose business it is to win a victory for his employer (in this case, God), and to care for his soldiers (that is, his subjects) only in relation to that victory.

Here, the belief in *telocracy* revealed itself in all its characteristic details. The 'ruler' was bound by no rules. He was recognized as the organizer of an all-embracing social-religious purpose. His duty was to permit no divergence from this purpose.

Each subject was recognized as a servant of this purpose, an agent of government. He had no rights but the comprehensive right to be ruled in this manner and (if he were obedient) to remain a member of this 'holy community'.

Otherwise, his destiny was to be suppressed, expelled, or executed.

But, what should be noticed, is that Geneva (for example) displayed a *telocratic* disposition towards government, not because religious uniformity was imposed. Many governments in modern times have imposed religious uniformity without displaying any disposition towards *telocracy*.

What made Geneva a *telocratic* state was the belief that the proper business of government was to impose a comprehensive uniformity upon its subjects understood in a religious idiom.

6

The second version of this *telocratic* belief I want to notice is that which in the eighteenth century was called 'enlightened despotism' or 'enlightened absolutism'.

I think it is better called, simply, 'enlightened government', because it was a belief about the business of governing which did not necessarily carry with it any particular belief about the authority of government.

This belief about the proper business of governing had its beginnings in the sixteenth century, and in the eighteenth century it spread itself over a large part of Europe. But it did not, at that time, penetrate English thought at all significantly.

It is a specifically modern belief. I do not think there is any exact counterpart to it in any other political experience.

It was explored, first, by a German school of writers known as the 'Cameralists': J. H. G. von Justi (of Göttingen), F. K. von Moser and Joseph Sonnenfels (of Vienna), Christian Wolff and G. F. Lamprecht. Frederick the Great of Prussia made a significant contribution to this literature in his *Testament politique*.

The belief was reflected, with varying clearness, in the governments of Prussia, Saxony, Baden, Württemberg, the Austrian empire (Joseph II), Tuscany, Naples, Spain (Charles III), Portugal (Pombal), Denmark (Christian VII and his minister Struensee), Sweden (Gustavus III), Poland (Stanislaus Augustus) and Russia (Catherine II).

A supreme example of it appeared in the France of the *ancien régime*. And one of the best descriptions of this belief is to be found in Alexis de Tocqueville's *The Old Regime and the French Revolution*.

The first principle of 'enlightened government' was the belief that a ruler or a government was the servant, not of God or his subjects, but of a 'cause'. The business of governing was to promote this 'cause' relentlessly and efficiently.

This 'cause' was a substantive condition of things which came to be spoken of as 'welfare'. The belief was an early vision of what we have come to call a 'welfare state'.

'Welfare', however, was not a vague expression. It signified a single, uniform condition of things, imposed by a government, which included material prosperity and a large measure of security from the vicissitudes of life, and in relation to which all activities and enterprises whatever were judged to be valuable.

It had, above all, nothing whatever to do with what the mass of ordinary people might actually want; nor was it a condition of things which allowed for individual choice or preference.

And the reason why, in this belief about the business of governing, no account was to be taken of individual preferences, was not merely that to do so would upset the desired uniformity.

It was based upon the belief that the mass of ordinary people were ignorant, helpless, 'unenlightened' *canaille*, whose activities would remain fruitless and inconsequent unless a single, overall purpose were imposed upon them. Subjects were children; they had to be organized and educated.

Moreover, every 'state' was understood to be a mess of ages of mismanagement and misgovernment.

The first task of a ruler was to sweep away obsolete rights, laws and practices; particularly the privileges of aristocracies and the property rights of all.

In this manner a clean sheet would appear upon which it was the business of a government to write the rules and regulations which would constitute the desired uniform and enlightened manner of life.

Here, then, in the beliefs about the business of governing which constituted the doctrine of 'enlightened government' was a secular counterpart to the religious *telocracy* characteristic, for example, of sixteenth-century Geneva.

The office of government was to impose a single end upon all the activities of its subjects, and to organize those activities in detail so that they contributed to the achievement of this end.

This is what J. H. G. von Justi says of it:

> A properly constituted 'state' must be exactly analogous to a machine in which all the wheels and gears are precisely adjusted to one another; and the ruler must be the operator, the mainspring or the soul (if one may use the expression) which sets everything in motion and directs it to the purpose for which it was designed.

In this belief about the business of governing, then, 'enlightenment' appeared, first, in the formulation of the 'social policy' or 'purpose' to be imposed, to which all activities whatsoever were to be subordinated – art, literature, education, religion, work, and play.

But 'enlightenment' appeared, secondly, in devising the means by which a government should perform its office in a 'state'.

And it was here that the 'Cameralists' broke new ground.

They inspired the belief that governing a 'state' should be a 'scientific' operation, an activity of 'social engineering'. And the 'science' required was understood to be the 'science of administration'.

Indeed, all these writers were professors of public administration; and it may be conjectured that their belief in *telocracy* sprang largely from their belief that they had discovered the administrative techniques necessary to operate a *telocracy*.

Governing, as they understood it, was a matter of manipulating human conduct so that a 'state' should be an association of human beings moved by a single purpose.

What was required for this was, not only an 'enlightened' ruler, but also a properly trained corps of *Beamten*, officials, administrators, inspectors, schoolmasters, preachers, public relations officers, planners, tax gatherers, accountants, agricultural and industrial advisers, and so on, whose 'vocation' was to be the efficient agents of 'enlightened' government in its task of the total organization of the activities of its subjects.

This so-called 'theory' of 'enlightened' government is, perhaps, the most fully elaborated of all the versions of *telocratic* belief in modern times. And since its first emergence, it has remained one of the strongest dispositions of European thought about the business of governing.

You are, no doubt, familiar with it in contemporary writing; but you will make a mistake if you imagine it to be an invention of our own generation to meet the alleged needs of our time.

It was, in fact, a seventeenth-century invention; and there has been no significant modification of the doctrine since the 'Cameralists' first set it out. What has, of course, been extended is the comprehensiveness of the vision of a *telocratic* 'state'; and this has largely been inspired by the belief that modern techniques bring within the bounds of possibility what for the seventeenth century could be no more than a dream.

7

All versions of the belief in *telocratic* government are variations on a single theme. Consequently it is often difficult to separate one from another. And the next version we have to consider has much in common with that which belonged to the doctrine of 'enlightened' government.

It is distinguished by the single 'purpose' or 'end' which it is understood to be the business of government to impose upon its subjects.

In 'enlightened' government this end was understood to be a certain sort of compulsory 'welfare', or (as was sometimes said) 'happiness'. In this next version the end to be imposed, and to which all other activities were to be subordinated, is understood to be the maximum exploitation of the natural resources of the 'state'.

This end has been denoted by the words 'productivity' and 'development'; but it must be understood that the subjects of a government, in this belief about its office, have always been included in the 'natural resources' of the 'state'.

The first writer to take up with it, clearly and unambiguously, was Francis Bacon in the sixteenth century. And his statement of this belief was so cogent that for the next three centuries every writer who embraced this version of the *telocratic* doctrine acknowledged a debt to Bacon.

Bacon goes to the root of the matter and provides a complete set of reasons in support of this doctrine.

(1) The choice of this end or purpose is not arbitrary. As Bacon understands it, the enterprise of exploiting, to the maximum, the natural resources of the world is the proper occupation of mankind – proper, because it had been imposed upon mankind by God himself. It is *the* religious duty upon which all human energy and intelligence should be focused; and all other activities (art, learning, education, literature, etc.) should be regarded as the servants of this enterprise.

(2) Hitherto, Bacon thought, this enterprise had been pursued in a very haphazard and inefficient manner. 'Nature' had never yet been made to yield all that it was capable of yielding. What the enterprise required was organization and central direction.

(3) The proper business of government was precisely to be the organizer and director of the 'productive' activities of its subjects.

To rule is to direct man's efforts in the recovery of 'that right over nature which belongs to them by divine bequest' and which they have been sadly reluctant to enjoy.

Thus, in the Baconian version of *telocratic* belief, a 'state' is understood as an 'economy', the managing director of which is the government.

The 'subjects' of this government, no less than the mineral, agricultural, and industrial potential of the 'state', are the resources to be exploited. Each man is recognized as a 'unit' in this productive enterprise.

To impede this enterprise is 'treason'; to make a notable contribution to it is to earn a place in the calendar of *Stakhanovite* 'saints'.

Education is learning to take your place in this enterprise; leisure is preparation for more effective work.

It is a collection of ideas about the business of government which is thoroughly familiar to us.

8

There is one other important version of this belief in *telocratic* government to be considered.

It appeared in the nineteenth century, although there had been intimations of it in the seventeenth century, especially in English writers.

It is the belief that the proper business of government is to be the organizer and director, not of the 'productive' efforts of its subjects, but of the distribution of the product.

The substantive condition of things to be imposed by government is, here, understood, not to be 'work', 'abundance', 'affluence', or 'prosperity', but 'equality' and 'security'.

That this version of *telocratic* belief should have appeared fairly late in modern European history is not surprising. No sane man could attribute the office of 'distributor' to a government unless there was clearly something to be distributed.

But during the nineteenth century the 'productive' efforts of European peoples had been successful enough to generate this belief that the proper office of government was, not to see that its subjects 'worked', but to organize the distribution of what they produced.

The 'social purpose', the 'end', of which government was to be the organizer and director, was the determination of how the national income was to be spent.

9

These, then, are some of the versions in which a belief in *telocracy* has appeared in modern European thought. Nearly all of them are old; but even the oldest has its contemporary adherents.

But, like everything else in recent times, when the belief in *telocracy* reached the twentieth century, it had come to include so many reminiscences of earlier opinions that it appears to us more like an anthology of beliefs than a coherent doctrine about the business of governing.

For example, the somewhat miscellaneous collection of beliefs which is called 'socialism' certainly contains (among much else) a *telocratic* disposition. But in it the sharp distinctions between, for example, the 'puritan', the 'enlightened', the 'productivist', and the 'distributivist' idioms of *telocracy* have been worn smooth.

On the whole, twentieth-century *telocratic* belief owes more to circumstance than to any fresh consideration of the virtues of *telocracy*.

Two major wars, the great increase in the populations of modern 'states', and the invention of new administrative techniques and instruments of government have all given to the old notion of *telocracy* a new apparent appropriateness.

And there is a whole contemporary literature devoted to expounding the belief that the conjunction of *telocracy* (that is, government understood as the organization of a 'state' in pursuit of a single, premeditated end) with 'democracy' (that is, government constituted in a certain manner) has generated a unique style of governing.

10

Let me remind you that what we have been considering is one of the two major dispositions of belief in modern times about the proper business of governing.

In varying degrees this disposition of thought reveals itself in nearly every political writer in modern times, in the program of nearly every political party, and in nearly every imaginative projection of what may be hoped or feared from the government of a modern 'state'.

But it is not the only disposition of thought on this matter. And next week I want to say something about another understanding of the business of governing which, almost everywhere, has been its companion.

Editorial Note

LSE 1/1/21, file 5, fos. 501–15. Photocopy of a typescript.

Thirty-two

The Office of Government (2)

1

We are considering beliefs about the proper business of government which have been current in modern times.

Beliefs and opinions on this subject – the activities of government – are, of course, connected with beliefs about the authority of government, but there is no *necessary* connection between what we believe a government should be doing and what we believe about the source of its authority.

But there is likely to be a fairly close connection between what we think a government should be doing and what sort of a collectivity of human beings we understand a 'state' to be.

I suggested that beliefs about the business of government in modern times divide themselves into two main dispositions of thought. And I called them, respectively, *telocracy* and *nomocracy*.

Last week I said something about the fortunes in modern times of the belief in *telocracy* – that is, the opinion that the proper business of government is organizing its subjects in the pursuit of a single, premeditated 'end' or 'purpose'.

This week I want to say something about the fortunes of the belief in *nomocracy*.

2

Nomocracy means, literally, 'government understood as the rule of its subjects by means of law'.

More elaborately, it means the belief that the proper office of government is: (1) To be the custodian of a system of legal rights and duties in the enjoyment and observation of which the subjects of the government may pursue their own chosen ends and purposes while still remaining a single association.

(2) To be the custodian of the interests of the association in relation to other similar associations.

Now, this view of the business of government is to be recognized, in the first place, as a formal denial of a belief in *telocracy*. It denies that the office of government is that of imposing upon its subjects a substantive condition of things representing a single 'purpose' pursued by all.

But to understand *nomocracy* merely as a formal denial of a belief in *telocracy* is to misunderstand it.

First, so far as modern Europe is concerned, it is a belief about government which antedates a belief in *telocracy*.

Secondly, to understand *nomocracy* merely in terms of what it denies is to understand it imperfectly. It has a positive character.

The word *nomocracy* ('government by law') when used to denote a belief about the proper business of government seems, at first sight, to be only obliquely opposed to *telocracy*.

It seems to stand for a belief about the form, and not the substance, of the activities of government.

And the form it prescribes is a form which, we have seen, is not forbidden in *telocratic* belief. A *telocracy* *may* impose its single and premeditated 'end' upon its subjects by making and administering laws.

This indicates that the significant difference between these two dispositions of thought lies in the fact that for the believer in *nomocracy*, *how* a government acts is a more important consideration than *what* it does; while for the believer in *telocracy* it does not matter *how* a government acts so long as *what* it does promotes the chosen 'end' in view.

And while, in a *telocracy*, rule by law is not forbidden, it is never something valued on its own account: the only thing valued on its own account is the pursuit and achievement of the chosen end, which is a substantive condition of things.

The broad outline of the difference between these two beliefs about the business of government appears in the different meanings which each attributes to the expressions 'rights' and 'duties'.

A belief in *telocracy* attributes to the subjects of government a single comprehensive 'right' – the 'right' to the enjoyment of the substantive condition of things which it is the business of the government to impose; and one single comprehensive 'duty' – the 'duty' to participate in the achievement of this premeditated 'end'.

If, for example, the end is material prosperity, then all subjects have the duty of contributing to this end, and the right to their share in the product.

A belief in *nomocracy*, on the other hand, understands 'rights' to be numerous and to be opportunities of which subjects may or may not avail themselves; and it understands 'duties' as numerous and as concerned with the relations between subjects and only in exceptional circumstances the relations between subjects and their government.

3

But, a belief in *nomocracy* reveals its full character in the assumptions it makes about 'states', 'subjects', and 'governments'.

It assumes:

- That a 'state' is to be understood as a contingent association of dissimilar, adult individuals.
- That these individuals are such that they may be expected to entertain a variety of religious and moral beliefs; to be engaged in multifarious and rapidly changing activities, occupations, and enterprises; to have (each of them) something to do on his own account; to have 'private' lives.
- That these individuals greatly prize the freedom to make choices for themselves, to seek their own happiness in their own, often different, ways.
- That, as members of a 'state' they have, to a significant extent in common, a number of what Aristotle called 'admitted, or agreed, goods'; and (more important) they recognize a number of 'admitted, or agreed, evils'.

  Among the most cherished of these 'admitted goods' is the freedom to make choices for themselves; and among their strongest antipathies is interference with this freedom.
- They live under a system of law, and enjoy a system of rights and duties in respect of one another and in respect of their government.

  This system of law defines their lawful relations to one another and the lawful demands they may make upon one another and those which their government may make upon them. It reflects, in the main, the collection of 'admitted goods' they hold in common.

- This system of rights and duties was never designed by anyone; and it does not represent any single substantive condition of things.

  In order to remain serviceable, this system of rights and duties must often be emended and less often enlarged. It is understood to be more like the rules of a game than like anything else.
- The office of government is twofold. The distinction between its two kinds of activity is important. It corresponds roughly to the distinction of medieval political thought between a government's *jurisdictio* and a government's *gubernaculum*.

  (a) The government is the custodian of this law and of the processes in which it may be emended; and it is the sole judge and punisher of failures to observe its provisions.

  (b) In emergencies (such as war, natural calamities, etc.) this government is permitted to exceed its normal activities and impose abnormal and temporary duties upon its subjects or require them, for a time, to surrender their normal rights. It may even, temporarily, impose an overall purpose upon all the activities of its subjects.

  But 'good cause' must be shown for doing this; the argument of 'necessity' must not be over-pressed; and the occasion must be one in which the 'survival' of the association seems to be threatened in such a manner that this 'survival' becomes, temporarily, the chief 'admitted good'. It is, of course, always among the 'admitted goods'.

4

In seeking analogies with which to illuminate this understanding of the business of government, European thought in modern times has often settled upon analogies drawn from judicial activity. For it may be seen that even lawmaking, in this conception of government, is a quasi-judicial process: a balancing of one 'admitted good' against another, and not the imposition of an overall pattern of life.

Thus, the activity of governing has been likened to that of a judge, or an arbitrator, or an umpire, or a referee. And opponents of this view of government have likened it to the activity of a 'night watchman', and have suggested that it has only a 'negative' office to perform.

None of these analogies fits this understanding of the business of governing with any exactness. And it is particularly important to understand why the analogy of an 'arbitrator' does not fit the belief in *nomocracy*; and why, perhaps, that of a 'judge' fits a little less inexactly.

(1) Two opposed interests may be modified into coexistence by mutual agreement; and this mutual agreement may be promoted by an 'arbitrator'.

When this happens the interests come to follow a line of a resolution of forces: a line which bisects the angle of divergence. The differing 'weights' of the divergent interests determine the line agreed, or suggested by the 'arbitrator'.

In short, there is a compromise which reflects the relative current strengths of the divergent interests and reflects nothing else.

This is what may happen in a wage dispute when it is settled by agreement between the parties concerned, or by 'arbitration'.

(2) But when a law, or a government acting as a legislator, is the means by which collisions of interests are resolved, both the situation and the result are quite different.

(a) The law itself, the current system of rights and duties, and not the differing 'weights' or 'strengths' of the divergent interests, either provides or suggests the solution.

That is to say, the permanent (though modifiable) system of legal rights and duties, here, constitutes a third and interested party in every such situation. It acts, not as an 'arbitrator', but as a 'judge' versed in the law.

(b) The solution achieved in this manner will not relate merely to one particular occasion (as it would in mutual agreement or arbitration).

Either the solution is found in the law itself; or, if it is not to be found there, it will be written by legislators into the law as new legal rights and duties, applicable not merely to these disputants but to all subjects of the government.

A *nomocratic* government, then, rules either by applying the known law, or by making new law. And to make new law is to make a rule which has three characteristics to distinguish it from a merely agreed, or 'arbitrated', resolution of a dispute:

First, the rule is consistent with the current system of rules; it is not merely new, it is also old. It reflects the 'admitted goods' of the association, but it is not part of a 'policy' to impose a substantive condition of things.

Secondly, the rule is common to the whole association and is not merely appropriate to a particular dispute. Indeed, it is a general maxim that hard cases make bad law.

Thirdly, it is, henceforth, known in advance and is perpetually available for the settlement of divergencies of interest.

To believe in *nomocracy*, then, is not to attribute a merely negative office to government. A government, in this understanding of its office, is the positive and perpetually operative guardian of the 'admitted goods' of the society.

And if an analogy is sought for this conception of government, it is, perhaps, more nearly to be found in the 'governor' of an engine than anywhere else.

The function of the 'governor' of an engine is not to make it go, but is merely to control the speed at which its parts move in relation to one another.

One further observation about this *nomocratic* belief.

It is commonly confused with the already deeply confused idea denoted in the expression *laissez-faire*.

The expressions *laissez-faire* and its companion *laissez-aller* do not stand for beliefs about the proper business of government. They were expressions, invented in the eighteenth century, designed to recommend that there were some things which a *telocratically* inclined government would be well advised not to do if its chosen end were 'abundance' or 'material prosperity'.

In short, the belief in *nomocracy* is not even remotely connected with the belief that the proper business of government is to do as little as it can possibly manage to do – a belief which is sometimes read into the expression *laissez-faire* and which belongs only to the lunatic fringe of modern European political thought.

The difference between *telocracy* and *nomocracy* is a difference, not between two different amounts of activity, but between two different kinds of activity.

5

Now, it is important to understand that the belief in *nomocracy* is not an arbitrary and unaccountable disposition of thought in modern Europe. No less than *telocracy* it has a context of circumstances which makes it intelligible.

(1) Every modern European 'state' began in diversity: diversities of the communities of which it was composed, diversity of moral and religious belief, diversity of occupations and activities.

In short, there was much in every modern European 'state' as it emerged to resist the pressures of *telocracy* and to make *nomocracy* appropriate.

(2) Every modern European 'state' began in the enjoyment of a legal order, a system of rights and duties which defined the relationships of subjects to one another and to their government.

This system of legal rights and duties was not the invention of these modern governments, although it was, in most 'states', greatly modified in legislative activity.

Thus, a government believed to be the custodian of a system of law, and not of an overall 'social purpose', was familiar and easily recognizable.

(3) The early lawmaking activities of modern governments were largely directed to emancipating their subjects from feudal and corporate obligations. This was recognized and welcomed as an emancipation, a process in which freedom of movement and choice was increased.

A money economy, where the business of a government is recognized to be the custodian of a stable currency (and not the direction of the disposal of the national income) is, itself, the counterpart of *nomocracy*. And of the features of a modern European 'state' was its disposition to become a money economy.

(4) There were, as I have said, some great problems which emerged with modern European 'states' and which provoked a belief in the necessity of *telocracy*.

The chief of these was the 'problem of the poor' – that is, the problem of those who, because they were unable to make choices for themselves, were eligible for the imposition upon them, by governments, of a uniform substantive condition of life. And the response of *telocracy* to this problem in modern Europe has been the 'pauperization' of all subjects; that is, the substitution of government choices for individual choices for all its subjects.

But in every modern 'state' there was a significant number of 'subjects' who could resist the *telocratic* tendency; and in so far as they were able to impress themselves upon government, ruling was turned in a *nomocratic* direction.

(5) Many 'states' in the sixteenth and seventeenth centuries became the battle ground on which two or more different version of *telocratic* belief contended for supremacy.

And often the only escape from this civil war of *telocracies* was a government turn in a *nomocratic* direction, whose office was to maintain peace and the more elementary 'admitted goods' by means of a substantively neutral legal order.

This was so in France in the sixteenth century, where *nomocracy* was the belief of the *politiques*; and in England at the restoration.

(6) Lastly, there was one important religious belief which did much to promote a belief in *nomocracy*.

It was a tenet of orthodox Christianity that God himself did not rule mankind *telocratically*; so why should it be considered the proper business of kings and governments to rule their subjects *telocratically*?

God, no doubt, had a single 'purpose' which he desired the human race to pursue. But he had expressly given men the ability and the opportunity to diverge from this 'purpose', the opportunity to conform or to diverge from his design.

He periodically corrected their errors and rescued them from the consequences of their mistakes. But he never showed any disposition to compel them to toe a single line. He gave them a law, not a 'plan'.

If, then, God ruled mankind *nomocratically*, why should it be believed that human rulers should rule their subjects other than *nomocratically*?

6

There was, then, much in the political and intellectual experience associated with modern European 'states' to promote and to make persuasive a belief in *nomocracy*.

Much of the fortunes of the belief in *telocracy* in modern times is the story of the various overall 'ends' or 'purposes' which it has been considered proper for governments to impose upon their subjects: rectitude, virtue, happiness, production, distribution, etc.

Now the belief in *nomocracy* is, precisely, the rejection of the view that the business of a government is to impose an overall 'end' or 'purpose' on its subjects. And therefore its history in modern times is not one of that sort.

It is a history of the various attempts that have been made to discern its character and to understand its implications more fully.

The writers who have engaged in this enterprise are numerous and diverse. They include: Hobbes, Locke, Halifax, Hume, Burke, Kant, Adam Smith, Tom Paine, the authors of the *Federalist*, Benjamin Franklin, J. S. Mill, Proudhon, von Humboldt, Tocqueville, Acton, T. H. Green, Bosanquet, etc., etc.

These writers, of course, diverge from one another on many questions; they arise together here because on this question of the business of governing they represent the same disposition of thought.

I want now to illustrate this belief about government by considering its particulars in the writings of two or three of its advocates.

7: Kant

Kant was a philosopher, so we may expect from him something more than the declaration of a preference for *nomocracy* and a recommendation of it on grounds that are alleged to be appropriate analogies. His design is to explain its necessary character.

Kant may be said to begin with some general beliefs about human beings. They are not exclusive to himself; but they are the beliefs in terms of which he understands the business of governing human beings.

Each man naturally (but not exclusively) seeks his own 'happiness'. This 'happiness' is something individual to himself.

That is to say, there is no substantive condition of human life which may be called 'happiness in general', and which an enlightened *telocrat* could discover and impose upon all his subjects alike.

We are capable of contributing to the 'happiness' of others, but only on the condition that we recognize that their 'happiness' is not necessarily to be found in the same things as our 'happiness'.

But further, each man is a 'moral being'.

This means that he is capable of choosing how he shall act in respect of his external circumstances and in relation to his own inclinations. And as a 'moral being', he is capable of choosing for himself between right and wrong conduct.

That is to say, there is no substantive condition of human life which may be called the 'good' or the 'virtuous' life, and which a *telocrat* could discern and impose upon all his subjects.

The essence of the 'good life' is the 'good will' – conduct which is governed by an individual choice to do what it is believed should be done.

Thus, for a ruler to impose an overall 'end' or 'purpose' upon all his subjects conflicts with both the nature of 'good' and the 'moral' nature of human beings: it turns them into slaves by making their moral judgments for them.

But men (particularly if they are powerful) are apt to impose themselves on one another. They are apt to claim this moral autonomy for themselves and to deny it to others. They are apt to treat others as means to their own ends.

A *telocrat* is a person of this sort, although he is apt to disguise this character by alleging that the 'end' he wishes to impose is not his 'own' but is the 'end' proper to be pursued by all.

This is an illusion: there is no 'end' proper to be pursued by all except the 'end' of living as an autonomous moral being.

The problem of governing, then, is how to rule 'moral beings' without depriving them of their 'moral' character.

A 'state' is an association of morally autonomous beings living under the rule of a government.

The business of this government is twofold. It is to prevent the naturally powerful from imposing themselves upon the naturally less powerful and treating them merely as means to their own ends. And it is to do this without depriving its subjects of their moral autonomy.

To rule by imposing general laws or rules of conduct upon all its subjects alike is a device in which this twofold object may be achieved.

The proper office of government is, not to supply its subjects with a substantive condition of life called 'happiness' or 'virtue', not to impose upon them a uniform 'social purpose' or 'end' to be pursued, but to supply them with a law.

The design of this law is to determine the relations between those under in such a manner that the 'moral autonomy' of each is respected. This is what Kant calls 'justice'.

There are, no doubt, defects in this theory of *nomocracy*; and Hegel was quick to point some of them out. But it has the virtue of linking a view of what human beings are with a view of what the business of governing human beings must be.

8: Adam Smith

Kant's elucidation of *nomocratic* belief was in the language of 'moral freedom'. Adam Smith's is in a much more common-sense language. It runs something like this; and it is not to be confused with his economic doctrines. This is politics.

Each human being is a creature of wants rather than needs. He has tastes and preferences of his own, and he is concerned to satisfy these tastes and preferences.

Moreover, he often wishes to enjoy a wider variety of satisfactions than he can easily procure for himself unaided by others.

This circumstance makes barter, exchange, the division of labour, and human association and co-operation at once desirable and intelligible.

Further, it may be observed that a human being is not merely interested in himself, and that his interest in others is not merely a recognition that they may be of use to him. He is, of course, liable to be self-centred and egoistic; but he is also capable of friendship, generosity, sympathy, benevolence, and good will.

Now, a 'state' is a contingent, historic association of such human beings which is ruled by a government. What, in these circumstances, is the proper business of this government?

From the point of view of governing a 'state', the most important thing about human beings is, neither their aptitude for selfishness, nor their aptitude for benevolence, but their capacity for doing actual 'injury' to one another.

The 'injuries' they may do to one another may be of various kinds. They include not only physical harm, but also 'injury' to property, credit, and reputation. But 'injury' is always committed in an overt action, and in this respect it is quite different from merely having malicious thoughts.

Smith calls this capacity to 'injure' one another the capacity human beings have for being 'unjust' to one another.

'Justice', then, is not a readiness to love others, to sympathize with them, or to wish them well. It is a readiness to refrain from doing 'injury' to others.

No man has a 'natural' claim to the generosity, good will, and love of other people; all men have a 'natural' claim to be treated justly, that is, not to be 'injured', by their fellows.

The business of government is with 'justice'. It is to assure each of its subjects of the enjoyment of this 'natural' right not to be 'injured' by others. And it performs this function by maintaining a system of legal rights and duties designed to limit the injury that one man may do to another.

It is the business of government to see that each of its subjects has redress for injury done him; and to see that those who prove themselves in their conduct to be injurious to others are deterred by 'punishment'.

The system of law, if it is to serve its purpose, must, of course, be appropriate to the kind of relationships which the members of the association are apt to enter into, and the kind of injuries they are most apt to do one another.

It, therefore, falls to government not only to administer the law, but also to see that this law is appropriate to its subjects.

Now, all this may be understood as a designed avoidance of *telocracy*. The business of government is not to impose an overall pattern of life upon its subjects, or to give a 'purpose' or 'end' to the activities of subjects who might otherwise not know what they should be doing.

'Justice' is not itself 'the good life'. It is something much narrower. But it is something essential to a civilized life. And it is what government is concerned with.

9: Bentham

Bentham is disposed to answer the question: What is the proper business of government? in terms of the answer he gives to another question: What sort of people are the members of a modern European 'state', and what do they require for their government.

The members of a modern European 'state' are sentient, rational human beings moved by a desire for pleasure and an aversion from pain.

They are engaged in multifarious activities, both in competition and in cooperation with one another.

Each has a 'private' life; they live in separate dwellings, but they are apt to associate with one another; and they have both benevolent and selfish propensities.

But, though they are members of an association, this association cannot be supposed to have an 'interest' or a 'good' of its own. There is no common 'end' or 'purpose' which a *telocratic* government might justifiably impose upon its subjects, because each of them must be understood to know better than any other man (whether ruler or fellow subject) what in fact pleases him.

Now, in consequence of both their benevolent and their selfish impulses, human beings are apt to be intolerant of one another's beliefs, opinions, conduct, and manner of life; and they are apt to try to impose themselves upon one another, particularly the powerful upon the less powerful.

This intolerance of others reveals itself in a disposition to get pleasure out of imposing one's own beliefs about happiness upon others. Indeed, men may be found bonding themselves together in groups, not merely to pursue their own interests, but to impose upon all their arbitrary conclusions about human conduct.

Indeed, some governments are themselves of this character – those moved by a belief in *telocracy*.

This intolerance, however, is out of place. It conflicts with the principle that every man is an adult and knows best where his own happiness lies.

And it generates a situation in which there is less, rather than more, happiness in the world.

This, moreover, is particularly the case when self-preference takes the form, not of overt egoism, but of benevolence – that is, the disposition to impose upon others what I believe to be 'good' for them.

And this is where the activity of 'governing' comes in.

It is the business of government to maintain a system of legal rights and duties, enjoyed by all subjects alike, in which each subject is protected against the selfishness (particularly the benevolent selfishness) of all others.

In short, the proper office of government is not to make choices for its subjects, not to impose upon them a 'government happiness', not to organize them in the pursuit of a common 'social good', not to 'improve' or to 'educate' them; it is to oblige them, under threat of 'punishment', to tolerate in one another what the law itself tolerates in all its subjects.

This is how Bentham himself formulates his belief in *nomocracy*:

> The principal business of laws, the only business which is evidently and incontestably necessary, is the preventing of individuals from pursuing their own happiness by the destruction of the greater portion of the happiness of others.
>
> To impose restraints upon the individual, to make choices on his behalf for his own welfare, is the business of education; it is the duty of the old towards the young; of the keeper towards the madman; it is rarely the duty of the legislator towards the people.

10

Now, none of these writers may be said to offer us a very thorough, or a very subtle, elucidation of *nomocratic* belief.

Perhaps, their chief defect is that, too often, they fail to grasp the distinction between an 'arbitrator' and a 'judge'. And it is here that a writer like Hegel shows his superiority.

But I have said enough to show that there is here a substantial belief about the proper business of government, neither naive, nor inappropriate to a modern European 'state', nor capable of becoming inappropriate merely by the march of events.

The main circumstance hostile to a belief in *nomocracy* in modern Europe has not, I think, arisen from reflection upon its demerits; it has been war and the solidarity of purpose which war imposes upon a 'state'.

War is the paradigm case of a situation in which the variety of 'admitted goods' in a society is reduced, or almost reduced, to one; a 'state' at war is a paradigm case of *telocracy*. And it is not insignificant that the rhetoric of *telocratic* belief is always liberally sprinkled with military analogy.

11

In this discussion of modern European beliefs about the proper business of governing I have been concerned with two dispositions of thought.

Neither of these dispositions of thought has been exactly reproduced in the activities of any European government, or in the organizations of beliefs which constitute political parties.

Every government and every political party in modern times has felt the pull of both *telocratic* and *nomocratic* belief. Indeed, modern Europe has invented for itself a political vocabulary in which each word has two meanings – one appropriate to *telocracy* and the other to *nomocracy*.

These dispositions of thought are the poles between which European belief on this topic has, so to speak, arced for four and a half centuries. And I think the politics of modern Europe, if it is to be understood, must be recognized as what has emerged from the tension between these two dispositions.

Indeed, if either of these dispositions of belief were to disappear from the scene, it would be a signal warning us that a new political experience was emerging over the horizon, as unlike that of current Europe as the political experience of modern Europe is unlike that of ancient Greece.

No doubt this will happen sometime. No political experience lasts forever. But if something new were to emerge, I would expect it to be something other than the mere triumph of either *telocratic* or *nomocratic* belief.

Editorial Note

LSE 1/1/21, file 5, fos. 516–31. Photocopy of a typescript. Some additions have been made to the lecture in an unknown hand, not reproduced here.

Index of Names
of Persons and Places

Index of Subjects

Index of Works